Older Americans

A CHANGING MARKET

Older Americans

A CHANGING MARKET

5th EDITION

BY THE NEW STRATEGIST EDITORS

New Strategist Publications, Inc.
Ithaca, New York

New Strategist Publications, Inc.
P.O. Box 242, Ithaca, New York 14851
800/848-0842; 607/273-0913
www.newstrategist.com

ISBN 1-885070-91-8

Printed in the United States of America

Table of Contents

Tables

Chapter 7. Population

Chapter 8. Spending

Chapter 9. Time Use

Illustrations

Chapter 5. Labor Force

Chapter 6. Living Arrangements

Chapter 7. Population

Chapter 8. Spending

Chapter 9. Time Use

Chapter 10. Wealth

Introduction

A revolution is underway. In 2006, the oldest members of the Baby-Boom generation turn 60, continuing the radical transformation of the 55-or-older age group.

No segment of the population will change as much as older Americans during the next two decades. Not only is the age group becoming increasingly sophisticated as it fills with well-educated Boomers, but the number of older Americans is expanding rapidly. And because older men and women are more likely to vote than younger adults, the number-one priority of politicians, policymakers, and businesses in the years ahead will be to cater to the wants and needs of people aged 55 or older.

The fifth edition of *Older Americans: A Changing Market* reveals the characteristics of the older population today and tomorrow. It shows the lifestyles, incomes, and spending patterns of fifty-, sixty-, and seventysomethings. Those who peruse these pages will see the changes that lie ahead as Boomers increasingly dominate the age group.

Already, the 55-to-64 age group is breaking new ground. Labor force participation rates are rising (see the Labor Force chapter). Householders aged 55 to 64 were the only ones to make income gains between 2000 and 2004, and men in the age group saw their incomes grow faster than men younger or older (see the Income chapter). The net worth of householders aged 55 to 64 surged between 2001 and 2004, rising 29 percent compared with a paltry 1.5 percent gain for all households (see the Wealth chapter).

Are these trends a sign of progress for older Americans, or are they a harbinger of trouble to come? With early retirement becoming less common, 55-to-64-year-olds are staying on the job longer, boosting incomes and wealth. But will they ever be able to achieve a financially secure retirement? Once they retire, will they still be healthy enough to enjoy their time off? Only 42 percent of workers aged 55 or older have saved at least $100,000, according to the 2005 Retirement Confidence Survey (see the Wealth chapter). Only 20 percent are very confident in having enough money for a comfortable retirement. Among the 51 percent with an IRA or 401(k)-type plan, the median balances are just $19,000 and $25,000, respectively. As older Americans look toward retirement, their biggest concerns are that they won't be healthy enough and that they won't have enough money, according to a survey by Pulte Homes (see the Labor Force chapter). Those two issues—health status and financial wellbeing—will continue to top the charts as Boomers flood the older age groups.

So far, the nation's politicians and businesses have done little to prepare for the changing priorities of older Americans. Businesses are naturally more concerned with the bottom line than sheltering older workers from financial turmoil. Politicians are often more concerned with pleasing corporate lobbyists than helping their aging and anxious constituents. These facts will not go unnoticed by Boomers as they march into old age. Already accounting for 40 percent of voters, the political power of Boomers will grow as they get older and their voting rate rises. How aging Boomers decide to solve the problems of health care and economic security, the nation's most pressing domestic concerns, will reshape the American social and economic landscape for decades to come.

Those who understand the changing wants and needs of the older population will be prepared for the future. *Older Americans: A Changing Market* will help you prepare for what lies ahead.

How to use this book

Older Americans: A Changing Market is designed for easy use. It is divided into ten chapters, organized alphabetically: Education, Health, Housing, Income, Labor Force, Living Arrangements, Population, Spending, Time Use, and Wealth.

The fifth edition of *Older Americans* includes the latest statistics on the health, living arrangements, incomes, spending, and wealth of the 55-or-older age group. The socioeconomic estimates presented here are the all-important mid-decade demographics, offering enough of a trend line into the 21st century to guide researchers in their business plans or government policies. *Older Americans* presents labor force data for 2005, including the government's updated labor force projections which reveal rising labor force participation among men and women aged 55 and older. It contains new data on the health of the population, including updated estimates of the overweight and obese. The Census Bureau's latest population projections are also included in the book, showing the enormous growth of the older population already in progress. *Older Americans* also presents the latest estimates of household wealth from the recently released Federal Reserve Board's 2004 Survey of Consumer Finances. New to this edition is the Time Use chapter, with many tables based on the Bureau of Labor Statistics' new American Time Use Survey. The results show that today's older Americans have more leisure time than any other age group, watch more television than younger Americans, and spend more time cleaning and cooking. Will aging Boomers follow in their footsteps or will they be forced to stay in the rat race just to make ends meet?

Most of the tables in *Older Americans* are based on data collected by the federal government, in particular the Census Bureau, the Bureau of Labor Statistics, the National Center for Education Statistics, the National Center for Health Statistics, and the Federal Reserve Board. The federal government is the best source of up-to-date, reliable information on the changing characteristics of Americans.

Older Americans includes the demographic and lifestyle data most important to researchers. Most of the tables are based on data collected by the federal government, but they are not simply reprints of government spreadsheets—as is the case in many reference books. Instead, each table is individually compiled and created by New Strategist's editors, with calculations designed to reveal the trends. The task of extracting and processing raw data from the government's web sites at times requires hours of effort to create a single table. The effort is worthwhile, however, because each table tells a story about older Americans, a story explained by the accompanying text and chart, which analyze the data and highlight future trends. If you need more information than the tables and text provide, you can plumb the original source listed at the bottom of each table.

The book contains a comprehensive table list to help you locate the information you need. For a more detailed search, see the index at the back of the book. Also at the back of the book are the bibliography and the glossary, which defines the terms and describes the many surveys referenced in the tables and text.

With *Older Americans: A Changing Market* in hand, you can position your organization to benefit from the coming revolution.

1

Education

■ One of the most dramatic changes of the past half-century is the rise in the educational attainment of the older population. As recently as 1970, a minority of men and women aged 55 or older were high school graduates. Today, nearly 80 percent have a high school diploma.

■ The older population is educationally diverse. Eighty-eight percent of men aged 55 to 59 have a high school diploma versus only 70 percent of men aged 75 or older.

■ Among men aged 55 or older, 81 percent of Asians and 84 percent of non-Hispanic whites are high school graduates. This compares with only 63 percent of blacks and a 49 percent minority of Hispanics.

■ Thirty-five percent of people aged 55 to 59 took part in work-related courses in 2003, and 56 percent participated in less-formal work-related learning activities.

Big Gains in Educational Attainment

Until 1980, the majority of older Americans had not completed high school.

Of all the social revolutions that have occurred over the past half-century, one of the most dramatic is the rise in the educational attainment of the nation's older population. Even as recently as 1970, a minority of men and women aged 55 or older were high school graduates. Today, nearly 80 percent have a high school diploma.

Twenty-nine percent of men aged 55 or older are college graduates today, up from only 5 percent in 1950 and 9 percent in 1970. Among women, the figure has grown from 3 percent in 1950 to 18 percent today. The gap in the educational attainment of men and women will close in the years ahead as better-educated generations enter the age group.

■ The health and wealth of older Americans are improving because of their rising educational attainment. As well-educated Baby Boomers fill the age group, the sophistication of the 55-or-older population will continue to grow.

The educational attainment of older Americans has grown sharply

(percent of people aged 55 or older who are high school graduates, by sex, 1950 and 2004)

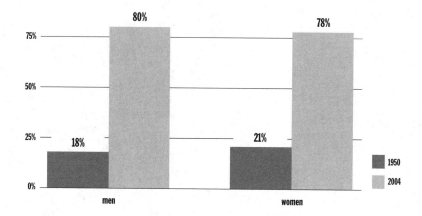

Table 1.1 Educational Attainment of People Aged 55 or Older, 1950 to 2004

(percent distribution of people aged 55 or older by sex and educational attainment, 1950 to 2004)

	total	not a high school graduate	high school graduate or more	some college or more	college, four years or more
Men aged 55 or older					
2004	100.0%	20.2%	79.8%	49.4%	28.8%
2000	100.0	24.9	75.1	43.9	24.3
1990	100.0	38.5	61.5	30.2	18.1
1980	100.0	50.4	49.6	22.5	12.6
1970	100.0	65.9	34.1	15.8	8.9
1960	100.0	79.2	20.8	11.1	5.3
1950	100.0	81.5	18.5	9.1	4.8
Women aged 55 or older					
2004	100.0	21.6	78.4	40.1	18.2
2000	100.0	25.8	74.2	34.6	14.6
1990	100.0	38.2	61.8	22.9	10.6
1980	100.0	49.4	50.6	17.7	7.9
1970	100.0	62.8	37.2	14.0	6.3
1960	100.0	75.4	24.6	11.1	4.0
1950	100.0	78.8	21.2	8.7	3.4

Source: Bureau of the Census, Educational Attainment, Historical Tables; Internet site http://www.census.gov/population/www/ socdemo/educ-attn.html; calculations by New Strategist

Older Americans Are the Least Educated

Generation X is the most highly educated generation.

The percentage of Americans with a college degree peaks among Generation Xers and Baby Boomers. Thirty-one percent of Generation Xers have a college degree, the highest level of education among the generations. Boomers are not far behind, at 30 percent. Among older Americans (aged 55 or older), only 23 percent are college graduates—a figure on the rise now that Boomers are filling the older age groups.

Although Generation X is the best educated generation overall, the oldest Boomer men are better educated than any other Americans. Thirty-four percent of men aged 55 to 59 have a college degree, thanks to draft deferments offered to college students during the Vietnam War. These men are boosting the educational attainment of older age groups.

■ The educational attainment of older women is also rising as Boomers enter the 55-or-older age groups, but the increase will not be as rapid as the one for older men.

Fewer than one in four older Americans has a college degree

(percent of people aged 25 or older with a bachelor's degree by generation, 2004)

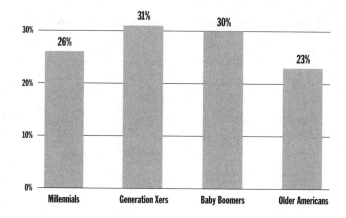

Table 1.2 Educational Attainment by Generation, 2004

(number and percent distribution of people aged 25 or older by highest level of education, 2004; numbers in thousands)

	total 25 or older	Millennials (25 to 27)	Generation X (28 to 39)	Boomers (40 to 58)	older Americans (55 or older)
Total people	**186,877**	**11,424**	**48,569**	**77,313**	**63,033**
Not a high school graduate	27,744	1,590	5,961	8,612	13,197
High school graduate	59,810	3,438	14,276	24,281	21,917
Some college, no degree	31,808	2,448	8,657	13,525	9,597
Associate's degree	15,764	932	4,496	7,658	3,836
Bachelor's degree	33,766	2,533	10,651	14,585	8,350
Master's degree	12,609	357	3,266	6,166	4,126
Professional degree	2,952	93	773	1,334	985
Doctoral degree	2,422	36	487	1,150	1,028
High school graduate or more	159,131	9,837	42,606	68,699	49,839
Some college or more	99,321	6,399	28,330	44,418	27,922
Bachelor's degree or more	51,749	3,019	15,177	23,235	14,489
Total people	**100.0%**	**100.0%**	**100.0%**	**100.0%**	**100.0%**
Not a high school graduate	14.8	13.9	12.3	11.1	20.9
High school graduate	32.0	30.1	29.4	31.4	34.8
Some college, no degree	17.0	21.4	17.8	17.5	15.2
Associate's degree	8.4	8.2	9.3	9.9	6.1
Bachelor's degree	18.1	22.2	21.9	18.9	13.2
Master's degree	6.7	3.1	6.7	8.0	6.5
Professional degree	1.6	0.8	1.6	1.7	1.6
Doctoral degree	1.3	0.3	1.0	1.5	1.6
High school graduate or more	85.2	86.1	87.7	88.9	79.1
Some college or more	53.1	56.0	58.3	57.5	44.3
Bachelor's degree or more	27.7	26.4	31.2	30.1	23.0

Note: Numbers by generation will not sum to total because of the overlap between Baby Boomers and older Americans.
Source: Bureau of the Census, Educational Attainment in the United States: 2004, detailed tables; Internet site http://www
.census.gov/population/www/socdemo/education/cps2004.html; calculations by New Strategist

Table 1.3 Educational Attainment of People Aged 55 or Older, 2004

(number and percent distribution of people aged 25 or older, aged 55 or older, and aged 55 or older in five-year age groups, by highest level of education, 2004; numbers in thousands)

	total 25 or older	aged 55 or older total	55 to 59	60 to 64	aged 65 or older total	65 to 69	70 to 74	75+
Total people	**186,877**	**63,033**	**16,158**	**12,217**	**34,659**	**9,818**	**8,420**	**16,421**
Not a high school graduate	27,744	13,197	1,955	1,901	9,339	2,143	2,170	5,025
High school graduate	59,810	21,917	5,054	4,382	12,482	3,610	3,005	5,867
Some college, no degree	31,808	9,597	2,886	1,938	4,771	1,492	1,179	2,100
Associate's degree	15,764	3,836	1,377	861	1,600	519	390	691
Bachelor's degree	33,766	8,350	2,732	1,823	3,794	1,191	926	1,677
Master's degree	12,609	4,126	1,531	901	1,694	559	497	639
Professional degree	2,952	985	292	176	517	129	139	250
Doctoral degree	2,422	1,028	332	233	462	175	114	173
High school grad. or more	159,131	49,839	14,204	10,314	25,320	7,675	6,250	11,397
Some college or more	99,321	27,922	9,150	5,932	12,838	4,065	3,245	5,530
Bachelor's degree or more	51,749	14,489	4,887	3,133	6,467	2,054	1,676	2,739
Total people	**100.0%**	**100.0%**	**100.0%**	**100.0%**	**100.0%**	**100.0%**	**100.0%**	**100.0%**
Not a high school graduate	14.8	20.9	12.1	15.6	26.9	21.8	25.8	30.6
High school graduate	32.0	34.8	31.3	35.9	36.0	36.8	35.7	35.7
Some college, no degree	17.0	15.2	17.9	15.9	13.8	15.2	14.0	12.8
Associate's degree	8.4	6.1	8.5	7.0	4.6	5.3	4.6	4.2
Bachelor's degree	18.1	13.2	16.9	14.9	10.9	12.1	11.0	10.2
Master's degree	6.7	6.5	9.5	7.4	4.9	5.7	5.9	3.9
Professional degree	1.6	1.6	1.8	1.4	1.5	1.3	1.7	1.5
Doctoral degree	1.3	1.6	2.1	1.9	1.3	1.8	1.4	1.1
High school grad. or more	85.2	79.1	87.9	84.4	73.1	78.2	74.2	69.4
Some college or more	53.1	44.3	56.6	48.6	37.0	41.4	38.5	33.7
Bachelor's degree or more	27.7	23.0	30.2	25.6	18.7	20.9	19.9	16.7

Source: Bureau of the Census, Educational Attainment in the United States: 2004, detailed tables; Internet site http://ww.census. gov/population/www/socdemo/education/cps2004.html; calculations by New Strategist

The Oldest Men Are the Least Educated

Men aged 55 to 59 are the best educated among all Americans.

The older population is educationally diverse. At the youthful end are the most-educated people in the nation. At the older end are the least educated.

Eighty-eight percent of men aged 55 to 59 (an age group now filled with the oldest Boomers) have a high school diploma versus only 70 percent of men aged 75 or older. The 60 percent majority of men aged 55 to 59 have college experience, and 34 percent have a college degree. In contrast, only 39 percent of men aged 75 or older have been to college and just 23 percent have a bachelor's degree. Draft deferments for college students during the Vietnam War are behind the high level of educational attainment among men aged 55 to 59, giving them an incentive to go to college and stay in school until they earned their degree.

■ Better health is linked with greater educational attainment. As better-educated men replace older men with little education, the older population is becoming increasingly healthy and active.

More than one-third of men aged 55 to 59 have a college degree

(percent of men aged 55 or older who are college graduates, 2004)

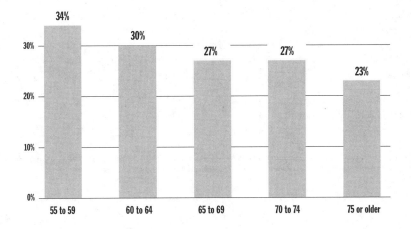

Table 1.4 Educational Attainment of Men Aged 55 or Older, 2004

(number and percent distribution of men aged 25 or older, aged 55 or older, and aged 55 or older in five-year age groups, by highest level of education, 2004; numbers in thousands)

| | | aged 55 or older | | | | | | |
| | | | | | aged 65 or older | | | |
	total 25 or older	total	55 to 59	60 to 64	total	65 to 69	70 to 74	75+
Total men	**89,558**	**28,347**	**7,852**	**5,699**	**14,797**	**4,566**	**3,789**	**6,441**
Not a high school graduate	13,569	5,714	943	936	3,837	973	917	1,949
High school graduate	27,889	8,631	2,189	1,867	4,575	1,455	1,153	1,967
Some college, no degree	15,012	4,290	1,399	855	2,035	671	548	816
Associate's degree	6,751	1,550	625	333	594	232	160	203
Bachelor's degree	16,632	4,417	1,451	939	2,026	685	503	839
Master's degree	6,158	2,189	772	467	952	325	306	321
Professional degree	1,925	757	222	130	404	92	107	205
Doctoral degree	1,621	796	251	172	373	135	97	141
High school grad. or more	75,988	22,630	6,909	4,763	10,959	3,595	2,874	4,492
Some college or more	48,099	13,999	4,720	2,896	6,384	2,140	1,721	2,525
Bachelor's degree or more	26,336	8,159	2,696	1,708	3,755	1,237	1,013	1,506
Total men	**100.0%**	**100.0%**	**100.0%**	**100.0%**	**100.0%**	**100.0%**	**100.0%**	**100.0%**
Not a high school graduate	15.2	20.2	12.0	16.4	25.9	21.3	24.2	30.3
High school graduate	31.1	30.4	27.9	32.8	30.9	31.9	30.4	30.5
Some college, no degree	16.8	15.1	17.8	15.0	13.8	14.7	14.5	12.7
Associate's degree	7.5	5.5	8.0	5.8	4.0	5.1	4.2	3.2
Bachelor's degree	18.6	15.6	18.5	16.5	13.7	15.0	13.3	13.0
Master's degree	6.9	7.7	9.8	8.2	6.4	7.1	8.1	5.0
Professional degree	2.1	2.7	2.8	2.3	2.7	2.0	2.8	3.2
Doctoral degree	1.8	2.8	3.2	3.0	2.5	3.0	2.6	2.2
High school grad. or more	84.8	79.8	88.0	83.6	74.1	78.7	75.9	69.7
Some college or more	53.7	49.4	60.1	50.8	43.1	46.9	45.4	39.2
Bachelor's degree or more	29.4	28.8	34.3	30.0	25.4	27.1	26.7	23.4

Source: Bureau of the Census, Educational Attainment in the United States: 2004, detailed tables; Internet site http://www .census.gov/population/www/socdemo/education/cps2004.html; calculations by New Strategist

Educated Women Will Reinvent Old Age

Women aged 55 to 59 are more than twice as likely to be college graduates as those aged 75 or older.

The educational diversity of older women is striking. Women in their late fifties (an age group now filled with the oldest Boomers) are much more likely to have finished high school than women aged 75 or older, 88 versus 69 percent. While more than half of women aged 55 to 59 have some college experience, the proportion is just 30 percent among the oldest women. And while only 12 percent of women aged 75 or older are college graduates, more than one in four women aged 55 to 59 has a bachelor's degree.

Women comprise the great majority of the older population. As the well-educated Baby-Boom generation fills the 55-or-older age group, the educational attainment of older women will climb. This ongoing socioeconomic revolution will transform what it means to be old in America.

■ The stereotypical image of the elderly as frail and vulnerable will give way to a more active and demanding view of old age.

More than one in four women aged 55 to 59 is a college graduate

(percent of women aged 55 or older who are college graduates, 2004)

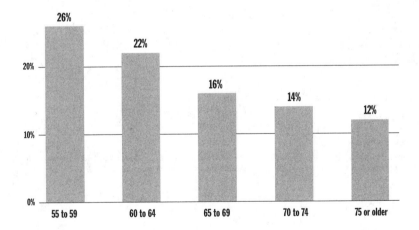

Table 1.5 Educational Attainment of Women Aged 55 or Older, 2004

(number and percent distribution of women aged 25 or older, aged 55 or older, and aged 55 or older in five-year age groups, by highest level of education, 2004; numbers in thousands)

	total 25 or older	aged 55 or older total	55 to 59	60 to 64	aged 65 or older total	65 to 69	70 to 74	75+
Total women	**97,319**	**34,686**	**8,307**	**6,517**	**19,862**	**5,252**	**4,631**	**9,980**
Not a high school graduate	14,175	7,483	1,010	965	5,502	1,172	1,253	3,077
High school graduate	31,921	13,285	2,865	2,515	7,907	2,155	1,853	3,899
Some college, no degree	16,796	5,306	1,486	1,083	2,736	821	631	1,284
Associate's degree	9,013	2,288	754	529	1,006	287	232	487
Bachelor's degree	17,134	3,932	1,281	883	1,767	506	423	838
Master's degree	6,451	1,935	759	435	742	234	191	317
Professional degree	1,027	229	71	46	114	37	32	45
Doctoral degree	801	229	81	61	89	40	17	31
High school grad. or more	83,143	27,204	7,297	5,552	14,361	4,080	3,379	6,901
Some college or more	51,222	13,919	4,432	3,037	6,454	1,925	1,526	3,002
Bachelor's degree or more	25,413	6,325	2,192	1,425	2,712	817	663	1,231
Total women	**100.0%**	**100.0%**	**100.0%**	**100.0%**	**100.0%**	**100.0%**	**100.0%**	**100.0%**
Not a high school graduate	14.6	21.6	12.2	14.8	27.7	22.3	27.1	30.8
High school graduate	32.8	38.3	34.5	38.6	39.8	41.0	40.0	39.1
Some college, no degree	17.3	15.3	17.9	16.6	13.8	15.6	13.6	12.9
Associate's degree	9.3	6.6	9.1	8.1	5.1	5.5	5.0	4.9
Bachelor's degree	17.6	11.3	15.4	13.5	8.9	9.6	9.1	8.4
Master's degree	6.6	5.6	9.1	6.7	3.7	4.5	4.1	3.2
Professional degree	1.1	0.7	0.9	0.7	0.6	0.7	0.7	0.5
Doctoral degree	0.8	0.7	1.0	0.9	0.4	0.8	0.4	0.3
High school grad. or more	85.4	78.4	87.8	85.2	72.3	77.7	73.0	69.1
Some college or more	52.6	40.1	53.4	46.6	32.5	36.7	33.0	30.1
Bachelor's degree or more	26.1	18.2	26.4	21.9	13.7	15.6	14.3	12.3

Source: Bureau of the Census, Educational Attainment in the United States: 2004, detailed tables; Internet site http://www .census.gov/population/www/socdemo/education/cps2004.html; calculations by New Strategist

Asians Are the Best-Educated Older Americans

Most older Hispanics have not even graduated from high school.

Among people aged 55 or older, Asians, blacks, and non-Hispanic whites are far better educated than Hispanics. Among men aged 55 or older, from 81 to 84 percent of Asians and non-Hispanic whites are high school graduates. This compares with only 63 percent of blacks and a 49 percent minority of Hispanics. Fully 46 percent of Asian men aged 55 or older are college graduates versus 31 percent of non-Hispanic whites, 13 percent of blacks, and 12 percent of Hispanics.

Among older women, Asians are less likely than non-Hispanic whites to be high school graduates (71 versus 83 percent). But 32 percent of Asian women aged 55 or older are college graduates versus a smaller 19 percent of non-Hispanic whites, 13 percent of blacks, and just 8 percent of Hispanics.

■ The educational attainment of older blacks will rise as Boomers with much more education enter the age group. In contrast, the educational attainment of older Hispanics will not rise much because Hispanic Boomers lag in education.

Among older Hispanics, a minority has graduated from high school

(percent of men aged 55 or older with a high school diploma, 2004)

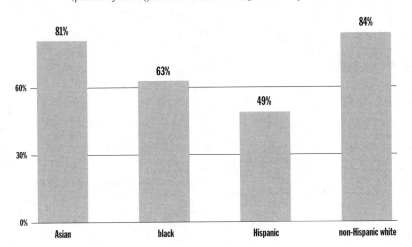

Table 1.6 Educational Attainment of Men Aged 55 or Older by Race and Hispanic Origin, 2004

(number and percent distribution of men aged 55 or older by educational attainment, race, and Hispanic origin, 2004; numbers in thousands)

	total	Asian	black	Hispanic	non-Hispanic white
Total men aged 55 or older	**28,347**	**979**	**2,368**	**1,904**	**22,840**
Not a high school graduate	5,714	182	869	972	3,650
High school graduate	8,631	197	747	414	7,212
Some college, no degree	4,290	85	313	223	3,596
Associate's degree	1,550	69	119	67	1,277
Bachelor's degree	4,417	236	169	142	3,830
Master's degree	2,189	100	90	55	1,926
Professional degree	757	47	29	16	663
Doctoral degree	796	63	22	22	682
High school graduate or more	22,630	797	1,489	939	19,186
Some college or more	13,999	600	742	525	11,974
Bachelor's degree or more	8,159	446	310	235	7,101
Total men aged 55 or older	**100.0%**	**100.0%**	**100.0%**	**100.0%**	**100.0%**
Not a high school graduate	20.2	18.6	36.7	51.1	16.0
High school graduate	30.4	20.1	31.5	21.7	31.6
Some college, no degree	15.1	8.7	13.2	11.7	15.7
Associate's degree	5.5	7.0	5.0	3.5	5.6
Bachelor's degree	15.6	24.1	7.1	7.5	16.8
Master's degree	7.7	10.2	3.8	2.9	8.4
Professional degree	2.7	4.8	1.2	0.8	2.9
Doctoral degree	2.8	6.4	0.9	1.2	3.0
High school graduate or more	79.8	81.4	62.9	49.3	84.0
Some college or more	49.4	61.3	31.3	27.6	52.4
Bachelor's degree or more	28.8	45.6	13.1	12.3	31.1

Note: Asians and blacks are those identifying themselves as being of the race alone and those identifying themselves as being of the race in combination with other races; non-Hispanic whites are those identifying themselves as being white alone and not Hispanic. Numbers will not add to total because not all races are shown and Hispanics may be of any race.
Source: Bureau of the Census, Educational Attainment in the United States: 2004, detailed tables; Internet site http://www .census.gov/population/www/socdemo/education/cps2004.html; calculations by New Strategist

Table 1.7 Educational Attainment of Women Aged 55 or Older by Race and Hispanic Origin, 2004

(number and percent distribution of women aged 55 or older by educational attainment, race, and Hispanic origin, 2004; numbers in thousands)

	total	Asian	black	Hispanic	non-Hispanic white
Total women aged 55 or older	**34,686**	**1,144**	**3,392**	**2,338**	**27,541**
Not a high school graduate	7,483	323	1,170	1,277	4,637
High school graduate	13,285	280	1,116	554	11,241
Some college, no degree	5,306	103	459	226	4,472
Associate's degree	2,288	62	188	87	1,919
Bachelor's degree	3,932	266	263	129	3,245
Master's degree	1,935	60	159	43	1,659
Professional degree	229	28	18	6	173
Doctoral degree	229	14	8	17	191
High school graduate or more	27,204	813	2,211	1,062	22,900
Some college or more	13,919	533	1,095	508	11,659
Bachelor's degree or more	6,325	368	448	195	5,268
Total women aged 55 or older	**100.0%**	**100.0%**	**100.0%**	**100.0%**	**100.0%**
Not a high school graduate	21.6	28.2	34.5	54.6	16.8
High school graduate	38.3	24.5	32.9	23.7	40.8
Some college, no degree	15.3	9.0	13.5	9.7	16.2
Associate's degree	6.6	5.4	5.5	3.7	7.0
Bachelor's degree	11.3	23.3	7.8	5.5	11.8
Master's degree	5.6	5.2	4.7	1.8	6.0
Professional degree	0.7	2.4	0.5	0.3	0.6
Doctoral degree	0.7	1.2	0.2	0.7	0.7
High school graduate or more	78.4	71.1	65.2	45.4	83.1
Some college or more	40.1	46.6	32.3	21.7	42.3
Bachelor's degree or more	18.2	32.2	13.2	8.3	19.1

Note: Asians and blacks are those identifying themselves as being of the race alone and those identifying themselves as being of the race in combination with other races; non-Hispanic whites are those identifying themselves as being white alone and not Hispanic. Numbers will not add to total because not all races are shown and Hispanics may be of any race.
Source: Bureau of the Census, Educational Attainment in the United States: 2004, detailed tables; Internet site http://www .census.gov/population/www/socdemo/education/cps2004.html; calculations by New Strategist

Few Older Americans Are in School

Of the nation's 75 million students, only 372,000 are aged 55 or older.

Just 0.6 percent of people aged 55 or older are currently enrolled in school. This figure is much smaller than the proportion of middle-aged Americans in school, but it is likely to grow as the well-educated Baby-Boom generation enters the age group. The more educated the person, the more likely he or she is to return to school to get even more education.

Among older students, women outnumber men—214,000 to 157,000. In the 55-or-older age group, those aged 55 to 59 are most likely to be students, with 1.2 percent enrolled in school.

■ As well-educated Boomers age into their sixties, expect to see school enrollment rise among older Americans.

Older women outnumber older men in school

(number of people aged 55 or older enrolled in school, by sex, 2004)

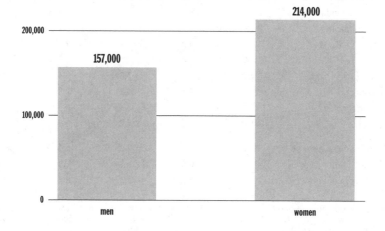

Table 1.8 School Enrollment by Sex and Age, 2004

(total number of people aged 3 or older, and number and percent enrolled in school by sex and age, 2004; numbers in thousands)

		enrolled	
	total	number	percent
Total people	**277,467**	**75,461**	**27.2%**
Under age 55	213,425	75,091	35.2
Aged 55 or older	64,042	372	0.6
Aged 55 to 59	16,578	203	1.2
Aged 60 to 64	12,747	107	0.8
Aged 65 or older	34,717	62	0.2
Total females	**141,957**	**38,012**	**26.8**
Under age 55	106,756	37,796	35.4
Aged 55 or older	35,201	214	0.6
Aged 55 to 59	8,569	117	1.4
Aged 60 to 64	6,665	53	0.8
Aged 65 or older	19,967	44	0.2
Total males	**135,510**	**37,449**	**27.6**
Under age 55	106,666	37,290	35.0
Aged 55 or older	28,842	157	0.5
Aged 55 to 59	8,009	85	1.1
Aged 60 to 64	6,082	54	0.9
Aged 65 or older	14,751	18	0.1

Source: Bureau of the Census, School Enrollment—Social and Economic Characteristics of Students: October 2004, detailed tables; Internet site http://www.census.gov/population/www/socdemo/school/cps2004.html; calculations by New Strategist

Few Older Students Attend College Full-Time

Eight out of 10 graduate students aged 55 or older are part-timers.

As the number of older college students has grown over the past few decades, so has the number of students who attend college part-time. Many of the older Americans enrolled in college work during the day and take classes at night. Others are actively pursuing a college degree while also enjoying retirement.

Overall, 347,000 people aged 55 or older are in college, accounting for just 2 percent of total college enrollment. The age group represents 3 percent of part-time undergraduates and 8 percent of part-time graduate students.

■ Look for college enrollment among people aged 55 or older to rise as the well-educated Baby-Boom generation enters the age group.

Older students are part-timers

(percent of total college students and college students aged 55 or older who attend school part-time, 2004)

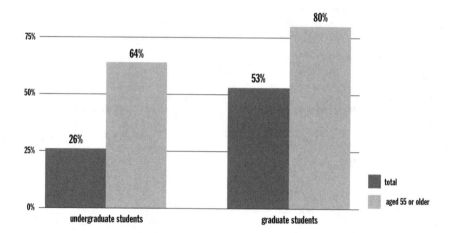

Table 1.9 College Students by Age and Attendance Status, 2004

(number and percent distribution of people aged 15 or older enrolled in institutions of higher education, by age and full- or part-time attendance status, 2004; numbers in thousands)

	total	undergraduate total	full-time	part-time	graduate total	full-time	part-time
Total enrolled	**17,383**	**14,005**	**10,418**	**3,587**	**3,378**	**1,572**	**1,806**
Under age 55	17,039	13,830	10,357	3,473	3,207	1,537	1,670
Aged 55 or older	347	174	62	112	171	34	137
Aged 55 to 59	194	117	43	74	75	18	57
Aged 60 to 64	104	33	10	23	72	12	60
Aged 65 or older	49	24	9	15	24	4	20
PERCENT DISTRIBUTION BY ATTENDANCE STATUS							
Total enrolled	–	**100.0%**	**74.4%**	**25.6%**	**100.0%**	**46.5%**	**53.5%**
Under age 55	–	100.0	74.9	25.1	100.0	47.9	52.1
Aged 55 or older	–	100.0	35.6	64.4	100.0	19.9	80.1
Aged 55 to 59	–	100.0	36.8	63.2	100.0	24.0	76.0
Aged 60 to 64	–	100.0	30.3	69.7	100.0	16.7	83.3
Aged 65 or older	–	100.0	37.5	62.5	100.0	16.7	83.3
PERCENT DISTRIBUTION BY AGE							
Total enrolled	**100.0%**	**100.0%**	**100.0%**	**100.0%**	**100.0%**	**100.0%**	**100.0%**
Under age 55	98.0	98.8	99.4	96.8	94.9	97.8	92.5
Aged 55 or older	2.0	1.2	0.6	3.1	5.1	2.2	7.6
Aged 55 to 59	1.1	0.8	0.4	2.1	2.2	1.1	3.2
Aged 60 to 64	0.6	0.2	0.1	0.6	2.1	0.8	3.3
Aged 65 or older	0.3	0.2	0.1	0.4	0.7	0.3	1.1

Note: "–" means not applicable.
Source: Bureau of the Census, School Enrollment—Social and Economic Characteristics of Students: October 2004, detailed tables; Internet site http://www.census.gov/population/www/socdemo/school/cps2004.html; calculations by New Strategist

Many Older Americans Participate in Adult Education for Job-Related Reasons

Life-long learning is becoming a necessity for job security.

As job security dwindles, many workers are turning to the educational system to try to stay on track. Overall, 33 percent of Americans aged 17 or older participated in work-related adult education during the past 12 months. An even larger 58 percent participated in less-formal work-related learning activities, such as seminars offered by employers.

Not surprisingly, the percentage of older Americans involved in work-related courses falls with age, from 35 percent of people aged 55 to 59 to just 5 percent of those aged 70 or older. The percentage participating in less-formal work-related learning activities ranges from 56 percent in the 55-to-59 age group to 13 percent among those aged 70 or older.

■ Many Americans who participate in work-related education are retraining themselves to compete in the increasingly global economy.

A substantial percentage of older Americans participate in work-related courses

(percent of people aged 17 or older participating in job- or career-related courses, by age, 2003)

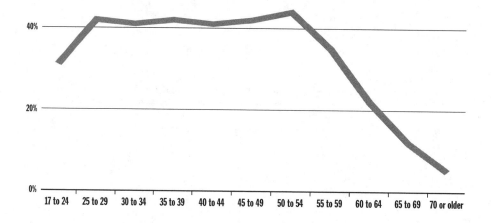

Table 1.10 Participation in Adult Education for Work-Related Reasons, 2003

(percent of people aged 17 or older participating in work-related adult education during the past 12 months, by age and type, 2003; numbers in thousands)

	career- or job-related courses	less formal work-related learning activities
Total people	**33.2%**	**58.3%**
Aged 17 to 24	30.9	73.4
Aged 25 to 29	42.4	75.4
Aged 30 to 34	40.7	68.4
Aged 35 to 39	41.6	67.5
Aged 40 to 44	40.7	70.4
Aged 45 to 49	42.2	65.3
Aged 50 to 54	43.6	65.7
Aged 55 to 59	34.9	56.3
Aged 60 to 64	21.7	39.4
Aged 65 to 69	11.9	27.0
Aged 70 or older	4.7	12.9

Note: Adult education is defined as all education activities except full-time enrollment in higher education credential programs. Examples include part-time college attendance and classes or seminars given by employers.
Source: National Center for Education Statistics, Digest of Education Statistics, 2004, list of tables, Internet site http:// nces.ed.gov/programs/digest/d04/list_tables3.asp#c3b_1; calculations by New Strategist

2

Health

■ The percentage of people who rate their health as very good or excellent declines with age to just 36 percent in the 65-or-older age group.

■ Americans have a weight problem, and older Americans are no exception. Among people aged 50 or older, the average man weighs more than 190 pounds. The average woman weighs more than 160.

■ Medical expenses for people aged 65 or older stood at a median of $3,649 in 2003. Medicare covered 53 percent of those expenses, while 19 percent was paid for out-of-pocket.

■ Eighty-five percent of people aged 65 or older took at least one prescription drug in the past month, and 52 percent took three or more.

■ The percentage of people with difficulties in physical functioning rises to 28 percent in the 65-to-74 age group and peaks at 48 percent among those aged 75 or older.

■ People aged 65 or older account for 25 percent of doctor visits, 14 percent of visits to hospital outpatient departments, 15 percent of visits to emergency rooms, and 38 percent of hospital discharges.

■ In 1900, the average 65-year-old could expect to live 11.9 more years. By 2003, life expectancy for 65-year-olds had increased to 18.5 years.

Fewer than Half of 55-to-64-Year-Olds Say Their Health Is Very Good or Excellent

At every age, however, the percentage saying their health is very good or excellent exceeds the proportion saying it is only fair or poor.

The 54 percent majority of Americans aged 18 or older say their health is very good or excellent. The figure peaks at 64 percent in the 25-to-34 age group, then declines with age as chronic conditions become more common. The percentage of people who report very good to excellent health falls below 50 percent in the 55-to-64 age group and bottoms out at 36 percent among those aged 65 or older. Even in the oldest age group, however, the proportion of people reporting very good or excellent health (36 percent) surpasses the share of those reporting fair or poor health (28 percent).

As people age, the number of days they experience poor physical health rises. From a low of about 2 days per month among 18-to-34-year-olds, the figure peaks at 6.4 days among people aged 75 or older. Interestingly, the number of days per month of poor mental health peaks in the 25-to-54 age group at 3.7, than falls to 2.2 days among people aged 65 or older.

■ Medical advances that allow people to manage their chronic conditions more easily should boost the proportion of older Americans who report very good or excellent health.

More than one-third of the oldest Americans say their health is very good or excellent

(percent of people aged 18 or older who say their health is very good or excellent, by age, 2004)

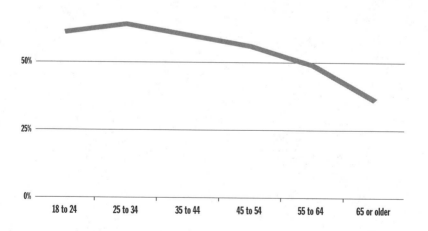

Table 2.1 Health Status by Age, 2004

(percent distribution of people aged 18 or older by self-reported health status, by age, 2004)

	excellent	very good	good	fair	poor
Total people	**20.8%**	**33.6%**	**29.8%**	**10.8%**	**3.9%**
Aged 18 to 24	24.6	36.5	30.3	6.7	0.8
Aged 25 to 34	26.5	37.6	27.9	6.2	1.0
Aged 35 to 44	24.4	35.8	28.6	8.1	2.3
Aged 45 to 54	21.4	34.2	28.6	10.0	4.3
Aged 55 to 64	18.5	30.5	30.5	12.3	6.5
Aged 65 or older	10.6	25.7	34.5	19.8	8.6

Source: Centers for Disease Control and Prevention, Behavioral Risk Factor Surveillance System Prevalence Data, 2004, Internet site http://apps.nccd.cdc.gov/brfss/

Table 2.2 Health Problems in Past 30 Days by Age, 2004

(average number of days during the past 30 days people aged 18 or older reported poor physical or mental health, and average number of days of activity limitation due to poor health, by age, 2004)

	days with poor physical health	days with poor mental health	days with activity limitations due to poor health
Total people	**3.6**	**3.5**	**2.1**
Aged 18 to 24	2.2	4.3	1.4
Aged 25 to 34	2.1	3.7	1.4
Aged 35 to 44	3.0	3.7	1.9
Aged 45 to 54	3.9	3.7	2.6
Aged 55 to 64	4.9	3.2	2.9
Aged 65 to 74	5.1	2.2	2.4
Aged 75 or older	6.4	2.2	3.1

Source: Centers for Disease Control and Prevention, National Center for Chronic Disease Prevention and Health Promotion, Prevalence Data, Internet site http://apps.nccd.cdc.gov/HRQOL/

Weight Problems Are the Norm for Older Americans

Many are trying to lose weight.

Americans have a weight problem, with the average person having put on 24 to 25 pounds over the past four decades. Older Americans are no exception. The average older man weighs more than 190 pounds. The average older woman weighs more than 160. The percentage of people aged 55 or older who are overweight ranges from 60 to 72 percent among women and from 67 to 76 percent among men.

Not surprisingly, many Americans are trying to lose weight. Nationally, 38 percent are trying to shed pounds, with the figure standing at 43 percent among people aged 55 to 64. Among people aged 65 or older, a smaller 31 percent are trying to lose weight.

Although most older Americans are overweight, only 18 percent of 55-to-64-year-olds and 11 percent of people aged 65 or older have been advised by a health professional to lose weight. Many of those trying to lose weight say they are using physical activity or exercise to do so. But fewer than one-third of people aged 55 or older engage in regular physical activity.

■ Although most Americans are overweight, surprisingly few have been advised by the medical community to lose weight.

Older Americans weigh more

(average weight in pounds of people aged 60 to 74, by sex, 1960–62 and 1999–02)

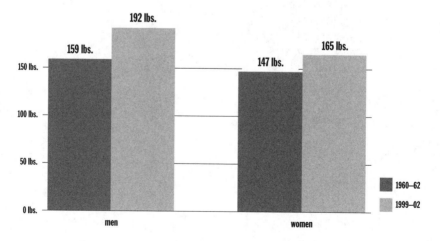

Table 2.3 Average Measured Weight by Sex and Age, 1960–62 and 1999–02

(average weight in pounds of people aged 20 to 74, by sex and age, 1960–62 and 1999–02; change in pounds 1960–62 to 1999–02)

	1999–02	1960–62	change in pounds
Men aged 20 to 74	**191.0 lbs.**	**166.3 lbs.**	**24.7 lbs.**
Aged 20 to 29	183.4	163.9	19.5
Aged 30 to 39	189.1	169.9	19.2
Aged 40 to 49	196.0	169.1	26.9
Aged 50 to 59	195.4	167.7	27.7
Aged 60 to 74	191.5	158.9	32.6
Women aged 20 to 74	**164.3**	**140.2**	**24.1**
Aged 20 to 29	156.5	127.7	28.8
Aged 30 to 39	163.0	138.8	24.2
Aged 40 to 49	168.2	142.8	25.4
Aged 50 to 59	169.2	146.5	22.7
Aged 60 to 74	164.7	147.3	17.4

Note: Data are based on measured weight of a sample of the civilian noninstitutionalized population.
Source: National Center for Health Statistics, Mean Body Weight, Height, and Body Mass Index, United States 1960–2002, Advance Data, No. 347, 2004, Internet site http://www.cdc.gov/nchs/pressroom/04news/americans.htm; calculations by New Strategist

Table 2.4 Weight Status by Sex and Age, 1999–02

(percent distribution of people aged 20 or older by weight status, by sex and age, 1999–02)

	healthy weight	overweight total	overweight obese
Total people	**32.9%**	**65.2%**	**30.5%**
Total men	**30.4**	**68.6**	**27.5**
Aged 20 to 34	40.3	57.4	21.7
Aged 35 to 44	29.0	70.5	28.5
Aged 45 to 54	24.0	75.7	30.6
Aged 55 to 64	23.8	75.4	35.5
Aged 65 to 74	22.8	76.2	31.9
Aged 75 or older	32.0	67.4	18.0
Total women	**35.4**	**62.0**	**33.4**
Aged 20 to 34	42.6	52.8	28.4
Aged 35 to 44	37.1	60.6	32.1
Aged 45 to 54	33.1	65.1	36.9
Aged 55 to 64	27.6	72.2	42.1
Aged 65 to 74	26.4	70.9	39.3
Aged 75 or older	36.9	59.9	23.6

Note: Data are based on measured height and weight of a sample of the civilian noninstitutionalized population. Being overweight is defined as having a body mass index of 25 or higher. Obesity is defined as a body mass index of 30 or higher. Body mass index is calculated by dividing weight in kilograms by height in meters squared.
Source: National Center for Health Statistics, Health, United States, 2005, Internet site http://www.cdc.gov/nchs/hus.htm

Table 2.5 Weight Loss Behavior by Age, 2000

(percent of people aged 18 or older engaging in selected weight loss behaviors, by age, 2000)

	total	18 to 24	25 to 34	35 to 44	45 to 54	55 to 64	65 or older
Trying to lose weight	38.0%	30.2%	38.0%	40.4%	44.7%	42.6%	30.6%
Trying to maintain weight	58.9	51.9	56.9	59.8	63.1	60.8	58.4
Eating fewer calories to lose/ maintain weight*	13.5	11.4	12.1	13.9	15.2	13.2	12.0
Eating less fat to lose/maintain weight*	27.4	25.3	25.8	27.7	28.3	29.1	29.4
Eating fewer calories and less fat to lose/maintain weight*	29.6	25.5	27.0	30.1	32.6	33.0	29.0
Using physical activity or exercise to lose/maintain weight*	60.7	74.7	67.7	64.0	60.5	55.4	43.3
Advised by health professional to lose weight	11.7	4.0	8.4	11.3	16.0	17.7	11.2

* Among those trying to lose or maintain weight.
Source: Centers for Disease Control and Prevention, Behavioral Risk Factor Surveillance System Prevalence Data, 2000, Internet site http://apps.nccd.cdc.gov/brfss/index.asp

Few Older Americans Are Physically Active

The majority of those aged 75 or older are physically inactive.

Although many people claim to exercise, few older Americans participate in regular leisure-time physical activities. Forty-one percent of people aged 55 to 64 are physically inactive during their leisure time, a figure that rises to 46 percent among people aged 65 to 74 and to the 58 percent majority among people aged 75 or older.

Only 28 to 29 percent of people aged 55 to 74 participate regularly in leisure-time physical activities. The figure falls to just 18 percent among those aged 75 or older.

■ If more communities encouraged walking rather than driving, the proportion of Americans who regularly exercise might increase.

Most people do not exercise regularly

(percent of people aged 18 or older who participate regularly in leisure-time physical activity, by age, 2003)

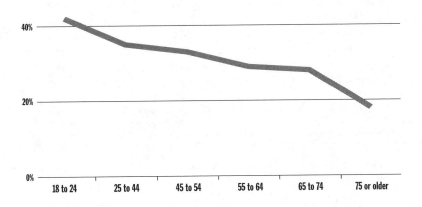

Table 2.6 Leisure-Time Physical Activity Level by Sex and Age, 2003

(percent distribution of people aged 18 or older by leisure-time physical activity level, by sex and age, 2003)

	total	physically inactive	at least some physical activity	regular physical activity
Total people	**100.0%**	**37.6%**	**29.6%**	**32.8%**
Aged 18 to 24	100.0	29.6	28.2	42.3
Aged 25 to 44	100.0	34.0	31.0	34.9
Aged 45 to 54	100.0	36.5	30.8	32.8
Aged 55 to 64	100.0	40.8	30.1	29.2
Aged 65 to 74	100.0	45.8	25.8	28.4
Aged 75 or older	100.0	57.5	24.8	17.7
Total men	**100.0**	**35.4**	**29.2**	**35.4**
Aged 18 to 44	100.0	30.9	29.5	39.6
Aged 45 to 54	100.0	36.4	30.5	33.2
Aged 55 to 64	100.0	39.5	29.7	30.8
Aged 65 to 74	100.0	43.0	24.9	32.1
Aged 75 or older	100.0	48.1	28.9	23.0
Total women	**100.0**	**39.5**	**29.9**	**30.6**
Aged 18 to 44	100.0	34.9	31.1	34.0
Aged 45 to 54	100.0	36.5	31.1	32.4
Aged 55 to 64	100.0	41.9	30.4	27.6
Aged 65 to 74	100.0	48.0	26.6	25.4
Aged 75 or older	100.0	63.7	22.0	14.3

Note: "Physically inactive" are those with no sessions of light/moderate or vigorous leisure-time physical activity of at least 10 minutes duration during past week. "At least some physical activity" includes those who performed at least one light/moderate or vigorous leisure-time physical activity of at least 10 minutes duration during past week, but did not meet the definition for regular leisure-time activity. "Regular physical activity" includes those with three or more sessions per week of vigorous activity lasting at least 20 minutes or five or more sessions per week of light/moderate activity lasting at least 30 minutes.
Source: National Center for Health Statistics, Health, United States, 2005, Internet site http://www.cdc.gov/nchs/hus.htm

Smoking Declines Sharply with Age

Only 9 percent of people aged 65 or older smoke cigarettes.

The percentage of Americans who smoke cigarettes is sharply lower than what it was a few decades ago. Nevertheless, a substantial 21 percent of people aged 18 or older were current smokers in 2004. The figure peaks among 18-to-24-year-olds at 27 percent. Among people aged 55 to 64, a smaller 18 percent smoke, and the figure is only half that (9 percent) among people aged 65 or older. Former smokers greatly outnumber current smokers among people aged 55 or older.

Drinking is more popular than smoking among older Americans. Overall, 57 percent of people aged 18 or older have had an alcoholic beverage in the past month. The proportion peaks at 63 percent in the 25-to-34 age group, then declines with age. A 40 percent minority of people aged 65 or older have had a drink in the past month.

Few older Americans have ever used illicit drugs, but that is about to change. Among people aged 55 to 59, a substantial 38 percent have used illicit drugs at some time during their lives, a figure that will climb as younger Boomers enter the age group. The proportion of people aged 55 or older who have used illicit drugs during the past year is 5 percent or less.

■ As health problems increase with age, smoking and drinking become less common.

Many older Americans have quit smoking

(percent distribution of people aged 65 or older by cigarette smoking status, 2004)

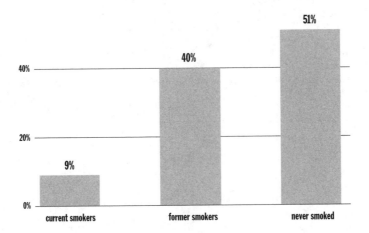

Table 2.7 Cigarette Smoking Status by Age, 2004

(percent distribution of people aged 18 or older by age and cigarette smoking status, 2004)

	total	current smoker total	smoke every day	smoke some days	former smoker	never smoked
Total people	**100.0%**	**20.9%**	**15.6%**	**5.3%**	**23.9%**	**54.9%**
Aged 18 to 24	100.0	26.9	18.5	8.4	8.0	64.1
Aged 25 to 34	100.0	24.9	17.4	7.5	14.3	59.8
Aged 35 to 44	100.0	23.7	18.4	5.3	17.2	58.0
Aged 45 to 54	100.0	22.4	17.4	5.0	25.6	50.9
Aged 55 to 64	100.0	18.2	14.6	3.6	36.3	45.5
Aged 65 or older	100.0	9.0	6.9	2.1	39.5	51.0

Source: Centers for Disease Control and Prevention, Behavioral Risk Factor Surveillance System Prevalence Data, 2004, Internet site http://apps.nccd.cdc.gov/brfss/index.asp; calculations by New Strategist

Table 2.8 Alcohol Use by Age, 2004

(percent distribution of people aged 18 or older by whether they have had at least one drink of alcohol within the past 30 days, by age, 2004)

	yes	no
Total people	**56.8%**	**43.1%**
Aged 18 to 24	58.4	40.8
Aged 25 to 34	62.9	37.0
Aged 35 to 44	60.6	39.3
Aged 45 to 54	58.5	41.4
Aged 55 to 64	53.3	46.6
Aged 65 or older	39.9	60.0

Source: Centers for Disease Control and Prevention, Behavioral Risk Factor Surveillance System Prevalence Data, 2004, Internet site http://apps.nccd.cdc.gov/brfss/index.asp

Table 2.9 Illicit Drug Use by Age, 2004

(percent of people aged 12 or older who ever used any illicit drug, who used an illicit drug in the past year, and who used an illicit drug in the past month, by age, 2004)

	ever used	used in past year	used in past month
Total people	**45.8%**	**14.5%**	**7.9%**
Aged 12 to 17	30.0	21.0	10.6
Aged 18 to 25	59.2	33.9	19.4
Aged 26 to 29	60.0	23.5	13.2
Aged 30 to 34	54.5	15.7	9.4
Aged 35 to 39	59.4	14.1	7.2
Aged 40 to 44	64.9	14.4	7.5
Aged 45 to 49	61.8	11.8	6.8
Aged 50 to 54	56.3	9.0	4.8
Aged 55 to 59	38.2	5.1	2.6
Aged 60 to 64	24.2	2.0	1.1
Aged 65 or older	8.3	0.9	0.4

Note: Illicit drugs include marijuana/hashish, cocaine (including crack), heroin, hallucinogens, inhalants, or any prescription-type psychotherapeutic used nonmedically.
Source: SAMHSA, Office of Applied Studies, National Survey on Drug Use and Health, 2004, Internet site http://oas.samhsa .gov/nsduh/2k4nsduh/2k4Results/apph.htm

Many 55-to-64-Year-Olds Lack Health Insurance

Nearly 4 million 55-to-64-year-olds are not insured.

Among all Americans, 46 million lacked health insurance in 2004—or 16 percent of the population. While the figure is a smaller 13 percent among 55-to-64-year-olds, the chance of illness in that age group is much greater than average. Nearly everyone aged 65 or older has health insurance through the federal government's Medicare program.

Two-thirds of 55-to-64-year-olds have employment-based health insurance coverage, although only half have coverage through their own employer. Just 18 percent have government health insurance, including 7 percent with Medicaid coverage and 6 percent with military insurance. Fully 95 percent of people aged 65 or older are covered by Medicare, the government's health insurance program for the elderly.

■ As Baby Boomers become eligible for Medicare, entrepreneurialism will rise among them because health insurance needs will no longer tie them to an employer.

Thirteen percent of 55-to-64-year-olds have no health insurance

(percent of people without health insurance coverage, by age, 2004)

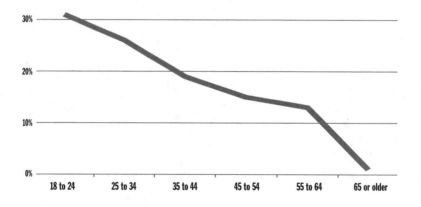

Table 2.10 Health Insurance Coverage by Age, 2004

(number and percent distribution of people by age and health insurance coverage status, 2004; numbers in thousands)

	total	with health insurance coverage during year			not covered at any time during the year
		total	private	government	
Total people	**291,155**	**245,335**	**198,262**	**79,086**	**45,820**
Under age 18	73,821	65,553	48,462	21,922	8,269
Aged 18 to 24	27,972	19,200	16,229	4,022	8,772
Aged 25 to 34	39,307	29,130	25,765	4,578	10,177
Aged 35 to 44	43,350	35,240	31,883	4,680	8,110
Aged 45 to 54	41,960	35,700	32,414	4,847	6,260
Aged 55 to 64	29,532	25,596	22,174	5,442	3,936
Aged 65 or older	35,213	34,916	21,336	33,595	297
PERCENT DISTRIBUTION BY COVERAGE STATUS					
Total people	**100.0%**	**84.3%**	**68.1%**	**27.2%**	**15.7%**
Under age 18	100.0	88.8	65.6	29.7	11.2
Aged 18 to 24	100.0	68.6	58.0	14.4	31.4
Aged 25 to 34	100.0	74.1	65.5	11.6	25.9
Aged 35 to 44	100.0	81.3	73.5	10.8	18.7
Aged 45 to 54	100.0	85.1	77.2	11.6	14.9
Aged 55 to 64	100.0	86.7	75.1	18.4	13.3
Aged 65 or older	100.0	99.2	60.6	95.4	0.8
PERCENT DISTRIBUTION BY AGE					
Total people	**100.0%**	**100.0%**	**100.0%**	**100.0%**	**100.0%**
Under age 18	25.4	26.7	24.4	27.7	18.0
Aged 18 to 24	9.6	7.8	8.2	5.1	19.1
Aged 25 to 34	13.5	11.9	13.0	5.8	22.2
Aged 35 to 44	14.9	14.4	16.1	5.9	17.7
Aged 45 to 54	14.4	14.6	16.3	6.1	13.7
Aged 55 to 64	10.1	10.4	11.2	6.9	8.6
Aged 65 or older	12.1	14.2	10.8	42.5	0.6

Note: Numbers may not add to total because some people have more than one type of health insurance coverage.
Source: Bureau of the Census, 2005 Current Population Survey, Internet site http://pubdb3.census.gov/macro/032005/health/ h01_000.htm; calculations by New Strategist

Table 2.11 Private Health Insurance Coverage by Age, 2004

(number and percent distribution of people by age and private health insurance coverage status, 2004; numbers in thousands)

| | | with private health insurance | | | |
| | | total | employment based | | |
	total	total	total	own	direct purchase
Total people	**291,155**	**198,262**	**174,174**	**91,709**	**26,961**
Under age 18	73,821	48,462	44,892	237	4,166
Aged 18 to 24	27,972	16,229	12,966	5,122	1,495
Aged 25 to 34	39,307	25,765	24,027	18,151	2,266
Aged 35 to 44	43,350	31,883	29,824	21,335	2,773
Aged 45 to 54	41,960	32,414	30,088	22,141	3,215
Aged 55 to 64	29,532	22,174	19,872	14,907	3,066
Aged 65 or older	35,213	21,336	12,505	9,817	9,979
PERCENT DISTRIBUTION BY COVERAGE STATUS					
Total people	**100.0%**	**68.1%**	**59.8%**	**31.5%**	**9.3%**
Under age 18	100.0	65.6	60.8	0.3	5.6
Aged 18 to 24	100.0	58.0	46.4	18.3	5.3
Aged 25 to 34	100.0	65.5	61.1	46.2	5.8
Aged 35 to 44	100.0	73.5	68.8	49.2	6.4
Aged 45 to 54	100.0	77.2	71.7	52.8	7.7
Aged 55 to 64	100.0	75.1	67.3	50.5	10.4
Aged 65 or older	100.0	60.6	35.5	27.9	28.3
PERCENT DISTRIBUTION BY AGE					
Total people	**100.0%**	**100.0%**	**100.0%**	**100.0%**	**100.0%**
Under age 18	25.4	24.4	25.8	0.3	15.5
Aged 18 to 24	9.6	8.2	7.4	5.6	5.5
Aged 25 to 34	13.5	13.0	13.8	19.8	8.4
Aged 35 to 44	14.9	16.1	17.1	23.3	10.3
Aged 45 to 54	14.4	16.3	17.3	24.1	11.9
Aged 55 to 64	10.1	11.2	11.4	16.3	11.4
Aged 65 or older	12.1	10.8	7.2	10.7	37.0

Note: Numbers may not add to total because some people have more than one type of health insurance coverage.
Source: Bureau of the Census, 2005 Current Population Survey, Internet site http://pubdb3.census.gov/macro/032005/health/h01_000.htm; calculations by New Strategist

Table 2.12 Government Health Insurance Coverage by Age, 2004

(number and percent distribution of people by age and government health insurance coverage status, 2004; numbers in thousands)

	total	with government health insurance			
		total	Medicaid	Medicare	military
Total people	**291,155**	**79,086**	**37,514**	**39,745**	**10,680**
Under age 18	73,821	21,922	19,847	500	2,045
Aged 18 to 24	27,972	4,022	3,196	212	804
Aged 25 to 34	39,307	4,578	3,408	482	982
Aged 35 to 44	43,350	4,680	3,135	900	1,129
Aged 45 to 54	41,960	4,847	2,595	1,548	1,425
Aged 55 to 64	29,532	5,442	2,036	2,651	1,785
Aged 65 or older	35,213	33,595	3,297	33,452	2,509
PERCENT DISTRIBUTION BY COVERAGE STATUS					
Total people	**100.0%**	**27.2%**	**12.9%**	**13.7%**	**3.7%**
Under age 18	100.0	29.7	26.9	0.7	2.8
Aged 18 to 24	100.0	14.4	11.4	0.8	2.9
Aged 25 to 34	100.0	11.6	8.7	1.2	2.5
Aged 35 to 44	100.0	10.8	7.2	2.1	2.6
Aged 45 to 54	100.0	11.6	6.2	3.7	3.4
Aged 55 to 64	100.0	18.4	6.9	9.0	6.0
Aged 65 or older	100.0	95.4	9.4	95.0	7.1
PERCENT DISTRIBUTION BY AGE					
Total people	**100.0%**	**100.0%**	**100.0%**	**100.0%**	**100.0%**
Under age 18	25.4	27.7	52.9	1.3	19.1
Aged 18 to 24	9.6	5.1	8.5	0.5	7.5
Aged 25 to 34	13.5	5.8	9.1	1.2	9.2
Aged 35 to 44	14.9	5.9	8.4	2.3	10.6
Aged 45 to 54	14.4	6.1	6.9	3.9	13.3
Aged 55 to 64	10.1	6.9	5.4	6.7	16.7
Aged 65 or older	12.1	42.5	8.8	84.2	23.5

Note: Numbers may not add to total because some people have more than one type of health insurance coverage.
Source: Bureau of the Census, 2005 Current Population Survey, Internet site http://pubdb3.census.gov/macro/032005/health/ h01_000.htm; calculations by New Strategist

Older Americans Spend Big on Health Care

Some expenses are covered by Medicare, but many are not.

Medical expenses are the norm for Americans regardless of age. But people aged 65 or older, because they have more medical problems, spend much more than younger adults on medical care.

In 2003, medical expenses for people aged 65 or older stood at a hefty median of $3,649, according to the federal government's Medical Expenditure Panel Survey. Medicare covered only 53 percent of the cost, while 19 percent was paid for out-of-pocket.

Among the 81 percent of people aged 55 to 64 with prescription drug expenses, the median expense was a considerable $864. Among the 91 percent of people aged 65 or older with prescription drug expenses, the median expense was $1,219. People aged 55 to 64 paid for 41 percent of their prescription drug expenses out-of-pocket. Among people aged 65 or older, 54 percent of prescription drug expenses were paid for out-of-pocket.

■ It remains to be seen how the new Medicare prescription drug plan will change the spending of older Americans on drugs.

Prescription drug expenses among older Americans exceed $1,000 per year

(median amount spent on medical care by people aged 65 or older with expense, by type of service, 2003)

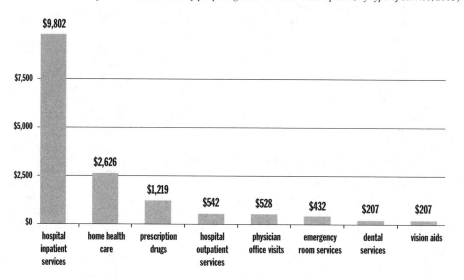

Table 2.13 Spending on Health Care by Age, 2003

(percent of people with health care expense, median expense per person, total expenses, and percent distribution of total expenses by source of payment, by age, 2003)

	total (thousands)	percent with expense	median expense per person	total expenses amount (millions)	total expenses percent distribution
Total people	**290,604**	**85.6%**	**$1,021**	**$895,527**	**100.0%**
Under age 18	72,996	86.4	425	80,187	9.0
Aged 18 to 44	111,141	79.0	758	228,017	25.5
Aged 45 to 54	40,295	87.9	1,539	134,724	15.0
Aged 55 to 59	16,180	90.9	2,163	88,150	9.8
Aged 60 to 64	13,293	93.4	2,646	74,167	8.3
Aged 65 or older	36,699	96.3	3,649	290,283	32.4
Aged 65 to 69	9,994	94.1	2,775	67,130	7.5
Aged 70 to 74	9,074	96.6	3,681	76,549	8.5
Aged 75 to 79	7,839	97.3	4,189	61,536	6.9
Aged 80 or older	9,792	97.6	4,418	85,068	9.5

PERCENT DISTRIBUTION OF TOTAL EXPENSES BY SOURCE OF PAYMENT

	total	out of pocket	private insurance	Medicare	Medicaid	other
Total people	**100.0%**	**19.6%**	**42.4%**	**19.9%**	**9.2%**	**8.9%**
Under age 18	100.0	20.5	50.3	–	22.6	6.3
Aged 18 to 44	100.0	18.8	52.9	–	13.2	13.0
Aged 45 to 54	100.0	22.0	55.2	–	7.9	8.6
Aged 55 to 59	100.0	17.7	60.9	–	6.2	8.9
Aged 60 to 64	100.0	22.4	56.3	–	7.0	6.4
Aged 65 or older	100.0	18.8	16.7	53.0	4.3	7.2
Aged 65 to 69	100.0	18.2	27.8	42.0	4.5	7.5
Aged 70 to 74	100.0	16.4	16.9	55.3	3.6	7.7
Aged 75 to 79	100.0	20.5	13.5	54.8	3.6	7.6
Aged 80 or older	100.0	20.3	10.1	58.1	5.2	6.3

Note: "Other" insurance includes Department of Veterans Affairs (except Tricare), American Indian Health Service, state and local clinics, worker's compensation, homeowner's and automobile insurance, etc. "–" means not applicable or sample is too small to make a reliable estimate.
Source: Agency for Healthcare Research and Quality, Medical Expenditure Panel Survey, 2003, Internet site http://www.meps .ahrq.gov/CompendiumTables/TC_TOC.htm; calculations by New Strategist

Table 2.14 Health Care Expenditures of People Aged 55 to 64, 2003

(percent of people aged 55 to 64 with health care expense, median amount spent by those with expense, total expenses and percent distribution by type, and percent distribution of expenses by source of payment, 2003)

	percent with expense	median amount spent by those with expense	total expenses (millions)	total expenses percent distribution
Any health care expense	**92.0%**	**$2,410**	**$162,316**	**100.0%**
Prescription medicine	80.8	864	37,823	23.3
Dental services	47.0	239	8,215	5.1
Vision aids	20.1	245	1,648	1.0
Hospital inpatient services	8.7	10,014	56,184	34.6
Emergency room services	12.1	531	4,141	2.6
Hospital outpatient services	29.9	725	18,194	11.2
Physician office visits	78.8	398	21,297	13.1
Home health care	2.5	–	–	–

PERCENT DISTRIBUTION OF TOTAL EXPENSES BY SOURCE OF PAYMENT

	total	out of pocket	private insurance	Medicare	Medicaid	other
Any health care expense	**100.0%**	**19.9%**	**58.8%**	**–**	**6.6%**	**7.7%**
Prescription medicine	100.0	41.3	44.0	–	10.3	3.5
Dental services	100.0	53.9	40.7	–	1.7	3.7
Vision aids	100.0	75.7	19.7	–	2.7	1.6
Hospital inpatient services	100.0	1.9	73.5	–	4.3	8.0
Emergency room services	100.0	9.3	65.0	–	4.6	13.1
Hospital outpatient services	100.0	8.1	71.1	–	5.5	9.8
Physician office visits	100.0	16.7	57.1	–	6.3	12.6
Home health care	100.0	–	–	–	–	–

Note: "Other" insurance includes Department of Veterans Affairs (except Tricare), American Indian Health Service, state and local clinics, worker's compensation, homeowner's and automobile insurance, etc. Subcategories will not add to total expenses because not all health care expenses are shown. "–" means sample is too small to make a reliable estimate or not applicable.
Source: Agency for Healthcare Research and Quality, Medical Expenditure Panel Survey, 2003, Internet site http://www.meps.ahrq.gov/CompendiumTables/TC_TOC.htm; calculations by New Strategist

Table 2.15 Health Care Expenditures of People Aged 65 or older, 2003

(percent of people aged 65 or older with health care expense, median amount spent by those with expense, total expenses and percent distribution by type, and percent distribution of expenses by source of payment, 2003)

	percent with expense	median amount spent by those with expense	total expenses (millions)	total expenses percent distribution
Any health care expense	**96.3%**	**$3,649**	**$290,283**	**100.0%**
Prescription medicine	91.0	1,219	59,637	20.5
Dental services	38.5	207	7,227	2.5
Vision aids	18.8	207	1,676	0.6
Hospital inpatient services	19.8	9,802	116,265	40.1
Emergency room services	19.4	432	5,154	1.8
Hospital outpatient services	37.9	542	26,084	9.0
Physician office visits	88.6	528	35,218	12.1
Home health care	9.9	2,626	19,790	6.8

PERCENT DISTRIBUTION OF TOTAL EXPENSES BY SOURCE OF PAYMENT

	total	out of pocket	private insurance	Medicare	Medicaid	other
Any health care expense	**100.0%**	**18.8%**	**16.7%**	**53.0%**	**4.3%**	**7.2%**
Prescription medicine	100.0	53.5	22.0	8.1	8.7	7.7
Dental services	100.0	72.1	20.9	2.2	1.0	3.7
Vision aids	100.0	76.2	12.2	4.4	4.9	2.4
Hospital inpatient services	100.0	1.2	13.4	78.2	1.2	5.9
Emergency room services	100.0	6.6	14.1	69.6	2.8	6.9
Hospital outpatient services	100.0	4.0	19.2	67.3	0.9	8.5
Physician office visits	100.0	8.5	21.7	58.8	1.9	9.2
Home health care	100.0	26.5	1.6	44.7	19.7	7.5

Note: "Other" insurance includes Department of Veterans Affairs (except Tricare), American Indian Health Service, state and local clinics, worker's compensation, homeowner's and automobile insurance, etc. Subcategories will not add to total expenses because not all health care expenses are shown.
Source: Agency for Healthcare Research and Quality, Medical Expenditure Panel Survey, 2003, Internet site http://www.meps .ahrq.gov/CompendiumTables/TC_TOC.htm; calculations by New Strategist

Health Problems Are Common in the 65-or-Older Age Group

Hypertension and arthritis are the most common health conditions among people aged 65 or older.

Fifty to 55 percent of Americans aged 65 or older have hypertension, making it one of the two most common health conditions in the age group. The other is arthritis, with 47 to 56 percent have been diagnosed. Thirty-two to 49 percent of people aged 65 or older have hearing problems, and 19 to 25 percent cancer.

The percentage of people who experience health problems rises steeply with age for most conditions. The percentage of people with hypertension rises from just 7 percent of 18-to-44-year-olds to more than half of those aged 75 or older. Similarly, the prevalence of arthritis rises from 8 to 56 percent. Hearing problems increase from just 8 to 49 percent.

As Americans became more aware of the problems associated with high cholesterol over the past few decades, rates have dropped in most age groups. The same cannot be said for high blood pressure. The majority of men aged 65 or older and women aged 55 or older had high blood pressure or were taking hypertensive medication in 1999–02, a significantly larger share than in 1988–94.

■ As the Baby-Boom generation ages into the 65-or-older age group, the number of people with hypertension, arthritis, and hearing problems will surge.

The percentage of people with arthritis rises with age

(percent of people diagnosed with arthritis, by age, 2004)

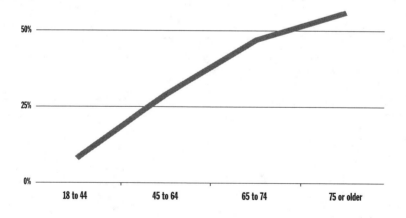

Table 2.16 Health Conditions among People Aged 18 or Older by Age, 2004

(number of people aged 18 or older with selected health conditions, by type of condition and age, 2004; numbers in thousands)

	total	18 to 44	45 to 64	65 to 74	75 or older
NUMBER					
Total people	**215,191**	**110,417**	**70,182**	**18,360**	**16,232**
Selected circulatory diseases					
Heart disease, all types	24,666	4,953	8,636	4,994	6,082
Coronary	13,621	1,184	4,858	3,358	4,221
Hypertension	47,493	8,133	21,303	9,089	8,968
Stroke	5,519	510	1,750	1,257	2,002
Selected respiratory conditions					
Emphysema	3,576	309	1,393	904	970
Asthma					
Ever	21,300	10,959	6,973	1,893	1,474
Still	14,358	7,058	4,871	1,368	1,061
Hay fever	18,629	8,777	7,252	1,475	1,126
Sinusitis	30,789	13,976	11,769	2,780	2,265
Chronic bronchitis	9,047	3,483	3,413	1,126	1,026
Cancer, any	**15,024**	**2,046**	**5,551**	**3,428**	**3,999**
Breast cancer (men and women)	2,581	160	1,089	555	778
Cervical cancer	1,108	506	430	79	93
Prostate cancer	1,688	–	379	488	815
Other selected diseases and conditions					
Diabetes	15,126	2,173	6,963	3,393	2,598
Ulcers	14,828	4,956	5,722	2,002	2,148
Kidney disease	3,652	972	1,250	629	801
Liver disease	2,860	878	1,449	263	270
Arthritic diagnosis	46,515	8,841	20,169	8,496	9,008
Chronic joint symptoms	58,005	17,349	24,439	8,181	8,036
Migraines or severe headaches	32,923	20,279	10,523	1,292	830
Pain in neck	31,742	13,721	13,050	2,540	2,430
Pain in lower back	58,394	26,382	21,543	5,225	5,243
Pain in face or jaw	9,215	4,939	3,272	598	406
Selected sensory problems					
Hearing trouble	35,135	8,459	12,960	5,800	7,917
Vision trouble	19,086	5,624	7,641	2,591	3,230
Absence of all natural teeth	16,814	2,016	5,927	3,909	4,962

(continued)

	total	18 to 44	45 to 64	65 to 74	75 or older
Selected mental health problems					
Sadness	24,232	11,215	8,984	1,948	2,085
Hopelessness	13,259	6,570	5,006	741	942
Worthlessness	10,400	5,033	3,816	603	947
Everything is an effort	29,686	15,395	9,783	2,133	2,375
Nervousness	33,450	17,899	10,996	2,311	2,244
Restlessness	36,172	19,322	11,909	2,573	2,367

Note: The conditions shown are those that have ever been diagnosed by a doctor, except as noted. Hay fever, sinusitis, and chronic bronchitis have been diagnosed in the past twelve months. Kidney and liver disease have been diagnosed in the past twelve months and exclude kidney stones, bladder infections, and incontinence. Chronic joint symptoms are shown if the respondent had pain, aching, or stiffness in or around a joint (excluding back and neck) and the condition began more than three months ago. Migraines, pain in neck, lower back, face, or jaw are shown only if pain lasted a whole day or more. Hearing trouble is anyone saying they had at least "a little trouble." Vision trouble is anyone with "any trouble seeing" even when wearing glasses or contacts. Mental health problems are indicated if the person had the feeling during the past 30 days at least "some of the time." "–" means sample is too small to make a reliable estimate.
Source: National Center for Health Statistics, Summary Health Statistics for U.S. Adults: National Health Interview Survey, 2004, Series 10, No. 228, 2005, Internet site http://www.cdc.gov/nchs/nhis.htm; calculations by New Strategist

Table 2.17 Percent with Health Condition by Age, 2004

(percent of people aged 18 or older with selected health conditions, by type of condition and age, 2004)

	total	18 to 44	45 to 64	65 to 74	75 or older
PERCENT WITH CONDITION					
Total people	**100.0%**	**100.0%**	**100.0%**	**100.0%**	**100.0%**
Selected circulatory diseases					
Heart disease, all types	11.5	4.5	12.3	27.3	37.6
Coronary	6.3	1.1	6.9	18.4	26.1
Hypertension	22.1	7.4	30.5	49.8	55.4
Stroke	2.6	0.5	2.5	6.9	12.4
Selected respiratory conditions					
Emphysema	1.7	0.3	2.0	4.9	6.0
Asthma					
Ever	9.9	9.9	10.0	10.3	9.1
Still	6.7	6.4	7.0	7.5	6.6
Hay fever	8.7	8.0	10.4	8.0	7.0
Sinusitis	14.3	12.7	16.8	15.2	14.0
Chronic bronchitis	4.2	3.2	4.9	6.1	6.3
Cancer, any	**7.0**	**1.9**	**7.9**	**18.7**	**24.7**
Breast cancer (men and women)	1.2	0.1	1.6	3.0	4.8
Cervical cancer	1.0	0.9	1.2	0.8	0.9
Prostate cancer	1.6	–	1.1	5.8	13.0
Other selected diseases and conditions					
Diabetes	7.1	2.0	10.1	18.9	16.4
Ulcers	6.9	4.5	8.2	10.9	13.3
Kidney disease	1.7	0.9	1.8	3.4	4.9
Liver disease	1.3	0.8	2.1	1.4	1.7
Arthritic diagnosis	21.7	8.0	28.8	46.5	55.8
Chronic joint symptoms	27.0	15.7	35.0	44.7	49.8
Migraines or severe headaches	15.3	18.4	15.0	7.1	5.1
Pain in neck	14.8	12.4	18.7	13.9	15.0
Pain in lower back	27.2	23.9	30.8	28.5	32.5
Pain in face or jaw	4.3	4.5	4.7	3.3	2.5
Selected sensory problems					
Hearing trouble	16.3	7.7	18.5	31.7	48.9
Vision trouble	8.9	5.1	10.9	14.1	19.9
Absence of all natural teeth	7.8	1.8	8.5	21.3	30.7

(continued)

	total	18 to 44	45 to 64	65 to 74	75 or older
Selected mental health problems					
Sadness	11.4%	10.3%	13.0%	10.8%	13.3%
Hopelessness	6.3	6.1	7.3	4.1	6.1
Worthlessness	4.9	4.6	5.5	3.4	6.1
Everything is an effort	14.1	14.2	14.2	11.9	15.2
Nervousness	15.8	16.4	15.9	12.8	14.3
Restlessness	17.1	17.7	17.2	14.3	15.1

Note: The conditions shown are those that have ever been diagnosed by a doctor, except as noted. Hay fever, sinusitis, and chronic bronchitis have been diagnosed in the past twelve months. Kidney and liver disease have been diagnosed in the past twelve months and exclude kidney stones, bladder infections, and incontinence. Chronic joint symptoms are shown if the respondent had pain, aching, or stiffness in or around a joint (excluding back and neck) and the condition began more than three months ago. Migraines, pain in neck, lower back, face, or jaw are shown only if pain lasted a whole day or more. Hearing trouble is anyone saying they had at least "a little trouble." Vision trouble is anyone with "any trouble seeing" even when wearing glasses or contacts. Mental health problems are indicated if the person had the feeling during the past 30 days at least "some of the time." "–" means sample is too small to make a reliable estimate.

Source: National Center for Health Statistics, Summary Health Statistics for U.S. Adults: National Health Interview Survey, 2004, Series 10, No. 228, 2005, Internet site http://www.cdc.gov/nchs/nhis.htm; calculations by New Strategist

Table 2.18 Distribution of Health Conditions by Age, 2004

(percent distribution of people aged 18 or older with selected health conditions, by type of condition and age, 2004)

	total	18 to 44	45 to 64	65 to 74	75 or older
PERCENT DISTRIBUTION					
Total people	**100.0%**	**51.3%**	**32.6%**	**8.5%**	**7.5%**
Selected circulatory diseases					
Heart disease, all types	100.0	20.1	35.0	20.2	24.7
Coronary	100.0	8.7	35.7	24.7	31.0
Hypertension	100.0	17.1	44.9	19.1	18.9
Stroke	100.0	9.2	31.7	22.8	36.3
Selected respiratory conditions					
Emphysema	100.0	8.6	39.0	25.3	27.1
Asthma					
Ever	100.0	51.5	32.7	8.9	6.9
Still	100.0	49.2	33.9	9.5	7.4
Hay fever	100.0	47.1	38.9	7.9	6.0
Sinusitis	100.0	45.4	38.2	9.0	7.4
Chronic bronchitis	100.0	38.5	37.7	12.4	11.3
Cancer, any	**100.0**	**13.6**	**36.9**	**22.8**	**26.6**
Breast cancer (men and women)	100.0	6.2	42.2	21.5	30.1
Cervical cancer	100.0	45.7	38.8	7.1	8.4
Prostate cancer	100.0	–	22.5	28.9	48.3
Other selected diseases and conditions					
Diabetes	100.0	14.4	46.0	22.4	17.2
Ulcers	100.0	33.4	38.6	13.5	14.5
Kidney disease	100.0	26.6	34.2	17.2	21.9
Liver disease	100.0	30.7	50.7	9.2	9.4
Arthritic diagnosis	100.0	19.0	43.4	18.3	19.4
Chronic joint symptoms	100.0	29.9	42.1	14.1	13.9
Migraines or severe headaches	100.0	61.6	32.0	3.9	2.5
Pain in neck	100.0	43.2	41.1	8.0	7.7
Pain in lower back	100.0	45.2	36.9	8.9	9.0
Pain in face or jaw	100.0	53.6	35.5	6.5	4.4
Selected sensory problems					
Hearing trouble	100.0	24.1	36.9	16.5	22.5
Vision trouble	100.0	29.5	40.0	13.6	16.9
Absence of all natural teeth	100.0	12.0	35.3	23.2	29.5

(continued)

	total	18 to 44	45 to 64	65 to 74	75 or older
Selected mental health problems					
Sadness	100.0%	46.3%	37.1%	8.0%	8.6%
Hopelessness	100.0	49.6	37.8	5.6	7.1
Worthlessness	100.0	48.4	36.7	5.8	9.1
Everything is an effort	100.0	51.9	33.0	7.2	8.0
Nervousness	100.0	53.5	32.9	6.9	6.7
Restlessness	100.0	53.4	32.9	7.1	6.5

Note: The conditions shown are those that have ever been diagnosed by a doctor, except as noted. Hay fever, sinusitis, and chronic bronchitis have been diagnosed in the past twelve months. Kidney and liver disease have been diagnosed in the past twelve months and exclude kidney stones, bladder infections, and incontinence. Chronic joint symptoms are shown if the respondent had pain, aching, or stiffness in or around a joint (excluding back and neck) and the condition began more than three months ago. Migraines, pain in neck, lower back, face, or jaw are shown only if pain lasted a whole day or more. Hearing trouble is anyone saying they had at least "a little trouble." Vision trouble is anyone with "any trouble seeing" even when wearing glasses or contacts. Mental health problems are indicated if the person had the feeling during the past 30 days at least "some of the time." "–" means sample is too small to make a reliable estimate.

Source: National Center for Health Statistics, Summary Health Statistics for U.S. Adults: National Health Interview Survey, 2004, Series 10, No. 228, 2005, Internet site http://www.cdc.gov/nchs/nhis.htm; calculations by New Strategist

Table 2.19 High Cholesterol by Sex and Age, 1988–94 and 1999–02

(percent of people aged 20 or older who have high serum cholesterol, by sex and age, 1988–94 and 1999–02; percentage point change, 1988–94 to 1999–02)

	1999–02	1988–94	percentage point change
Total people	**17.3%**	**19.6%**	**−2.3**
Total men	**16.6**	**17.7**	**−1.1**
Aged 20 to 34	9.8	8.2	1.6
Aged 35 to 44	19.8	19.4	0.4
Aged 45 to 54	23.6	26.6	−3.0
Aged 55 to 64	19.9	28.0	−8.1
Aged 65 to 74	13.7	21.9	−8.2
Aged 75 or older	10.2	20.4	−10.2
Total women	**18.0**	**21.3**	**−3.3**
Aged 20 to 34	8.9	7.3	1.6
Aged 35 to 44	12.4	12.3	0.1
Aged 45 to 54	21.4	26.7	−5.3
Aged 55 to 64	25.6	40.9	−15.3
Aged 65 to 74	32.3	41.3	−9.0
Aged 75 or older	26.5	38.2	−11.7

Note: High cholesterol is defined as 240 mg/dL or more.
Source: National Center for Health Statistics, Health, United States, 2005, Internet site http://www.cdc.gov/nchs/hus.htm; calculations by New Strategist

Table 2.20 High Blood Pressure by Sex and Age, 1988–94 and 1999–02

(percent of people aged 20 or older with hypertension or who take antihypertensive medication, by sex and age, 1988–94 and 1999–02; percentage point change, 1988–94 to 1999–02)

	1999–02	1988–94	percentage point change
Total people	**30.2%**	**24.1%**	**6.1**
Total men	**27.6**	**23.8**	**3.8**
Aged 20 to 34	8.1	7.1	1.0
Aged 35 to 44	17.1	17.1	0.0
Aged 45 to 54	31.0	29.2	1.8
Aged 55 to 64	45.0	40.6	4.4
Aged 65 to 74	59.6	54.4	5.2
Aged 75 or older	69.0	60.4	8.6
Total women	**32.7**	**24.4**	**8.3**
Aged 20 to 34	2.7	2.9	–0.2
Aged 35 to 44	15.1	11.2	3.9
Aged 45 to 54	31.8	23.9	7.9
Aged 55 to 64	53.9	42.6	11.3
Aged 65 to 74	72.7	56.2	16.5
Aged 75 or older	83.1	73.6	9.5

Note: A person with hypertension is defined as someone who has systolic pressure of at least 140 mmHg or diastolic pressure of at least 90 mmHg, or who takes antihypertensive medication.
Source: National Center for Health Statistics, Health, United States, 2005, Internet site http://www.cdc.gov/nchs/hus.htm; calculations by New Strategist

Prescription Drug Use Is Increasing

More Americans use a growing number of prescriptions.

The use of prescription drugs to treat a variety of illnesses, particularly chronic conditions, increased substantially between 1988–94 and 1999-02. The percentage of people who took at least one drug in the past month rose from 38 to 45 percent during those years. The percentage of those who used three or more prescription drugs in the past month climbed from 11 to 18 percent. Eighty-five percent of people aged 65 or older took at least one prescription drug in the past month, and 52 percent took three or more.

Regardless of age, most people have incurred a prescription drug expense during the past year, with the proportion rising from a low of 53 percent among children to a high of 91 percent among people aged 65 or older, according to the federal government's Medical Expenditure Panel Survey. Expenses for prescription drugs rise with age, to more than $1,200 per year for people aged 65 or older. Among the elderly, the 54 percent majority of prescription drug expenses are paid for out-of-pocket. These figures will change as the new Medicare prescription drug benefit alters payment patterns.

■ Behind the increase in the use of prescriptions is the introduction and marketing of new drugs to treat chronic health problems.

Most people have prescription drug expenses

(percent of people with prescription drug expenses, by age, 2003)

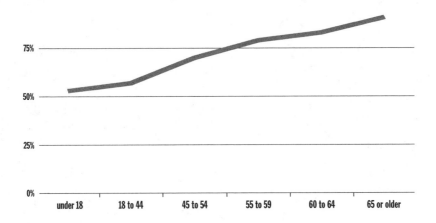

Table 2.21 Prescription Drug Use by Sex and Age, 1988–94 and 1999–02

(percent of people aged 18 or older who took at least one or three or more prescription drugs in the past month, by sex and age, 1988–94 and 1999–02; percentage point change, 1988–94 to 1999–02)

	at least one			three or more		
	1999–02	1988–94	percentage point change	1999–02	1988–94	percentage point change
Total people	**45.1%**	**37.8%**	**7.3**	**17.6%**	**11.0%**	**6.6**
Under age 18	24.2	20.5	3.7	4.1	2.4	1.7
Aged 18 to 44	35.9	31.3	4.6	8.4	5.7	2.7
Aged 45 to 64	64.1	54.8	9.3	30.8	20.0	10.8
Aged 65 or older	84.7	73.6	11.1	51.6	35.3	16.3
Total females	**51.2**	**44.6**	**6.6**	**21.1**	**13.6**	**7.5**
Under age 18	22.0	20.6	1.4	3.9	2.3	1.6
Aged 18 to 44	44.6	40.7	3.9	10.2	7.6	2.6
Aged 45 to 64	72.0	62.0	10.0	37.4	24.7	12.7
Aged 65 or older	88.1	78.3	9.8	55.7	38.2	17.5
Total males	**38.7**	**30.6**	**8.1**	**13.9**	**8.3**	**5.6**
Under age 18	26.2	20.4	5.8	4.3	2.6	1.7
Aged 18 to 44	27.1	21.5	5.6	6.7	3.6	3.1
Aged 45 to 64	55.6	47.2	8.4	23.5	15.1	8.4
Aged 65 or older	80.1	67.2	12.9	46.0	31.3	14.7

Source: National Center for Health Statistics, Health, United States, 2005, Internet site http://www.cdc.gov/nchs/hus.htm; calculations by New Strategist

Table 2.22 Spending on Prescription Medications by Age, 2003

(percent of people with prescription medication expense, median expense per person, total expenses, and percent distribution of total expenses by source of payment, by age, 2003)

	total (thousands)	percent with expense	median expense per person	total expenses amount (millions)	total expenses percent distribution
Total people	**290,604**	**64.4%**	**$306**	**$177,653**	**100.0%**
Under age 18	72,996	53.2	72	10,464	5.9
Aged 18 to 44	111,141	56.5	184	38,082	21.4
Aged 45 to 54	40,295	70.0	475	31,647	17.8
Aged 55 to 59	16,180	79.0	779	19,801	11.1
Aged 60 to 64	13,293	82.9	983	18,022	10.1
Aged 65 or older	36,699	91.0	1,219	59,637	33.6
Aged 65 to 69	9,994	87.2	1,043	15,009	8.4
Aged 70 to 74	9,074	91.1	1,255	15,566	8.8
Aged 75 to 79	7,839	92.8	1,329	13,335	7.5
Aged 80 or older	9,792	93.5	1,253	15,726	8.9

PERCENT DISTRIBUTION OF TOTAL EXPENSES BY SOURCE OF PAYMENT

	total	out of pocket	private insurance	Medicare	Medicaid	other
Total people	**100.0%**	**44.9%**	**35.1%**	**3.3%**	**12.4%**	**4.3%**
Under age 18	100.0	38.3	37.4	–	24.2	0.1
Aged 18 to 44	100.0	40.9	38.4	–	17.6	1.9
Aged 45 to 54	100.0	40.0	44.3	–	11.9	3.2
Aged 55 to 59	100.0	38.5	45.5	–	11.0	4.7
Aged 60 to 64	100.0	44.5	42.4	–	9.5	2.2
Aged 65 or older	100.0	53.5	22.0	8.1	8.7	7.7
Aged 65 to 69	100.0	48.6	27.4	6.8	10.2	7.0
Aged 70 to 74	100.0	50.7	26.1	7.7	7.6	7.8
Aged 75 to 79	100.0	53.6	19.6	11.2	6.3	9.4
Aged 80 or older	100.0	60.9	14.9	7.3	10.3	6.6

Note: "Other" insurance includes Department of Veterans Affairs (except Tricare), American Indian Health Service, state and local clinics, worker's compensation, homeowner's and automobile insurance, etc. "–" means sample is too small to make a reliable estimate or not applicable.
Source: Agency for Healthcare Research and Quality, Medical Expenditure Panel Survey, 2003, Internet site http://www.meps.ahrq.gov/CompendiumTables/TC_TOC.htm; calculations by New Strategist

Millions of Older Americans Are Disabled

Nearly half of those aged 75 or older have physical difficulties.

Population surveys and censuses measure disability in many different ways. But the results are the same. The percentage of Americans with a disability rises with age. A survey by the National Center for Health Statistics finds the percentage of people with difficulties in physical functioning stands at 6 percent among those aged 18 to 44, rises to 28 percent in the 65-to-74 age group and peaks at 48 percent among those aged 75 or older.

The Census Bureau's Current Population Survey reports that 11 percent of people aged 16 to 74 had a work disability in 2005—meaning a health problem that prevented them from working or limited the amount or kind of work they can do. The figure stands at 21 to 23 percent among people aged 55 to 74. The more educated the worker, the less likely he or she is to have a work disability. Only 10 to 13 percent of college-educated workers aged 55 to 74 have a work disability.

■ Many people have difficulties in physical functioning because of their expanding waistlines.

Difficulties in physical functioning are common among older Americans

(percent of people with difficulties in physical functioning, by age, 2004)

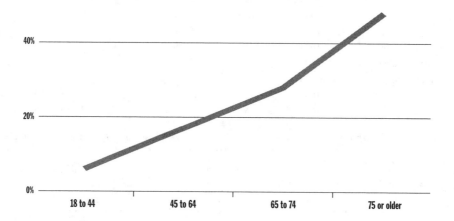

| 40% |
| 20% |
| 0% |

| 18 to 44 | 45 to 64 | 65 to 74 | 75 or older |

Table 2.23 Difficulties in Physical Functioning by Age, 2004

(number of people aged 18 or older with difficulties in physical functioning, by type of difficulty and age, 2004; numbers in thousands)

	total	18 to 44	45 to 64	65 to 74	75 or older
TOTAL PEOPLE	**215,191**	**110,417**	**70,182**	**18,360**	**16,232**
Total with any physical difficulty	**31,671**	**6,339**	**12,249**	**5,226**	**7,856**
Walk quarter of a mile	14,979	2,036	5,431	2,752	4,759
Climb up ten steps without resting	11,268	1,324	4,233	1,975	3,737
Stand for two hours	18,443	3,068	6,929	3,170	5,277
Sit for two hours	6,739	1,832	3,164	809	933
Stoop, bend, or kneel	18,259	3,158	7,384	3,179	4,539
Reach over head	5,292	662	2,337	876	1,417
Grasp or handle small objects	3,841	501	1,748	560	1,032
Lift or carry ten pounds	9,214	1,105	3,645	1,617	2,847
Push or pull large objects	14,026	2,392	5,634	2,233	3,766

PERCENT WITH PHYSICAL DIFFICULTY BY AGE

	total	18 to 44	45 to 64	65 to 74	75 or older
TOTAL PEOPLE	**100.0%**	**100.0%**	**100.0%**	**100.0%**	**100.0%**
Total with any physical difficulty	**14.7**	**5.7**	**17.5**	**28.5**	**48.4**
Walk quarter of a mile	7.0	1.8	7.7	15.0	29.3
Climb up 10 steps without resting	5.2	1.2	6.0	10.8	23.0
Stand for two hours	8.6	2.8	9.9	17.3	32.5
Sit for two hours	3.1	1.7	4.5	4.4	5.7
Stoop, bend, or kneel	8.5	2.9	10.5	17.3	28.0
Reach over head	2.5	0.6	3.3	4.8	8.7
Grasp or handle small objects	1.8	0.5	2.5	3.1	6.4
Lift or carry ten pounds	4.3	1.0	5.2	8.8	17.5
Push or pull large objects	6.5	2.2	8.0	12.2	23.2

PERCENT DISTRIBUTION OF THOSE WITH PHYSICAL DIFFICULTIES BY AGE

	total	18 to 44	45 to 64	65 to 74	75 or older
TOTAL PEOPLE	**100.0%**	**51.3%**	**32.6%**	**8.5%**	**7.5%**
Total with any physical difficulty	**100.0**	**20.0**	**38.7**	**16.5**	**24.8**
Walk quarter of a mile	100.0	13.6	36.3	18.4	31.8
Climb up 10 steps without resting	100.0	11.8	37.6	17.5	33.2
Stand for two hours	100.0	16.6	37.6	17.2	28.6
Sit for two hours	100.0	27.2	47.0	12.0	13.8
Stoop, bend, or kneel	100.0	17.3	40.4	17.4	24.9
Reach over head	100.0	12.5	44.2	16.6	26.8
Grasp or handle small objects	100.0	13.0	45.5	14.6	26.9
Lift or carry ten pounds	100.0	12.0	39.6	17.5	30.9
Push or pull large objects	100.0	17.1	40.2	15.9	26.9

Note: Respondents were classified as having difficulties if they responded "very difficult" or "can't do at all."
Source: National Center for Health Statistics, Summary Health Statistics for U.S. Adults: National Health Interview Survey, 2004, Series 10, No. 228, 2005, Internet site http://www.cdc.gov/nchs/nhis.htm; calculations by New Strategist

Table 2.24 People Aged 55 to 74 with a Work Disability, 2005

(number and percent of people aged 16 or older with a work disability, by selected age groups, education, and severity of disability, 2005; numbers in thousands)

| | | with a work disability | | | | | |
| | | total | | not severe | | severe | |
	total	number	percent	number	percent	number	percent
Total aged 16 to 74	**208,411**	**23,848**	**11.4%**	**8,143**	**3.9%**	**15,705**	**7.5%**
Not a high school graduate	37,643	6,664	17.7	1,530	4.1	5,134	13.6
High school graduate	63,247	8,895	14.1	2,848	4.5	6,047	9.6
Associate's degree or some college	56,009	5,416	9.7	2,277	4.1	3,139	5.6
Bachelor's degree or more	51,512	2,872	5.6	1,488	2.9	1,384	2.7
Total aged 55 to 64	**29,518**	**6,327**	**21.4**	**1,703**	**5.8**	**4,623**	**15.7**
Not a high school graduate	4,039	1,772	43.9	245	6.1	1,527	37.8
High school graduate	9,605	2,306	24.0	609	6.3	1,697	17.7
Associate's degree or some college	7,471	1,393	18.6	490	6.6	903	12.1
Bachelor's degree or more	8,403	856	10.2	360	4.3	496	5.9
Total aged 65 to 69	**10,124**	**2,310**	**22.8**	**1,363**	**13.5**	**946**	**9.3**
Not a high school graduate	2,127	796	37.4	356	16.7	441	20.7
High school graduate	3,773	816	21.6	528	14.0	288	7.6
Associate's degree or some college	2,098	418	19.9	269	12.8	148	7.1
Bachelor's degree or more	2,126	280	13.2	211	9.9	69	3.2
Total aged 70 to 74	**8,264**	**1,882**	**22.8**	**1,366**	**16.5**	**516**	**6.2**
Not a high school graduate	1,981	641	32.4	353	17.8	288	14.5
High school graduate	3,075	666	21.7	523	17.0	144	4.7
Associate's degree or some college	1,565	351	22.5	303	19.3	49	3.1
Bachelor's degree or more	1,644	223	13.6	187	11.4	36	2.2

Note: A person is considered to have a work disability if any of the following conditions are met:
1. Identified by the March supplement question "Does anyone in this household have a health problem or disability which prevents them from working or which limits the kind or amount of work they can do?"
2. Identified by the March supplement question "Is there anyone in this household who ever retired or left a job for health reasons?"
3. Identified by the core questionnaire as currently not in the labor force because of a disability.
4. Identified by the March supplement as a person who did not work at all in the previous year because of illness or disability.
5. Under 65 years old and covered by Medicare in previous year.
6. Under 65 years old and received Supplemental Security Income (SSI) in previous year.
7. Received VA disability income in previous year.
If one or more of conditions 3, 4, 5, or 6 are met, the person is considered to have a severe work disability.
Source: Bureau of the Census, 2005 Current Population Survey Annual Social and Economic Supplement, Internet site http:// www.census.gov/hhes/www/disability/disabcps.html

Older Americans Account for One in Four Physician Visits

Most of those in the doctor's office are women.

In 2003, Americans visited physicians a total of 906 million times. People aged 65 or older accounted for 25 percent of those visits. Women account for the 58 percent majority of people aged 65 or older who visited a doctor because women outnumber men in the age group.

People aged 65 or older account for only 14 percent of visits to hospital outpatient departments. Most older Americans who visit outpatient departments do so because of chronic problems rather than acute conditions. The 65-or-older age group accounts for 15 percent of visits to emergency rooms. But among emergency room visitors, those aged 65 or older are most likely to be classified as having an "emergent" problem, which means a true emergency.

People aged 65 or older accounted for more than 13 million discharges from short-stay hospitals in 2003—a hefty 38 percent of the total. Heart disease is the most common first-listed diagnosis for those aged 65 or older discharged from the hospital, followed by respiratory disease.

When people who visited a doctor or health care clinic are asked to rate the care they receive, fewer than half give it the highest rating (a 9 or 10 on a scale of 0 to 10). The proportion of consumers who rate their experience a 9 or 10 rises with age to a peak of 58 percent among Medicare recipients.

■ As the Baby-Boom generation ages, older Americans will become a larger share of health care consumers, boosting demand for physicians trained in geriatric medicine.

People aged 65 or older go to the doctor six to eight times a year

(average number of physician visits per person per year, by age, 2003)

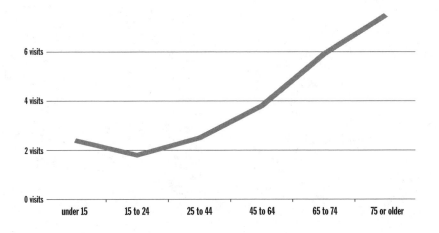

Table 2.25 **Physician Office Visits by Sex and Age, 2003**

(total number, percent distribution, and number of physician office visits per person per year, by sex and age, 2003; numbers in thousands)

	total	percent distribution	average visits per year
Total visits	**906,023**	**100.0%**	**3.2**
Under age 15	145,245	16.0	2.4
Aged 15 to 24	72,447	8.0	1.8
Aged 25 to 44	203,553	22.5	2.5
Aged 45 to 64	257,258	28.4	3.8
Aged 65 to 74	106,424	11.7	5.9
Aged 75 or older	121,096	13.4	7.5
Visits by females	**537,298**	**59.3**	**3.7**
Under age 15	67,442	7.4	2.3
Aged 15 to 24	46,705	5.2	2.3
Aged 25 to 44	136,881	15.1	3.3
Aged 45 to 64	153,417	16.9	4.4
Aged 65 to 74	60,449	6.7	6.1
Aged 75 or older	72,404	8.0	7.3
Visits by males	**368,724**	**40.7**	**2.6**
Under age 15	77,802	8.6	2.5
Aged 15 to 24	25,742	2.8	1.3
Aged 25 to 44	66,672	7.4	1.6
Aged 45 to 64	103,841	11.5	3.1
Aged 65 to 74	45,975	5.1	5.6
Aged 75 or older	48,692	5.4	7.8

Source: National Center for Health Statistics, National Ambulatory Medical Care Survey: 2003 Summary, Advance Data No. 365, 2005, Internet site http://www.cdc.gov/nchs/about/major/ahcd/adata.htm

Table 2.26 Hospital Outpatient Department Visits by Age and Reason, 2003

(number and percent distribution of visits to hospital outpatient departments by age and major reason for visit, 2003; numbers in thousands)

	total	major reason for visit					
		acute problem	chronic problem, routine	chronic problem, flare-up	pre- or post-surgery	preventive care	unknown
Total visits	**94,578**	**38,339**	**27,355**	**6,135**	**3,974**	**17,053**	**1,721**
Under age 15	21,822	10,354	4,762	1,273	581	4,423	427
Aged 15 to 24	11,521	4,847	2,007	436	280	3,783	168
Aged 25 to 44	24,784	10,812	5,839	1,332	1,003	5,449	348
Aged 45 to 64	23,307	8,123	8,894	2,053	1,394	2,388	454
Aged 65 to 74	7,077	2,070	3,236	588	412	598	173
Aged 75 or older	6,067	2,133	2,616	452	303	412	150
PERCENT DISTRIBUTION BY AGE							
Total visits	**100.0%**	**100.0%**	**100.0%**	**100.0%**	**100.0%**	**100.0%**	**100.0%**
Under age 15	23.1	27.0	17.4	20.7	14.6	25.9	24.8
Aged 15 to 24	12.2	12.6	7.3	7.1	7.0	22.2	9.8
Aged 25 to 44	26.2	28.2	21.3	21.7	25.2	32.0	20.2
Aged 45 to 64	24.6	21.2	32.5	33.5	35.1	14.0	26.4
Aged 65 to 74	7.5	5.4	11.8	9.6	10.4	3.5	10.1
Aged 75 or older	6.4	5.6	9.6	7.4	7.6	2.4	8.7
PERCENT DISTRIBUTION BY MAJOR REASON							
Total visits	**100.0%**	**40.5%**	**28.9%**	**6.5%**	**4.2%**	**18.0%**	**1.8%**
Under age 15	100.0	47.4	21.8	5.8	2.7	20.3	2.0
Aged 15 to 24	100.0	42.1	17.4	3.8	2.4	32.8	1.5
Aged 25 to 44	100.0	43.6	23.6	5.4	4.0	22.0	1.4
Aged 45 to 64	100.0	34.9	38.2	8.8	6.0	10.2	1.9
Aged 65 to 74	100.0	29.2	45.7	8.3	5.8	8.4	2.4
Aged 75 or older	100.0	35.2	43.1	7.5	5.0	6.8	2.5

Source: National Center for Health Statistics, National Hospital Ambulatory Medical Care Survey: 2003 Outpatient Department Summary, Advance Data No. 366, 2005, Internet site http://www.cdc.gov/nchs/about/major/ahcd/adata.htm; calculations by New Strategist

Table 2.27 Emergency Department Visits by Age and Urgency of Problem, 2003

(number of visits to emergency rooms and percent distribution by urgency of problem, by age, 2003; numbers in thousands)

| | number | percent distribution | percent distribution by urgency of problem | | | | | |
			total	emergent	urgent	semiurgent	nonurgent	unknown
Total visits	**113,903**	**100.0%**	**100.0%**	**15.2%**	**35.2%**	**20.0%**	**12.8%**	**16.7%**
Under age 15	24,733	21.7	100.0	10.8	33.7	22.3	15.5	17.7
Aged 15 to 24	17,731	15.6	100.0	11.9	34.6	22.0	15.1	16.5
Aged 25 to 44	32,906	28.9	100.0	13.3	35.8	20.9	13.8	16.2
Aged 45 to 64	20,992	18.4	100.0	17.7	35.7	18.3	11.5	16.9
Aged 65 to 74	7,153	6.3	100.0	24.5	36.3	15.3	7.2	16.6
Aged 75 or older	10,389	9.1	100.0	25.5	36.5	15.5	5.9	16.7

Note: Emergent is a status in which the patient should be seen in less than 15 minutes; urgent is a status in which the patient should be seen within 15 to 60 minutes; semiurgent is a status in which the patient should be seen within 61 to 120 minutes; nonurgent is a status in which the patient should be seen within 121 minutes to 24 hours; unknown denotes a visit with no mention of immediacy or triage or the patient was dead on arrival.

Source: National Center for Health Statistics, National Hospital Ambulatory Medical Care Survey: 2003 Emergency Department Summary, Advance Data No. 358, 2005, Internet site http://www.cdc.gov/nchs/about/major/ahcd/adata.htm

Table 2.28 Hospital Discharges by Diagnosis and Age, 2003

(number and percent of hospital discharges from nonfederal short-stay hospitals by first-listed diagnosis and age, 2003; numbers in thousands)

	total	under 45		45 to 64		65 or older	
		number	percent of total	number	percent of total	number	percent of total
All conditions	**34,738**	**13,402**	**38.6%**	**8,120**	**23.4%**	**13,216**	**38.0%**
Infectious and parasitic diseases	928	351	37.8	192	20.7	385	41.5
Neoplasms	1,692	340	20.1	627	37.1	726	42.9
Endocrine, nutritional, and metabolic diseases and immunity disorders	1,785	585	32.8	478	26.8	722	40.4
Diabetes mellitus	597	187	31.3	204	34.2	205	34.3
Diseases of the blood and blood-forming organs	445	166	37.3	94	21.1	186	41.8
Mental disorders	2,292	1,409	61.5	618	27.0	265	11.6
Diseases of the nervous system and sense organs	532	214	40.2	123	23.1	194	36.5
Diseases of the circulatory system	6,434	477	7.4	1,898	29.5	4,060	63.1
Heart disease	4,445	293	6.6	1,325	29.8	2,828	63.6
Acute myocardial infarction	767	44	5.7	227	29.6	496	64.7
Cerebrovascular disease	966	47	4.9	231	23.9	684	70.8
Diseases of the respiratory system	3,802	1,175	30.9	777	20.4	1,850	48.7
Diseases of the digestive system	3,468	1,045	30.1	1,033	29.8	1,389	40.1
Diseases of the genitourinary system	1,888	664	35.2	478	25.3	746	39.5
Complications of pregnancy, childbirth, and the puerperium	552	551	99.8	–	–	–	–
Diseases of the skin, subcutaneous tissue	656	187	28.5	174	26.5	214	32.6
Diseases of the musculoskeletal system and connective tissue	1,854	368	19.8	651	35.1	834	45.0
Congenital anomalies	183	158	86.3	18	9.8	7	3.8
Certain conditions originating in the perinatal period	191	191	100.0	0	0.0	0	0.0
Symptoms, signs, ill-defined conditions	271	154	56.8	56	20.7	61	22.5
Injury and poisoning	2,833	1,073	37.9	679	24.0	1,081	38.2
Supplementary classifications	4,933	4,215	85.4	221	4.5	496	10.1

Note: "–" means category not applicable or sample is too small to make a reliable estimate.
Source: National Center for Health Statistics, 2003 National Hospital Discharge Survey, Advance Data, No. 359, 2005, Internet site http://www.cdc.gov/nchs/about/major/hdasd/listpubs.htm; calculations by New Strategist

Table 2.29 Rating of Health Care Received from Doctor's Office or Clinic, 2003

(number of people aged 18 or older who visited a doctor or health care clinic in past 12 months, and percent distribution by rating for health care received on a scale from 0 (worst) to 10 (best), by age, 2003; people in thousands)

	with health care visit		rating		
	number	percent	9 to 10	7 to 8	6 or lower
Total people	**147,294**	**100.0%**	**47.2%**	**37.8%**	**14.2%**
Aged 18 to 44	65,979	100.0	42.1	40.6	16.5
Aged 45 to 54	28,471	100.0	45.1	39.3	14.9
Aged 55 to 59	12,499	100.0	50.4	36.8	12.0
Aged 60 to 64	10,615	100.0	51.0	35.9	12.7
Aged 65 or older	29,730	100.0	57.7	31.2	10.1
Aged 65 to 69	8,161	100.0	54.9	33.7	10.5
Aged 70 to 74	7,810	100.0	60.1	27.6	11.1
Aged 75 to 79	6,301	100.0	61.5	28.7	9.0
Aged 80 or older	7,458	100.0	55.1	34.4	9.4

Source: Agency for Healthcare Research and Quality, Medical Expenditure Panel Survey, 2003, Internet site http://www.meps .ahrq.gov/CompendiumTables/TC_TOC.htm; calculations by New Strategist

More than 1 Million Use Home Health Care

But more of the elderly are in nursing homes than receiving home health care.

Home health care surged during the 1990s as insurance companies pressured hospitals to discharge patients sooner. But growth in home health care has slowed as government cost-cutters and insurance companies have asked families to shoulder more of the patient care burden. In 2000, 1.4 million people—most of them aged 65 or older—received home health care services. Diseases of the circulatory system are the most common reason for receiving home health care.

The latest census of the nursing home population counted 1.5 million people aged 65 or older living in nursing homes, 74 percent of them women. More than half the elderly in nursing homes are aged 85 or older. Eighty percent of the elderly in nursing homes are mobility dependent, 66 percent are incontinent, and 47 percent cannot eat independently.

More than 600,000 people were discharged from hospice care in 2000—most of them due to death. Eighty percent of hospice care discharges are people aged 65 or older. The median length of stay in hospice care was 16 days.

■ If home health care services are curtailed to save costs, a larger burden falls on family caregivers. For the elderly living alone, this can mean institutionalization.

Among the elderly in nursing homes, most are very old

(percent distribution of nursing home residents aged 65 or older, by age, 1999)

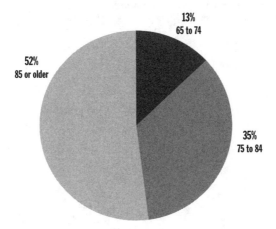

Table 2.30　Home Health Care Patients, 2000

(number and percent distribution of home health care patients by sex, age, and primary admission diagnosis, 2000)

	number	percent distribution
Total home health care patients	**1,355,290**	**100.0%**
Sex		
Females	878,228	64.8
Males	477,062	35.2
Age		
Under age 65	399,811	29.5
Aged 65 or older	955,479	70.5
Aged 65 to 74	234,465	17.3
Aged 75 to 84	424,206	31.3
Aged 85 or older	296,809	21.9
Primary admission diagnosis		
Malignant neoplasms	66,409	4.9
Diabetes	105,713	7.8
Diseases of the nervous system and sense organs	82,673	6.1
Diseases of the circulatory system	319,848	23.6
Diseases of the heart	147,727	10.9
Cerebrovascular diseases	98,936	7.3
Diseases of the respiratory system	92,160	6.8
Decubitus ulcers	25,751	1.9
Diseases of the musculoskeletal system and connective tissue	132,818	9.8
Osteoarthritis	47,435	3.5
Fractures, all sites	55,567	4.1
Fracture of neck of femur (hip)	20,329	1.5
Other	472,996	34.9

Source: National Center for Health Statistics, Health, United States, 2005, Internet site http://www.cdc.gov/nchs/hus.htm; calculations by New Strategist

Table 2.31 Nursing Home Residents Aged 65 or Older, 1999

(number and percent distribution of nursing home residents aged 65 or older, residents per 1,000 population, and percent with functional problems, by sex and age, 1999)

				percent with functional problems			
	number	percent distribution	residents per 1,000 population	dependent mobility	incontinent	dependent eating	dependent eating, mobility, and incontinent
Total residents aged 65 or older	**1,469,500**	**100.0%**	**42.9**	**80.4%**	**65.7%**	**47.4%**	**37.0%**
Aged 65 to 74	194,800	13.3	10.8	73.9	58.5	43.1	31.7
Aged 75 to 84	517,600	35.2	43.0	77.8	64.2	46.6	35.4
Aged 85 or older	757,100	51.5	182.5	83.8	68.6	49.0	39.4
Female residents	**1,091,700**	**74.3**	**54.6**	**81.9**	**65.6**	**48.1**	**37.7**
Aged 65 to 74	110,700	7.5	11.2	76.4	57.7	41.6	29.3
Aged 75 to 84	368,100	25.0	51.2	78.2	62.2	47.7	35.6
Aged 85 or older	612,900	41.7	210.5	85.2	69.0	49.7	40.4
Male residents	**377,800**	**25.7**	**26.5**	**75.9**	**66.0**	**45.1**	**35.0**
Aged 65 to 74	84,100	5.7	10.3	70.5	59.6	45.0	34.8
Aged 75 to 84	149,500	10.2	30.8	76.9	68.9	44.7	35.2
Aged 85 or older	144,200	9.8	116.5	78.1	66.8	45.7	34.9

Source: National Center for Health Statistics, 1999 National Nursing Home Survey, Internet site http://www.cdc.gov/nchs/about/ major/nnhsd/nnhsd.htm; calculations by New Strategist

Table 2.32 Hospice Discharges by Age, 2000

(number, percent distribution, average and median length of service for patients discharged from hospice care, by age, 2000)

	number	percent distribution	average length of service (in days)	median length of service (in days)
Total hospice discharges	**621,100**	**100.0%**	**46.9**	**15.6**
Under age 65	126,900	20.4	43.9	15.0
Aged 65 or older	494,300	79.6	47.7	16.3
Aged 65 to 74	153,100	24.6	41.2	16.4
Aged 75 to 84	176,400	28.4	50.6	16.5
Aged 85 or older	164,800	26.5	50.5	–

Note: "–" means sample is too small to make a reliable estimate.
Source: National Center for Health Statistics, Characteristics of Hospice Care Discharges and Their Length of Service: United States, 2000, Vital and Health Statistics Report, Series 13, No. 154, 2003, Internet site http://www.cdc.gov/nchs/pressroom/03facts/ hospicecare.htm

Heart Disease and Cancer Are the Biggest Killers

Cancer is the leading cause of death among people aged 55 to 74.

Among the 2.4 million people who died in 2002, 85 percent were aged 55 or older. More than half (57 percent) were aged 75 or older. The 55-or-older age group accounts for 92 percent of deaths due to heart disease, 94 percent of deaths due to influenza and pneumonia, and nearly 100 percent of deaths due to Alzheimer's disease. But the age group accounts for only 39 percent of accidental deaths, 29 percent of suicides, and 9 percent of homicides.

While heart disease is the number one cause of death among people aged 75 or older, cancer is the leading cause of death among 55-to-74-year-olds. Together, the two diseases account for 54 percent of all deaths in the 55-or-older age group. Among the oldest Americans, those aged 85 or older, heart disease causes 37 percent of deaths, while cancer accounts for only 12 percent.

■ With most Americans living to old age, growing numbers must cope with the disabilities of aging. The demands of the disabled drive up health care costs, but they provide opportunities for the health care industry.

Heart disease overtakes cancer as a cause of death in old age

(percent of deaths due to heart disease or cancer, by age, 2002)

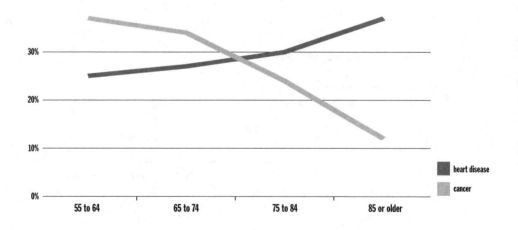

Table 2.33 Deaths from the 15 Leading Causes of Death, 2002: Number of Deaths

(number of deaths from the 15 leading causes of death, by age, 2002; ranked by total number of deaths)

	total	aged 55 or older				
		total	55 to 64	65 to 74	75 to 84	85+
Total deaths	**2,443,387**	**2,065,062**	**253,342**	**422,990**	**707,654**	**681,076**
Diseases of the heart	696,947	640,535	64,234	112,547	213,581	250,173
Malignant neoplasms	557,271	484,392	93,391	144,757	167,062	79,182
Cerebrovascular disease	162,672	153,190	9,897	21,992	54,889	66,412
Chronic lower respiratory disease	124,816	119,593	11,280	29,788	49,241	29,284
Accidents (unintentional injuries)	106,742	41,986	8,345	8,086	12,904	12,651
Diabetes mellitus	73,249	64,737	10,022	16,709	23,282	14,724
Influenza and pneumonia	65,681	61,813	2,987	6,847	19,984	31,995
Alzheimer's disease	58,866	58,799	510	3,602	20,135	34,552
Nephritis, nephrotic syndrome, and nephrosis	40,974	37,771	3,455	7,164	13,896	13,256
Septicemia	33,865	30,030	3,360	6,336	11,010	9,324
Suicide	31,655	9,166	3,618	2,463	2,259	826
Chronic liver disease and cirrhosis	27,257	16,463	6,097	5,381	4,000	985
Essential (primary) hypertension and hypertensive renal disease	20,261	18,871	1,526	2,922	6,138	8,285
Homicide	17,638	1,653	841	421	296	95
Pneumonitis due to solids and liquids	17,593	16,907	671	1,793	5,900	8,543

Note: Numbers will not add to total because age not stated is not shown.
Source: National Center for Health Statistics, Deaths: Final Data for 2002, National Vital Statistics Reports, Vol. 53, No. 5, 2004,
Internet site http://www.cdc.gov/nchs/products/pubs/pubd/nvsr/53/53-21.htm; calculations by New Strategist

Table 2.34 Deaths from the 15 Leading Causes of Death, 2002: Distribution by Cause

(percent distribution of deaths by cause for total people and people aged 55 or older, 2002; ranked by total number of deaths)

	total	aged 55 or older				
		total	55 to 64	65 to 74	75 to 84	85+
Total deaths	**100.0%**	**100.0%**	**100.0%**	**100.0%**	**100.0%**	**100.0%**
Diseases of the heart	28.5	31.0	25.4	26.6	30.2	36.7
Malignant neoplasms	22.8	23.5	36.9	34.2	23.6	11.6
Cerebrovascular disease	6.7	7.4	3.9	5.2	7.8	9.8
Chronic lower respiratory disease	5.1	5.8	4.5	7.0	7.0	4.3
Accidents (unintentional injuries)	4.4	2.0	3.3	1.9	1.8	1.9
Diabetes mellitus	3.0	3.1	4.0	4.0	3.3	2.2
Influenza and pneumonia	2.7	3.0	1.2	1.6	2.8	4.7
Alzheimer's disease	2.4	2.8	0.2	0.9	2.8	5.1
Nephritis, nephrotic syndrome, and nephrosis	1.7	1.8	1.4	1.7	2.0	1.9
Septicemia	1.4	1.5	1.3	1.5	1.6	1.4
Suicide	1.3	0.4	1.4	0.6	0.3	0.1
Chronic liver disease and cirrhosis	1.1	0.8	2.4	1.3	0.6	0.1
Essential (primary) hypertension and hypertensive renal disease	0.8	0.9	0.6	0.7	0.9	1.2
Homicide	0.7	0.1	0.3	0.1	0.0	0.0
Pneumonitis due to solids and liquids	0.7	0.8	0.3	0.4	0.8	1.3

Source: National Center for Health Statistics, Deaths: Final Data for 2002, National Vital Statistics Reports, Vol. 53, No. 5, 2004, Internet site http://www.cdc.gov/nchs/products/pubs/pubd/nvsr/53/53-21.htm; calculations by New Strategist

Table 2.35   **Deaths from the 15 Leading Causes of Death, 2002: Distribution by Age**

(percent distribution of deaths by age for total people and people aged 55 or older, 2002; ranked by total number of deaths)

	total	aged 55 or older				
		total	55 to 64	65 to 74	75 to 84	85+
Total deaths	**100.0%**	**84.5%**	**10.4%**	**17.3%**	**29.0%**	**27.9%**
Diseases of the heart	100.0	91.9	9.2	16.1	30.6	35.9
Malignant neoplasms	100.0	86.9	16.8	26.0	30.0	14.2
Cerebrovascular disease	100.0	94.2	6.1	13.5	33.7	40.8
Chronic lower respiratory disease	100.0	95.8	9.0	23.9	39.5	23.5
Accidents (unintentional injuries)	100.0	39.3	7.8	7.6	12.1	11.9
Diabetes mellitus	100.0	88.4	13.7	22.8	31.8	20.1
Influenza and pneumonia	100.0	94.1	4.5	10.4	30.4	48.7
Alzheimer's disease	100.0	99.9	0.9	6.1	34.2	58.7
Nephritis, nephrotic syndrome, and nephrosis	100.0	92.2	8.4	17.5	33.9	32.4
Septicemia	100.0	88.7	9.9	18.7	32.5	27.5
Suicide	100.0	29.0	11.4	7.8	7.1	2.6
Chronic liver disease and cirrhosis	100.0	60.4	22.4	19.7	14.7	3.6
Essential (primary) hypertension and hypertensive renal disease	100.0	93.1	7.5	14.4	30.3	40.9
Homicide	100.0	9.4	4.8	2.4	1.7	0.5
Pneumonitis due to solids and liquids	100.0	96.1	3.8	10.2	33.5	48.6

Source: National Center for Health Statistics, Deaths: Final Data for 2002, National Vital Statistics Reports, Vol. 53, No. 5, 2004, Internet site http://www.cdc.gov/nchs/products/pubs/pubd/nvsr/53/53-21.htm; calculations by New Strategist

Table 2.36 Leading Causes of Death for People Aged 55 to 64, 2002

(number and percent distribution of deaths accounted for by the ten leading causes of death for people aged 55 to 64, 2002)

	number	percent distribution
All causes	**253,342**	**100.0%**
1. Malignant neoplasms (cancer) (2)	93,391	36.9
2. Diseases of heart (1)	64,234	25.4
3. Chronic lower respiratory disease (4)	11,280	4.5
4. Diabetes mellitus (6)	10,022	4.0
5. Cerebrovascular diseases (3)	9,897	3.9
6. Accidents (unintentional injuries) (5)	8,345	3.3
7. Chronic liver disease and cirrhosis (12)	6,097	2.4
8. Suicide (11)	3,618	1.4
9. Nephritis, nephrotic syndrome, and nephrosis (9)	3,455	1.4
10. Septicemia (10)	3,360	1.3
All other causes	39,643	15.6

Note: Number in parentheses shows rank for all Americans if the cause of death is among the top fifteen.
Source: National Center for Health Statistics, Deaths: Final Data for 2002, National Vital Statistics Reports, Vol. 53, No. 5, 2004, Internet site http://www.cdc.gov/nchs/products/pubs/pubd/nvsr/53/53-21.htm; calculations by New Strategist

Table 2.37 Leading Causes of Death for People Aged 65 to 74, 2002

(number and percent distribution of deaths accounted for by the ten leading causes of death for people aged 65 to 74, 2002)

	number	percent distribution
All causes	**422,990**	**100.0%**
1. Malignant neoplasms (cancer) (2)	144,757	34.2
2. Diseases of the heart (1)	112,547	26.6
3. Chronic lower respiratory disease (4)	29,788	7.0
4. Cerebrovascular diseases (3)	21,992	5.2
5. Diabetes mellitus (6)	16,709	4.0
6. Accidents (unintentional injuries) (5)	8,086	1.9
7. Nephritis, nephrotic syndrome, and nephrosis (9)	7,164	1.7
8. Influenza and pneumonia (7)	6,847	1.6
9. Septicemia (10)	6,336	1.5
10. Chronic liver disease and cirrhosis (12)	5,381	1.3
All other causes	63,383	15.0

Note: Number in parentheses shows rank for all Americans if the cause of death is among the top fifteen.
Source: National Center for Health Statistics, Deaths: Final Data for 2002, National Vital Statistics Reports, Vol. 53, No. 5, 2004, Internet site http://www.cdc.gov/nchs/products/pubs/pubd/nvsr/53/53-21.htm; calculations by New Strategist

Table 2.38 Leading Causes of Death for People Aged 75 to 84, 2002

(number and percent distribution of deaths accounted for by the 10 leading causes of death for people aged 75 to 84, 2002)

	number	percent distribution
All causes	**707,654**	**100.0%**
1. Diseases of the heart (1)	213,581	30.2
2. Malignant neoplasms (cancer) (2)	167,062	23.6
3. Cerebrovascular diseases (3)	54,889	7.8
4. Chronic lower respiratory disease (4)	49,241	7.0
5. Diabetes mellitus (6)	23,282	3.3
6. Alzheimer's disease (8)	20,135	2.8
7. Influenza and pneumonia (7)	19,984	2.8
8. Nephritis, nephrotic syndrome, nephrosis (9)	13,896	2.0
9. Accidents (unintentional injuries) (5)	12,904	1.8
10. Septicemia (10)	11,010	1.6
All other causes	121,670	17.2

Note: Number in parentheses shows rank for all Americans if the cause of death is among the top fifteen.
Source: National Center for Health Statistics, Deaths: Final Data for 2002, National Vital Statistics Reports, Vol. 53, No. 5, 2004, Internet site http://www.cdc.gov/nchs/products/pubs/pubd/nvsr/53/53-21.htm; calculations by New Strategist

Table 2.39 Leading Causes of Death for People Aged 85 or Older, 2002

(number and percent distribution of deaths accounted for by the ten leading causes of death for people aged 85 or older, 2002)

	number	percent distribution
All causes	**681,076**	**100.0%**
1. Diseases of the heart (1)	250,173	36.7
2. Malignant neoplasms (cancer) (2)	79,182	11.6
3. Cerebrovascular diseases (3)	66,412	9.8
4. Alzheimer's disease (8)	34,552	5.1
5. Influenza and pneumonia (7)	31,995	4.7
6. Chronic lower respiratory disease (4)	29,284	4.3
7. Diabetes mellitus (6)	14,724	2.2
8. Nephritis, nephrotic syndrome, nephrosis (9)	13,256	1.9
9. Accidents (unintentional injuries) (5)	12,651	1.9
10. Septicemia (10)	9,324	1.4
All other causes	139,523	20.5

Note: Number in parenthses shows rank for all Americans if the cause of death is among the top fifteen.
Source: National Center for Health Statistics, Deaths: Final Data for 2002, National Vital Statistics Reports, Vol. 53, No. 5, 2004, Internet site http://www.cdc.gov/nchs/products/pubs/pubd/nvsr/53/53-21.htm; calculations by New Strategist

Life Expectancy Has Grown at Older Ages

The biggest gains have been made since 1950.

Between 1900 and 2003, life expectancy at age 65 grew by 6.6 years. In 1900, the average 65-year-old could expect to live 11.9 more years. In 2003, a 65-year-old could expect to live 18.5 more years. The gain in life expectancy is due primarily to the success of medical science at curtailing deaths from heart disease, the biggest killer of Americans.

Life expectancy at birth stood at 74.8 years for males and 80.1 years for females in 2003. At all ages, the life expectancy of females is greater than that of males. Among people aged 85, men can expect to live another 6.1 years, while women can expect 7.2 more years of life.

■ Perhaps more important than length of life is quality of life, particularly in very old age. While medical science has made great strides in lengthening life, older Americans are now demanding improved quality of life as well.

More years remain at the end of life

(number of years of life remaining for people aged 65 or older, 1900 and 2003)

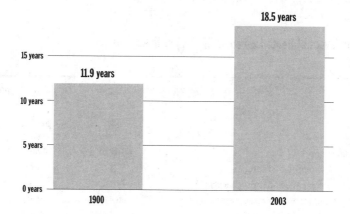

Table 2.40 Life Expectancy by Age, 1900 to 2003

(years of life remaining at birth and age 65, 1900 to 2003; change in years of life remaining for selected years)

	at birth	age 65
2003	77.6	18.5
2002	77.4	18.2
2001	77.2	18.1
2000	76.9	17.9
1999	76.7	17.7
1998	76.7	17.8
1997	76.5	17.7
1996	76.1	17.5
1995	75.8	17.4
1994	75.7	17.4
1993	75.5	17.3
1992	75.8	17.5
1991	75.5	17.4
1990	75.4	17.2
1980	73.7	16.4
1970	70.8	15.2
1960	69.7	14.3
1950	68.2	13.9
1900	47.3	11.9
Change		
1990 to 2003	2.2	1.3
1900 to 2003	30.3	6.6

Source: National Center for Health Statistics, Health, United States, 2005; and Deaths: Preliminary Data for 2003, National Vital Statistics Report, Vol. 53, No. 15, 2005, Internet site http://www.cdc.gov/nchs/products/pubs/pubd/nvsr/53/53-21.htm; calculations by New Strategist

Table 2.41 Life Expectancy by Age and Sex, 2003

(years of life remaining at selected ages, by sex, 2003)

	total	females	males
At birth	**77.6**	**80.1**	**74.8**
Aged 1	77.1	79.6	74.4
Aged 5	73.2	75.7	70.5
Aged 10	68.2	70.8	65.6
Aged 15	63.3	65.8	60.7
Aged 20	58.5	60.9	55.9
Aged 25	53.8	56.1	51.3
Aged 30	49.0	51.2	46.6
Aged 35	44.3	46.4	41.9
Aged 40	39.6	41.7	37.3
Aged 45	35.0	37.0	32.8
Aged 50	30.6	32.5	28.5
Aged 55	26.4	28.0	24.4
Aged 60	22.3	23.8	20.5
Aged 65	18.5	19.8	16.8
Aged 70	15.0	16.1	13.5
Aged 75	11.8	12.7	10.6
Aged 80	9.1	9.7	8.1
Aged 85	6.9	7.2	6.1
Aged 90	5.1	5.3	4.5
Aged 95	3.8	4.0	3.4
Aged 100	2.9	3.0	2.7

Source: National Center for Health Statistics, Deaths: Preliminary Data for 2003, National Vital Statistics Report, Vol. 53, No. 15, 2005, Internet site http://www.cdc.gov/nchs/products/pubs/pubd/nvsr/53/53-21.htm; calculations by New Strategist

3

Housing

■ In 2005, 69 percent of the nation's householders owned their home—including 81 percent of householders aged 65 or older.

■ Sixty-nine percent of householders aged 65 or older live in a single-family, detached home. Nineteen percent live in an apartment building, while 7 percent live in a mobile home.

■ Older Americans are no less likely to have a home outfitted with amenities than is the average household. Fully 84 percent have a porch, deck, balcony, or patio, 54 percent have central air conditioning, and most have a dishwasher.

■ When asked how they would rate their housing unit on a scale of 1 (worst) to 10 (best), 79 percent of householders aged 65 or older rate their home an 8 or higher. Seventy-five percent rate their neighborhood an 8 or higher.

■ Housing costs are lowest for homeowners aged 65 or older regardless of household type. Median monthly housing costs for married homeowners aged 65 or older were just $398 in 2003.

■ Older Americans are less likely to move than the average person. Among movers, however, people aged 55 or older are more likely to settle in a different state. Nineteen percent of all movers moved to a different state, but the proportion rises as high as 29 to 30 percent among movers aged 60 to 64.

Older Americans Are Most Likely to Own a Home

People aged 65 to 74 have the highest homeownership rate.

The percentage of householders who own their home has been rising, thanks to the aging of the population and low mortgage interest rates. In 2005, 68.9 percent of the nation's house-holders owned their home—including 81 percent of householders aged 65 or older.

Between 1990 and 2005, householders aged 65 or older experienced big gains in homeownership, with their rate rising by 4.3 percentage points, from 76.3 to 80.6 percent. Behind the increase was the entry of a more affluent generation into the age group. Between 2000 and 2005, however, the homeownership rate fell slightly among 65-to-69-year-olds, although it continued to rise among Americans aged 70 or older. The youngest adults are least likely to own a home. Only 43 percent of householders under age 35 are homeowners.

■ Since older Americans are most likely to own a home, the nation's homeownership rate should continue to climb as the population ages.

Homeownership rate peaks in the 65-to-74 age group

(percent of householders who own their home, by age, 2005)

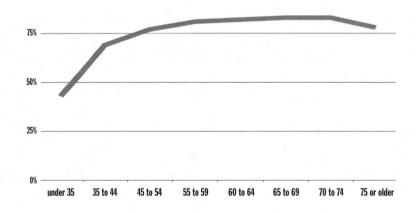

Table 3.1 Homeownership by Age of Householder, 1990 to 2005

(percentage of householders who own their home by age of householder, 1990 to 2005; percentage point change, 2000–05 and 1990–2005)

	2005	2000	1990	percentage point change	
				2000–05	1990–2005
Total households	**68.9%**	**67.4%**	**63.9%**	**1.5**	**5.0**
Under age 35	43.0	40.8	38.5	2.2	4.5
Aged 35 to 44	69.3	67.9	66.3	1.4	3.0
Aged 45 to 54	76.6	76.5	75.2	0.1	1.4
Aged 55 to 59	80.6	80.4	78.8	0.2	1.8
Aged 60 to 64	81.9	80.3	79.8	1.6	2.1
Aged 65 or older	80.6	80.4	76.3	0.2	4.3
Aged 65 to 69	82.8	83.0	80.0	–0.2	2.8
Aged 70 to 74	82.9	82.6	78.4	0.3	4.5
Aged 75 or older	78.4	77.7	72.3	0.7	6.1

Source: Bureau of the Census, Housing Vacancies and Homeownership Survey, Internet site http://www.census.gov/hhes/www/ housing/hvs/annual05/ann05t15.html; calculations by New Strategist

Homeownership Rises with Age

People aged 65 or older account for nearly one in four homeowners.

The housing industry is booming because the population is aging, and older people are more likely to own a home than young adults. A minority of householders under age 35 owns a home. The homeownership rate climbs sharply as people age into their thirties and forties, topping 80 percent among those aged 55 to 74. The rate drops slightly among the oldest householders.

The percentage of householders who rent falls from the 57 percent majority of those under age 35 to less than 20 percent among those aged 55 to 74. Among householders aged 75 or older, a slightly larger 22 percent are renters as elderly widows sell their home and move into smaller apartments, often to be closer to their adult children.

■ The 65 percent majority of the nation's homeowners are aged 45 or older, while the 62 percent majority of renters are under age 45.

Homeowners outnumber renters by far among older householders

(percent distribution of householders aged 55 or older by homeownership status and age, 2005)

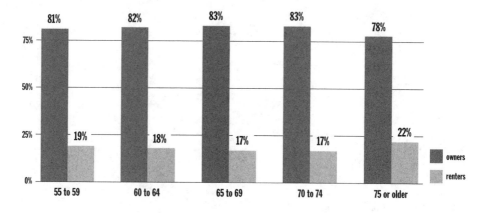

Table 3.2 Owners and Renters by Age of Householder, 2005

(number and percent distribution of householders by homeownership status, and owner and renter share of total, by age of householder, 2005; numbers in thousands)

	total	owners			renters		
		number	percent distribution	share of total	number	percent distribution	share of total
Total households	**108,231**	**74,553**	**100.0%**	**68.9%**	**33,678**	**100.0%**	**31.1%**
Under age 35	24,909	10,723	14.4	43.0	14,186	42.1	57.0
Aged 35 to 44	22,248	15,412	20.7	69.3	6,836	20.3	30.7
Aged 45 to 54	22,375	17,129	23.0	76.6	5,246	15.6	23.4
Aged 55 to 59	9,504	7,661	10.3	80.6	1,843	5.5	19.4
Aged 60 to 64	7,336	6,007	8.1	81.9	1,329	3.9	18.1
Aged 65 or older	21,859	17,622	23.6	80.6	4,237	12.6	19.4
Aged 65 to 69	5,900	4,886	6.6	82.8	1,014	3.0	17.2
Aged 70 to 74	5,016	4,156	5.6	82.9	860	2.6	17.1
Aged 75 or older	10,943	8,580	11.5	78.4	2,363	7.0	21.6

Source: Bureau of the Census, Housing Vacancies and Homeownership Survey, Internet site http://www.census.gov/hhes/www/ housing/hvs/annual05/ann05t15.html; calculations by New Strategist

Married Couples Are Most Likely to Be Homeowners

The majority of older householders own their home, however, regardless of household type.

The homeownership rate among all married couples was a lofty 84 percent in 2005, much higher than the 69 percent rate for all households. Among married couples aged 50 or older, the homeownership rate tops 90 percent, peaking at 93 percent among those aged 65 to 74.

Among householders aged 55 or older, homeownership is lowest for those who live alone. Regardless of household type, however, the majority of older householders are homeowners. Among men aged 65 or older who live alone, 68 percent are homeowners. The rate is a slightly higher 70 percent for their female counterparts. For female- and male-headed family householders in the age group, 82 to 83 percent are homeowners.

■ As the large Baby-Boom generation moves into the older age groups, its homeownership rate will climb, continuing to fuel the housing industry.

Most householders aged 65 or older own their home

(percent of householders aged 65 or older who own their home, by household type, 2005)

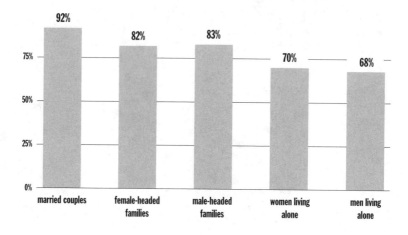

Table 3.3 Homeownership Rate by Age of Householder and Type of Household, 2005

(percent of households owning their home, by age of householder and type of household, 2005)

| | | family households | | | people living alone | |
	total	married couples	female hh, no spouse present	male hh, no spouse present	females	males
Total households	**68.9%**	**84.2%**	**51.0%**	**59.1%**	**59.6%**	**50.3%**
Under age 25	25.7	39.1	25.7	44.6	13.6	17.8
Aged 25 to 29	40.9	58.5	23.6	38.9	26.0	30.2
Aged 30 to 34	56.8	72.6	32.2	49.7	37.0	37.5
Aged 35 to 39	66.6	81.7	44.6	55.4	45.0	45.5
Aged 40 to 44	71.7	85.5	52.9	62.7	51.6	47.6
Aged 45 to 49	75.0	88.5	60.1	67.4	53.9	52.2
Aged 50 to 54	78.3	90.6	65.8	72.4	60.2	53.6
Aged 55 to 59	80.6	91.4	68.5	73.1	66.8	58.4
Aged 60 to 64	81.9	92.3	71.3	75.7	69.7	61.3
Aged 65 or older	80.6	92.2	82.0	83.4	70.2	68.1
Aged 65 to 69	82.8	92.8	77.5	76.1	71.5	63.3
Aged 70 to 74	82.9	93.3	81.6	82.3	71.5	66.5
Aged 75 or older	78.4	90.9	84.3	88.2	69.3	71.2

Source: Bureau of the Census, Housing Vacancies and Homeownership Survey, Internet site http://www.census.gov/hhes/www/ housing/hvs/annual05/ann05t15.html; calculations by New Strategist

Most Blacks and Hispanics Are Not Homeowners

The homeownership rate rises above 50 percent for those aged 45 or older, however.

The homeownership rate of blacks and Hispanics is well below average. The overall homeownership rate stood at 68.3 percent for all households in 2003 (the latest data available by race, Hispanic origin, and age). Among blacks, the rate was a smaller 47.6 percent. The Hispanic rate was an even lower 46.3 percent.

Homeownership rises above 50 percent for black householders aged 45 to 54. Among Hispanics, the rate reaches 50 percent in the 35-to-44 age group. Homeownership peaks in the 75-or-older age group for both blacks and Hispanics.

■ Blacks are less likely to be homeowners because a smaller share of their households are headed by married couples.

Most older Americans are homeowners, regardless of race or Hispanic origin

(homeownership rate of total households and householders aged 65 to 74, by race and Hispanic origin, 2003)

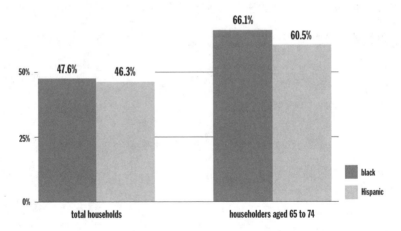

Table 3.4 Black and Hispanic Homeownership Rate by Age, 2003

(percent of total, black, and Hispanic households owning their home, by age of householder, 2003)

	total	black	Hispanic
Total households	**68.3%**	**47.6%**	**46.3%**
Under age 25	20.9	12.1	13.5
Aged 25 to 29	41.1	23.0	26.7
Aged 30 to 34	55.3	33.0	36.9
Aged 35 to 44	68.4	45.4	50.0
Aged 45 to 54	76.3	55.6	57.9
Aged 55 to 64	81.1	63.9	63.5
Aged 65 to 74	82.3	66.1	60.5
Aged 75 or older	78.1	66.6	64.6

Note: Blacks include only those identifying themselves as black alone. Hispanics may be of any race.
Source: Bureau of the Census, American Housing Survey for the United States: 2003, Current Housing Reports, Internet site http://www.census.gov/hhes/www/ahs.html; calculations by New Strategist

Among Older Americans, Homeownership Is Highest in the South

Their rate of homeownership is also highest in nonmetropolitan areas.

Among all age groups, the Midwest has the highest homeownership rate (73 percent in 2003), but among people aged 65 or older homeownership is highest in the South at 85 percent. In every region, older Americans are much more likely to own a home than is the average householder. In the West, the contrast is particularly striking, with 78 percent of householders aged 65 or older owning a home versus a much smaller 64 percent average.

Regardless of their metropolitan status, the majority of older householders are homeowners. The figures range from a high of 86 percent in nonmetropolitan areas to a low of 70 percent in central cities.

■ With the population aging, homeownership rates should rise in every region during the next few decades.

Most older Americans own their home, regardless of region

(percent of householders aged 65 or older who own their home, by region, 2003)

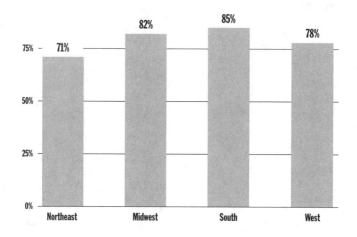

Table 3.5 Households by Region, Homeownership Status, and Age, 2003

(number and percent distribution of total households and households headed by people aged 65 or older by region of residence and homeownership status, 2003; numbers in thousands)

	total households			householders aged 65 or older		
	total	owner	renter	total	owner	renter
Total households	**105,842**	**72,238**	**33,604**	**21,627**	**17,350**	**4,277**
Northeast	20,133	12,964	7,169	4,617	3,291	1,325
Midwest	24,488	17,889	6,599	5,188	4,271	917
South	38,145	26,699	11,446	7,678	6,543	1,135
West	23,077	14,686	8,390	4,144	3,244	900
PERCENT DISTRIBUTION BY HOMEOWNERSHIP STATUS						
Total households	**100.0%**	**68.3%**	**31.7%**	**100.0%**	**80.2%**	**19.8%**
Northeast	100.0	64.4	35.6	100.0	71.3	28.7
Midwest	100.0	73.1	26.9	100.0	82.3	17.7
South	100.0	70.0	30.0	100.0	85.2	14.8
West	100.0	63.6	36.4	100.0	78.3	21.7
PERCENT DISTRIBUTION BY REGION						
Total households	**100.0%**	**100.0%**	**100.0%**	**100.0%**	**100.0%**	**100.0%**
Northeast	19.0	17.9	21.3	21.3	19.0	31.0
Midwest	23.1	24.8	19.6	24.0	24.6	21.4
South	36.0	37.0	34.1	35.5	37.7	26.5
West	21.8	20.3	25.0	19.2	18.7	21.0

Source: Bureau of the Census, American Housing Survey for the United States in 2003, Internet site http://www.census.gov/hhes/www/housing/ahs/ahs03/ahs03.html; calculations by New Strategist

Table 3.6 Households by Metropolitan Residence, Homeownership Status, and Age, 2003

(number and percent distribution of total households and households headed by people aged 65 or older by metropolitan residence and homeownership status, 2003; numbers in thousands)

	total households			householders aged 65 or older		
	total	owner	renter	total	owner	renter
Total households	**105,842**	**72,238**	**33,604**	**21,627**	**17,350**	**4,277**
In metropolitan areas	85,065	56,425	28,640	16,308	12,787	3,521
In central cities	31,300	16,701	14,599	5,853	4,121	1,732
In suburbs	53,765	39,724	14,041	10,455	8,666	1,789
Outside metropolitan areas	20,778	15,813	4,965	5,318	4,563	756
PERCENT DISTRIBUTION BY HOMEOWNERSHIP STATUS						
Total households	**100.0%**	**68.3%**	**31.7%**	**100.0%**	**80.2%**	**19.8%**
In metropolitan areas	100.0	66.3	33.7	100.0	78.4	21.6
In central cities	100.0	53.4	46.6	100.0	70.4	29.6
In suburbs	100.0	73.9	26.1	100.0	82.9	17.1
Outside metropolitan areas	100.0	76.1	23.9	100.0	85.8	14.2
PERCENT DISTRIBUTION BY METROPOLITAN RESIDENCE						
Total households	**100.0%**	**100.0%**	**100.0%**	**100.0%**	**100.0%**	**100.0%**
In metropolitan areas	80.4	78.1	85.2	75.4	73.7	82.3
In central cities	29.6	23.1	43.4	27.1	23.8	40.5
In suburbs	50.8	55.0	41.8	48.3	49.9	41.8
Outside metropolitan areas	19.6	21.9	14.8	24.6	26.3	17.7

Source: Bureau of the Census, American Housing Survey for the United States in 2003, Internet site http://www.census.gov/hhes/ www/housing/ahs/ahs03/ahs03.html; calculations by New Strategist

Most Older Americans Live in Single-Family Homes

The majority of elderly homeowners have three or more bedrooms.

Sixty-nine percent of householders aged 65 or older live in single-family, detached homes. Nineteen percent live in apartment buildings, while 7 percent live in mobile homes. Not surprisingly, older homeowners are much more likely to live in single-family homes than older renters (81 versus 21 percent).

Despite their smaller household size, many older householders have large homes. Sixty-eight percent of elderly homeowners have three or more bedrooms, and 48 percent have two or more bathrooms. Among homeowners aged 65 or older, the median home size is 1,715 square feet. Among renters in the age group, the median home size is 1,283 square feet.

■ Many Americans downsize their home as they age, but others want extra bedrooms and bathrooms for visiting children and grandchildren.

Most older homeowners have three or more bedrooms

(percent distribution of homeowners aged 65 or older, by number of bedrooms in home, 2003)

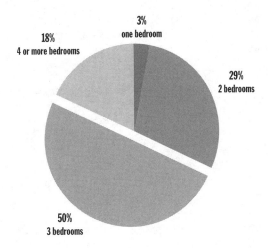

Table 3.7 Number of Units in Structure by Age of Householder, 2003

(number and percent distribution of households by age of householder and number of units in structure, 2003; numbers in thousands)

	total	one, detached	one, attached	multi-unit dwellings total	2 to 4	5 to 9	10 to 19	20 to 49	50 or more	mobile homes
Total households	**105,842**	**67,753**	**6,272**	**24,963**	**8,474**	**5,135**	**4,468**	**3,294**	**3,592**	**6,854**
Under age 55	68,811	41,723	4,240	18,506	6,372	4,133	3,642	2,407	1,952	4,340
Aged 55 to 64	15,404	11,069	898	2,411	907	411	393	287	412	1,026
Aged 65 or older	21,627	14,960	1,134	4,046	1,194	590	434	600	1,228	1,488
Aged 65 to 74	10,782	7,719	546	1,742	531	290	247	259	416	775
Aged 75 or older	10,845	7,241	588	2,304	663	300	187	341	812	713
Median age (years)	47	49	44	40	40	37	36	39	51	48

PERCENT DISTRIBUTION BY AGE OF HOUSEHOLDER

	total	one, detached	one, attached	multi-unit dwellings total	2 to 4	5 to 9	10 to 19	20 to 49	50 or more	mobile homes
Total households	**100.0%**	**100.0%**	**100.0%**	**100.0%**	**100.0%**	**100.0%**	**100.0%**	**100.0%**	**100.0%**	**100.0%**
Under age 55	65.0	61.6	67.6	74.1	75.2	80.5	81.5	73.1	54.3	63.3
Aged 55 to 64	14.6	16.3	14.3	9.7	10.7	8.0	8.8	8.7	11.5	15.0
Aged 65 or older	20.4	22.1	18.1	16.2	14.1	11.5	9.7	18.2	34.2	21.7
Aged 65 to 74	10.2	11.4	8.7	7.0	6.3	5.6	5.5	7.9	11.6	11.3
Aged 75 or older	10.2	10.7	9.4	9.2	7.8	5.8	4.2	10.4	22.6	10.4

PERCENT DISTRIBUTION BY UNITS IN STRUCTURE

	total	one, detached	one, attached	multi-unit dwellings total	2 to 4	5 to 9	10 to 19	20 to 49	50 or more	mobile homes
Total households	**100.0%**	**64.0%**	**5.9%**	**23.6%**	**8.0%**	**4.9%**	**4.2%**	**3.1%**	**3.4%**	**6.5%**
Under age 55	100.0	60.6	6.2	26.9	9.3	6.0	5.3	3.5	2.8	6.3
Aged 55 to 64	100.0	71.9	5.8	15.7	5.9	2.7	2.6	1.9	2.7	6.7
Aged 65 or older	100.0	69.2	5.2	18.7	5.5	2.7	2.0	2.8	5.7	6.9
Aged 65 to 74	100.0	71.6	5.1	16.2	4.9	2.7	2.3	2.4	3.9	7.2
Aged 75 or older	100.0	66.8	5.4	21.2	6.1	2.8	1.7	3.1	7.5	6.6

Source: Bureau of the Census, American Housing Survey for the United States in 2003, Internet site http://www.census.gov/hhes/www/housing/ahs/ahs03/ahs03.html; calculations by New Strategist

Table 3.8 Number of Units in Structures Occupied by Householders Aged 65 or Older, 2003

(number and percent distribution of householders aged 65 or older by number of units in structure and homeownership status, 2003; numbers in thousands)

	total	owner	renter
Total householders aged 65 or older	**21,627**	**17,350**	**4,277**
1 unit, detached	14,961	14,071	890
1 unit, attached	1,134	867	267
2 to 4 units	1,194	379	815
5 to 9 units	590	135	455
10 to 19 units	433	146	287
20 to 49 units	600	146	454
50 or more units	1,228	242	986
Mobile home	1,487	1,364	123

PERCENT DISTRIBUTION BY HOMEOWNERSHIP STATUS

Total householders aged 65 or older	**100.0%**	**80.2%**	**19.8%**
1 unit, detached	100.0	94.1	5.9
1 unit, attached	100.0	76.5	23.5
2 to 4 units	100.0	31.7	68.3
5 to 9 units	100.0	22.9	77.1
10 to 19 units	100.0	33.7	66.3
20 to 49 units	100.0	24.3	75.7
50 or more units	100.0	19.7	80.3
Mobile home	100.0	91.7	8.3

PERCENT DISTRIBUTION BY NUMBER OF UNITS IN STRUCTURE

Total householders aged 65 or older	**100.0%**	**100.0%**	**100.0%**
1 unit, detached	69.2	81.1	20.8
1 unit, attached	5.2	5.0	6.2
2 to 4 units	5.5	2.2	19.1
5 to 9 units	2.7	0.8	10.6
10 to 19 units	2.0	0.8	6.7
20 to 49 units	2.8	0.8	10.6
50 or more units	5.7	1.4	23.1
Mobile home	6.9	7.9	2.9

Source: Bureau of the Census, American Housing Survey for the United States in 2003, Internet site http://www.census.gov/hhes/ www/housing/ahs/ahs03/ahs03.html; calculations by New Strategist

Table 3.9 Size of Housing Unit Occupied by Householders Aged 65 or Older, 2003

(number and percent distribution of householders aged 65 or older by size of unit and homeownership status, 2003; numbers in thousands)

	number			percent distribution by homeownership status			percent distribution by size of unit		
	total	owner	renter	total	owner	renter	total	owner	renter
Total householders aged 65 or older	**21,627**	**17,350**	**4,277**	**100.0%**	**80.2%**	**19.8%**	**100.0%**	**100.0%**	**100.0%**
Number of bedrooms									
None	152	12	140	100.0	7.9	92.1	0.7	0.1	3.3
One	2,389	587	1,801	100.0	24.6	75.4	11.0	3.4	42.1
Two	6,644	4,962	1,682	100.0	74.7	25.3	30.7	28.6	39.3
Three	9,261	8,731	530	100.0	94.3	5.7	42.8	50.3	12.4
Four or more	3,182	3,058	124	100.0	96.1	3.9	14.7	17.6	2.9
Number of bathrooms									
None	162	100	62	100.0	61.7	38.3	0.7	0.6	1.4
One	8,540	5,266	3,274	100.0	61.7	38.3	39.5	30.4	76.5
One-and-one-half	4,007	3,645	362	100.0	91.0	9.0	18.5	21.0	8.5
Two or more	8,918	8,339	579	100.0	93.5	6.5	41.2	48.1	13.5
Rooms used for business									
With room(s) used for business	2,931	2,489	441	100.0	84.9	15.0	13.6	14.3	10.3
Median square footage of unit	**1,687**	**1,715**	**1,283**	–	–	–	–	–	–

Note: "–" means not applicable.
Source: Bureau of the Census, American Housing Survey for the United States in 2003, Internet site http://www.census.gov/hhes/www/housing/ahs/ahs03/ahs03.html; calculations by New Strategist

Few Older Homeowners Live in New Homes

Householders under age 55 are more likely to live in new homes.

Overall, only 6 percent of homeowners live in a new home—meaning one built in the past four years. Among homeowners aged 55 to 64, a smaller 4 percent live in a new home. Among those aged 65 or older, the proportion is just 3 percent.

Householders aged 55 or older account for 41 percent of the nation's homeowners, but for only 23 percent of the owners of homes built in the past four years. They account for only 20 percent of renters in new rental units.

■ With many older adults living in older homes, they are a large and growing market for home remodeling and repair services.

Older householders account for a small share of the owners of recently built homes

(percent distribution of homeowners living in homes built in the past four years, by age of householder, 2003)

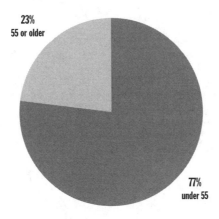

23%
55 or older

77%
under 55

Table 3.10 Owners and Renters of New Homes by Age of Householder, 2003

(number of total occupied housing units, number and percent built in the past four years, and percent distribution of new units by housing tenure and age of householder, 2003; numbers in thousands)

		new homes		
	total	number	percent of total	percent distribution
Total households	**105,842**	**5,691**	**5.4%**	**100.0%**
Under age 55	68,811	4,436	6.4	77.9
Aged 55 to 64	15,404	582	3.8	10.2
Aged 65 or older	21,627	672	3.1	11.8
Aged 65 to 74	10,782	430	4.0	7.6
Aged 75 or older	10,845	242	2.2	4.3
Total owner households	**72,238**	**4,673**	**6.5**	**100.0**
Under age 55	42,391	3,619	8.5	77.4
Aged 55 to 64	12,497	518	4.1	11.1
Aged 65 or older	17,350	535	3.1	11.4
Aged 65 to 74	8,876	363	4.1	7.8
Aged 75 or older	8,474	172	2.0	3.7
Total renter households	**33,604**	**1,018**	**3.0**	**100.0**
Under age 55	26,420	816	3.1	80.2
Aged 55 to 64	2,906	64	2.2	6.3
Aged 65 or older	4,277	137	3.2	13.5
Aged 65 to 74	1,907	67	3.5	6.6
Aged 75 or older	2,370	70	3.0	6.9

Source: Bureau of the Census, American Housing Survey for the United States in 2003, Internet site http://www.census.gov/hhes/ www/housing/ahs/ahs03/ahs03.html; calculations by New Strategist

Most Older Americans Depend on Piped Gas for Heat

Renters are more likely than homeowners to heat with electricity.

Piped gas was the main heating fuel for the 53 percent majority of the nation's elderly households in 2003. Among homeowners aged 65 or older, 55 percent depend on piped gas as their main heating fuel. Among renters, the figure is a smaller 42 percent. Electricity is the second most common heating fuel, used by 24 percent of elderly homeowners and 40 percent of renters.

More than one in ten older homeowners use fuel oil as their primary heating fuel. A hardy 2 percent depend primarily on wood.

■ Households in the South are more likely than those in other regions to use electricity as the primary heating fuel. As the South gains residents, a growing share of households will use electricity as the primary heating fuel.

Piped gas is the most widely used heating fuel among older Americans

(percent distribution of householders aged 65 or older, by primary heating fuel used, 2003)

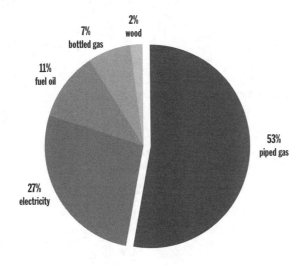

Table 3.11 Main Home Heating Fuel Used by Householders Aged 65 or Older, 2003

(number and percent distribution of housing units occupied by a householder aged 65 or older by main house heating fuel and homeownership status, 2003; numbers in thousands)

	total	owner	renter
Total households headed by people aged 65 or older using heating fuel	**21,566**	**17,304**	**4,261**
Piped gas	11,360	9,584	1,776
Electricity	5,767	4,080	1,688
Fuel oil	2,365	1,790	575
Bottled gas	1,494	1,362	133
Wood	360	314	47
Kerosene/other liquid fuel	156	126	29
Coal or coke	41	40	2
Solar energy	2	0	2
Other	19	9	10

PERCENT DISTRIBUTION BY TYPE OF HEATING FUEL

	total	owner	renter
Total households headed by people aged 65 or older using heating fuel	**100.0%**	**100.0%**	**100.0%**
Piped gas	52.7	55.4	41.7
Electricity	26.7	23.6	39.6
Fuel oil	11.0	10.3	13.5
Bottled gas	6.9	7.9	3.1
Wood	1.7	1.8	1.1
Kerosene/other liquid fuel	0.7	0.7	0.7
Coal or coke	0.2	0.2	0.0
Solar energy	0.0	0.0	0.0
Other	0.1	0.1	0.2

Source: Bureau of the Census, American Housing Survey for the United States in 2003, Internet site http://www.census.gov/hhes/ www/housing/ahs/ahs03/ahs03.html; calculations by New Strategist

Older Americans' Homes Have Many Amenities

Most have dishwashers, central air conditioning, and garages or carports.

The homes of older Americans are outfitted with amenities. Fully 84 percent have a porch, deck, balcony, or patio. Washing machines are also in 84 percent of the homes of older Americans, while clothes dryers are in 79 percent. Sixty-eight percent have a garage or carport, and 54 percent have central air conditioning. Fifty-eight percent have a dishwasher.

Older homeowners are much more likely than older renters to have amenities in the home. Sixty-two percent of elderly homeowners have a dishwasher, for example, compared with 40 percent of renters. Thirty-seven percent of elderly homeowners have a useable fireplace versus only 7 percent of renters.

■ Although older Americans were raised with few amenities, they have outfitted their homes with most of the conveniences.

Most older householders have a home with central air conditioning

(percent of households headed by people aged 65 or older with selected amenities, 2003)

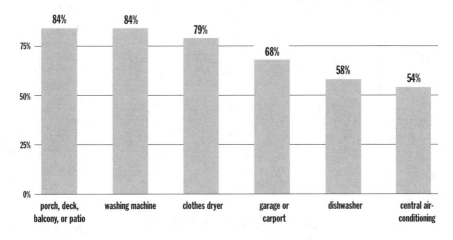

Table 3.12 Amenities of Housing Units Occupied by Householders Aged 65 or Older, 2003

(number and percent distribution of households headed by people aged 65 or older by amenities in unit and homeownership status, 2003; numbers in thousands)

	total	owner	renter
Total households headed by people aged 65 or older	**21,627**	**17,350**	**4,277**
Porch, deck, balcony, or patio	18,271	15,626	2,645
Telephone	21,145	16,992	4,153
Washing machine	18,253	16,452	1,801
Clothes dryer	17,112	15,567	1,545
Garage or carport	14,602	13,341	1,261
Dishwasher	11,781	10,527	1,254
Central air conditioning	12,487	10,775	1,712
Separate dining room	10,173	9,274	899
Disposal in kitchen sink	9,202	7,492	1,711
Usable fireplace	6,737	6,444	293
With two or more living/ recreation rooms	6,080	5,871	209

PERCENT DISTRIBUTION BY AMENITY

	total	owner	renter
Total households headed by people aged 65 or older	**100.0%**	**100.0%**	**100.0%**
Porch, deck, balcony, or patio	84.5	90.1	61.8
Telephone	97.8	97.9	97.1
Washing machine	84.4	94.8	42.1
Clothes dryer	79.1	89.7	36.1
Garage or carport	67.5	76.9	29.5
Central air conditioning	54.5	60.7	29.3
Dishwasher	57.7	62.1	40.0
Separate dining room	47.0	53.5	21.0
Disposal in kitchen sink	42.5	43.2	40.0
Usable fireplace	31.2	37.1	6.9
With two or more living/ recreation rooms	28.1	33.8	4.9

Source: Bureau of the Census, American Housing Survey for the United States in 2003, Internet site http://www.census.gov/hhes/ www/housing/ahs/ahs03/ahs03.html; calculations by New Strategist

Most of the Elderly Are Satisfied with Their Home and Neighborhood

Homeowners are happier than renters, but few renters are dissatisfied.

When asked how they would rate their housing unit on a scale of 1 (worst) to 10 (best), 79 percent of householders aged 65 or older rate their home an 8 or higher. Homeowners rate their homes more highly than renters—81 percent of owners and 72 percent of renters give their home at least an 8. Forty-one percent of homeowners and 36 percent of renters give their home the highest rating of 10.

Opinions are almost as positive when older householders are asked to rate their neighborhood. Seventy-five percent rate their neighborhood an 8 or higher, including 77 percent of homeowners and 70 percent of renters.

■ Older householders rate their home and neighborhood highly because, over the years, those who were unhappy found a new place to live.

Most older householders rate their home and neighborhood highly

(percent of householders aged 65 or older who rate their home and neighborhood an 8 or higher on a scale of 1 to 10, with 1 being worst and 10 being best, 2003)

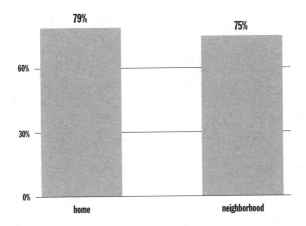

Table 3.13 Opinion of Housing Unit among Householders Aged 65 or Older By Homeownership Status, 2003

(number and percent distribution of housing units occupied by householders aged 65 or older by householder's opinion of housing unit and homeownership status, 2003; numbers in thousands)

	total	owner	renter
Total householders aged 65 or older	**21,627**	**17,350**	**4,277**
1 (worst)	76	45	31
2	33	22	11
3	76	54	22
4	114	71	43
5	807	549	259
6	693	497	196
7	1,741	1,327	414
8	5,163	4,160	1,002
9	3,342	2,781	562
10 (best)	8,593	7,067	1,526

PERCENT DISTRIBUTION BY OPINION OF HOUSING UNIT

Total householders aged 65 or older	**100.0%**	**100.0%**	**100.0%**
1 (worst)	0.4	0.3	0.7
2	0.2	0.1	0.3
3	0.4	0.3	0.5
4	0.5	0.4	1.0
5	3.7	3.2	6.1
6	3.2	2.9	4.6
7	8.1	7.6	9.7
8	23.9	24.0	23.4
9	15.5	16.0	13.1
10 (best)	39.7	40.7	35.7

PERCENT DISTRIBUTION BY HOMEOWNERSHIP STATUS

Total householders aged 65 or older	**100.0%**	**80.2%**	**19.8%**
1 (worst)	100.0	59.2	40.8
2	100.0	66.7	33.3
3	100.0	71.1	28.9
4	100.0	62.3	37.7
5	100.0	68.0	32.1
6	100.0	71.7	28.3
7	100.0	76.2	23.8
8	100.0	80.6	19.4
9	100.0	83.2	16.8
10 (best)	100.0	82.2	17.8

Note: Numbers will not add to total because "not reported" is not shown.
Source: Bureau of the Census, American Housing Survey for the United States in 2003, Internet site http://www.census.gov/hhes/ www/housing/ahs/ahs03/ahs03.html; calculations by New Strategist

Table 3.14 Opinion of Neighborhood among Householders Aged 65 or Older By Homeownership Status, 2003

(number and percent distribution of housing units occupied by householders aged 65 or older by householder's opinion of neighborhood and homeownership status, 2003; numbers in thousands)

	total	owner	renter
Total householders aged 65 or older	**21,627**	**17,350**	**4,277**
1 (worst)	90	68	22
2	72	62	10
3	101	71	30
4	176	113	63
5	1,005	728	277
6	847	647	200
7	1,852	1,441	412
8	5,245	4,277	968
9	3,360	2,769	590
10 (best)	7,675	6,240	1,435

PERCENT DISTRIBUTION BY OPINION OF NEIGHBORHOOD

Total householders aged 65 or older	**100.0%**	**100.0%**	**100.0%**
1 (worst)	0.4	0.4	0.5
2	0.3	0.4	0.2
3	0.5	0.4	0.7
4	0.8	0.7	1.5
5	4.6	4.2	6.5
6	3.9	3.7	4.7
7	8.6	8.3	9.6
8	24.3	24.7	22.6
9	15.5	16.0	13.8
10 (best)	35.5	36.0	33.6

PERCENT DISTRIBUTION BY HOMEOWNERSHIP STATUS

Total householders aged 65 or older	**100.0%**	**80.2%**	**19.8%**
1 (worst)	100.0	75.6	24.4
2	100.0	86.1	13.9
3	100.0	70.3	29.7
4	100.0	64.2	35.8
5	100.0	72.4	27.6
6	100.0	76.4	23.6
7	100.0	77.8	22.2
8	100.0	81.5	18.5
9	100.0	82.4	17.6
10 (best)	100.0	81.3	18.7

Note: Numbers will not add to total because "not reported" is not shown.
Source: Bureau of the Census, American Housing Survey for the United States in 2003, Internet site http://www.census.gov/hhes/ www/housing/ahs/ahs03/ahs03.html; calculations by New Strategist

Many Older Americans Live near Open Space, Woodlands

Few are bothered by crime, street noise, or other problems.

Of the 22 million householders aged 65 or older in the United States, 79 percent report having single-family, detached houses within 300 feet of their home—82 percent of homeowners and 63 percent of renters. Thirty-four percent of homeowners and 28 percent of renters report having open space, park, woods, farm, or ranchland close by.

Many older householders have commercial or institutional buildings within 300 feet of their home—14 percent of homeowners and 40 percent of renters. Just 2 percent report industries or factories nearby, while a larger 10 percent say a four-lane highway, railroad, or airport is within 300 feet.

Few older householders report bothersome neighborhood problems. The biggest problem is street noise or traffic, reported by 7 percent of homeowners and 9 percent of renters. Crime ranks second but is bothersome to only 4 percent of homeowners and 7 percent of renters. People are the third biggest neighborhood problem, bothering 3 percent of older householders nationwide.

■ Despite media reports of crime problems in many neighborhoods, few older householders say crime is bothersome where they live.

The biggest neighborhood problem among the elderly is street noise

(percent of householders aged 65 or older saying they are bothered by selected neighborhood problems, 2003)

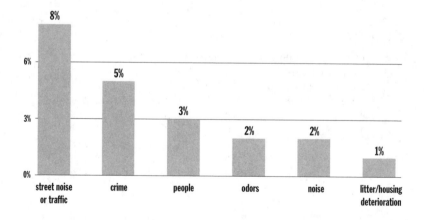

Table 3.15 Characteristics of Neighborhoods among Householders Aged 65 or Older By Homeownership Status, 2003

(number and percent distribution of housing units occupied by householders aged 65 or older by description of area within 300 feet, by homeownership status, 2003; numbers in thousands)

	total	owner	renter
Total householders aged 65 or older	**21,627**	**17,350**	**4,277**
Single-family detached houses	17,012	14,300	2,712
Single-family attached houses	2,341	1,581	761
1 to 3 story multi-unit	3,343	1,628	1,715
4 to 6 story multi-unit	1,065	367	698
7 or more story multi-unit	614	177	437
Mobile homes	2,558	2,341	216
Commercial/institutional buildings	4,229	2,500	1,729
Industrial buildings or factories	534	334	201
Open space, park, woods, farm, or ranch	7,149	5,932	1,218
Four or more lane highway, railroad, or airport	2,188	1,494	694
Waterfront property	761	687	74

PERCENT DISTRIBUTION BY DESCRIPTION OF NEIGHBORHOOD

Total householders aged 65 or older	**100.0%**	**100.0%**	**100.0%**
Single-family detached houses	78.7	82.4	63.4
Single-family attached houses	10.8	9.1	17.8
1 to 3 story multi-unit	15.5	9.4	40.1
4 to 6 story multi-unit	4.9	2.1	16.3
7 or more story multi-unit	2.8	1.0	10.2
Mobile homes	11.8	13.5	5.1
Commercial/institutional buildings	19.6	14.4	40.4
Industrial buildings or factories	2.5	1.9	4.7
Open space, park, woods, farm, or ranch	33.1	34.2	28.5
Four or more lane highway, railroad, or airport	10.1	8.6	16.2
Waterfront property	3.5	4.0	1.7

PERCENT DISTRIBUTION BY HOMEOWNERSHIP STATUS

Total householders aged 65 or older	**100.0%**	**80.2%**	**19.8%**
Single-family detached houses	100.0	84.1	15.9
Single-family attached houses	100.0	67.5	32.5
1 to 3 story multi-unit	100.0	48.7	51.3
4 to 6 story multi-unit	100.0	34.5	65.5
7 or more story multi-unit	100.0	28.8	71.2
Mobile homes	100.0	91.5	8.4
Commercial/institutional buildings	100.0	59.1	40.9
Industrial buildings or factories	100.0	62.5	37.6
Open space, park, woods, farm, or ranch	100.0	83.0	17.0
Four or more lane highway, railroad, or airport	100.0	68.3	31.7
Waterfront property	100.0	90.3	9.7

Note: Numbers will not add to total because more than one category may apply to unit.
Source: Bureau of the Census, American Housing Survey for the United States in 2003, Internet site http://www.census.gov/hhes/ www/housing/ahs/ahs03/ahs03.html; calculations by New Strategist

Table 3.16 Neighborhood Problems Reported by Householders Aged 65 or Older By Homeownership Status, 2003

(number and percent of housing units occupied by householders aged 65 or older by neighborhood conditions considered bothersome by householder, and percent distribution of bothersome conditions by homeownership status, 2003; numbers in thousands)

	total	owner	renter
Total householders aged 65 or older	**21,627**	**17,350**	**4,277**
Street noise or traffic	1,684	1,301	383
Crime	1,051	754	297
Odors	475	364	111
Noise	388	295	93
Litter or housing deterioration	316	265	51
Poor city or county services	124	102	23
Undesirable commercial/institutional/industrial	102	89	13
People	608	476	132
PERCENT WITH PROBLEM			
Total householders aged 65 or older	**100.0%**	**100.0%**	**100.0%**
Street noise or traffic	7.8	7.5	9.0
Crime	4.9	4.3	6.9
Odors	2.2	2.1	2.6
Noise	1.8	1.7	2.2
Litter or housing deterioration	1.5	1.5	1.2
Poor city or county services	0.6	0.6	0.5
Undesirable commercial/institutional/industrial	0.5	0.5	0.3
People	2.8	2.7	3.1
PERCENT DISTRIBUTION OF PROBLEMS BY HOMEOWNERSHIP STATUS			
Total householders aged 65 or older	**100.0%**	**80.2%**	**19.8%**
Street noise or traffic	100.0	77.3	22.7
Crime	100.0	71.7	28.3
Odors	100.0	76.6	23.4
Noise	100.0	76.0	24.0
Litter or housing deterioration	100.0	83.9	16.1
Poor city or county services	100.0	82.3	18.5
Undesirable commercial/institutional/industrial	100.0	87.3	12.7
People	100.0	78.3	21.7

Note: Numbers will not add to total because "not reported" is not shown.
Source: Bureau of the Census, American Housing Survey for the United States in 2003, Internet site http://www.census.gov/hhes/www/housing/ahs/ahs03/ahs03.html; calculations by New Strategist

Housing Costs Are Lower for Older Americans

Most elderly homeowners have paid off their mortgage.

Housing costs are lowest for homeowners aged 65 or older regardless of household type. Median monthly housing costs for married homeowners aged 65 or older were just $398 in 2003. For all couples who own a home, median monthly housing costs were a much higher $843.

Among married couples, homeowners have higher monthly housing costs than renters until age 65. Among couples aged 65 or older, renters pay more for housing. The same pattern holds true for elderly men and women who live alone.

Behind the lower housing costs of elderly homeowners is the fact that most have paid off their mortgage. Only 22 percent of homeowners aged 65 or older have a mortgage. Consequently, elderly homeowners must devote only 18 percent of their monthly income to housing. Among elderly renters, the figure is a much higher 39 percent.

■ As Boomers enter the 65-or-older age group, the percentage of elderly homeowners with mortgages is likely to rise because many Boomers have refinanced their home to pay off other debts.

Housing costs are lowest for the oldest homeowners

(median monthly housing costs for married couples, by age of householder, 2003)

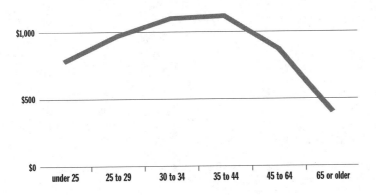

Table 3.17 Median Monthly Housing Costs by Household Type and Age of Householder, 2003

(median monthly housing costs and indexed costs by type of household, age of householder, and housing tenure, 2003)

	median monthly cost			indexed cost		
	total	owners	renters	total	owners	renters
Total households	**$684**	**$717**	**$651**	**100**	**105**	**95**
TWO-OR-MORE-PERSON HOUSEHOLDS	**761**	**806**	**704**	**111**	**118**	**103**
Married couples	**810**	**843**	**740**	**118**	**123**	**108**
Under age 25	688	779	653	101	114	95
Aged 25 to 29	825	969	700	121	142	102
Aged 30 to 34	954	1,100	756	139	161	111
Aged 35 to 44	1,023	1,117	792	150	163	116
Aged 45 to 64	852	869	763	125	127	112
Aged 65 or older	416	398	661	61	58	97
Other male householder	**740**	**752**	**734**	**108**	**110**	**107**
Aged 15 to 44	773	867	740	113	127	108
Aged 45 to 64	721	734	705	105	107	103
Aged 65 or older	479	416	714	70	61	104
Other female householder	**654**	**673**	**645**	**96**	**98**	**94**
Aged 15 to 44	679	778	642	99	114	94
Aged 45 to 64	693	742	656	101	108	96
Aged 65 or older	408	350	630	60	51	92
SINGLE-PERSON HOUSEHOLDS	**512**	**433**	**567**	**75**	**63**	**83**
Male householder	**557**	**517**	**574**	**81**	**76**	**84**
Aged 15 to 44	644	759	605	94	111	88
Aged 45 to 64	551	562	544	81	82	80
Aged 65 or older	354	307	478	52	45	70
Female householder	**474**	**391**	**559**	**69**	**57**	**82**
Aged 15 to 44	656	774	617	96	113	90
Aged 45 to 64	566	600	536	83	88	78
Aged 65 or older	329	294	470	48	43	69

Note: Housing costs include utilities, mortgages, real estate taxes, property insurance, and regime fees.
Source: Bureau of the Census, American Housing Survey for the United States in 2003, Internet site http://www.census.gov/hhes/ www/housing/ahs/ahs03/ahs03.html; calculations by New Strategist

Table 3.18 Monthly Housing Costs of Householders Aged 65 or Older by Homeownership Status, 2003

(total median monthly housing costs, monthly housing costs as a percent of current income, and median monthly amount paid for selected services and utilities, for householders aged 65 or older by homeownership status, 2003)

	householders aged 65 or older		
	total	owner	renter
Total median monthly housing cost	**$377**	**$350**	**$534**
Monthly housing cost as a percent of current income	**20.8%**	**18.1%**	**39.0%**
Median monthly cost of electricity	$57	$60	$42
Median monthly cost of piped gas	52	54	39
Median monthly cost of fuel oil	74	76	61
Median monthly cost of property insurance	41	42	17
Median monthly cost of water	28	28	23
Median monthly cost of trash removal	16	16	14
Percent with a mortgage	–	22.5%	–
Median monthly payment for principal and interest	–	$501	–
Median monthly real estate taxes	–	87	–

Note: Median costs are for those with expense; "–" means not applicable.
Source: Bureau of the Census, American Housing Survey for the United States in 2003, Internet site http://www.census.gov/hhes/www/housing/ahs/ahs03/ahs03.html; calculations by New Strategist

The Value of the Homes Owned by Older Americans Is below Average

Home values peak in middle age.

The median value of the homes owned by people aged 65 or older stood at $122,789 in 2003, substantially below the $140,269 value of the average owned home. Behind the lesser value is the fact that elderly homeowners are more likely to live in older and smaller homes than the average homeowner. The homes owned by elderly married couples were valued at a median of $142,851 in 2003—close to the national average. Eighteen percent of married-couple homeowners aged 65 or older own a home worth $300,000 or more.

Older homeowners have built substantial equity in their homes because many have paid off their mortgages. The median purchase price of the homes owned by the elderly was just $32,904. Some will spend this equity on living expenses as they age, while others will leave it to their children.

■ Home values have been rising steadily and are now significantly higher than the 2003 figures shown in this section.

Home values are lower among the elderly

(median value of homes owned by married couples, by age of householder, 2003)

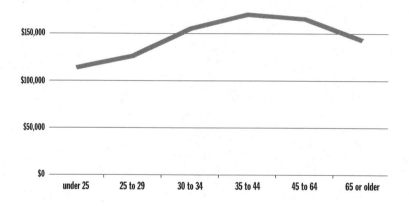

Table 3.19 Value of Owner-Occupied Homes by Type of Household and Age of Householder, 2003

(number of homeowners by value of home, median value of housing unit, and indexed median value, by type of household and age of householder, 2003)

	number (in 000s)	under $100,000	$100,000 to $149,999	$150,000 to $199,999	$200,000 to $249,999	$250,000 to $299,999	$300,000 or more	median value of home	indexed median value
Total homeowners	**72,238**	**24,630**	**14,266**	**9,989**	**6,358**	**4,561**	**12,434**	**$140,269**	**100**
TWO-OR-MORE-PERSON HOUSEHOLDS	**56,783**	**17,689**	**11,119**	**8,104**	**5,287**	**3,869**	**10,715**	**148,124**	**106**
Married couples	**44,684**	**12,562**	**8,767**	**6,655**	**4,382**	**3,214**	**9,103**	**157,610**	**112**
Under age 25	465	200	119	51	36	12	47	113,675	81
Aged 25 to 29	1,948	699	529	288	163	91	178	126,086	90
Aged 30 to 34	3,848	1,062	794	671	406	261	656	155,125	111
Aged 35 to 44	10,719	2,675	2,031	1,610	1,110	855	2,439	170,314	121
Aged 45 to 64	19,197	5,132	3,595	2,817	1,947	1,425	4,282	165,485	118
Aged 65 or older	8,506	2,796	1,701	1,218	720	570	1,501	142,851	102
Other male householder	**4,363**	**1,730**	**862**	**517**	**351**	**242**	**660**	**126,163**	**90**
Under age 45	2,220	923	492	248	142	96	319	119,009	85
Aged 45 to 64	1,594	580	289	195	136	106	288	137,391	98
Aged 65 or older	548	225	81	73	74	40	54	129,563	92
Other female householder	**7,737**	**3,398**	**1,491**	**932**	**554**	**412**	**951**	**115,815**	**83**
Under age 45	3,130	1,471	627	377	218	155	282	107,453	77
Aged 45 to 64	3,102	1,269	588	394	219	165	468	124,079	88
Aged 65 or older	1,506	657	276	161	117	92	202	117,197	84
SINGLE-PERSON HOUSEHOLDS	**15,455**	**6,940**	**3,147**	**1,886**	**1,071**	**692**	**1,719**	**112,510**	**80**
Male householder	**6,078**	**2,732**	**1,189**	**674**	**443**	**239**	**800**	**112,898**	**80**
Under age 45	2,074	907	449	253	130	56	279	114,450	82
Aged 45 to 64	2,340	1,038	437	255	202	99	309	115,075	82
Aged 65 or older	1,664	786	304	167	111	83	213	107,475	77
Female householder	**9,376**	**4,208**	**1,957**	**1,211**	**627**	**454**	**919**	**112,274**	**80**
Under age 45	1,325	487	357	198	95	48	140	124,647	89
Aged 45 to 64	2,925	1,206	629	374	218	179	319	120,388	86
Aged 65 or older	5,126	2,515	972	639	315	227	459	102,482	73

Source: Bureau of the Census, American Housing Survey for the United States in 2003, Internet site http://www.census.gov/hhes/ www/housing/ahs/ahs03/ahs03.html; calculations by New Strategist

Table 3.20 Housing Value and Purchase Price for Homeowners Aged 65 or Older, 2003

(number and percent distribution of homeowners aged 65 or older by value of home and purchase price, 2003; numbers in thousands)

	number	percent distribution
Total homeowners aged 65 or older	**17,350**	**100.0%**
Value of home		
Under $50,000	2,342	13.5
$50,000 to $99,999	4,638	26.7
$100,000 to $149,999	3,333	19.2
$150,000 to $199,999	2,258	13.0
$200,000 to $249,999	1,337	7.7
$250,000 to $299,999	1,012	5.8
$300,000 or more	2,429	14.0
Median value	$122,789	–
Purchase price of homes purchased or built		
Under $50,000	9,419	54.3
$50,000 to $99,999	2,885	16.6
$100,000 to $149,999	1,228	7.1
$150,000 to $199,999	696	4.0
$200,000 to $249,999	297	1.7
$250,000 to $299,999	175	1.0
$300,000 or more	321	1.9
Received as inheritance or gift	776	4.5
Median purchase price	$32,904	–

Note: Numbers may not add to total because "not reported" is not shown; "–" means not applicable.
Source: Bureau of the Census, American Housing Survey for the United States in 2003, Internet site http://www.census.gov/hhes/www/housing/ahs/ahs03/ahs03.html; calculations by New Strategist

Mobility Rate Is Low in Old Age

Behind the lower mobility of older Americans are high rates of homeownership and strong community ties.

While 14 percent of Americans aged 1 or older moved between March 2003 and March 2004, the proportion was a much smaller 4 percent among people aged 65 or older. Among movers, however, older adults are more likely to move to a different state. Nineteen percent of all movers moved to a different state, but the proportion rises as high as 29 to 30 percent among movers aged 60 to 64 and 36 percent among movers aged 80 to 84. Many of the 60-to-64-year-olds moving between states are retirees heading to warmer climates. Many in the older group are moving closer to adult children as they become increasingly frail with age.

Not surprisingly, people aged 65 or older are more likely than those younger to report moving for "other" reasons, a category that includes change of climate and health. A survey by Pulte Homes shows that only 47 percent of people aged 41 to 69 plan to stay in their current home throughout retirement. Among those planning to move, 45 percent say they will move out of state. About two-thirds of those planning to move will do so because they want a more affordable house or location. A smaller 46 percent say they will move to live in a warmer climate.

■ Americans are moving less than they once did. Several factors are behind the lower mobility rate, including the aging of the population, greater homeownership, and more dual-income couples.

Older movers are more likely than younger ones to head to a different state

(percent of movers who moved to a different state between March 2003 and March 2004, by age)

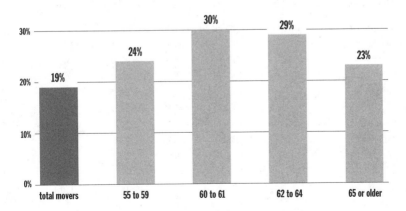

Table 3.21 Geographical Mobility of People by Age, 2003 to 2004

(total number and percent distribution of people aged 1 or older by mobility status between March 2003 and March 2004, by selected age groups; numbers in thousands)

	total	movers total	same county	different county, same state	different state	abroad
Total, aged 1 or older	**284,367**	**38,995**	**22,551**	**7,842**	**7,330**	**1,272**
Under age 55	221,334	35,714	20,877	7,106	6,520	1,211
Aged 55 to 59	16,158	1,047	533	241	252	21
Aged 60 to 61	5,454	334	159	69	100	6
Aged 62 to 64	6,762	385	169	88	112	16
Aged 65 or older	34,660	1,513	812	338	344	19
Aged 65 to 69	9,818	472	249	131	86	6
Aged 70 to 74	8,420	342	205	59	70	8
Aged 75 to 79	7,631	320	153	79	85	3
Aged 80 to 84	5,220	225	109	36	80	0
Aged 85 or older	3,571	154	96	33	23	2

PERCENT DISTRIBUTION BY MOBILITY STATUS

	total	movers total	same county	different county, same state	different state	abroad
Total, aged 1 or older	**100.0%**	**13.7%**	**7.9%**	**2.8%**	**2.6%**	**0.4%**
Under age 55	100.0	16.1	9.4	3.2	2.9	0.5
Aged 55 to 59	100.0	6.5	3.3	1.5	1.6	0.1
Aged 60 to 61	100.0	6.1	2.9	1.3	1.8	0.1
Aged 62 to 64	100.0	5.7	2.5	1.3	1.7	0.2
Aged 65 or older	100.0	4.4	2.3	1.0	1.0	0.1
Aged 65 to 69	100.0	4.8	2.5	1.3	0.9	0.1
Aged 70 to 74	100.0	4.1	2.4	0.7	0.8	0.1
Aged 75 to 79	100.0	4.2	2.0	1.0	1.1	0.0
Aged 80 to 84	100.0	4.3	2.1	0.7	1.5	0.0
Aged 85 or older	100.0	4.3	2.7	0.9	0.6	0.1

PERCENT DISTRIBUTION OF MOVERS BY TYPE OF MOVE

	total	movers total	same county	different county, same state	different state	abroad
Total, aged 1 or older	–	**100.0%**	**57.8%**	**20.1%**	**18.8%**	**3.3%**
Under age 55	–	100.0	58.5	19.9	18.3	3.4
Aged 55 to 59	–	100.0	50.9	23.0	24.1	2.0
Aged 60 to 61	–	100.0	47.6	20.7	29.9	1.8
Aged 62 to 64	–	100.0	43.9	22.9	29.1	4.2
Aged 65 or older	–	100.0	53.7	22.3	22.7	1.3
Aged 65 to 69	–	100.0	52.8	27.8	18.2	1.3
Aged 70 to 74	–	100.0	59.9	17.3	20.5	2.3
Aged 75 to 79	–	100.0	47.8	24.7	26.6	0.9
Aged 80 to 84	–	100.0	48.4	16.0	35.6	0.0
Aged 85 or older	–	100.0	62.3	21.4	14.9	1.3

Note: "–" means not applicable.
Source: Bureau of the Census, Geographical Mobility: 2004, Detailed Tables, Internet site http://www.census.gov/population/www/socdemo/migrate/cps2004.html; calculations by New Strategist

Table 3.22 Reason for Moving by Age, 2003 to 2004

(number and percent distribution of movers by primary reason for move between March 2003 and March 2004, by age; numbers in thousands)

	total	family reasons	employment reasons	housing reasons	other
Total movers	**38,995**	**9,475**	**6,624**	**20,577**	**2,319**
Under age 45	32,450	7,929	5,619	17,058	1,843
Aged 45 to 64	5,030	1,141	893	2,744	252
Aged 65 or older	1,516	404	113	776	223
Aged 65 to 74	816	196	71	469	80
Aged 75 or older	700	208	42	307	143
Total movers	**100.0%**	**24.3%**	**17.0%**	**52.8%**	**5.9%**
Under age 45	100.0	24.4	17.3	52.6	5.7
Aged 45 to 64	100.0	22.7	17.8	54.6	5.0
Aged 65 or older	100.0	26.6	7.5	51.2	14.7
Aged 65 to 74	100.0	24.0	8.7	57.5	9.8
Aged 75 or older	100.0	29.7	6.0	43.9	20.4

Note: "Other" includes to attend or leave college, change of climate, and health reasons.
Source: Bureau of the Census, Geographical Mobility: 2004, Detailed Tables, Internet site http://www.census.gov/population/ www/socdemo/migrate/cps2004.html; calculations by New Strategist

Table 3.23 Plans for Moving after Retirement, 2005

(percent distribution of people aged 41 to 69 by attitudes toward moving after retirement, 2005)

	total	41 to 49	50 to 59	60 to 69
"What plans do you have for a home now that you are retured/when you retire?"				
• Stay in current home for entire retirement	47%	39%	46%	62%
• Stay in current home first, buy a new home	23	24	23	24
• Buy new home before retiring, make it retirement home	17	25	19	3
• Buy and move to new home as soon as I can after I retire	8	10	8	6
• Sell current home, move to rental property	4	3	5	6
"Where do you plan for your new retirement home to be located?" (asked of respondents who are planning to move)				
• Out of state I currently live in	45	45	48	38
• Within same area I currently live in	29	26	30	34
• In same state, different area	27	29	22	28
"How important would each of the following reasons for moving be in making your decision to move at retirement?" (percent saying extremely/very important among those planning to move)				
• More affordable housing	67	63	70	72
• More affordable location	66	65	67	67
• Better community lifestyle	60	60	66	51
• Warmer climate	46	45	54	36
• To be closer to family	42	40	42	44

Source: Pulte Homes, 2005 Del Webb Baby Boomer Survey; Internet site http://phx.corporate-ir.net/phoenix. zhtml?c=147717&p=delWebb

4

Income

■ Householders aged 55 to 64 saw their median income climb 2 percent between 2000 and 2004. Although small, this increase stands in contrast to the 3 percent decline in the median income of householders aged 65 or older.

■ Household income falls as people age and retire from the labor force. Median household income in 2004 stood at $50,400 for householders aged 55 to 64, $30,854 for those aged 65 to 74, and $20,467 for those aged 75 or older.

■ The most-affluent older householders are couples aged 55 to 59 because most are still in the labor force. Their median income was a lofty $75,388 in 2004, and one-third had incomes of $100,000 or more.

■ Between 2000 and 2004, the median income of men and women aged 55 to 74 rose 3 to 12 percent, after adjusting for inflation. The median income of people aged 75 or older fell slightly during those years.

■ Among Americans aged 65 or older, from 90 to 92 percent received Social Security income in 2004, making it the most-common source of income for the age group.

■ Poverty rates are below average for older Americans. Ten percent of people aged 55 or older are poor compared with a larger 13 percent of all Americans.

The Incomes of Older Householders Have Fallen Since 2000

But the median income of householders aged 65 or older is still above its 1990 level.

Householders aged 55 to 64 saw their median income climb 2 percent between 2000 and 2004. Although small, this increase stands in contrast to the 3 percent decline in the median income of householders aged 65 or older. Despite the decline, the median income of householders aged 65 or older was 4 percent greater in 2004 than in 1990, after adjusting for inflation—rising from $23,621 to $24,509.

The incomes of householders aged 55 to 64 are growing because fewer are opting for early retirement. The median income of householders aged 55 to 64 climbed from $45,357 in 1990 to $50,400 in 2004, an 11 percent increase after adjusting for inflation.

■ The incomes of households headed by 55-to-64-year-olds will continue to grow as Baby Boomers fill the age group and early retirement becomes less common.

Householders aged 55 to 64 have made gains

(percent change in median income of total households and households headed by people aged 55 or older, by age, 2000–04; in 2004 dollars)

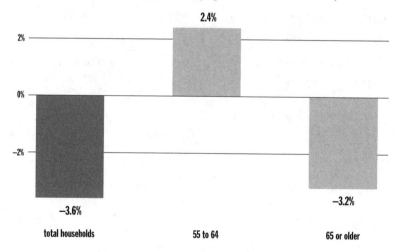

Table 4.1 Median Income of Households Headed by People Aged 55 or older, 1990 to 2004

(median income of total households and households headed by people aged 55 or older, 1990 to 2004; percent change for selected years; in 2004 dollars)

	total households	55 to 64	householders aged 65 or older		
			total	65 to 74	75 to 84
2004	$44,389	$50,400	$24,509	$30,854	$20,467
2003	44,482	50,538	24,426	30,437	19,993
2002	44,546	49,582	24,319	29,593	20,273
2001	45,062	48,942	24,669	30,063	20,461
2000	46,058	49,199	25,320	30,879	20,637
1999	46,129	50,627	25,840	31,002	21,709
1998	45,003	49,959	25,148	30,220	20,699
1997	43,430	48,537	24,366	29,684	20,045
1996	42,544	47,726	23,312	28,063	19,173
1995	41,943	46,868	23,505	28,348	18,884
1994	40,677	44,419	22,814	27,008	18,572
1993	40,217	43,092	22,851	27,433	18,445
1992	40,422	44,851	22,608	26,878	17,971
1991	40,746	45,044	22,959	27,135	18,844
1990	41,963	45,357	23,621	28,438	18,429
Percent change					
2000 to 2004	–3.6%	2.4%	–3.2%	–0.1%	–0.8%
1990 to 2004	5.8	11.1	3.8	8.5	11.1

Source: Bureau of the Census, Current Population Survey Annual Social and Economic Supplements, Internet site http:// www.census.gov/hhes//www/income/histinc/inchhtoc.html; calculations by New Strategist

Many Older Householders Have High Incomes

Nearly 5 million have incomes of $100,000 or more.

Household income falls as people age because many retire from the labor force and live on savings, pensions, and Social Security benefits. While the $50,400 median income of house-holders aged 55 to 64 exceeds that of the average household, the $24,509 median income of householders aged 65 or older is well below average. Median income bottoms out at $20,467 among householders aged 75 or older.

Many older householders are affluent, however. Twenty-two percent of householders aged 55 to 59 have annual incomes of $100,000 or more, as do 6 percent of those aged 65 or older. Among the nation's 18 million households with $100,000-plus incomes, 27 percent are aged 55 or older.

■ The household incomes of 55-to-64-year-olds will grow substantially as working Baby Boomers fill the age group.

Incomes decline with age

(median income of households by age of householder, 2004)

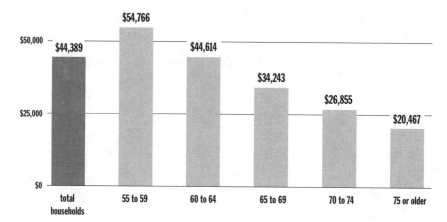

Table 4.2 Income of Households Headed by People Aged 55 or Older, 2004: Total Households

(number and percent distribution of total households and households headed by people aged 55 or older, by income, 2004; households in thousands as of 2005)

						aged 55 or older				
							aged 65 or older			
			aged 55 to 64					aged 65 to 74		
	total	total	total	55–59	60–64	total	total	65–69	70–74	75+
Total households	113,146	40,611	17,476	9,747	7,729	23,135	11,519	6,204	5,315	11,616
Under $10,000	9,805	4,475	1,496	727	769	2,979	1,348	660	688	1,632
$10,000 to $19,999	14,754	8,154	1,772	847	927	6,382	2,331	1,099	1,232	4,051
$20,000 to $29,999	14,263	6,300	2,020	1,032	986	4,280	1,932	970	963	2,349
$30,000 to $39,999	12,641	4,586	1,767	926	840	2,819	1,548	816	732	1,271
$40,000 to $49,999	10,743	3,333	1,602	878	724	1,731	1,044	580	464	686
$50,000 to $59,999	9,229	2,786	1,508	842	667	1,278	756	462	294	522
$60,000 to $69,999	8,078	2,150	1,265	708	556	885	594	382	212	290
$70,000 to $79,999	6,457	1,714	1,067	636	431	647	447	268	178	199
$80,000 to $89,999	5,294	1,313	873	523	350	440	295	190	106	145
$90,000 to $99,999	4,068	1,043	734	454	280	309	203	128	75	105
$100,000 or more	17,814	4,755	3,370	2,172	1,198	1,385	1,018	647	370	367
Median income	$44,389	$36,235	$50,400	$54,766	$44,614	$24,509	$30,854	$34,243	$26,855	$20,467
Total households	100.0%	100.0%	100.0%	100.0%	100.0%	100.0%	100.0%	100.0%	100.0%	100.0%
Under $10,000	8.7	11.0	8.6	7.5	9.9	12.9	11.7	10.6	12.9	14.0
$10,000 to $19,999	13.0	20.1	10.1	8.7	12.0	27.6	20.2	17.7	23.2	34.9
$20,000 to $29,999	12.6	15.5	11.6	10.6	12.8	18.5	16.8	15.6	18.1	20.2
$30,000 to $39,999	11.2	11.3	10.1	9.5	10.9	12.2	13.4	13.2	13.8	10.9
$40,000 to $49,999	9.5	8.2	9.2	9.0	9.4	7.5	9.1	9.3	8.7	5.9
$50,000 to $59,999	8.2	6.9	8.6	8.6	8.6	5.5	6.6	7.4	5.5	4.5
$60,000 to $69,999	7.1	5.3	7.2	7.3	7.2	3.8	5.2	6.2	4.0	2.5
$70,000 to $79,999	5.7	4.2	6.1	6.5	5.6	2.8	3.9	4.3	3.3	1.7
$80,000 to $89,999	4.7	3.2	5.0	5.4	4.5	1.9	2.6	3.1	2.0	1.2
$90,000 to $99,999	3.6	2.6	4.2	4.7	3.6	1.3	1.8	2.1	1.4	0.9
$100,000 or more	15.7	11.7	19.3	22.3	15.5	6.0	8.8	10.4	7.0	3.2

Source: Bureau of the Census, 2005 Current Population Survey Annual Social and Economic Supplement, Internet site http:// pubdb3.census.gov/macro/032003/hhinc/new02_000.htm; calculations by New Strategist

Non-Hispanic Whites Have Higher Incomes than Blacks or Hispanics

Among older Americans, Asians have the highest incomes, however.

Households headed by non-Hispanic whites aged 55 to 64 had a median income of $53,544 in 2004, much greater than the $32,281 black median and the $37,522 Hispanic median. Asian householders aged 55 to 64 had a median income of $59,155, surpassing that of non-Hispanic whites. Thirty-one percent of Asian and 21 percent of non-Hispanic white householders aged 55 to 64 had an income of $100,000 or more in 2004. This compares with only 9 percent of blacks and 11 percent of Hispanics.

Income disparities are not as great among householders aged 65 or older. The median income of Asian households headed by people aged 65 or older was $26,899 in 2004 versus a slightly lower $25,741 for non-Hispanic whites. Among their Hispanic counterparts, median household income was just $19,153, while the black median stood at an even lower $17,236. Black householders aged 75 or older have the lowest incomes, just $14,507.

■ The income disparities among older householders by race and Hispanic origin will persist because the underlying factors—the scarcity of married-couples among blacks and the poor educational level of Hispanics—are also true among younger generations of Americans.

Among householders aged 65 or older, blacks have the lowest incomes

(median income of households headed by people aged 65 or older, by race and Hispanic origin, 2004)

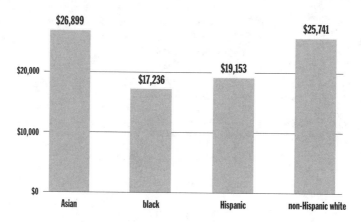

Table 4.3 Income of Households Headed by People Aged 55 or Older, 2004: Asian Households

(number and percent distribution of total Asian households and Asian households headed by people aged 55 or older, by income, 2004; households in thousands as of 2005)

		aged 55 or older								
						aged 65 or older				
			aged 55 to 64				aged 65 to 74			
	total	total	total	55–59	60–64	total	total	65–69	70–74	75+
Total Asian households	4,360	1,106	583	360	223	523	315	189	126	208
Under $10,000	331	128	45	25	19	83	39	20	19	43
$10,000 to $19,999	373	180	51	27	24	129	63	35	28	65
$20,000 to $29,999	405	128	57	44	13	71	44	16	29	27
$30,000 to $39,999	355	77	29	9	21	48	30	13	16	18
$40,000 to $49,999	420	86	59	41	19	27	12	8	5	15
$50,000 to $59,999	371	101	55	32	25	46	32	23	8	13
$60,000 to $69,999	315	58	48	28	18	10	6	3	2	3
$70,000 to $79,999	267	33	19	10	9	14	11	8	3	3
$80,000 to $89,999	236	38	21	15	5	17	10	8	1	5
$90,000 to $99,999	195	39	19	11	6	20	16	13	1	4
$100,000 or more	1,093	243	181	119	62	62	51	39	13	11
Median income	$57,475	$43,902	$59,155	$61,892	$57,000	$26,899	$32,709	$50,536	$23,038	$19,290
Total Asian households	100.0%	100.0%	100.0%	100.0%	100.0%	100.0%	100.0%	100.0%	100.0%	100.0%
Under $10,000	7.6	11.6	7.7	6.9	8.5	15.9	12.4	10.6	15.1	20.7
$10,000 to $19,999	8.6	16.3	8.7	7.5	10.8	24.7	20.0	18.5	22.2	31.3
$20,000 to $29,999	9.3	11.6	9.8	12.2	5.8	13.6	14.0	8.5	23.0	13.0
$30,000 to $39,999	8.1	7.0	5.0	2.5	9.4	9.2	9.5	6.9	12.7	8.7
$40,000 to $49,999	9.6	7.8	10.1	11.4	8.5	5.2	3.8	4.2	4.0	7.2
$50,000 to $59,999	8.5	9.1	9.4	8.9	11.2	8.8	10.2	12.2	6.3	6.3
$60,000 to $69,999	7.2	5.2	8.2	7.8	8.1	1.9	1.9	1.6	1.6	1.4
$70,000 to $79,999	6.1	3.0	3.3	2.8	4.0	2.7	3.5	4.2	2.4	1.4
$80,000 to $89,999	5.4	3.4	3.6	4.2	2.2	3.3	3.2	4.2	0.8	2.4
$90,000 to $99,999	4.5	3.5	3.3	3.1	2.7	3.8	5.1	6.9	0.8	1.9
$100,000 or more	25.1	22.0	31.0	33.1	27.8	11.9	16.2	20.6	10.3	5.3

Note: Asians include those identifying themselves as being Asian alone and those identifying themselves as being Asian in combination with one or more other races.
Source: Bureau of the Census, 2005 Current Population Survey Annual Social and Economic Supplement, Internet site http://pubdb3.census.gov/macro/032003/hhinc/new02_000.htm; calculations by New Strategist

Table 4.4 Income of Households Headed by People Aged 55 or Older, 2004: Black Households

(number and percent distribution of total black households and black households headed by people aged 55 or older, by income, 2004; households in thousands as of 2005)

						aged 55 or older				
			aged 55 to 64				aged 65 or older			
								aged 65 to 74		
	total	total	total	55–59	60–64	total	total	65–69	70–74	75+
Total black households	14,127	4,053	1,918	1,097	821	2,135	1,221	683	538	914
Under $10,000	2,496	862	270	126	144	592	308	150	157	285
$10,000 to $19,999	2,334	915	314	163	150	601	307	168	139	294
$20,000 to $29,999	2,167	655	309	180	129	346	210	109	102	134
$30,000 to $39,999	1,799	410	205	121	82	205	125	77	50	78
$40,000 to $49,999	1,290	288	166	92	74	122	79	46	32	42
$50,000 to $59,999	922	223	157	91	65	66	50	35	15	15
$60,000 to $69,999	842	185	133	88	43	52	29	20	10	21
$70,000 to $79,999	578	119	80	45	36	39	35	19	15	7
$80,000 to $89,999	416	75	58	37	21	17	12	10	2	5
$90,000 to $99,999	341	80	54	34	20	26	16	11	7	10
$100,000 or more	941	244	174	120	54	70	50	41	8	21
Median income	$30,268	$24,356	$32,281	$36,130	$28,231	$17,236	$19,886	$21,428	$17,039	$14,507
Total black households	100.0%	100.0%	100.0%	100.0%	100.0%	100.0%	100.0%	100.0%	100.0%	100.0%
Under $10,000	17.7	21.3	14.1	11.5	17.5	27.7	25.2	22.0	29.2	31.2
$10,000 to $19,999	16.5	22.6	16.4	14.9	18.3	28.1	25.1	24.6	25.8	32.2
$20,000 to $29,999	15.3	16.2	16.1	16.4	15.7	16.2	17.2	16.0	19.0	14.7
$30,000 to $39,999	12.7	10.1	10.7	11.0	10.0	9.6	10.2	11.3	9.3	8.5
$40,000 to $49,999	9.1	7.1	8.7	8.4	9.0	5.7	6.5	6.7	5.9	4.6
$50,000 to $59,999	6.5	5.5	8.2	8.3	7.9	3.1	4.1	5.1	2.8	1.6
$60,000 to $69,999	6.0	4.6	6.9	8.0	5.2	2.4	2.4	2.9	1.9	2.3
$70,000 to $79,999	4.1	2.9	4.2	4.1	4.4	1.8	2.9	2.8	2.8	0.8
$80,000 to $89,999	2.9	1.9	3.0	3.4	2.6	0.8	1.0	1.5	0.4	0.5
$90,000 to $99,999	2.4	2.0	2.8	3.1	2.4	1.2	1.3	1.6	1.3	1.1
$100,000 or more	6.7	6.0	9.1	10.9	6.6	3.3	4.1	6.0	1.5	2.3

Note: Blacks include those identifying themselves as being black alone and those identifying themselves as being black in combination with one or more other races.
Source: Bureau of the Census, 2005 Current Population Survey Annual Social and Economic Supplement, Internet site http:// pubdb3.census.gov/macro/032003/hhinc/new02_000.htm; calculations by New Strategist

Table 4.5 Income of Households Headed by People Aged 55 or Older, 2004: Hispanic Households

(number and percent distribution of total Hispanic households and Hispanic households headed by people aged 55 or older, by income, 2004; households in thousands as of 2004)

						aged 55 or older				
							aged 65 or older			
			aged 55 to 64					aged 65 to 74		
	total	total	total	55–59	60–64	total	total	65–69	70–74	75+
Total Hispanic households	12,181	2,489	1,272	724	547	1,217	719	402	317	497
Under $10,000	1,303	428	153	67	87	275	156	78	76	120
$10,000 to $19,999	1,957	551	188	104	84	363	178	103	75	185
$20,000 to $29,999	2,040	406	189	114	76	217	143	76	66	76
$30,000 to $39,999	1,631	281	142	86	57	139	79	45	35	60
$40,000 to $49,999	1,326	183	120	66	55	63	50	31	20	14
$50,000 to $59,999	1,018	168	106	68	40	62	36	27	8	26
$60,000 to $69,999	694	116	94	57	36	22	20	14	7	2
$70,000 to $79,999	562	71	53	28	25	18	15	10	5	4
$80,000 to $89,999	378	57	48	30	19	9	8	1	6	1
$90,000 to $99,999	293	46	34	22	12	12	9	5	4	3
$100,000 or more	980	172	140	85	56	32	25	12	13	6
Median income	$34,241	$28,540	$37,522	$39,121	$35,024	$19,153	$21,366	$21,560	$21,017	$16,364
Total Hispanic households	100.0%	100.0%	100.0%	100.0%	100.0%	100.0%	100.0%	100.0%	100.0%	100.0%
Under $10,000	10.7	17.2	12.0	9.3	15.9	22.6	21.7	19.4	24.0	24.1
$10,000 to $19,999	16.1	22.1	14.8	14.4	15.4	29.8	24.8	25.6	23.7	37.2
$20,000 to $29,999	16.7	16.3	14.9	15.7	13.9	17.8	19.9	18.9	20.8	15.3
$30,000 to $39,999	13.4	11.3	11.2	11.9	10.4	11.4	11.0	11.2	11.0	12.1
$40,000 to $49,999	10.9	7.4	9.4	9.1	10.1	5.2	7.0	7.7	6.3	2.8
$50,000 to $59,999	8.4	6.7	8.3	9.4	7.3	5.1	5.0	6.7	2.5	5.2
$60,000 to $69,999	5.7	4.7	7.4	7.9	6.6	1.8	2.8	3.5	2.2	0.4
$70,000 to $79,999	4.6	2.9	4.2	3.9	4.6	1.5	2.1	2.5	1.6	0.8
$80,000 to $89,999	3.1	2.3	3.8	4.1	3.5	0.7	1.1	0.2	1.9	0.2
$90,000 to $99,999	2.4	1.8	2.7	3.0	2.2	1.0	1.3	1.2	1.3	0.6
$100,000 or more	8.0	6.9	11.0	11.7	10.2	2.6	3.5	3.0	4.1	1.2

Source: Bureau of the Census, 2005 Current Population Survey Annual Social and Economic Supplement, Internet site http:// pubdb3.census.gov/macro/032003/hhinc/new02_000.htm; calculations by New Strategist

Table 4.6 Income of Households Headed by People Aged 55 or Older, 2004: Non-Hispanic White Households

(number and percent distribution of total non-Hispanic white households and non-Hispanic white households headed by people aged 55 or older, by income, 2004; households in thousands as of 2005)

						aged 55 or older				
							aged 65 or older			
				aged 55 to 64				aged 65 to 74		
	total	total	total	55–59	60–64	total	total	65–69	70–74	75+
Total non-Hispanic white households	**81,445**	**32,621**	**13,533**	**7,482**	**6,051**	**19,088**	**9,173**	**4,882**	**4,291**	**9,915**
Under $10,000	5,593	3,008	1,007	496	511	2,001	839	408	432	1,162
$10,000 to $19,999	9,937	6,435	1,200	548	651	5,235	1,753	776	977	3,482
$20,000 to $29,999	9,578	5,070	1,447	688	759	3,623	1,525	767	757	2,099
$30,000 to $39,999	8,687	3,775	1,367	698	669	2,408	1,301	673	628	1,106
$40,000 to $49,999	7,623	2,752	1,242	673	572	1,510	897	494	404	611
$50,000 to $59,999	6,830	2,265	1,174	645	528	1,091	629	371	259	461
$60,000 to $69,999	6,131	1,776	982	529	453	794	534	344	190	260
$70,000 to $79,999	4,984	1,474	908	550	357	566	382	229	153	185
$80,000 to $89,999	4,203	1,135	741	434	306	394	262	168	94	132
$90,000 to $99,999	3,223	874	623	385	239	251	161	99	62	88
$100,000 or more	14,654	4,057	2,841	1,835	1,005	1,216	889	553	335	327
Median income	$48,977	$37,275	$53,544	$59,834	$47,610	$25,741	$33,529	$36,995	$29,655	$21,290
Total non-Hispanic white households	**100.0%**	**100.0%**	**100.0%**	**100.0%**	**100.0%**	**100.0%**	**100.0%**	**100.0%**	**100.0%**	**100.0%**
Under $10,000	6.9	9.2	7.4	6.6	8.4	10.5	9.1	8.4	10.1	11.7
$10,000 to $19,999	12.2	19.7	8.9	7.3	10.8	27.4	19.1	15.9	22.8	35.1
$20,000 to $29,999	11.8	15.5	10.7	9.2	12.5	19.0	16.6	15.7	17.6	21.2
$30,000 to $39,999	10.7	11.6	10.1	9.3	11.1	12.6	14.2	13.8	14.6	11.2
$40,000 to $49,999	9.4	8.4	9.2	9.0	9.5	7.9	9.8	10.1	9.4	6.2
$50,000 to $59,999	8.4	6.9	8.7	8.6	8.7	5.7	6.9	7.6	6.0	4.6
$60,000 to $69,999	7.5	5.4	7.3	7.1	7.5	4.2	5.8	7.0	4.4	2.6
$70,000 to $79,999	6.1	4.5	6.7	7.4	5.9	3.0	4.2	4.7	3.6	1.9
$80,000 to $89,999	5.2	3.5	5.5	5.8	5.1	2.1	2.9	3.4	2.2	1.3
$90,000 to $99,999	4.0	2.7	4.6	5.1	3.9	1.3	1.8	2.0	1.4	0.9
$100,000 or more	18.0	12.4	21.0	24.5	16.6	6.4	9.7	11.3	7.8	3.3

Note: Non-Hispanic whites are those identifying themselves as being white alone and not Hispanic.
Source: Bureau of the Census, 2005 Current Population Survey Annual Social and Economic Supplement, Internet site http:// pubdb3.census.gov/macro/032003/hhinc/new02_000.htm; calculations by New Strategist

Many Older Couples Are Comfortably Well Off

Older men and women who live alone have much lower incomes.

Among householders aged 55 to 64, the median income of married couples stood at $68,301 in 2004—nearly $18,000 greater than the median income of the average household in the age group. For couples aged 65 or older, median household income was $36,724, well above the $24,509 average. The most affluent older householders are couples aged 55 to 59 because most are still in the labor force. Their median income was $75,388 in 2004. One in three had an income of $100,000 or more.

The median income of male-headed families surpasses that of married couples among householders aged 70 or older. Behind the higher incomes of male-headed families is the likely presence of an additional earner in the household—such as a grown son or daughter in the labor force.

Women who live alone have the lowest incomes. Among householders aged 75 or older, women who live alone had a median income of just $13,719 in 2004, well below the $20,467 median for all households in the age group.

■ The household incomes of older Americans should rise in the years ahead as Baby Boomers enter the 55-or-older age groups and postpone retirement.

Women who live alone have the lowest incomes

(median income of householders aged 65 or older, by household type, 2004)

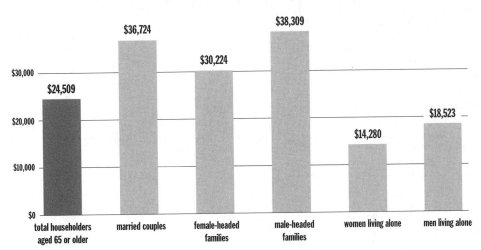

Table 4.7 Income of Households by Household Type, 2004: Aged 55 or Older

(number and percent distribution of households headed by people aged 55 or older, by income and household type, 2004; households in thousands as of 2005)

	total	family households			nonfamily households			
		married couples	female hh, no spouse present	male hh, no spouse present	female householder		male householder	
					total	living alone	total	living alone
Total households headed by people aged 55 or older	**40,611**	**19,924**	**3,268**	**927**	**11,163**	**10,688**	**5,329**	**4,823**
Under $10,000	4,475	641	337	46	2,548	2,512	902	885
$10,000 to $19,999	8,154	1,947	566	112	4,115	4,063	1,415	1,365
$20,000 to $29,999	6,300	2,854	577	150	1,811	1,748	909	843
$30,000 to $39,999	4,586	2,442	447	131	956	886	608	539
$40,000 to $49,999	3,333	1,873	368	92	568	523	430	359
$50,000 to $59,999	2,786	1,824	282	81	369	318	228	183
$60,000 to $69,999	2,150	1,399	241	65	241	213	205	172
$70,000 to $79,999	1,714	1,234	138	39	175	140	125	94
$80,000 to $89,999	1,313	937	90	51	109	95	124	103
$90,000 to $99,999	1,043	786	65	35	63	47	96	81
$100,000 or more	4,755	3,985	155	124	203	143	287	200
Median income	$36,235	$52,654	$33,815	$43,950	$17,895	$17,302	$24,261	$22,406
Total households headed by people aged 55 or older	**100.0%**	**100.0%**	**100.0%**	**100.0%**	**100.0%**	**100.0%**	**100.0%**	**100.0%**
Under $10,000	11.0	3.2	10.3	5.0	22.8	23.5	16.9	18.3
$10,000 to $19,999	20.1	9.8	17.3	12.1	36.9	38.0	26.6	28.3
$20,000 to $29,999	15.5	14.3	17.7	16.2	16.2	16.4	17.1	17.5
$30,000 to $39,999	11.3	12.3	13.7	14.1	8.6	8.3	11.4	11.2
$40,000 to $49,999	8.2	9.4	11.3	9.9	5.1	4.9	8.1	7.4
$50,000 to $59,999	6.9	9.2	8.6	8.7	3.3	3.0	4.3	3.8
$60,000 to $69,999	5.3	7.0	7.4	7.0	2.2	2.0	3.8	3.6
$70,000 to $79,999	4.2	6.2	4.2	4.2	1.6	1.3	2.3	1.9
$80,000 to $89,999	3.2	4.7	2.8	5.5	1.0	0.9	2.3	2.1
$90,000 to $99,999	2.6	3.9	2.0	3.8	0.6	0.4	1.8	1.7
$100,000 or more	11.7	20.0	4.7	13.4	1.8	1.3	5.4	4.1

Source: Bureau of the Census, 2005 Current Population Survey Annual Social and Economic Supplement, Internet site http:// pubdb3.census.gov/macro/032003/hhinc/new02_000.htm; calculations by New Strategist

Table 4.8 Income of Households by Household Type, 2004: Aged 55 to 64

(number and percent distribution of households headed by people aged 55 to 64, by income and household type, 2004; households in thousands as of 2005)

| | | family households | | | nonfamily households | | | |
| | | | | | female householder | | male householder | |
	total	married couples	female hh, no spouse present	male hh, no spouse present	total	living alone	total	living alone
Total households headed by 55-to-64-year-olds	**17,476**	**10,051**	**1,467**	**459**	**3,272**	**3,001**	**2,227**	**1,920**
Under $10,000	1,496	343	142	18	619	595	375	364
$10,000 to $19,999	1,772	549	223	42	610	588	349	319
$20,000 to $29,999	2,020	776	221	70	598	569	354	320
$30,000 to $39,999	1,767	806	180	56	441	406	283	253
$40,000 to $49,999	1,602	864	159	45	325	295	209	161
$50,000 to $59,999	1,508	984	150	55	188	156	131	97
$60,000 to $69,999	1,265	820	146	38	140	120	123	104
$70,000 to $79,999	1,067	782	70	23	112	89	78	58
$80,000 to $89,999	873	662	36	31	68	60	75	62
$90,000 to $99,999	734	570	39	21	43	30	62	53
$100,000 or more	3,370	2,894	100	61	128	93	187	128
Median income	$50,400	$68,301	$38,223	$49,702	$26,130	$25,042	$30,910	$28,276
Total households headed by 55-to-64-year-olds	**100.0%**	**100.0%**	**100.0%**	**100.0%**	**100.0%**	**100.0%**	**100.0%**	**100.0%**
Under $10,000	8.6	3.4	9.7	3.9	18.9	19.8	16.8	19.0
$10,000 to $19,999	10.1	5.5	15.2	9.2	18.6	19.6	15.7	16.6
$20,000 to $29,999	11.6	7.7	15.1	15.3	18.3	19.0	15.9	16.7
$30,000 to $39,999	10.1	8.0	12.3	12.2	13.5	13.5	12.7	13.2
$40,000 to $49,999	9.2	8.6	10.8	9.8	9.9	9.8	9.4	8.4
$50,000 to $59,999	8.6	9.8	10.2	12.0	5.7	5.2	5.9	5.1
$60,000 to $69,999	7.2	8.2	10.0	8.3	4.3	4.0	5.5	5.4
$70,000 to $79,999	6.1	7.8	4.8	5.0	3.4	3.0	3.5	3.0
$80,000 to $89,999	5.0	6.6	2.5	6.8	2.1	2.0	3.4	3.2
$90,000 to $99,999	4.2	5.7	2.7	4.6	1.3	1.0	2.8	2.8
$100,000 or more	19.3	28.8	6.8	13.3	3.9	3.1	8.4	6.7

Source: Bureau of the Census, 2005 Current Population Survey Annual Social and Economic Supplement, Internet site http:// pubdb3.census.gov/macro/032003/hhinc/new02_000.htm; calculations by New Strategist

Table 4.9 Income of Households by Household Type, 2004: Aged 55 to 59

(number and percent distribution of households headed by people aged 55 to 59, by income and household type, 2004; households in thousands as of 2005)

| | | family households | | | nonfamily households | | | |
| | | | | | female householder | | male householder | |
	total	married couples	female hh, no spouse present	male hh, no spouse present	total	living alone	total	living alone
Total households headed by 55-to-59-year-olds	**9,747**	**5,632**	**891**	**275**	**1,695**	**1,524**	**1,254**	**1,077**
Under $10,000	727	163	90	9	287	271	176	170
$10,000 to $19,999	847	256	121	20	264	247	188	173
$20,000 to $29,999	1,032	339	131	48	302	291	212	188
$30,000 to $39,999	926	372	112	28	249	224	164	153
$40,000 to $49,999	878	449	81	19	196	181	134	97
$50,000 to $59,999	842	527	90	36	115	93	73	54
$60,000 to $69,999	708	446	91	29	75	65	70	58
$70,000 to $79,999	636	474	49	15	61	44	37	32
$80,000 to $89,999	523	395	21	13	54	46	41	35
$90,000 to $99,999	454	336	28	10	35	22	46	40
$100,000 or more	2,172	1,875	79	46	57	40	115	78
Median income	$54,766	$75,388	$39,321	$51,704	$29,638	$27,252	$32,008	$30,285
Total households headed by 55-to-59-year-olds	**100.0%**	**100.0%**	**100.0%**	**100.0%**	**100.0%**	**100.0%**	**100.0%**	**100.0%**
Under $10,000	7.5	2.9	10.1	3.3	16.9	17.8	14.0	15.8
$10,000 to $19,999	8.7	4.5	13.6	7.3	15.6	16.2	15.0	16.1
$20,000 to $29,999	10.6	6.0	14.7	17.5	17.8	19.1	16.9	17.5
$30,000 to $39,999	9.5	6.6	12.6	10.2	14.7	14.7	13.1	14.2
$40,000 to $49,999	9.0	8.0	9.1	6.9	11.6	11.9	10.7	9.0
$50,000 to $59,999	8.6	9.4	10.1	13.1	6.8	6.1	5.8	5.0
$60,000 to $69,999	7.3	7.9	10.2	10.5	4.4	4.3	5.6	5.4
$70,000 to $79,999	6.5	8.4	5.5	5.5	3.6	2.9	3.0	3.0
$80,000 to $89,999	5.4	7.0	2.4	4.7	3.2	3.0	3.3	3.2
$90,000 to $99,999	4.7	6.0	3.1	3.6	2.1	1.4	3.7	3.7
$100,000 or more	22.3	33.3	8.9	16.7	3.4	2.6	9.2	7.2

Source: Bureau of the Census, 2005 Current Population Survey Annual Social and Economic Supplement, Internet site http://pubdb3.census.gov/macro/032003/hhinc/new02_000.htm; calculations by New Strategist

Table 4.10 Income of Households by Household Type, 2004: Aged 60 to 64

(number and percent distribution of households headed by people aged 60 to 64, by income and household type, 2004; households in thousands as of 2005)

| | | family households | | | nonfamily households | | | |
| | | | | | female householder | | male householder | |
	total	married couples	female hh, no spouse present	male hh, no spouse present	total	living alone	total	living alone
Total households headed by 60-to-64-year-olds	**7,729**	**4,419**	**576**	**184**	**1,577**	**1,478**	**973**	**843**
Under $10,000	769	180	51	8	332	324	199	195
$10,000 to $19,999	927	293	102	24	347	342	161	147
$20,000 to $29,999	986	437	91	21	295	278	144	133
$30,000 to $39,999	840	433	68	28	191	181	118	101
$40,000 to $49,999	724	416	78	26	130	114	76	63
$50,000 to $59,999	667	456	60	19	72	63	58	43
$60,000 to $69,999	556	374	55	8	65	56	52	46
$70,000 to $79,999	431	307	23	7	52	44	43	26
$80,000 to $89,999	350	267	17	18	15	15	35	27
$90,000 to $99,999	280	235	11	11	8	8	15	13
$100,000 or more	1,198	1,019	22	15	71	53	72	50
Median income	$44,614	$59,845	$36,005	$45,457	$23,526	$22,444	$28,921	$26,511
Total households headed by 60-to-64-year-olds	**100.0%**	**100.0%**	**100.0%**	**100.0%**	**100.0%**	**100.0%**	**100.0%**	**100.0%**
Under $10,000	9.9	4.1	8.9	4.3	21.1	21.9	20.5	23.1
$10,000 to $19,999	12.0	6.6	17.7	13.0	22.0	23.1	16.5	17.4
$20,000 to $29,999	12.8	9.9	15.8	11.4	18.7	18.8	14.8	15.8
$30,000 to $39,999	10.9	9.8	11.8	15.2	12.1	12.2	12.1	12.0
$40,000 to $49,999	9.4	9.4	13.5	14.1	8.2	7.7	7.8	7.5
$50,000 to $59,999	8.6	10.3	10.4	10.3	4.6	4.3	6.0	5.1
$60,000 to $69,999	7.2	8.5	9.5	4.3	4.1	3.8	5.3	5.5
$70,000 to $79,999	5.6	6.9	4.0	3.8	3.3	3.0	4.4	3.1
$80,000 to $89,999	4.5	6.0	3.0	9.8	1.0	1.0	3.6	3.2
$90,000 to $99,999	3.6	5.3	1.9	6.0	0.5	0.5	1.5	1.5
$100,000 or more	15.5	23.1	3.8	8.2	4.5	3.6	7.4	5.9

Source: Bureau of the Census, 2005 Current Population Survey Annual Social and Economic Supplement, Internet site http:// pubdb3.census.gov/macro/032003/hhinc/new02_000.htm; calculations by New Strategist

Table 4.11 Income of Households by Household Type, 2004: Aged 65 or Older

(number and percent distribution of households headed by people aged 65 or older, by income and household type, 2004; households in thousands as of 2005)

| | | family households | | | nonfamily households | | | |
| | | | | | female householder | | male householder | |
	total	married couples	female hh, no spouse present	male hh, no spouse present	total	living alone	total	living alone
Total households headed by people aged 65 or older	**23,135**	**9,873**	**1,801**	**468**	**7,891**	**7,687**	**3,102**	**2,903**
Under $10,000	2,979	298	195	28	1,929	1,917	527	521
$10,000 to $19,999	6,382	1,398	343	70	3,505	3,475	1,066	1,046
$20,000 to $29,999	4,280	2,078	356	80	1,213	1,179	555	523
$30,000 to $39,999	2,819	1,636	267	75	515	480	325	286
$40,000 to $49,999	1,731	1,009	209	47	243	228	221	198
$50,000 to $59,999	1,278	840	132	26	181	162	97	86
$60,000 to $69,999	885	579	95	27	101	93	82	68
$70,000 to $79,999	647	452	68	16	63	51	47	36
$80,000 to $89,999	440	275	54	20	41	35	49	41
$90,000 to $99,999	309	216	26	14	20	17	34	28
$100,000 or more	1,385	1,091	55	63	75	50	100	72
Median income	$24,509	$36,724	$30,224	$38,309	$14,481	$14,280	$19,488	$18,523
Total households headed by people aged 65 or older	**100.0%**	**100.0%**	**100.0%**	**100.0%**	**100.0%**	**100.0%**	**100.0%**	**100.0%**
Under $10,000	12.9	3.0	10.8	6.0	24.4	24.9	17.0	17.9
$10,000 to $19,999	27.6	14.2	19.0	15.0	44.4	45.2	34.4	36.0
$20,000 to $29,999	18.5	21.0	19.8	17.1	15.4	15.3	17.9	18.0
$30,000 to $39,999	12.2	16.6	14.8	16.0	6.5	6.2	10.5	9.9
$40,000 to $49,999	7.5	10.2	11.6	10.0	3.1	3.0	7.1	6.8
$50,000 to $59,999	5.5	8.5	7.3	5.6	2.3	2.1	3.1	3.0
$60,000 to $69,999	3.8	5.9	5.3	5.8	1.3	1.2	2.6	2.3
$70,000 to $79,999	2.8	4.6	3.8	3.4	0.8	0.7	1.5	1.2
$80,000 to $89,999	1.9	2.8	3.0	4.3	0.5	0.5	1.6	1.4
$90,000 to $99,999	1.3	2.2	1.4	3.0	0.3	0.2	1.1	1.0
$100,000 or more	6.0	11.1	3.1	13.5	1.0	0.7	3.2	2.5

Source: Bureau of the Census, 2005 Current Population Survey Annual Social and Economic Supplement, Internet site http:// pubdb3.census.gov/macro/032003/hhinc/new02_000.htm; calculations by New Strategist

Table 4.12 Income of Households by Household Type, 2004: Aged 65 to 74

(number and percent distribution of households headed by people aged 65 to 74, by income and household type, 2004; households in thousands as of 2005)

		family households			nonfamily households			
					female householder		male householder	
	total	married couples	female hh, no spouse present	male hh, no spouse present	total	living alone	total	living alone
Total households headed by 65-to-74-year-olds	**11,519**	**5,998**	**858**	**252**	**2,956**	**2,856**	**1,454**	**1,356**
Under $10,000	1,348	190	106	15	736	728	301	298
$10,000 to $19,999	2,331	676	159	39	1,064	1,053	394	385
$20,000 to $29,999	1,932	1,002	151	39	516	492	224	215
$30,000 to $39,999	1,548	950	137	46	232	218	184	166
$40,000 to $49,999	1,044	667	98	25	134	130	118	106
$50,000 to $59,999	756	537	65	11	82	79	62	52
$60,000 to $69,999	594	419	50	15	56	52	51	42
$70,000 to $79,999	447	329	29	11	48	37	31	21
$80,000 to $89,999	295	211	23	14	20	19	26	25
$90,000 to $99,999	203	164	9	4	11	8	14	12
$100,000 or more	1,018	852	30	33	56	38	46	34
Median income	$30,854	$42,341	$31,011	$38,509	$16,269	$15,839	$21,182	$19,839
Total households headed by 65-to-74-year-olds	**100.0%**	**100.0%**	**100.0%**	**100.0%**	**100.0%**	**100.0%**	**100.0%**	**100.0%**
Under $10,000	11.7	3.2	12.4	6.0	24.9	25.5	20.7	22.0
$10,000 to $19,999	20.2	11.3	18.5	15.5	36.0	36.9	27.1	28.4
$20,000 to $29,999	16.8	16.7	17.6	15.5	17.5	17.2	15.4	15.9
$30,000 to $39,999	13.4	15.8	16.0	18.3	7.8	7.6	12.7	12.2
$40,000 to $49,999	9.1	11.1	11.4	9.9	4.5	4.6	8.1	7.8
$50,000 to $59,999	6.6	9.0	7.6	4.4	2.8	2.8	4.3	3.8
$60,000 to $69,999	5.2	7.0	5.8	6.0	1.9	1.8	3.5	3.1
$70,000 to $79,999	3.9	5.5	3.4	4.4	1.6	1.3	2.1	1.5
$80,000 to $89,999	2.6	3.5	2.7	5.6	0.7	0.7	1.8	1.8
$90,000 to $99,999	1.8	2.7	1.0	1.6	0.4	0.3	1.0	0.9
$100,000 or more	8.8	14.2	3.5	13.1	1.9	1.3	3.2	2.5

Source: Bureau of the Census, 2005 Current Population Survey Annual Social and Economic Supplement, Internet site http:// pubdb3.census.gov/macro/032003/hhinc/new02_000.htm; calculations by New Strategist

Table 4.13 Income of Households by Household Type, 2004: Aged 65 to 69

(number and percent distribution of households headed by people aged 65 to 69, by income and household type, 2004; households in thousands as of 2005)

	total	family households			nonfamily households			
		married couples	female hh, no spouse present	male hh, no spouse present	female householder total	female householder living alone	male householder total	male householder living alone
Total households headed by 65-to-69-year-olds	**6,204**	**3,407**	**461**	**153**	**1,395**	**1,326**	**788**	**724**
Under $10,000	660	100	70	8	342	338	139	137
$10,000 to $19,999	1,099	345	82	31	421	411	222	217
$20,000 to $29,999	970	486	79	21	262	247	122	117
$30,000 to $39,999	816	497	64	28	116	104	111	102
$40,000 to $49,999	580	365	53	13	90	86	61	48
$50,000 to $59,999	462	330	38	8	52	49	33	27
$60,000 to $69,999	382	267	30	11	44	41	30	24
$70,000 to $79,999	268	205	14	6	27	20	17	10
$80,000 to $89,999	190	135	16	11	12	11	16	15
$90,000 to $99,999	128	111	4	2	3	–	8	6
$100,000 or more	647	568	13	16	25	14	25	19
Median income	$34,243	$47,183	$30,135	$37,108	$18,244	$17,544	$22,518	$20,762
Total households headed by 65-to-69-year-olds	**100.0%**	**100.0%**	**100.0%**	**100.0%**	**100.0%**	**100.0%**	**100.0%**	**100.0%**
Under $10,000	10.6	2.9	15.2	5.2	24.5	25.5	17.6	18.9
$10,000 to $19,999	17.7	10.1	17.8	20.3	30.2	31.0	28.2	30.0
$20,000 to $29,999	15.6	14.3	17.1	13.7	18.8	18.6	15.5	16.2
$30,000 to $39,999	13.2	14.6	13.9	18.3	8.3	7.8	14.1	14.1
$40,000 to $49,999	9.3	10.7	11.5	8.5	6.5	6.5	7.7	6.6
$50,000 to $59,999	7.4	9.7	8.2	5.2	3.7	3.7	4.2	3.7
$60,000 to $69,999	6.2	7.8	6.5	7.2	3.2	3.1	3.8	3.3
$70,000 to $79,999	4.3	6.0	3.0	3.9	1.9	1.5	2.2	1.4
$80,000 to $89,999	3.1	4.0	3.5	7.2	0.9	0.8	2.0	2.1
$90,000 to $99,999	2.1	3.3	0.9	1.3	0.2	–	1.0	0.8
$100,000 or more	10.4	16.7	2.8	10.5	1.8	1.1	3.2	2.6

Note: "–" means sample is too small to make a reliable estimate.
Source: Bureau of the Census, 2005 Current Population Survey Annual Social and Economic Supplement, Internet site http:// pubdb3.census.gov/macro/032003/hhinc/new02_000.htm; calculations by New Strategist

Table 4.14 Income of Households by Household Type, 2004: Aged 70 to 74

(number and percent distribution of households headed by people aged 70 to 74, by income and household type, 2004; households in thousands as of 2005)

| | | family households | | | nonfamily households | | | |
| | | | | | female householder | | male householder | |
	total	married couples	female hh, no spouse present	male hh, no spouse present	total	living alone	total	living alone
Total households headed by 70-to-74-year-olds	**5,315**	**2,591**	**397**	**99**	**1,561**	**1,530**	**666**	**632**
Under $10,000	688	90	36	7	394	391	163	162
$10,000 to $19,999	1,232	332	78	8	643	641	173	168
$20,000 to $29,999	963	518	73	17	254	244	101	98
$30,000 to $39,999	732	453	72	17	116	114	72	65
$40,000 to $49,999	464	303	46	13	44	44	58	57
$50,000 to $59,999	294	207	27	5	29	29	27	25
$60,000 to $69,999	212	153	21	5	11	11	21	17
$70,000 to $79,999	178	125	14	4	21	17	15	11
$80,000 to $89,999	106	77	7	3	8	8	10	10
$90,000 to $99,999	75	54	5	2	8	8	6	6
$100,000 or more	370	283	17	17	32	24	21	15
Median income	$26,855	$37,793	$31,859	$40,552	$15,074	$14,909	$19,881	$19,082
Total households headed by 70-to-74-year-olds	**100.0%**	**100.0%**	**100.0%**	**100.0%**	**100.0%**	**100.0%**	**100.0%**	**100.0%**
Under $10,000	12.9	3.5	9.1	7.1	25.2	25.6	24.5	25.6
$10,000 to $19,999	23.2	12.8	19.6	8.1	41.2	41.9	26.0	26.6
$20,000 to $29,999	18.1	20.0	18.4	17.2	16.3	15.9	15.2	15.5
$30,000 to $39,999	13.8	17.5	18.1	17.2	7.4	7.5	10.8	10.3
$40,000 to $49,999	8.7	11.7	11.6	13.1	2.8	2.9	8.7	9.0
$50,000 to $59,999	5.5	8.0	6.8	5.1	1.9	1.9	4.1	4.0
$60,000 to $69,999	4.0	5.9	5.3	5.1	0.7	0.7	3.2	2.7
$70,000 to $79,999	3.3	4.8	3.5	4.0	1.3	1.1	2.3	1.7
$80,000 to $89,999	2.0	3.0	1.8	3.0	0.5	0.5	1.5	1.6
$90,000 to $99,999	1.4	2.1	1.3	2.0	0.5	0.5	0.9	0.9
$100,000 or more	7.0	10.9	4.3	17.2	2.0	1.6	3.2	2.4

Source: Bureau of the Census, 2005 Current Population Survey Annual Social and Economic Supplement, Internet site http:// pubdb3.census.gov/macro/032003/hhinc/new02_000.htm; calculations by New Strategist

Table 4.15 Income of Households by Household Type, 2004: Aged 75 or Older

(number and percent distribution of households headed by people aged 75 or older, by income and household type, 2004; households in thousands as of 2005)

| | total | family households | | | nonfamily households | | | |
		married couples	female hh, no spouse present	male hh, no spouse present	female householder total	living alone	male householder total	living alone
Total households headed by people aged 75 or older	**11,616**	**3,875**	**943**	**215**	**4,935**	**4,830**	**1,648**	**1,547**
Under $10,000	1,632	108	90	15	1,193	1,188	225	223
$10,000 to $19,999	4,051	722	183	31	2,441	2,421	671	662
$20,000 to $29,999	2,349	1,077	205	41	696	686	331	307
$30,000 to $39,999	1,271	685	130	30	284	261	140	119
$40,000 to $49,999	686	340	111	22	110	99	103	92
$50,000 to $59,999	522	304	68	15	99	86	37	34
$60,000 to $69,999	290	159	44	12	46	41	29	26
$70,000 to $79,999	199	123	40	4	15	13	15	14
$80,000 to $89,999	145	63	31	6	20	15	24	16
$90,000 to $99,999	105	52	15	10	8	8	20	17
$100,000 or more	367	240	25	30	19	12	54	38
Median income	$20,467	$30,346	$29,548	$37,880	$13,869	$13,719	$18,614	$17,843
Total households headed by people aged 75 or older	**100.0%**	**100.0%**	**100.0%**	**100.0%**	**100.0%**	**100.0%**	**100.0%**	**100.0%**
Under $10,000	14.0	2.8	9.5	7.0	24.2	24.6	13.7	14.4
$10,000 to $19,999	34.9	18.6	19.4	14.4	49.5	50.1	40.7	42.8
$20,000 to $29,999	20.2	27.8	21.7	19.1	14.1	14.2	20.1	19.8
$30,000 to $39,999	10.9	17.7	13.8	14.0	5.8	5.4	8.5	7.7
$40,000 to $49,999	5.9	8.8	11.8	10.2	2.2	2.0	6.3	5.9
$50,000 to $59,999	4.5	7.8	7.2	7.0	2.0	1.8	2.2	2.2
$60,000 to $69,999	2.5	4.1	4.7	5.6	0.9	0.8	1.8	1.7
$70,000 to $79,999	1.7	3.2	4.2	1.9	0.3	0.3	0.9	0.9
$80,000 to $89,999	1.2	1.6	3.3	2.8	0.4	0.3	1.5	1.0
$90,000 to $99,999	0.9	1.3	1.6	4.7	0.2	0.2	1.2	1.1
$100,000 or more	3.2	6.2	2.7	14.0	0.4	0.2	3.3	2.5

Source: Bureau of the Census, 2005 Current Population Survey Annual Social and Economic Supplement, Internet site http:// pubdb3.census.gov/macro/032003/hhinc/new02_000.htm; calculations by New Strategist

Some Older Americans Have Lost Ground

Those aged 55 to 64 have seen their incomes grow since 2000.

Between 2000 and 2004, the median income of men aged 75 or older fell 0.8 percent, after adjusting for inflation. The median income of women in the age group fell 2 percent. Behind the declines were falling interest rates, which cut the incomes of those collecting interest income. In contrast to the income decline among the oldest Americans, the incomes of men and women aged 55 to 74 rose between 2000 and 2004—up 3 to 12 percent among men and women in the age group, after adjusting for inflation. Behind the gains are rising labor force participation rates as workers postpone retirement.

Older Americans made significant gains in median income between 1990 and 2004. Among men, the median income of 55-to-64-year-olds rose 13 percent during those years, after adjusting for inflation. The gain was 6 percent for men aged 65 or older. Among women aged 55 to 64, median income rose a whopping 58 percent between 1990 and 2004 as career-oriented Boomer women filled the age group. The gain was a smaller 7 percent among women aged 65 or older.

■ The median income of men and women aged 55 to 64 should continue to climb thanks to rising labor force participation rates in the age group.

Incomes have grown since 2000 for 55-to-64-year-olds

(percent change in median income of people aged 55 or older, by sex, 2000–04; in 2004 dollars)

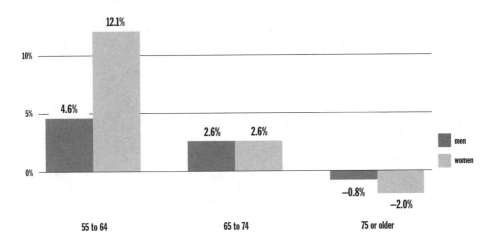

Table 4.16   Median Income of Men Aged 55 or Older, 1990 to 2004

(median income of men aged 15 or older and aged 55 or older, 1990 to 2004; percent change for selected years; in 2004 dollars)

	total men	55 to 64	aged 65 or older		
			total	65 to 74	75 or older
2004	$30,513	$39,212	$21,102	$24,161	$18,718
2003	30,735	39,961	20,910	23,783	18,258
2002	30,712	38,105	20,416	22,364	18,390
2001	31,054	38,028	21,009	23,151	18,697
2000	31,089	37,502	21,292	23,546	18,860
1999	30,937	37,955	21,877	24,325	19,243
1998	30,660	37,933	21,024	22,839	19,072
1997	29,590	36,567	20,853	23,063	18,082
1996	28,570	35,393	19,999	22,302	17,374
1995	27,771	35,671	20,290	22,583	17,429
1994	27,384	34,135	19,227	20,928	17,221
1993	27,165	32,362	19,288	20,965	17,278
1992	26,989	33,797	19,260	20,860	17,002
1991	27,684	34,435	19,418	20,741	17,633
1990	28,439	34,761	19,876	22,378	16,370
Percent change					
2000 to 2004	−1.9%	4.6%	−0.9%	2.6%	−0.8%
1990 to 2004	7.3	12.8	6.2	8.0	14.3

Source: Bureau of the Census, data from the Current Population Survey Annual Demographic Supplements, Internet site http://www.census.gov/hhes/income/histinc/p08ar.html; calculations by New Strategist

Table 4.17 Median Income of Women Aged 55 or Older, 1990 to 2004

(median income of women aged 15 or older and aged 55 or older, 1990 to 2004; percent change for selected years; in 2004 dollars)

	total women	55 to 64	aged 65 or older		
			total	65 to 74	75 or older
2004	$17,629	$20,810	$12,080	$12,279	$11,944
2003	17,723	20,915	12,163	12,469	11,947
2002	17,659	20,131	11,981	11,847	12,083
2001	17,729	19,019	12,072	11,953	12,161
2000	17,619	18,559	12,091	11,965	12,186
1999	17,347	18,070	12,421	12,444	12,404
1998	16,700	16,984	12,157	12,098	12,204
1997	16,082	16,872	11,809	11,902	11,732
1996	15,361	15,962	11,539	11,575	11,505
1995	14,930	15,239	11,515	11,419	11,603
1994	14,456	13,701	11,284	11,128	11,425
1993	14,220	13,940	10,941	11,131	10,768
1992	14,136	13,370	10,797	10,839	10,755
1991	14,169	13,393	11,076	11,003	11,146
1990	14,112	13,173	11,273	11,478	11,059
Percent change					
2000 to 2004	0.1%	12.1%	–0.1%	2.6%	–2.0%
1990 to 2004	24.9	58.0	7.2	7.0	8.0

Source: Bureau of the Census, data from the Current Population Survey Annual Demographic Supplements, Internet site http:// www.census.gov/hhes/income/histinc/p08ar.html; calculations by New Strategist

Among Workers, Older Men Command High Salaries

Income peaks among working men aged 55 or older.

Among men who work full-time, those with the highest incomes are aged 55 or older. Men aged 70 to 74 who work full-time had a median income of $55,145 in 2004, the highest among men of any age—but only 10 percent are full-time workers. Among the 65 percent of men aged 55 to 59 who work full-time, median income is a substantial $51,320.

Median income drops with age not because workers get paid less, but because fewer people work. The proportion working full-time drops from the 65 percent majority of men aged 55 to 59 to a 47 percent minority of men aged 60 to 64. Only 10 percent of men aged 65 or older work full-time.

Among men aged 55 or older, non-Hispanic whites have the highest incomes, a median of $30,575 in 2004. Asian men aged 55 or older have a far lower median, just $21,896. The median income of Asian men is higher than that of blacks or Hispanics, however. The median income of black men aged 55 or older stood at $19,640, while that of Hispanics was just $17,906.

■ Among older men, those with high earnings may be more likely to stay on the job than those who earn less, driving up the median income of older men who work full-time.

Incomes are high among older men who work full-time

(median income of men who work full-time, by age, 2004)

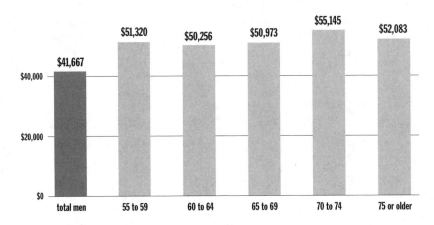

Table 4.18 Income of Men Aged 55 or Older, 2004: Total Men

(number and percent distribution of men aged 16 or older and aged 55 or older by income, 2004; median income by work status, and percent working year-round, full-time; men in thousands as of 2005)

		aged 55 or older								
						aged 65 or older				
			aged 55 to 64				aged 65 to 74			
	total	total	total	55–59	60–64	total	total	65–69	70–74	75+
TOTAL MEN	**111,686**	**29,198**	**14,047**	**8,003**	**6,044**	**15,151**	**8,466**	**4,814**	**3,652**	**6,685**
Without income	**9,909**	**766**	**451**	**251**	**200**	**315**	**187**	**114**	**73**	**128**
With income	**101,777**	**28,432**	**13,596**	**7,752**	**5,844**	**14,836**	**8,279**	**4,700**	**3,579**	**6,557**
Under $10,000	15,853	3,564	1,423	717	705	2,141	1,163	621	541	979
$10,000 to $19,999	18,096	6,831	1,936	947	990	4,895	2,290	1,202	1,088	2,606
$20,000 to $29,999	15,898	4,628	1,841	1,043	799	2,787	1,407	778	628	1,380
$30,000 to $39,999	13,391	3,375	1,684	876	808	1,691	1,131	665	467	559
$40,000 to $49,999	10,283	2,587	1,562	932	630	1,025	643	384	259	383
$50,000 to $59,999	7,376	1,732	1,147	721	426	585	441	285	156	144
$60,000 to $69,999	5,208	1,399	935	598	339	464	329	202	128	135
$70,000 to $79,999	3,767	937	682	408	274	255	162	87	75	92
$80,000 to $89,999	2,574	663	470	304	165	193	144	85	59	50
$90,000 to $99,999	1,881	536	371	264	107	165	119	80	39	45
$100,000 or more	7,452	2,184	1,546	943	603	638	453	314	140	185
Median income of men with income	$30,513	$28,333	$39,212	$42,090	$34,858	$21,102	$24,161	$26,368	$21,920	$18,718
Median income of full-time workers	41,667	51,222	50,949	51,320	50,256	51,403	51,366	50,973	55,145	52,083
Percent working full-time	53.8%	28.9%	57.1%	64.8%	47.0%	10.1%	15.0%	18.7%	10.2%	3.9%
TOTAL MEN	**100.0%**	**100.0%**	**100.0%**	**100.0%**	**100.0%**	**100.0%**	**100.0%**	**100.0%**	**100.0%**	**100.0%**
Without income	**8.9**	**2.6**	**3.2**	**3.1**	**3.3**	**2.1**	**2.2**	**2.4**	**2.0**	**1.9**
With income	**91.1**	**97.4**	**96.8**	**96.9**	**96.7**	**97.9**	**97.8**	**97.6**	**98.0**	**98.1**
Under $10,000	14.2	12.2	10.1	9.0	11.7	14.1	13.7	12.9	14.8	14.6
$10,000 to $19,999	16.2	23.4	13.8	11.8	16.4	32.3	27.0	25.0	29.8	39.0
$20,000 to $29,999	14.2	15.9	13.1	13.0	13.2	18.4	16.6	16.2	17.2	20.6
$30,000 to $39,999	12.0	11.6	12.0	10.9	13.4	11.2	13.4	13.8	12.8	8.4
$40,000 to $49,999	9.2	8.9	11.1	11.6	10.4	6.8	7.6	8.0	7.1	5.7
$50,000 to $59,999	6.6	5.9	8.2	9.0	7.0	3.9	5.2	5.9	4.3	2.2
$60,000 to $69,999	4.7	4.8	6.7	7.5	5.6	3.1	3.9	4.2	3.5	2.0
$70,000 to $79,999	3.4	3.2	4.9	5.1	4.5	1.7	1.9	1.8	2.1	1.4
$80,000 to $89,999	2.3	2.3	3.3	3.8	2.7	1.3	1.7	1.8	1.6	0.7
$90,000 to $99,999	1.7	1.8	2.6	3.3	1.8	1.1	1.4	1.7	1.1	0.7
$100,000 or more	6.7	7.5	11.0	11.8	10.0	4.2	5.4	6.5	3.8	2.8

Source: Bureau of the Census, 2005 Current Population Survey Annual Social and Economic Supplement, Internet site http:// pubdb3.census.gov/macro/032005/perinc/new01_000.htm; calculations by New Strategist

Table 4.19 Income of Men Aged 55 or Older, 2004: Asian Men

(number and percent distribution of Asian men aged 16 or older and aged 55 or older by income, 2004; median income by work status, and percent working year-round, full-time; men in thousands as of 2005)

	total	aged 55 or older — total	aged 55 to 64 — total	55–59	60–64	aged 65 or older — total	aged 65 to 74 — total	65–69	70–74	75+
TOTAL ASIAN MEN	5,038	997	513	305	208	484	316	187	129	168
Without income	654	59	22	9	13	37	21	12	9	17
With income	4,384	938	491	296	195	447	295	175	120	151
Under $10,000	695	178	50	26	24	128	79	38	41	50
$10,000 to $19,999	679	205	70	33	38	135	81	40	41	53
$20,000 to $29,999	607	123	69	45	23	54	40	20	20	14
$30,000 to $39,999	535	114	78	48	30	36	26	21	6	10
$40,000 to $49,999	388	52	37	26	11	15	8	5	3	7
$50,000 to $59,999	352	68	43	29	15	25	19	14	5	6
$60,000 to $69,999	205	33	23	13	10	10	9	9	0	1
$70,000 to $79,999	194	28	27	15	14	1	0	0	0	1
$80,000 to $89,999	154	17	13	7	7	4	1	1	0	3
$90,000 to $99,999	123	16	10	6	3	6	6	6	0	0
$100,000 or more	450	99	68	50	18	31	25	21	4	7
Median income of men with income	$32,419	$21,896	$36,608	$39,132	$33,573	$16,149	$17,263	$23,783	$13,704	$14,328
Median income of full-time workers	46,429	–	46,077	45,709	47,253	–	–	–	–	–
Percent working full-time	57.1%	27.9%	69.0%	75.1%	60.1%	11.8%	16.8%	21.4%	9.3%	2.4%
TOTAL ASIAN MEN	100.0%	100.0%	100.0%	100.0%	100.0%	100.0%	100.0%	100.0%	100.0%	100.0%
Without income	13.0	5.9	4.3	3.0	6.3	7.6	6.6	6.4	7.0	10.1
With income	87.0	94.1	95.7	97.0	93.8	92.4	93.4	93.6	93.0	89.9
Under $10,000	13.8	17.9	9.7	8.5	11.5	26.4	25.0	20.3	31.8	29.8
$10,000 to $19,999	13.5	20.6	13.6	10.8	18.3	27.9	25.6	21.4	31.8	31.5
$20,000 to $29,999	12.0	12.3	13.5	14.8	11.1	11.2	12.7	10.7	15.5	8.3
$30,000 to $39,999	10.6	11.4	15.2	15.7	14.4	7.4	8.2	11.2	4.7	6.0
$40,000 to $49,999	7.7	5.2	7.2	8.5	5.3	3.1	2.5	2.7	2.3	4.2
$50,000 to $59,999	7.0	6.8	8.4	9.5	7.2	5.2	6.0	7.5	3.9	3.6
$60,000 to $69,999	4.1	3.3	4.5	4.3	4.8	2.1	2.8	4.8	0.0	0.6
$70,000 to $79,999	3.9	2.8	5.3	4.9	6.7	0.2	0.0	0.0	0.0	0.6
$80,000 to $89,999	3.1	1.7	2.5	2.3	3.4	0.8	0.3	0.5	0.0	1.8
$90,000 to $99,999	2.4	1.6	1.9	2.0	1.4	1.2	1.9	3.2	0.0	0.0
$100,000 or more	8.9	9.9	13.3	16.4	8.7	6.4	7.9	11.2	3.1	4.2

Note: Asians are those identifying themselves as being Asian alone and those identifying themselves as being Asian in combination with one or more other races. "–" means sample is too small to make a reliable estimate.
Source: Bureau of the Census, 2005 Current Population Survey Annual Social and Economic Supplement, Internet site http://pubdb3.census.gov/macro/032005/perinc/new01_000.htm; calculations by New Strategist

Table 4.20 Income of Men Aged 55 or Older, 2004: Black Men

(number and percent distribution of black men aged 16 or older and aged 55 or older by income, 2004; median income by work status, and percent working year-round, full-time; men in thousands as of 2005)

	total	aged 55 or older total	aged 55 to 64 total	55–59	60–64	aged 65 or older total	aged 65 to 74 total	65–69	70–74	75+
TOTAL BLACK MEN	12,609	2,471	1,298	767	530	1,173	741	469	272	431
Without income	2,273	145	88	48	39	57	38	27	11	18
With income	10,336	2,326	1,210	719	491	1,116	703	442	261	413
Under $10,000	2,363	510	213	115	98	297	177	108	71	119
$10,000 to $19,999	2,115	661	255	130	125	406	233	131	103	172
$20,000 to $29,999	1,889	353	209	142	68	144	88	55	33	56
$30,000 to $39,999	1,456	275	159	86	71	116	91	68	24	25
$40,000 to $49,999	896	185	133	84	49	52	36	24	11	16
$50,000 to $59,999	594	103	72	46	26	31	31	22	8	0
$60,000 to $69,999	314	66	47	36	12	19	13	9	4	6
$70,000 to $79,999	211	40	32	16	16	8	6	3	3	3
$80,000 to $89,999	99	21	15	11	4	6	6	4	2	0
$90,000 to $99,999	120	22	15	9	4	7	2	2	0	5
$100,000 or more	280	88	60	43	18	28	19	18	1	9
Median income of men with income	$22,740	$19,640	$26,080	$27,343	$21,955	$15,021	$16,145	$17,724	$14,993	$13,527
Median income of full-time workers	31,724	40,130	36,659	36,494	36,966	42,619	40,762	43,854	–	–
Percent working full-time	46.2%	26.7%	47.8%	54.5%	38.1%	11.6%	14.7%	16.6%	11.8%	6.3%
TOTAL BLACK MEN	100.0%	100.0%	100.0%	100.0%	100.0%	100.0%	100.0%	100.0%	100.0%	100.0%
Without income	18.0	5.9	6.8	6.3	7.4	4.9	5.1	5.8	4.0	4.2
With income	82.0	94.1	93.2	93.7	92.6	95.1	94.9	94.2	96.0	95.8
Under $10,000	18.7	20.6	16.4	15.0	18.5	25.3	23.9	23.0	26.1	27.6
$10,000 to $19,999	16.8	26.8	19.6	16.9	23.6	34.6	31.4	27.9	37.9	39.9
$20,000 to $29,999	15.0	14.3	16.1	18.5	12.8	12.3	11.9	11.7	12.1	13.0
$30,000 to $39,999	11.5	11.1	12.2	11.2	13.4	9.9	12.3	14.5	8.8	5.8
$40,000 to $49,999	7.1	7.5	10.2	11.0	9.2	4.4	4.9	5.1	4.0	3.7
$50,000 to $59,999	4.7	4.2	5.5	6.0	4.9	2.6	4.2	4.7	2.9	0.0
$60,000 to $69,999	2.5	2.7	3.6	4.7	2.3	1.6	1.8	1.9	1.5	1.4
$70,000 to $79,999	1.7	1.6	2.5	2.1	3.0	0.7	0.8	0.6	1.1	0.7
$80,000 to $89,999	0.8	0.8	1.2	1.4	0.8	0.5	0.8	0.9	0.7	0.0
$90,000 to $99,999	1.0	0.9	1.2	1.2	0.8	0.6	0.3	0.4	0.0	1.2
$100,000 or more	2.2	3.6	4.6	5.6	3.4	2.4	2.6	3.8	0.4	2.1

Note: Blacks are those identifying themselves as being black alone and those identifying themselves as being black in combination with one or more other races. "–" means sample is too small to make a reliable estimate.
Source: Bureau of the Census, 2005 Current Population Survey Annual Social and Economic Supplement, Internet site http:// pubdb3.census.gov/macro/032005/perinc/new01_000.htm; calculations by New Strategist

Table 4.21 Income of Men Aged 55 or Older, 2004: Hispanic Men

(number and percent distribution of Hispanic men aged 16 or older and aged 55 or older by income, 2004; median income by work status, and percent working year-round, full-time; men in thousands as of 2005)

						aged 55 or older				
							aged 65 or older			
			aged 55 to 64					aged 65 to 74		
	total	total	total	55–59	60–64	total	total	65–69	70–74	75+
TOTAL HISPANIC MEN	15,223	2,031	1,101	665	437	930	567	322	245	363
Without income	1,968	137	62	38	25	75	44	27	16	31
With income	13,255	1,894	1,039	627	412	855	523	295	229	332
Under $10,000	2,239	449	153	72	81	296	169	84	84	128
$10,000 to $19,999	3,700	553	247	129	117	306	177	106	71	129
$20,000 to $29,999	2,823	282	185	133	52	97	55	30	25	42
$30,000 to $39,999	1,725	200	141	91	51	59	50	31	19	9
$40,000 to $49,999	1,027	146	101	62	38	45	30	18	13	15
$50,000 to $59,999	616	87	67	47	19	20	17	11	8	3
$60,000 to $69,999	370	47	40	22	17	7	6	5	2	1
$70,000 to $79,999	198	36	30	16	13	6	4	2	2	2
$80,000 to $89,999	130	31	24	18	5	7	7	3	4	0
$90,000 to $99,999	88	15	10	7	3	5	3	2	1	2
$100,000 or more	336	51	44	29	15	7	7	6	1	0
Median income of men with income	$21,559	$17,906	$26,319	$27,577	$21,309	$13,558	$14,664	$15,203	$13,523	$12,199
Median income of full-time workers	26,921	37,937	34,237	34,023	34,877	39,850	37,109	–	–	–
Percent working full-time	58.4%	28.5%	59.9%	66.8%	49.2%	12.3%	16.8%	21.7%	10.2%	5.0%
TOTAL HISPANIC MEN	100.0%	100.0%	100.0%	100.0%	100.0%	100.0%	100.0%	100.0%	100.0%	100.0%
Without income	12.9	6.7	5.6	5.7	5.7	8.1	7.8	8.4	6.5	8.5
With income	87.1	93.3	94.4	94.3	94.3	91.9	92.2	91.6	93.5	91.5
Under $10,000	14.7	22.1	13.9	10.8	18.5	31.8	29.8	26.1	34.3	35.3
$10,000 to $19,999	24.3	27.2	22.4	19.4	26.8	32.9	31.2	32.9	29.0	35.5
$20,000 to $29,999	18.5	13.9	16.8	20.0	11.9	10.4	9.7	9.3	10.2	11.6
$30,000 to $39,999	11.3	9.8	12.8	13.7	11.7	6.3	8.8	9.6	7.8	2.5
$40,000 to $49,999	6.7	7.2	9.2	9.3	8.7	4.8	5.3	5.6	5.3	4.1
$50,000 to $59,999	4.0	4.3	6.1	7.1	4.3	2.2	3.0	3.4	3.3	0.8
$60,000 to $69,999	2.4	2.3	3.6	3.3	3.9	0.8	1.1	1.6	0.8	0.3
$70,000 to $79,999	1.3	1.8	2.7	2.4	3.0	0.6	0.7	0.6	0.8	0.6
$80,000 to $89,999	0.9	1.5	2.2	2.7	1.1	0.8	1.2	0.9	1.6	0.0
$90,000 to $99,999	0.6	0.7	0.9	1.1	0.7	0.5	0.5	0.6	0.4	0.6
$100,000 or more	2.2	2.5	4.0	4.4	3.4	0.8	1.2	1.9	0.4	0.0

Note: "–" means sample is too small to make a reliable estimate.
Source: Bureau of the Census, 2005 Current Population Survey Annual Social and Economic Supplement, Internet site http:// pubdb3.census.gov/macro/032005/perinc/new01_000.htm; calculations by New Strategist

Table 4.22 Income of Men Aged 55 or Older, 2004: Non-Hispanic White Men

(number and percent distribution of non-Hispanic white men aged 16 or older and aged 55 or older by income, 2004; median income by work status, and percent working year-round, full-time; men in thousands as of 2005)

		aged 55 or older								
							aged 65 or older			
			aged 55 to 64					aged 65 to 74		
	total	total	total	55–59	60–64	total	total	65–69	70–74	75+
TOTAL NON-HISPANIC WHITE MEN	77,680	23,417	10,981	6,200	4,781	12,436	6,755	3,783	2,972	5,681
Without income	4,912	418	275	155	120	143	81	48	33	62
With income	72,768	22,999	10,706	6,045	4,661	12,293	6,674	3,735	2,939	5,619
Under $10,000	10,326	2,368	981	491	490	1,387	715	381	333	671
$10,000 to $19,999	11,441	5,340	1,327	640	687	4,013	1,774	909	865	2,239
$20,000 to $29,999	10,426	3,827	1,353	715	639	2,474	1,212	662	551	1,261
$30,000 to $39,999	9,557	2,765	1,294	648	647	1,471	959	546	413	510
$40,000 to $49,999	7,868	2,179	1,279	751	528	900	561	332	229	339
$50,000 to $59,999	5,717	1,462	958	596	363	504	370	236	134	133
$60,000 to $69,999	4,268	1,233	815	519	297	418	295	176	119	124
$70,000 to $79,999	3,137	827	587	358	229	240	151	81	71	87
$80,000 to $89,999	2,160	589	415	268	148	174	127	76	52	47
$90,000 to $99,999	1,535	479	333	241	94	146	108	69	38	37
$100,000 or more	6,334	1,928	1,359	819	540	569	400	266	134	169
Median income of men with income	$33,652	$30,575	$42,148	$46,708	$37,309	$22,389	$26,361	$28,567	$23,936	$19,517
Median income of full-time workers	46,986	55,164	54,737	55,862	52,215	55,466	55,413	52,374	59,760	55,921
Percent working full-time	54.0%	29.6%	57.6%	65.5%	47.4%	9.8%	14.9%	18.7%	10.1%	3.7%
TOTAL NON-HISPANIC WHITE MEN	100.0%	100.0%	100.0%	100.0%	100.0%	100.0%	100.0%	100.0%	100.0%	100.0%
Without income	6.3	1.8	2.5	2.5	2.5	1.1	1.2	1.3	1.1	1.1
With income	93.7	98.2	97.5	97.5	97.5	98.9	98.8	98.7	98.9	98.9
Under $10,000	13.3	10.1	8.9	7.9	10.2	11.2	10.6	10.1	11.2	11.8
$10,000 to $19,999	14.7	22.8	12.1	10.3	14.4	32.3	26.3	24.0	29.1	39.4
$20,000 to $29,999	13.4	16.3	12.3	11.5	13.4	19.9	17.9	17.5	18.5	22.2
$30,000 to $39,999	12.3	11.8	11.8	10.5	13.5	11.8	14.2	14.4	13.9	9.0
$40,000 to $49,999	10.1	9.3	11.6	12.1	11.0	7.2	8.3	8.8	7.7	6.0
$50,000 to $59,999	7.4	6.2	8.7	9.6	7.6	4.1	5.5	6.2	4.5	2.3
$60,000 to $69,999	5.5	5.3	7.4	8.4	6.2	3.4	4.4	4.7	4.0	2.2
$70,000 to $79,999	4.0	3.5	5.3	5.8	4.8	1.9	2.2	2.1	2.4	1.5
$80,000 to $89,999	2.8	2.5	3.8	4.3	3.1	1.4	1.9	2.0	1.7	0.8
$90,000 to $99,999	2.0	2.0	3.0	3.9	2.0	1.2	1.6	1.8	1.3	0.7
$100,000 or more	8.2	8.2	12.4	13.2	11.3	4.6	5.9	7.0	4.5	3.0

Note: Non-Hispanic whites are those identifying themselves as being white alone and not Hispanic.
Source: Bureau of the Census, 2005 Current Population Survey Annual Social and Economic Supplement, Internet site http:// pubdb3.census.gov/macro/032005/perinc/new01_000.htm; calculations by New Strategist

Older Women Have Low Incomes

Those who work are much better off than those who are not in the labor force.

The median income of women aged 55 or older who work full-time stood at $34,520 in 2004, more than double the $15,104 median for all women in the age group. Few older women work full-time, however. The proportion ranges from a high of 46 percent among women aged 55 to 59 to just 5 percent of women aged 65 or older.

Because most women aged 65 or older do not work, and because most did not spend much time in the labor force, their incomes are extremely low. Much of their financial support comes from Social Security. The median income of all women aged 65 or older was just $12,080 in 2004. Non-Hispanic white women in the age group have the highest incomes, a median of $12,679. Their Hispanic counterparts have the lowest incomes—a median of just $8,978. For black women the figure is $9,912, and for Asians, $9,557.

■ The incomes of older women will rise substantially in the years ahead as the working women of the Baby-Boom generation enter the 55-or-older age group.

Among older women, the incomes of workers are more than double the average

(median income of women aged 55 or older, by work status, 2004)

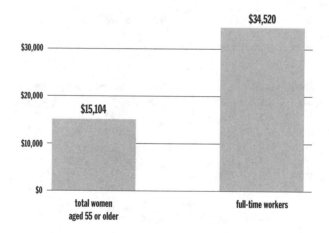

Table 4.23 Income of Women Aged 55 or Older, 2004: Total Women

(number and percent distribution of women aged 16 or older and aged 55 or older by income, 2004; median income by work status, and percent working year-round, full-time; women in thousands as of 2005)

		aged 55 or older								
							aged 65 or older			
			aged 55 to 64					aged 65 to 74		
	total	total	total	55–59	60–64	total	total	65–69	70–74	75+
TOTAL WOMEN	118,739	35,547	15,484	8,760	6,724	20,063	9,922	5,310	4,612	10,140
Without income	15,370	2,121	1,409	836	572	712	397	219	178	314
With income	103,369	33,426	14,075	7,924	6,152	19,351	9,525	5,091	4,434	9,826
Under $10,000	31,885	11,437	3,962	1,977	1,985	7,475	3,789	2,001	1,787	3,686
$10,000 to $19,999	23,868	9,992	2,843	1,492	1,352	7,149	2,989	1,442	1,547	4,160
$20,000 to $29,999	16,588	4,709	2,290	1,306	984	2,419	1,286	727	559	1,133
$30,000 to $39,999	11,583	2,623	1,693	1,054	639	930	541	313	228	388
$40,000 to $49,999	7,048	1,590	1,074	695	379	516	359	236	123	157
$50,000 to $59,999	4,128	1,012	693	438	256	319	180	125	55	140
$60,000 to $69,999	2,818	656	484	298	185	172	112	88	24	60
$70,000 to $79,999	1,737	402	280	174	106	122	94	63	30	28
$80,000 to $89,999	1,099	325	258	167	90	67	39	24	14	27
$90,000 to $99,999	675	183	142	98	44	41	29	11	19	12
$100,000 or more	1,939	494	355	224	131	139	109	61	48	31
Median income of women with income	$17,629	$15,104	$20,810	$23,235	$17,407	$12,080	$12,279	$12,715	$11,934	$11,944
Median income of full-time workers	32,101	34,520	34,910	35,220	33,458	34,314	34,685	36,682	31,524	32,390
Percent working full-time	35.7%	16.6%	38.7%	45.9%	29.4%	4.8%	8.2%	11.4%	4.6%	1.5%
TOTAL WOMEN	100.0%	100.0%	100.0%	100.0%	100.0%	100.0%	100.0%	100.0%	100.0%	100.0%
Without income	12.9	6.0	9.1	9.5	8.5	3.5	4.0	4.1	3.9	3.1
With income	87.1	94.0	90.9	90.5	91.5	96.5	96.0	95.9	96.1	96.9
Under $10,000	26.9	32.2	25.6	22.6	29.5	37.3	38.2	37.7	38.7	36.4
$10,000 to $19,999	20.1	28.1	18.4	17.0	20.1	35.6	30.1	27.2	33.5	41.0
$20,000 to $29,999	14.0	13.2	14.8	14.9	14.6	12.1	13.0	13.7	12.1	11.2
$30,000 to $39,999	9.8	7.4	10.9	12.0	9.5	4.6	5.5	5.9	4.9	3.8
$40,000 to $49,999	5.9	4.5	6.9	7.9	5.6	2.6	3.6	4.4	2.7	1.5
$50,000 to $59,999	3.5	2.8	4.5	5.0	3.8	1.6	1.8	2.4	1.2	1.4
$60,000 to $69,999	2.4	1.8	3.1	3.4	2.8	0.9	1.1	1.7	0.5	0.6
$70,000 to $79,999	1.5	1.1	1.8	2.0	1.6	0.6	0.9	1.2	0.7	0.3
$80,000 to $89,999	0.9	0.9	1.7	1.9	1.3	0.3	0.4	0.5	0.3	0.3
$90,000 to $99,999	0.6	0.5	0.9	1.1	0.7	0.2	0.3	0.2	0.4	0.1
$100,000 or more	1.6	1.4	2.3	2.6	1.9	0.7	1.1	1.1	1.0	0.3

Source: Bureau of the Census, 2005 Current Population Survey Annual Social and Economic Supplement, Internet site http://pubdb3.census.gov/macro/032005/perinc/new01_000.htm; calculations by New Strategist

Table 4.24 Income of Women Aged 55 or Older, 2004: Asian Women

(number and percent distribution of Asian women aged 16 or older and aged 55 or older by income, 2004; median income by work status, and percent working year-round, full-time; women in thousands as of 2005)

		aged 55 or older								
			aged 55 to 64			aged 65 or older		aged 65 to 74		
	total	total	total	55–59	60–64	total	total	65–69	70–74	75+
TOTAL ASIAN WOMEN	**5,484**	**1,233**	**604**	**359**	**245**	**629**	**347**	**198**	**148**	**283**
Without income	**1,176**	**199**	**110**	**56**	**54**	**89**	**52**	**27**	**24**	**38**
With income	**4,308**	**1,034**	**494**	**303**	**191**	**540**	**295**	**171**	**124**	**245**
Under $10,000	1,338	412	127	71	55	285	145	82	63	140
$10,000 to $19,999	762	253	96	67	31	157	87	49	39	69
$20,000 to $29,999	610	115	82	50	30	33	20	13	8	13
$30,000 to $39,999	483	73	61	30	28	12	6	3	3	4
$40,000 to $49,999	338	52	34	22	12	18	10	5	5	9
$50,000 to $59,999	230	30	18	11	7	12	5	5	0	5
$60,000 to $69,999	168	23	17	12	6	6	6	4	2	0
$70,000 to $79,999	111	18	14	11	2	4	4	3	1	0
$80,000 to $89,999	79	21	19	11	8	2	2	1	1	0
$90,000 to $99,999	39	11	9	8	2	2	0	0	0	2
$100,000 or more	151	27	18	11	7	9	8	5	3	2
Median income of women with income	$20,618	$13,374	$21,941	$21,484	$23,573	$9,557	$10,139	$10,457	$9,884	$9,081
Median income of full-time workers	36,491	–	34,409	32,585	36,221	–	–	–	–	–
Percent working full-time	37.5%	17.1%	43.0%	50.1%	32.7%	5.6%	8.1%	9.6%	6.1%	2.1%
TOTAL ASIAN WOMEN	**100.0%**	**100.0%**	**100.0%**	**100.0%**	**100.0%**	**100.0%**	**100.0%**	**100.0%**	**100.0%**	**100.0%**
Without income	**21.4**	**16.1**	**18.2**	**15.6**	**22.0**	**14.1**	**15.0**	**13.6**	**16.2**	**13.4**
With income	**78.6**	**83.9**	**81.8**	**84.4**	**78.0**	**85.9**	**85.0**	**86.4**	**83.8**	**86.6**
Under $10,000	24.4	33.4	21.0	19.8	22.4	45.3	41.8	41.4	42.6	49.5
$10,000 to $19,999	13.9	20.5	15.9	18.7	12.7	25.0	25.1	24.7	26.4	24.4
$20,000 to $29,999	11.1	9.3	13.6	13.9	12.2	5.2	5.8	6.6	5.4	4.6
$30,000 to $39,999	8.8	5.9	10.1	8.4	11.4	1.9	1.7	1.5	2.0	1.4
$40,000 to $49,999	6.2	4.2	5.6	6.1	4.9	2.9	2.9	2.5	3.4	3.2
$50,000 to $59,999	4.2	2.4	3.0	3.1	2.9	1.9	1.4	2.5	0.0	1.8
$60,000 to $69,999	3.1	1.9	2.8	3.3	2.4	1.0	1.7	2.0	1.4	0.0
$70,000 to $79,999	2.0	1.5	2.3	3.1	0.8	0.6	1.2	1.5	0.7	0.0
$80,000 to $89,999	1.4	1.7	3.1	3.1	3.3	0.3	0.6	0.5	0.7	0.0
$90,000 to $99,999	0.7	0.9	1.5	2.2	0.8	0.3	0.0	0.0	0.0	0.7
$100,000 or more	2.8	2.2	3.0	3.1	2.9	1.4	2.3	2.5	2.0	0.7

Note: Asians are those identifying themselves as being Asian alone and those identifying themselves as being Asian in combination with one or more other races. "–" means sample is too small to make a reliable estimate.
Source: Bureau of the Census, 2005 Current Population Survey Annual Social and Economic Supplement, Internet site http:// pubdb3.census.gov/macro/032005/perinc/new01_000.htm; calculations by New Strategist

Table 4.25 Income of Women Aged 55 or Older, 2004: Black Women

(number and percent distribution of black women aged 16 or older and aged 55 or older by income, 2004; median income by work status, and percent working year-round, full-time; women in thousands as of 2005)

						aged 55 or older				
							aged 65 or older			
			aged 55 to 64					aged 65 to 74		
	total	total	total	55–59	60–64	total	total	65–69	70–74	75+
TOTAL BLACK WOMEN	15,365	3,502	1,669	947	722	1,833	1,000	548	452	833
Without income	2,380	310	196	110	86	114	67	42	25	46
With income	12,985	3,192	1,473	837	636	1,719	933	506	427	787
Under $10,000	4,147	1,267	395	205	190	872	422	213	210	450
$10,000 to $19,999	2,946	896	370	210	158	526	298	157	141	229
$20,000 to $29,999	2,390	437	268	140	128	169	113	73	40	57
$30,000 to $39,999	1,571	258	182	113	71	76	46	27	19	31
$40,000 to $49,999	759	118	89	64	25	29	18	9	9	10
$50,000 to $59,999	415	58	42	25	16	16	11	10	1	5
$60,000 to $69,999	308	62	54	32	22	8	6	5	1	3
$70,000 to $79,999	176	35	25	19	7	10	9	7	3	0
$80,000 to $89,999	80	12	12	8	5	0	0	0	0	0
$90,000 to $99,999	55	15	11	8	3	4	4	2	2	0
$100,000 or more	137	29	23	14	9	6	4	2	2	2
Median income of women with income	$17,369	$12,583	$18,481	$20,181	$16,922	$9,912	$10,924	$11,601	$10,196	$9,178
Median income of full-time workers	29,191	28,082	30,434	30,857	29,193	27,017	30,340	–	–	–
Percent working full-time	39.7%	16.1%	38.5%	45.7%	29.1%	5.9%	8.8%	10.9%	6.0%	2.5%
TOTAL BLACK WOMEN	100.0%	100.0%	100.0%	100.0%	100.0%	100.0%	100.0%	100.0%	100.0%	100.0%
Without income	15.5	8.9	11.7	11.6	11.9	6.2	6.7	7.7	5.5	5.5
With income	84.5	91.1	88.3	88.4	88.1	93.8	93.3	92.3	94.5	94.5
Under $10,000	27.0	36.2	23.7	21.6	26.3	47.6	42.2	38.9	46.5	54.0
$10,000 to $19,999	19.2	25.6	22.2	22.2	21.9	28.7	29.8	28.6	31.2	27.5
$20,000 to $29,999	15.6	12.5	16.1	14.8	17.7	9.2	11.3	13.3	8.8	6.8
$30,000 to $39,999	10.2	7.4	10.9	11.9	9.8	4.1	4.6	4.9	4.2	3.7
$40,000 to $49,999	4.9	3.4	5.3	6.8	3.5	1.6	1.8	1.6	2.0	1.2
$50,000 to $59,999	2.7	1.7	2.5	2.6	2.2	0.9	1.1	1.8	0.2	0.6
$60,000 to $69,999	2.0	1.8	3.2	3.4	3.0	0.4	0.6	0.9	0.2	0.4
$70,000 to $79,999	1.1	1.0	1.5	2.0	1.0	0.5	0.9	1.3	0.7	0.0
$80,000 to $89,999	0.5	0.3	0.7	0.8	0.7	0.0	0.0	0.0	0.0	0.0
$90,000 to $99,999	0.4	0.4	0.7	0.8	0.4	0.2	0.4	0.4	0.4	0.0
$100,000 or more	0.9	0.8	1.4	1.5	1.2	0.3	0.4	0.4	0.4	0.2

Note: Blacks are those identifying themselves as being black alone and those identifying themselves as being black in combination with one or more other races. "–" means sample is too small to make a reliable estimate.
Source: Bureau of the Census, 2005 Current Population Survey Annual Social and Economic Supplement, Internet site http://pubdb3.census.gov/macro/032005/perinc/new01_000.htm; calculations by New Strategist

Table 4.26 Income of Women Aged 55 or Older, 2004: Hispanic Women

(number and percent distribution of Hispanic women aged 16 or older and aged 55 or older by income, 2004; median income by work status, and percent working year-round, full-time; women in thousands as of 2005)

| | | aged 55 or older | | | | | aged 65 or older | | | |
| | | | aged 55 to 64 | | | | | aged 65 to 74 | | |
	total	total	total	55–59	60–64	total	total	65–69	70–74	75+
TOTAL HISPANIC WOMEN	**14,381**	**2,479**	**1,215**	**678**	**536**	**1,264**	**749**	**428**	**321**	**515**
Without income	**3,992**	**354**	**215**	**129**	**85**	**139**	**91**	**48**	**43**	**47**
With income	**10,389**	**2,125**	**1,000**	**549**	**451**	**1,125**	**658**	**380**	**278**	**468**
Under $10,000	3,702	1,017	363	173	189	654	383	225	158	271
$10,000 to $19,999	2,880	580	276	156	120	304	162	83	79	143
$20,000 to $29,999	1,732	236	144	87	58	92	69	38	29	23
$30,000 to $39,999	944	107	81	42	39	26	16	12	4	10
$40,000 to $49,999	493	79	67	46	21	12	10	9	0	3
$50,000 to $59,999	232	48	26	14	13	22	12	9	2	10
$60,000 to $69,999	143	15	14	11	4	1	0	0	0	1
$70,000 to $79,999	101	16	10	7	3	6	3	3	0	3
$80,000 to $89,999	41	8	8	5	3	0	0	0	0	0
$90,000 to $99,999	29	5	5	5	0	0	0	0	0	0
$100,000 or more	95	12	5	4	1	7	5	1	4	3
Median income of women with income	$14,425	$10,821	$14,141	$15,572	$12,001	$8,978	$8,842	$8,503	$9,161	$9,126
Median income of full-time workers	24,255	–	26,308	26,437	25,529	–	–	–	–	–
Percent working full-time	32.9%	15.8%	33.5%	40.4%	24.8%	5.9%	8.7%	9.8%	7.2%	1.9%
TOTAL HISPANIC WOMEN	**100.0%**	**100.0%**	**100.0%**	**100.0%**	**100.0%**	**100.0%**	**100.0%**	**100.0%**	**100.0%**	**100.0%**
Without income	**27.8**	**14.3**	**17.7**	**19.0**	**15.9**	**11.0**	**12.1**	**11.2**	**13.4**	**9.1**
With income	**72.2**	**85.7**	**82.3**	**81.0**	**84.1**	**89.0**	**87.9**	**88.8**	**86.6**	**90.9**
Under $10,000	25.7	41.0	29.9	25.5	35.3	51.7	51.1	52.6	49.2	52.6
$10,000 to $19,999	20.0	23.4	22.7	23.0	22.4	24.1	21.6	19.4	24.6	27.8
$20,000 to $29,999	12.0	9.5	11.9	12.8	10.8	7.3	9.2	8.9	9.0	4.5
$30,000 to $39,999	6.6	4.3	6.7	6.2	7.3	2.1	2.1	2.8	1.2	1.9
$40,000 to $49,999	3.4	3.2	5.5	6.8	3.9	0.9	1.3	2.1	0.0	0.6
$50,000 to $59,999	1.6	1.9	2.1	2.1	2.4	1.7	1.6	2.1	0.6	1.9
$60,000 to $69,999	1.0	0.6	1.2	1.6	0.7	0.1	0.0	0.0	0.0	0.2
$70,000 to $79,999	0.7	0.6	0.8	1.0	0.6	0.5	0.4	0.7	0.0	0.6
$80,000 to $89,999	0.3	0.3	0.7	0.7	0.6	0.0	0.0	0.0	0.0	0.0
$90,000 to $99,999	0.2	0.2	0.4	0.7	0.0	0.0	0.0	0.0	0.0	0.0
$100,000 or more	0.7	0.5	0.4	0.6	0.2	0.6	0.7	0.2	1.2	0.6

Note: "–" means sample is too small to make a reliable estimate.
Source: Bureau of the Census, 2005 Current Population Survey Annual Social and Economic Supplement, Internet site http:// pubdb3.census.gov/macro/032005/perinc/new01_000.htm; calculations by New Strategist

Table 4.27 Income of Women Aged 55 or Older, 2004: Non-Hispanic White Women

(number and percent distribution of non-Hispanic white women aged 16 or older and aged 55 or older by income, 2004; median income by work status, and percent working year-round, full-time; women in thousands as of 2005)

		aged 55 or older								
						aged 65 or older				
		aged 55 to 64				aged 65 to 74				
	total	total	total	55–59	60–64	total	total	65–69	70–74	75+
TOTAL NON-HISPANIC WHITE WOMEN	**82,544**	**28,049**	**11,849**	**6,685**	**5,164**	**16,200**	**7,766**	**4,108**	**3,658**	**8,433**
Without income	**7,734**	**1,233**	**869**	**527**	**342**	**364**	**186**	**103**	**83**	**177**
With income	**74,810**	**26,816**	**10,980**	**6,158**	**4,822**	**15,836**	**7,580**	**4,005**	**3,575**	**8,256**
Under $10,000	22,391	8,638	3,034	1,504	1,530	5,604	2,809	1,467	1,340	2,795
$10,000 to $19,999	17,037	8,196	2,084	1,055	1,030	6,112	2,425	1,144	1,280	3,687
$20,000 to $29,999	11,753	3,899	1,780	1,017	764	2,119	1,082	602	480	1,037
$30,000 to $39,999	8,487	2,158	1,351	855	496	807	468	269	199	339
$40,000 to $49,999	5,402	1,326	873	559	316	453	317	212	105	136
$50,000 to $59,999	3,223	864	600	384	217	264	147	98	49	117
$60,000 to $69,999	2,180	548	390	237	153	158	101	79	20	56
$70,000 to $79,999	1,346	329	229	137	92	100	77	50	26	23
$80,000 to $89,999	895	281	217	144	74	64	36	23	14	27
$90,000 to $99,999	549	152	117	78	39	35	24	7	18	10
$100,000 or more	1,547	425	305	191	114	120	95	53	42	25
Median income of women with income	$18,379	$15,844	$21,690	$24,561	$18,018	$12,679	$13,013	$13,626	$12,486	$12,480
Median income of full-time workers	34,878	36,557	35,926	36,126	35,497	36,899	36,846	39,356	32,100	37,406
Percent working full-time	35.3%	16.7%	39.1%	46.3%	29.8%	4.6%	8.1%	11.7%	4.1%	1.4%
TOTAL NON-HISPANIC WHITE WOMEN	**100.0%**	**100.0%**	**100.0%**	**100.0%**	**100.0%**	**100.0%**	**100.0%**	**100.0%**	**100.0%**	**100.0%**
Without income	**9.4**	**4.4**	**7.3**	**7.9**	**6.6**	**2.2**	**2.4**	**2.5**	**2.3**	**2.1**
With income	**90.6**	**95.6**	**92.7**	**92.1**	**93.4**	**97.8**	**97.6**	**97.5**	**97.7**	**97.9**
Under $10,000	27.1	30.8	25.6	22.5	29.6	34.6	36.2	35.7	36.6	33.1
$10,000 to $19,999	20.6	29.2	17.6	15.8	19.9	37.7	31.2	27.8	35.0	43.7
$20,000 to $29,999	14.2	13.9	15.0	15.2	14.8	13.1	13.9	14.7	13.1	12.3
$30,000 to $39,999	10.3	7.7	11.4	12.8	9.6	5.0	6.0	6.5	5.4	4.0
$40,000 to $49,999	6.5	4.7	7.4	8.4	6.1	2.8	4.1	5.2	2.9	1.6
$50,000 to $59,999	3.9	3.1	5.1	5.7	4.2	1.6	1.9	2.4	1.3	1.4
$60,000 to $69,999	2.6	2.0	3.3	3.5	3.0	1.0	1.3	1.9	0.5	0.7
$70,000 to $79,999	1.6	1.2	1.9	2.0	1.8	0.6	1.0	1.2	0.7	0.3
$80,000 to $89,999	1.1	1.0	1.8	2.2	1.4	0.4	0.5	0.6	0.4	0.3
$90,000 to $99,999	0.7	0.5	1.0	1.2	0.8	0.2	0.3	0.2	0.5	0.1
$100,000 or more	1.9	1.5	2.6	2.9	2.2	0.7	1.2	1.3	1.1	0.3

Note: Non-Hispanic whites are those identifying themselves as being white alone and not Hispanic.
Source: Bureau of the Census, 2005 Current Population Survey Annual Social and Economic Supplement, Internet site http:// pubdb3.census.gov/macro/032005/perinc/new01_000.htm; calculations by New Strategist

Education Boosts Earnings of Older Americans

Men and women with a college degree earn the most.

College-educated men aged 55 to 64 who work full-time earned a median of $67,496 in 2004. This figure is 40 percent greater than the $48,236 earned by the average full-time worker in the age group. For women aged 55 to 64 who work full-time, those with a college degree earned a median of $48,939—52 percent more than the $32,215 average.

Getting an education boosts earnings not only because the college-educated command higher salaries, but because they are more likely to work full-time. Among men aged 55 to 64, fully 67 percent of those with a college degree work full-time versus a smaller 53 percent of those with only a high school diploma. Among women aged 55 to 64, 47 percent of the college educated work full-time compared with 35 percent of women with no more than a high school diploma.

Education plays an important role in earnings even among people aged 65 or older. Fourteen percent of men aged 65 or older with a college diploma work full-time, with median earnings of $60,503 in 2004. In contrast, only 9 percent of their high-school educated counterparts work full-time, with median earnings of $31,908. Among women aged 65 or older who work full-time, those with a college degree earn twice as much as those with only a high school diploma.

■ Education has long guaranteed higher earnings, but the warranty may be running out as the Internet allows educated workers in other countries to compete with Americans for the same jobs.

Among older Americans, college graduates earn more

(median earnings of full-time workers aged 55 to 64, by sex and educational attainment, 2004)

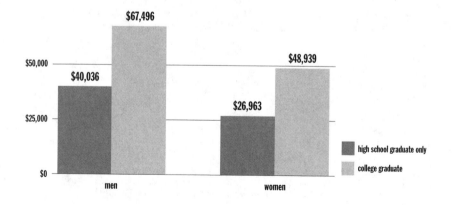

Table 4.28 Earnings of Men by Education, 2004: Aged 55 to 64

(number and percent distribution of men aged 55 to 64 by earnings and education, 2004; men in thousands as of 2005)

	total	less than 9th grade	9th to 12th grade, no degree	high school graduate, including GED	some college, no degree	associate's degree	bachelor's degree or more				
							total	bachelor's degree	master's degree	professional degree	doctoral degree
TOTAL MEN AGED 55 TO 64	14,047	883	1,093	4,134	2,309	1,066	4,562	2,515	1,268	341	438
Without earnings	3,738	403	459	1,308	589	243	736	445	222	37	32
With earnings	10,309	480	634	2,826	1,719	823	3,826	2,070	1,046	304	406
Under $10,000	897	65	101	281	171	46	235	146	66	13	10
$10,000 to $19,999	1,186	144	131	413	167	89	242	133	82	10	19
$20,000 to $29,999	1,362	142	159	469	235	109	250	165	64	5	13
$30,000 to $39,999	1,327	76	86	484	204	122	355	237	78	17	23
$40,000 to $49,999	1,238	37	72	427	233	112	359	226	80	23	29
$50,000 to $59,999	981	6	39	298	195	80	361	210	109	16	25
$60,000 to $69,999	833	7	26	175	161	98	364	192	119	12	41
$70,000 to $79,999	576	–	9	95	97	63	311	171	87	19	36
$80,000 to $89,999	379	–	1	60	74	29	215	124	61	4	26
$90,000 to $99,999	279	–	4	29	51	20	174	80	64	7	25
$100,000 or more	1,250	4	9	93	133	53	959	386	236	177	160
Median earnings of men with earnings	$41,673	$21,315	$25,022	$33,926	$41,918	$42,055	$61,246	$54,985	$61,510	$100,000+	$81,744
Median earnings of full-time workers	48,236	22,571	30,247	40,036	48,644	49,894	67,496	60,749	67,225	100,000+	90,756
Percent working full-time	57.1%	41.2%	39.5%	52.9%	57.0%	61.4%	67.3%	65.4%	64.3%	75.1%	81.1%

(continued)

	total	less than 9th grade	9th to 12th grade, no degree	high school graduate, including GED	some college, no degree	associate's degree	bachelor's degree or more				
							total	bachelor's degree	master's degree	professional degree	doctoral degree
TOTAL MEN AGED 55 TO 64	100.0%	100.0%	100.0%	100.0%	100.0%	100.0%	100.0%	100.0%	100.0%	100.0%	100.0%
Without earnings	26.6	45.6	42.0	31.6	25.5	22.8	16.1	17.7	17.5	10.9	7.3
With earnings	73.4	54.4	58.0	68.4	74.4	77.2	83.9	82.3	82.5	89.1	92.7
Under $10,000	6.4	7.4	9.2	6.8	7.4	4.3	5.2	5.8	5.2	3.8	2.3
$10,000 to $19,999	8.4	16.3	12.0	10.0	7.2	8.3	5.3	5.3	6.5	2.9	4.3
$20,000 to $29,999	9.7	16.1	14.5	11.3	10.2	10.2	5.5	6.6	5.0	1.5	3.0
$30,000 to $39,999	9.4	8.6	7.9	11.7	8.8	11.4	7.8	9.4	6.2	5.0	5.3
$40,000 to $49,999	8.8	4.2	6.6	10.3	10.1	10.5	7.9	9.0	6.3	6.7	6.6
$50,000 to $59,999	7.0	0.7	3.6	7.2	8.4	7.5	7.9	8.3	8.6	4.7	5.7
$60,000 to $69,999	5.9	0.8	2.4	4.2	7.0	9.2	8.0	7.6	9.4	3.5	9.4
$70,000 to $79,999	4.1	–	0.8	2.3	4.2	5.9	6.8	6.8	6.9	5.6	8.2
$80,000 to $89,999	2.7	–	0.1	1.5	3.2	2.7	4.7	4.9	4.8	1.2	5.9
$90,000 to $99,999	2.0	–	0.4	0.7	2.2	1.9	3.8	3.2	5.0	2.1	5.7
$100,000 or more	8.9	0.5	0.8	2.2	5.8	5.0	21.0	15.3	18.6	51.9	36.5

Note: "–" means number is less than 500 or sample is too small to make a reliable estimate.
Source: Bureau of the Census, 2005 Current Population Survey Annual Social and Economic Supplement, Internet site http://pubdb3.census.gov/macro/032005/perinc/new03_000.htm; calculations by New Strategist

Table 4.29 Earnings of Men by Education, 2004: Aged 65 or Older

(number and percent distribution of men aged 65 or older by earnings and education, 2004; men in thousands as of 2005)

	total	less than 9th grade	9th to 12th grade, no degree	high school graduate, including GED	some college, no degree	associate's degree	bachelor's degree or more				
							total	bachelor's degree	master's degree	professional degree	doctoral degree
TOTAL MEN AGED 65+	**15,151**	**2,004**	**1,803**	**4,797**	**2,125**	**663**	**3,759**	**2,134**	**904**	**376**	**345**
Without earnings	**11,653**	**1,736**	**1,530**	**3,796**	**1,596**	**482**	**2,514**	**1,469**	**611**	**229**	**205**
With earnings	**3,497**	**267**	**273**	**1,002**	**529**	**181**	**1,245**	**665**	**292**	**147**	**140**
Under $10,000	1,074	76	93	357	147	67	332	208	80	20	23
$10,000 to $19,999	638	86	75	200	79	21	178	115	38	10	13
$20,000 to $29,999	396	46	46	119	79	27	79	34	23	12	10
$30,000 to $39,999	375	23	28	111	73	13	128	84	26	7	11
$40,000 to $49,999	227	17	12	88	37	15	57	42	7	3	5
$50,000 to $59,999	165	5	7	37	29	13	72	35	21	9	7
$60,000 to $69,999	130	4	3	22	27	3	71	38	11	3	19
$70,000 to $79,999	113	1	1	21	17	9	62	24	12	13	13
$80,000 to $89,999	66	1	4	22	6	1	34	17	9	5	1
$90,000 to $99,999	33	3	–	7	9	2	13	2	6	4	1
$100,000 or more	281	4	6	19	27	9	216	66	55	59	35
Median earnings of men with earnings	$20,527	$13,319	$12,116	$16,497	$23,492	$20,239	$31,243	$21,137	$30,633	$76,494	$52,352
Median earnings of full-time workers	37,378	26,548	25,458	31,908	39,141	38,215	60,503	48,829	57,284	100,000+	–
Percent working full-time	10.1%	6.3%	6.3%	8.9%	11.6%	11.8%	14.5%	12.7%	14.2%	21.3%	18.6%

(continued)

TOTAL MEN AGED 65+	total	less than 9th grade	9th to 12th grade, no degree	high school graduate, including GED	some college, no degree	associate's degree	bachelor's degree or more				
							total	bachelor's degree	master's degree	professional degree	doctoral degree
	100.0%	100.0%	100.0%	100.0%	100.0%	100.0%	100.0%	100.0%	100.0%	100.0%	100.0%
Without earnings	76.9	86.6	84.9	79.1	75.1	72.7	66.9	68.8	67.6	60.9	59.4
With earnings	23.1	13.3	15.1	20.9	24.9	27.3	33.1	31.2	32.3	39.1	40.6
Under $10,000	7.1	3.8	5.2	7.4	6.9	10.1	8.8	9.7	8.8	5.3	6.7
$10,000 to $19,999	4.2	4.3	4.2	4.2	3.7	3.2	4.7	5.4	4.2	2.7	3.8
$20,000 to $29,999	2.6	2.3	2.6	2.5	3.7	4.1	2.1	1.6	2.5	3.2	2.9
$30,000 to $39,999	2.5	1.1	1.6	2.3	3.4	2.0	3.4	3.9	2.9	1.9	3.2
$40,000 to $49,999	1.5	0.8	0.7	1.8	1.7	2.3	1.5	2.0	0.8	0.8	1.4
$50,000 to $59,999	1.1	0.2	0.4	0.8	1.4	2.0	1.9	1.6	2.3	2.4	2.0
$60,000 to $69,999	0.9	0.2	0.2	0.5	1.3	0.5	1.9	1.8	1.2	0.8	5.5
$70,000 to $79,999	0.7	0.0	0.1	0.4	0.8	1.4	1.6	1.1	1.3	3.5	3.8
$80,000 to $89,999	0.4	0.0	0.2	0.5	0.3	0.2	0.9	0.8	1.0	1.3	0.3
$90,000 to $99,999	0.2	0.1	–	0.1	0.4	0.3	0.3	0.1	0.7	1.1	0.3
$100,000 or more	1.9	0.2	0.3	0.4	1.3	1.4	5.7	3.1	6.1	15.7	10.1

Note: "–" means number is less than 500 or sample is too small to make a reliable estimate.
Source: Bureau of the Census, 2005 Current Population Survey Annual Social and Economic Supplement, Internet site http://pubdb3.census.gov/macro/032005/perinc/new03_000.htm; calculations by New Strategist

Table 4.30 Earnings of Women by Education, 2004: Aged 55 to 64

(number and percent distribution of women aged 55 to 64 by earnings and education, 2004; women in thousands as of 2005)

	total	less than 9th grade	9th to 12th grade, no degree	high school graduate, including GED	some college, no degree	associate's degree	bachelor's degree or more total	bachelor's degree	master's degree	professional degree	doctoral degree
TOTAL WOMEN AGED 55 TO 64	15,484	836	1,227	5,476	2,671	1,429	3,845	2,308	1,255	137	145
Without earnings	6,144	567	768	2,384	974	415	1,036	710	266	38	22
With earnings	9,341	269	459	3,092	1,697	1,015	2,809	1,597	989	99	123
Under $10,000	1,617	95	128	605	294	127	368	242	111	9	6
$10,000 to $19,999	1,841	99	185	778	312	196	267	179	83	4	3
$20,000 to $29,999	1,863	53	92	800	407	186	326	236	75	10	6
$30,000 to $39,999	1,382	17	40	467	322	193	341	227	102	3	9
$40,000 to $49,999	911	2	5	211	160	129	404	233	142	17	13
$50,000 to $59,999	606	2	9	92	89	87	327	144	149	11	22
$60,000 to $69,999	411	–	1	66	37	59	247	140	99	4	3
$70,000 to $79,999	227	–	–	29	21	13	166	72	71	5	17
$80,000 to $89,999	154	–	–	24	20	5	105	43	44	10	8
$90,000 to $99,999	118	–	–	10	9	9	89	32	48	–	9
$100,000 or more	213	–	–	9	23	12	168	53	65	27	24
Median earnings of women with earnings	$25,738	$12,959	$15,525	$21,644	$24,981	$29,902	$41,506	$36,075	$47,905	$57,622	$60,861
Median earnings of full-time workers	32,215	18,674	19,775	26,963	30,757	35,277	48,939	43,517	53,007	76,555	78,734
Percent working full-time	38.7%	18.5%	21.4%	35.3%	42.7%	48.8%	47.0%	44.3%	49.6%	56.9%	57.9%

(continued)

TOTAL WOMEN AGED 55 TO 64	total	less than 9th grade	9th to 12th grade, no degree	high school graduate, including GED	some college, no degree	associate's degree	bachelor's degree or more				
							total	bachelor's degree	master's degree	professional degree	doctoral degree
TOTAL WOMEN AGED 55 TO 64	100.0%	100.0%	100.0%	100.0%	100.0%	100.0%	100.0%	100.0%	100.0%	100.0%	100.0%
Without earnings	**39.7**	**67.8**	**62.6**	**43.5**	**36.5**	**29.0**	**26.9**	**30.8**	**21.2**	**27.7**	**15.2**
With earnings	**60.3**	**32.2**	**37.4**	**56.5**	**63.5**	**71.0**	**73.1**	**69.2**	**78.8**	**72.3**	**84.8**
Under $10,000	10.4	11.4	10.4	11.0	11.0	8.9	9.6	10.5	8.8	6.6	4.1
$10,000 to $19,999	11.9	11.8	15.1	14.2	11.7	13.7	6.9	7.8	6.6	2.9	2.1
$20,000 to $29,999	12.0	6.3	7.5	14.6	15.2	13.0	8.5	10.2	6.0	7.3	4.1
$30,000 to $39,999	8.9	2.0	3.3	8.5	12.1	13.5	8.9	9.8	8.1	2.2	6.2
$40,000 to $49,999	5.9	0.2	0.4	3.9	6.0	9.0	10.5	10.1	11.3	12.4	9.0
$50,000 to $59,999	3.9	0.2	0.7	1.7	3.3	6.1	8.5	6.2	11.9	8.0	15.2
$60,000 to $69,999	2.7	—	0.1	1.2	1.4	4.1	6.4	6.1	7.9	2.9	2.1
$70,000 to $79,999	1.5	—	—	0.5	0.8	0.9	4.3	3.1	5.7	3.6	11.7
$80,000 to $89,999	1.0	—	—	0.4	0.7	0.3	2.7	1.9	3.5	7.3	5.5
$90,000 to $99,999	0.8	—	—	0.2	0.3	0.6	2.3	1.4	3.8	—	6.2
$100,000 or more	1.4	—	—	0.2	0.9	0.8	4.4	2.3	5.2	19.7	16.6

Note: "—" means number is less than 500, percentage is less than 0.05, or sample is too small to make a reliable estimate.
Source: Bureau of the Census, 2005 Current Population Survey Annual Social and Economic Supplement, Internet site http://pubdb3.census.gov/macro/032005/perinc/new03_000.htm; calculations by New Strategist

Table 4.31 Earnings of Women by Education, 2004: Aged 65 or Older

(number and percent distribution of women aged 65 or older by earnings and education, 2004; women in thousands as of 2005)

	total	less than 9th grade	9th to 12th grade, no degree	high school graduate, including GED	some college, no degree	associate's degree	bachelor's degree or more				
							total	bachelor's degree	master's degree	professional degree	doctoral degree
TOTAL WOMEN AGED 65+	20,063	2,717	2,659	8,004	2,675	1,139	2,868	1,902	788	114	64
Without earnings	17,212	2,561	2,419	6,927	2,177	874	2,254	1,532	606	84	33
With earnings	2,851	156	240	1,077	499	265	614	370	182	31	32
Under $10,000	1,225	64	145	432	230	90	265	165	80	3	16
$10,000 to $19,999	653	65	60	288	91	90	57	40	15	2	—
$20,000 to $29,999	427	19	20	205	73	40	69	40	22	7	—
$30,000 to $39,999	202	5	6	82	37	17	56	34	19	3	—
$40,000 to $49,999	103	—	7	25	16	9	46	31	12	2	—
$50,000 to $59,999	68	—	—	19	19	6	25	15	7	—	3
$60,000 to $69,999	49	3	—	8	10	5	23	16	2	1	4
$70,000 to $79,999	53	—	1	6	10	—	35	14	6	9	6
$80,000 to $89,999	20	—	—	4	—	—	16	5	11	—	—
$90,000 to $99,999	24	—	—	2	6	10	6	2	2	2	—
$100,000 or more	28	—	—	7	6	—	14	7	5	1	1
Median earnings of women with earnings	$11,789	$11,189	$6,997	$12,098	$11,797	$13,629	$14,467	$12,592	$14,012	—	—
Median earnings of full-time workers	26,640	—	—	22,465	30,557	27,235	45,263	42,679	—	—	—
Percent working full-time	4.8%	2.3%	2.6%	4.9%	5.7%	6.8%	7.7%	6.3%	8.2%	18.4%	21.9%

(continued)

TOTAL WOMEN AGED 65+	total	less than 9th grade	9th to 12th grade, no degree	high school graduate, including GED	some college, no degree	associate's degree	bachelor's degree or more				
							total	bachelor's degree	master's degree	professional degree	doctoral degree
	100.0%	100.0%	100.0%	100.0%	100.0%	100.0%	100.0%	100.0%	100.0%	100.0%	100.0%
Without earnings	**85.8**	**94.3**	**91.0**	**86.5**	**81.4**	**76.7**	**78.6**	**80.5**	**76.9**	**73.7**	**51.6**
With earnings	**14.2**	**5.7**	**9.0**	**13.5**	**18.7**	**23.3**	**21.4**	**19.5**	**23.1**	**27.2**	**50.0**
Under $10,000	6.1	2.4	5.5	5.4	8.6	7.9	9.2	8.7	10.2	2.6	25.0
$10,000 to $19,999	3.3	2.4	2.3	3.6	3.4	7.9	2.0	2.1	1.9	1.8	–
$20,000 to $29,999	2.1	0.7	0.8	2.6	2.7	3.5	2.4	2.1	2.8	6.1	–
$30,000 to $39,999	1.0	0.2	0.2	1.0	1.4	1.5	2.0	1.8	2.4	2.6	–
$40,000 to $49,999	0.5	–	0.3	0.3	0.6	0.8	1.6	1.6	1.5	1.8	–
$50,000 to $59,999	0.3	–	–	0.2	0.7	0.5	0.9	0.8	0.9	–	4.7
$60,000 to $69,999	0.2	0.1	–	0.1	0.4	0.4	0.8	0.8	0.3	0.9	6.3
$70,000 to $79,999	0.3	–	–	0.1	0.4	–	1.2	0.7	0.8	7.9	9.4
$80,000 to $89,999	0.1	–	–	–	–	–	0.6	0.3	1.4	–	–
$90,000 to $99,999	0.1	–	–	–	0.2	0.9	0.2	0.1	0.3	1.8	–
$100,000 or more	0.1	0.0	0.0	0.1	0.2	0.0	0.5	0.4	0.6	0.9	1.6

Note: "–" means number is less than 500, percentage is less than 0.05, or sample is too small to make a reliable estimate.
Source: Bureau of the Census, 2005 Current Population Survey Annual Social and Economic Supplement, Internet site http://pubdb3.census.gov/macro/032005/perinc/new03_000.htm; calculations by New Strategist

Most Older Americans Receive Social Security

The Social Security income of older Americans exceeds their pension or interest income.

Among Americans aged 65 or older, 90 to 92 percent received income from Social Security in 2004, making it the most-common source of income for the age group. The amount of Social Security income received by people aged 65 or older is modest, however, ranging from $8,879 for women to $12,573 for men. Among men and women aged 55 to 64, only 17 to 21 percent receive Social Security, most collecting it because they opted to retire at age 62.

Besides Social Security, the only other type of income received by the majority of people aged 65 or older is interest, which more than half receive. But the median amount of interest income received by older Americans is small, about $1,600 annually.

Forty-four percent of men aged 65 or older received pension income in 2004, collecting a median of $12,159. A much smaller 22 percent of women receive pension income, and the amount they collect is also smaller than that of men—a median of just $6,350 in 2004.

■ As Baby Boomers enter the 65-or-older age group, expect the percentage of older Americans with earnings to increase.

Social Security income is modest

(median annual Social Security income received by people aged 65 or older, by sex, 2004)

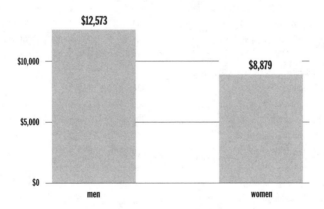

Table 4.32 Sources of Income for Men Aged 55 to 64, 2004

(number and percent distribution of men aged 55 to 64 with income and median income for those with income, by selected sources of income, 2004; men in thousands as of 2005; ranked by percent receiving source)

	number	percent with income	median income
Total men aged 55 to 64 with income	**13,596**	**100.0%**	**$39,212**
Earnings	10,309	75.8	41,673
Wages and salary	9,153	67.3	42,730
Nonfarm self-employment	1,409	10.4	21,074
Farm self-employment	271	2.0	3,649
Property income	8,338	61.3	1,792
Interest	7,866	57.9	1,521
Dividends	3,577	26.3	1,680
Rents, royalties, estates or trusts	1,286	9.5	2,223
Retirement income	2,750	20.2	18,490
Company or union retirement	1,559	11.5	14,479
State or local government retirement	520	3.8	23,462
Federal government retirement	256	1.9	24,891
Military retirement	255	1.9	16,760
Annuities	57	0.4	–
IRA, Keogh, or 401(k)	53	0.4	–
Railroad retirement	45	0.3	–
Pension income	2,462	18.1	18,338
Company or union retirement	1,463	10.8	14,101
State or local government retirement	465	3.4	25,630
Military retirement	241	1.8	16,514
Federal government retirement	238	1.8	28,091
Annuities	43	0.3	–
Railroad retirement	31	0.2	–
Social Security	2,336	17.2	12,162
SSI (Supplemental Security Income)	400	2.9	6,642
Veterans' benefits	603	4.4	9,128
Unemployment compensation	459	3.4	3,168
Disability benefits	299	2.2	13,260
Workers' compensation	194	1.4	2,819
Survivor benefits	99	0.7	19,234
Educational assistance	57	0.4	–
Financial assistance from other household	36	0.3	–
Public assistance	32	0.2	–
Alimony	5	0.0	–
Child support	3	0.0	–
Other income	63	0.5	–

Note: "–" means sample is too small to make a reliable estimate.
Source: Bureau of the Census, 2005 Current Population Survey Annual Social and Economic Supplement, Internet site http://pubdb3.census.gov/macro/032005/perinc/new08_000.htm; calculations by New Strategist

Table 4.33 Sources of Income for Men Aged 65 or Older, 2004

(number and percent distribution of men aged 65 or older with income and median income for those with income, by selected sources of income, 2004; men in thousands as of 2005; ranked by percent receiving source)

	number	percent with income	median income
Total men aged 65 or older with income	**14,836**	**100.0%**	**$21,102**
Social Security	13,315	89.7	12,573
Property income	9,009	60.7	1,953
Interest	8,446	56.9	1,648
Dividends	3,467	23.4	1,880
Rents, royalties, estates or trusts	1,423	9.6	2,329
Retirement income	6,826	46.0	12,302
Company or union retirement	4,545	30.6	9,226
State or local government retirement	1,018	6.9	20,153
Federal government retirement	713	4.8	23,716
Military retirement	348	2.3	16,710
IRA, Keogh, or 401(k)	220	1.5	7,067
Annuities	148	1.0	9,182
Railroad retirement	124	0.8	22,699
Pension income	6,487	43.7	12,159
Company or union retirement	4,434	29.9	9,225
State or local government retirement	967	6.5	20,367
Federal government retirement	677	4.6	24,158
Military retirement	336	2.3	15,856
Railroad retirement	121	0.8	22,857
Annuities	110	0.7	6,481
Earnings	3,497	23.6	20,527
Wages and salary	2,778	18.7	21,401
Nonfarm self-employment	689	4.6	12,375
Farm self-employment	226	1.5	2,261
Veterans' benefits	850	5.7	5,371
SSI (Supplemental Security Income)	361	2.4	4,652
Survivor benefits	281	1.9	9,277
Unemployment compensation	115	0.8	2,356
Disability benefits	100	0.7	15,118
Workers' compensation	53	0.4	–
Financial assistance from other household	52	0.4	–
Public assistance	10	0.1	–
Child support	5	0.0	–
Educational assistance	5	0.0	–
Alimony	3	0.0	–
Other income	39	0.3	–

Note: "–" means sample is too small to make a reliable estimate.
Source: Bureau of the Census, 2005 Current Population Survey Annual Social and Economic Supplement, Internet site http://pubdb3.census.gov/macro/032005/perinc/new08_000.htm; calculations by New Strategist

Table 4.34 Sources of Income for Men Aged 65 to 74, 2004

(number and percent distribution of men aged 65 to 74 with income and median income for those with income, by selected sources of income, 2004; men in thousands as of 2005; ranked by percent receiving source)

	number	percent with income	median income
Total men aged 65 to 74 with income	**8,279**	**100.0%**	**$24,161**
Social Security	7,257	87.7	12,861
Property income	5,056	61.1	1,976
Interest	4,747	57.3	1,668
Dividends	1,982	23.9	1,848
Rents, royalties, estates or trusts	816	9.9	2,449
Retirement income	3,627	43.8	14,761
Company or union retirement	2,379	28.7	10,695
State or local government retirement	547	6.6	21,634
Federal government retirement	379	4.6	23,401
Military retirement	219	2.6	17,658
IRA, Keogh, or 401(k)	124	1.5	7,410
Annuities	74	0.9	–
Railroad retirement	48	0.6	–
Pension income	3,468	41.9	14,479
Company or union retirement	2,325	28.1	10,772
State or local government retirement	521	6.3	21,647
Federal government retirement	362	4.4	23,883
Military retirement	216	2.6	17,650
Annuities	65	0.8	–
Railroad retirement	48	0.6	–
Earnings	2,694	32.5	22,089
Wages and salary	2,170	26.2	23,303
Nonfarm self-employment	525	6.3	14,979
Farm self-employment	161	1.9	2,027
Veterans' benefits	389	4.7	7,167
SSI (Supplemental Security Income)	230	2.8	4,567
Survivor benefits	120	1.4	8,945
Unemployment compensation	95	1.1	2,419
Disability benefits	56	0.7	–
Workers' compensation	41	0.5	–
Financial assistance from other household	27	0.3	–
Public assistance	6	0.1	–
Child support	5	0.1	–
Educational assistance	5	0.1	–
Alimony	0	0.0	–
Other income	36	0.4	–

Note: "–" means sample is too small to make a reliable estimate.
Source: Bureau of the Census, 2005 Current Population Survey Annual Social and Economic Supplement,.Internet site http://pubdb3.census.gov/macro/032005/perinc/new08_000.htm; calculations by New Strategist

Table 4.35 Sources of Income for Men Aged 75 or Older, 2004

(number and percent distribution of men aged 75 or older with income and median income for those with income, by selected sources of income, 2004; men in thousands as of 2005; ranked by percent receiving source)

	number	percent with income	median income
Total men aged 75 or older with income	**6,557**	**100.0%**	**$18,718**
Social Security	6,058	92.4	12,233
Property income	3,952	60.3	1,925
Interest	3,699	56.4	1,623
Dividends	1,484	22.6	1,925
Rents, royalties, estates or trusts	607	9.3	2,185
Retirement income	3,199	48.8	10,720
Company or union retirement	2,166	33.0	7,373
State or local government retirement	471	7.2	17,966
Federal government retirement	334	5.1	23,928
Military retirement	129	2.0	13,990
IRA, Keogh, or 401(k)	96	1.5	4,829
Railroad retirement	76	1.2	22,821
Annuities	74	1.1	–
Pension income	3,019	46.0	10,524
Company or union retirement	2,109	32.2	7,271
State or local government retirement	446	6.8	18,374
Federal government retirement	315	4.8	24,341
Military retirement	119	1.8	13,167
Railroad retirement	73	1.1	–
Annuities	45	0.7	–
Earnings	803	12.2	11,891
Wages and salary	608	9.3	12,192
Nonfarm self-employment	164	2.5	6,402
Farm self-employment	65	1.0	–
Veterans' benefits	460	7.0	4,682
Survivor benefits	161	2.5	9,530
SSI (Supplemental Security Income)	131	2.0	4,786
Disability benefits	44	0.7	–
Financial assistance from other household	25	0.4	–
Unemployment compensation	20	0.3	–
Workers' compensation	12	0.2	–
Public assistance	4	0.1	–
Alimony	3	0.0	–
Child support	0	0.0	–
Educational assistance	0	0.0	–
Other income	4	0.1	–

Note: "–" means sample is too small to make a reliable estimate.
Source: Bureau of the Census, 2005 Current Population Survey Annual Social and Economic Supplement, Internet site http://pubdb3.census.gov/macro/032005/perinc/new08_000.htm; calculations by New Strategist

Table 4.36 Sources of Income for Women Aged 55 to 64, 2004

(number and percent distribution of women aged 55 to 64 with income and median income for those with income, by selected sources of income, 2004; women in thousands as of 2005; ranked by percent receiving source)

	number	percent with income	median income
Total women aged 55 to 64 with income	**14,075**	**100.0%**	**$20,810**
Earnings	9,341	66.4	25,738
Wages and salary	8,666	61.6	26,371
Nonfarm self-employment	887	6.3	7,725
Farm self-employment	123	0.9	1,882
Property income	8,671	61.6	1,709
Interest	8,183	58.1	1,509
Dividends	3,473	24.7	1,652
Rents, royalties, estates or trusts	1,276	9.1	2,023
Social Security	2,902	20.6	7,768
Retirement income	1,936	13.8	11,332
Company or union retirement	995	7.1	8,173
State or local government retirement	619	4.4	16,720
Federal government retirement	152	1.1	19,414
Annuities	50	0.4	–
Military retirement	38	0.3	–
IRA, Keogh, or 401(k)	34	0.2	–
Railroad retirement	21	0.1	–
Pension income	1,460	10.4	13,169
Company or union retirement	793	5.6	8,414
State or local government retirement	527	3.7	18,328
Federal government retirement	93	0.7	23,936
Railroad retirement	20	0.1	–
Annuities	16	0.1	–
Military retirement	9	0.1	–
SSI (Supplemental Security Income)	543	3.9	5,465
Unemployment compensation	408	2.9	2,692
Survivor benefits	335	2.4	7,482
Disability benefits	243	1.7	8,346
Workers' compensation	183	1.3	5,212
Alimony	134	1.0	8,569
Child support	115	0.8	3,207
Public assistance	98	0.7	2,382
Educational assistance	85	0.6	1,696
Financial assistance from other household	84	0.6	2,042
Veterans' benefits	67	0.5	–
Other income	38	0.3	–

Note: "–" means sample is too small to make a reliable estimate.
Source: Bureau of the Census, 2005 Current Population Survey Annual Social and Economic Supplement, Internet site http:// pubdb3.census.gov/macro/032005/perinc/new08_000.htm; calculations by New Strategist

Table 4.37 Sources of Income for Women Aged 65 or Older, 2004

(number and percent distribution of women aged 65 or older with income and median income for those with income, by selected sources of income, 2004; women in thousands as of 2005; ranked by percent receiving source)

	number	percent with income	median income
Total women aged 65+ with income	**19,351**	**100.0%**	**$12,080**
Social Security	17,730	91.6	8,879
Property income	10,584	54.7	1,833
Interest	9,813	50.7	1,602
Dividends	3,603	18.6	1,710
Rents, royalties, estates or trusts	1,527	7.9	2,151
Retirement income	5,577	28.8	6,670
Company or union retirement	3,340	17.3	4,395
State or local government retirement	1,294	6.7	11,187
Federal government retirement	497	2.6	12,601
Annuities	191	1.0	5,266
IRA, Keogh, or 401(k)	146	0.8	4,904
Railroad retirement	144	0.7	11,419
Military retirement	93	0.5	7,408
Pension income	4,338	22.4	6,350
Company or union retirement	2,623	13.6	4,140
State or local government retirement	1,182	6.1	11,386
Federal government retirement	311	1.6	13,601
Railroad retirement	106	0.5	10,199
Annuities	74	0.4	–
Military retirement	10	0.1	–
Earnings	2,851	14.7	11,789
Wages and salary	2,543	13.1	12,291
Nonfarm self-employment	318	1.6	4,858
Farm self-employment	86	0.4	2,276
Survivor benefits	1,485	7.7	6,057
SSI (Supplemental Security Income)	818	4.2	3,487
Veterans' benefits	268	1.4	4,905
Financial assistance from other household	113	0.6	2,921
Workers' compensation	63	0.3	–
Unemployment compensation	60	0.3	–
Alimony	52	0.3	–
Disability benefits	49	0.3	–
Public assistance	39	0.2	–
Child support	22	0.1	–
Educational assistance	18	0.1	–
Other income	37	0.2	–

Note: "–" means sample is too small to make a reliable estimate.
Source: Bureau of the Census, 2005 Current Population Survey Annual Social and Economic Supplement, Internet site http:// pubdb3.census.gov/macro/032005/perinc/new08_000.htm; calculations by New Strategist

Table 4.38 Sources of Income for Women Aged 65 to 74, 2004

(number and percent distribution of women aged 65 to 74 with income and median income for those with income, by selected sources of income, 2004; women in thousands as of 2005)

	number	percent with income	median income
Total women aged 65 to 74 with income	**9,525**	**100.0%**	**$12,279**
Social Security	8,520	89.4	8,345
Property income	5,365	56.3	1,852
Interest	5,024	52.7	1,605
Dividends	1,882	19.8	1,718
Rents, royalties, estates or trusts	784	8.2	2,066
Retirement income	2,600	27.3	7,436
Company or union retirement	1,495	15.7	4,684
State or local government retirement	696	7.3	12,312
Federal government retirement	203	2.1	14,370
IRA, Keogh, or 401(k)	78	0.8	6,637
Railroad retirement	74	0.8	–
Annuities	52	0.5	–
Military retirement	44	0.5	–
Earnings	2,279	23.9	12,228
Wages and salary	2,051	21.5	12,947
Nonfarm self-employment	235	2.5	4,733
Farm self-employment	60	0.6	–
Pension income	2,161	22.7	7,417
Company or union retirement	1,253	13.2	4,613
State or local government retirement	653	6.9	12,826
Federal government retirement	139	1.5	15,217
Railroad retirement	54	0.6	–
Annuities	23	0.2	–
Military retirement	8	0.1	–
SSI (Supplemental Security Income)	405	4.3	3,457
Survivor benefits	517	5.4	5,665
Veterans' benefits	98	1.0	5,853
Financial assistance from other household	45	0.5	–
Unemployment compensation	42	0.4	–
Workers' compensation	41	0.4	–
Alimony	38	0.4	–
Disability benefits	34	0.4	–
Public assistance	29	0.3	–
Child support	17	0.2	–
Educational assistance	13	0.1	–
Other income	23	0.2	–

Note: "–" means sample is too small to make a reliable estimate.
Source: Bureau of the Census, 2005 Current Population Survey Annual Social and Economic Supplement, Internet site http:// pubdb3.census.gov/macro/032005/perinc/new08_000.htm; calculations by New Strategist

Table 4.39 Sources of Income for Women Aged 75 or Older, 2004

(number and percent distribution of women aged 75 or older with income and median income for those with income, by selected sources of income, 2004; women in thousands as of 2005)

	number	percent with income	median income
Total women aged 75+ with income	**9,826**	**100.0%**	**$11,944**
Social Security	9,210	93.7	9,405
Property income	5,218	53.1	1,814
Interest	4,789	48.7	1,599
Dividends	1,721	17.5	1,702
Rents, royalties, estates or trusts	743	7.6	2,248
Retirement income	2,977	30.3	6,063
Company or union retirement	1,846	18.8	4,157
State or local government retirement	598	6.1	10,458
Federal government retirement	294	3.0	11,852
Annuities	138	1.4	5,152
Railroad retirement	69	0.7	–
IRA, Keogh, or 401(k)	69	0.7	–
Military retirement	49	0.5	–
Pension income	2,177	22.2	5,460
Company or union retirement	1,370	13.9	3,734
State or local government retirement	529	5.4	10,266
Federal government retirement	173	1.8	12,419
Railroad retirement	53	0.5	–
Annuities	50	0.5	–
Military retirement	1	0.0	–
Earnings	572	5.8	9,743
Wages and salary	492	5.0	10,599
Nonfarm self-employment	82	0.8	5,557
Farm self-employment	26	0.3	–
Survivor benefits	968	9.9	6,241
SSI (Supplemental Security Income)	413	4.2	3,520
Veterans' benefits	170	1.7	4,689
Financial assistance from other household	67	0.7	–
Workers' compensation	22	0.2	–
Unemployment compensation	17	0.2	–
Disability benefits	15	0.2	–
Alimony	14	0.1	–
Public assistance	10	0.1	–
Educational assistance	5	0.1	–
Child support	4	0.0	–
Other income	13	0.1	–

Note: "–" means sample is too small to make a reliable estimate.
Source: Bureau of the Census, 2005 Current Population Survey Annual Social and Economic Supplement, Internet site http://pubdb3.census.gov/macro/032005/perinc/new08_000.htm; calculations by New Strategist

Table 4.40 Distribution of Average Annual Income by Source for People Aged 65 or Older, 2004

(average annual income of people aged 65 or older and percent distribution by source of income, by sex and age, 2004)

	total	men	women	65 to 69	70 to 74	75 to 79	80 to 84	85 or older
Average income	**22,801**	**31,371**	**16,329**	**28,082**	**23,597**	**20,278**	**19,118**	**17,325**
Total income	**100.0%**	**100.0%**	**100.0%**	**100.0%**	**100.0%**	**100.0%**	**100.0%**	**100.0%**
Social Security	41.8	35.2	51.4	31.6	40.5	48.2	51.9	59.1
Pensions, retirement plans	20.8	24.0	16.1	18.3	21.9	22.2	23.2	21.0
Income from assets	12.8	11.8	14.3	11.6	12.2	13.8	15.0	14.3
Earnings	22.7	26.9	16.8	36.9	23.6	14.2	7.1	3.4
Other	1.8	2.1	1.4	1.6	1.7	1.6	2.7	2.2

Note: Other income includes public assistance, Supplemental Security Income, unemployment compensation, workers' compensation, veterans benefits, nonpension survivors' benefits, nonpension disabilitiy benefits, educational assistance, child support, alimony, regular financial assistance from friends or relatives not living in household, and other sources.
Source: Employee Benefit Research Institute, "Income and the Elderly Population, Age 65 and Over, 2004," by Ken McDonnell, Notes, Vol. 27, No. 1, January 2006; Internet site http://www.ebri.org/

Poverty Rate Is below Average for Older Americans

Ten percent of people aged 55 or older are poor compared with a larger 13 percent of all Americans.

Of the nation's 37 million poor in 2004, just 17 percent were aged 55 or older. Older blacks and Hispanics are more than twice as likely to be poor as non-Hispanic whites, however. Among people aged 55 or older, only 8 to 11 percent of Asians and non-Hispanic whites are poor versus 17 percent of Hispanics and 21 percent of blacks.

Among Americans of all ages, non-Hispanic whites account for a 46 percent minority of the poor. Among Americans aged 55 or older, however, non-Hispanic whites account for the 63 percent majority of the poor. Blacks account for 20 percent of poor in the age group and Hispanics for 12 percent. Asians account for only 4 percent of poor people aged 55 or older.

■ The black and Hispanic share of poor people aged 55 or older will rise as more-diverse younger generations enter the 55-or-older age groups.

Among older Americans, blacks are most likely to be poor

(percent of people aged 55 or older living below poverty level, by race and Hispanic origin, 2004)

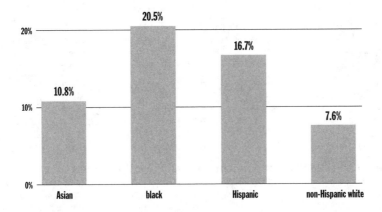

Table 4.41 People below Poverty Level by Age, Race, and Hispanic Origin, 2004

(number, percent, and percent distribution of people below poverty level by age, race, and Hispanic origin, 2004; people in thousands as of 2005)

	total	Asian	black	Hispanic	non-Hispanic white
NUMBER IN POVERTY					
Total people	**36,997**	**1,303**	**9,393**	**9,132**	**16,870**
Under age 55	30,798	1,061	8,167	8,382	12,968
Aged 55 or older	6,202	242	1,226	753	3,902
Aged 55 to 59	1,417	53	270	171	899
Aged 60 to 64	1,326	40	242	172	853
Aged 65 or older	3,459	149	714	410	2,150
Aged 65 to 74	1,723	86	386	250	982
Aged 75 to 84	1,253	53	240	119	829
Aged 85 or older	483	10	88	41	339
PERCENT IN POVERTY					
Total people	**12.7%**	**9.9%**	**24.7%**	**21.9%**	**8.6%**
Under age 55	13.6	9.5	25.5	22.5	9.0
Aged 55 or older	9.6	10.8	20.5	16.7	7.6
Aged 55 to 59	8.5	7.9	15.8	12.7	7.0
Aged 60 to 64	10.4	8.8	19.3	17.7	8.6
Aged 65 or older	9.8	13.4	23.8	18.7	7.5
Aged 65 to 74	9.4	13.0	22.2	19.0	6.8
Aged 75 to 84	9.7	14.2	25.5	17.2	7.6
Aged 85 or older	12.6	12.9	27.4	22.3	10.5
PERCENT DISTRIBUTION OF POOR BY AGE					
Total people	**100.0%**	**100.0%**	**100.0%**	**100.0%**	**100.0%**
Under age 55	83.2	81.4	86.9	91.8	76.9
Aged 55 or older	16.8	18.6	13.1	8.2	23.1
Aged 55 to 59	3.8	4.1	2.9	1.9	5.3
Aged 60 to 64	3.6	3.1	2.6	1.9	5.1
Aged 65 or older	9.3	11.4	7.6	4.5	12.7
Aged 65 to 74	4.7	6.6	4.1	2.7	5.8
Aged 75 to 84	3.4	4.1	2.6	1.3	4.9
Aged 85 or older	1.3	0.8	0.9	0.4	2.0
PERCENT DISTRIBUTION OF POOR BY RACE AND HISPANIC ORIGIN					
Total people	**100.0%**	**3.5%**	**25.4%**	**24.7%**	**45.6%**
Under age 55	100.0	3.4	26.5	27.2	42.1
Aged 55 or older	100.0	3.9	19.8	12.1	62.9
Aged 55 to 59	100.0	3.7	19.1	12.1	63.4
Aged 60 to 64	100.0	3.0	18.3	13.0	64.3
Aged 65 or older	100.0	4.3	20.6	11.9	62.2
Aged 65 to 74	100.0	5.0	22.4	14.5	57.0
Aged 75 to 84	100.0	4.2	19.2	9.5	66.2
Aged 85 or older	100.0	2.1	18.2	8.5	70.2

Note: Numbers will not add to total because Asians and blacks include those identifying themselves as being of the race alone and those identifying themselves as being of the race in combination with one or more other races, because Hispanics may be of any race, and because not all races are shown. Non-Hispanic whites include only those identifying themselves as white alone and not Hispanic.
Source: Bureau of the Census, 2005 Current Population Survey Annual Social and Economic Supplement, Internet site http://pubdb3.census.gov/macro/032005/pov/new34_100.htm; calculations by New Strategist

5

Labor Force

■ The end of early retirement can be seen in labor force participation trends among older Americans. Since 2000, the percentage of men aged 55 or older in the labor force has grown.

■ The sixties is a time of transition for most Americans, when their roles change from worker to retiree. The labor force participation rate drops sharply for men and women in their sixties.

■ Couples in which neither husband nor wife works become the majority in the 65-to-74 age group.

■ While only 11 percent of all men in the labor force work part-time, the proportion is 17 percent among men aged 55 or older.

■ Men and women aged 55 or older account for 30 percent of the self-employed, a much greater proportion than their share of all workers.

■ Job tenure is down for men aged 55 to 64. In 1991, men aged 55 to 64 had been with their current employer a median of 13.4 years. By 2004, the figure had fallen to 9.8 years.

■ Among men aged 55 or older, labor force participation should rise 2.6 percentage points between 2005 and 2014 compared with a decline of 0.3 percentage points among men under age 55.

Older Men Are More Likely to Work

The increase in participation has been especially sharp for men aged 62 to 74.

The end of early retirement can be seen clearly in labor force participation trends among older Americans. Since 2000—and despite (or perhaps because of) the weak economy—the percentage of men aged 55 or older in the labor force has grown, in some cases substantially. The labor force participation rate of men aged 62 to 64, the typical age of retirement, grew 5.5 percentage points between 2000 and 2005—to 52.5 percent. The figure had been as low as 45 percent in the mid-1990s. Among men aged 65 to 69, labor force participation increased 3.3 percentage points between 2000 and 2005—to 33.6 percent, the highest rate in more than two decades.

Among older women, the labor force participation rate rose substantially as well. Much of the increase has been due to the entry of a more career-oriented generation into the age group. Nevertheless, some of the rise is also due to declining stock market values and interest rates, driving older Americans back to work to supplement their dwindling retirement income.

■ As the Baby-Boom generation fills the 55-or-older age groups, the labor force participation rate of older Americans will continue to rise as early retirement becomes less common.

A growing share of men aged 62 to 74 are in the labor force

(percent of men aged 62 to 74 in the labor force, 2000 and 2005)

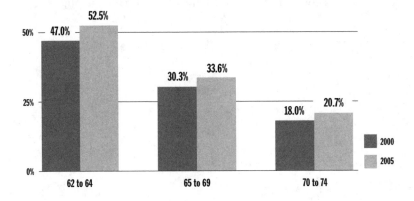

Table 5.1 Labor Force Participation Rate of People Aged 55 or Older by Sex, 1990 to 2005

(civilian labor force participation rate of people aged 16 or older and aged 55 or older, by sex, 1990 to 2005; percentage point change, 2000–2005 and 1990–2005)

	2005	2000	1990	percentage point change 2000–05	percentage point change 1990–2005
Men aged 16 or older	**73.3%**	**74.8%**	**76.4%**	**–1.5**	**–3.1**
Aged 55 to 64	69.3	67.3	67.8	2.0	1.5
Aged 55 to 59	77.6	77.0	79.9	0.6	–2.3
Aged 60 to 64	58.0	54.9	55.5	3.1	2.5
Aged 60 to 61	65.6	66.0	68.8	–0.4	–3.2
Aged 62 to 64	52.5	47.0	46.5	5.5	6.0
Aged 65 or older	19.8	17.7	16.3	2.1	3.5
Aged 65 to 69	33.6	30.3	26.0	3.3	7.6
Aged 70 to 74	20.7	18.0	15.4	2.7	5.3
Aged 75 or older	9.4	8.1	7.1	1.3	2.3
Women aged 16 or older	**59.3**	**59.9**	**57.5**	**–0.6**	**1.8**
Aged 55 to 64	57.0	51.9	45.2	5.1	11.8
Aged 55 to 59	65.6	61.4	55.3	4.2	10.3
Aged 60 to 64	45.8	40.2	35.5	5.6	10.3
Aged 60 to 61	53.8	49.0	42.9	4.8	10.9
Aged 62 to 64	40.0	34.1	30.7	5.9	9.3
Aged 65 or older	11.5	9.4	8.6	2.1	2.9
Aged 65 to 69	23.7	19.5	17.0	4.2	6.7
Aged 70 to 74	12.8	10.0	8.2	2.8	4.6
Aged 75 or older	4.5	3.6	2.7	0.9	1.8

Source: Bureau of Labor Statistics, Public Query Data Tool, Internet site http://www.bls.gov/data; and 2005 Current Population Survey, Internet site http://www.bls.gov/cps/home.htm; calculations by New Strategist

Labor Force Participation Rate Drops Sharply after Age 55

Most men aged 60 to 64 are in the labor force, but a minority of those aged 65 to 69 are still working.

The sixties is a time of transition for most Americans, when their roles change from worker to retiree. The labor force participation rate drops sharply with age. Among men aged 55 to 59, 78 percent are in the labor force. The figure falls to 58 percent among those aged 60 to 64, then drops to 34 percent among those aged 65 to 69. Only 9 percent of men aged 75 or older are in the labor force.

The 66 percent majority of women aged 55 to 59 are in the labor force, a figure that falls to a 46 percent minority among women aged 60 to 64. Only 24 percent of women aged 65 to 69 and 4 percent of those aged 75 or older are in the labor force.

■ The labor force participation rate of older Americans will rise in the coming decades as Baby Boomers postpone retirement.

Labor force participation falls with age

(percent of people aged 55 or older in the labor force, by sex, 2005)

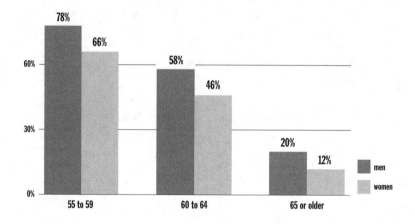

Table 5.2 Employment Status by Sex and Age, 2005

(number and percent of people aged 16 or older in the civilian labor force by sex and age, 2005; numbers in thousands)

	civilian noninstitutional population	civilian labor force			unemployed	
		total	percent of population	employed	number	percent of labor force
Total, aged 16 or older	**226,082**	**149,320**	**66.0%**	**141,730**	**7,591**	**5.1%**
Under age 55	160,849	125,064	77.8	118,287	6,777	5.4
Aged 55 or older	65,233	24,257	37.2	23,443	814	3.4
Aged 55 to 59	17,206	12,289	71.4	11,873	416	3.4
Aged 60 to 64	12,958	6,691	51.6	6,476	214	3.2
Aged 65 or older	35,068	5,278	15.1	5,094	184	3.5
Aged 65 to 69	10,048	2,846	28.3	2,748	98	3.4
Aged 70 to 74	8,358	1,366	16.3	1,316	50	3.7
Aged 75 or older	16,663	1,066	6.4	1,031	36	3.4
Men, aged 16 or older	**109,151**	**80,033**	**73.3**	**75,973**	**4,059**	**5.1**
Under age 55	79,706	67,029	84.1	63,403	3,626	5.4
Aged 55 or older	29,446	13,004	44.2	12,571	433	3.3
Aged 55 to 59	8,321	6,458	77.6	6,239	219	3.4
Aged 60 to 64	6,181	3,587	58.0	3,475	112	3.1
Aged 65 or older	14,944	2,959	19.8	2,857	102	3.4
Aged 65 to 69	4,678	1,571	33.6	1,519	52	3.3
Aged 70 to 74	3,745	775	20.7	748	27	3.5
Aged 75 or older	6,521	612	9.4	589	23	3.8
Women, aged 16 or older	**116,931**	**69,288**	**59.3**	**65,757**	**3,531**	**5.1**
Under age 55	81,143	58,034	71.5	54,883	3,151	5.4
Aged 55 or older	35,788	11,253	31.4	10,873	381	3.4
Aged 55 to 59	8,886	5,831	65.6	5,634	197	3.4
Aged 60 to 64	6,777	3,104	45.8	3,001	102	3.3
Aged 65 or older	20,125	2,319	11.5	2,238	82	3.5
Aged 65 to 69	5,370	1,275	23.7	1,228	46	3.6
Aged 70 to 74	4,613	591	12.8	568	23	3.9
Aged 75 or older	10,142	454	4.5	441	12	2.6

Source: Bureau of Labor Statistics, 2005 Current Population Survey, Internet site http://www.bls.gov/cps/home.htm; calculations by New Strategist

Labor Force Rates Differ by Race and Hispanic Origin

Ten percent of white men aged 75 or older are still in the labor force.

Labor force participation rates decline with advancing age, but the pace of the decline differs by race and Hispanic origin. Among men aged 55 to 59, nearly 85 percent of Asians are in the labor force. The participation rate in the age group is a smaller 79 percent among whites, 76 percent among Hispanics, and 66 percent among blacks. Asian men continue to have a higher labor force participation rate than blacks, Hispanics, or whites through the 65-to-69 age group. Among men aged 70 or older, however, Asians are least likely to work.

Among women aged 55 or older, Hispanic women have the lowest labor force participation rate. In the 55-to-59 age group, for example, just 58 percent of Hispanic women are in the labor force compared with 66 percent of Asian and white women. Regardless of race or Hispanic origin, the proportion of women who work falls below 50 percent in the 60-to-64 age group.

■ The labor force participation rate of older workers will rise as Baby-Boomers fill the 55-or-older age group in the years ahead.

Among men aged 55 to 64, Asians are most likely to work

(percent of men aged 55 to 64 in the labor force, by race and Hispanic origin, 2005)

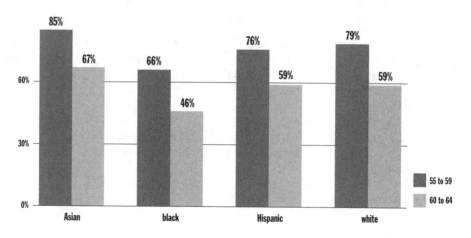

Table 5.3 Employment Status of Men by Race, Hispanic Origin, and Age, 2005

(number and percent of men aged 16 or older in the civilian labor force by race, Hispanic origin, and age, 2005; numbers in thousands)

	civilian noninstitutional population	civilian labor force total	percent of population	employed	unemployed number	percent of labor force
ASIAN MEN						
Total, aged 16 or older	**4,679**	**3,500**	**74.8%**	**3,359**	**141**	**4.0%**
Under age 55	3,685	3,005	81.5	2,884	121	4.0
Aged 55 or older	993	497	50.1	476	20	4.0
Aged 55 to 59	313	265	84.7	250	15	5.7
Aged 60 to 64	206	138	67.0	135	3	2.2
Aged 65 or older	474	94	19.8	91	3	3.2
Aged 65 to 69	174	64	36.8	61	2	3.1
Aged 70 to 74	119	19	16.0	19	–	–
Aged 75 or older	181	11	6.1	11	–	–
BLACK MEN						
Total, aged 16 or older	**11,882**	**7,998**	**67.3**	**7,155**	**844**	**10.6**
Under age 55	9,415	7,047	74.8	6,262	785	11.1
Aged 55 or older	2,467	952	38.6	893	59	6.2
Aged 55 to 59	754	496	65.8	464	32	6.5
Aged 60 to 64	565	260	46.0	247	13	5.0
Aged 65 or older	1,148	196	17.1	182	14	7.1
Aged 65 to 69	415	100	24.1	92	8	8.0
Aged 70 to 74	307	62	20.2	59	3	4.8
Aged 75 or older	426	34	8.0	31	3	8.8
HISPANIC MEN						
Total, aged 16 or older	**14,962**	**11,985**	**80.1**	**11,337**	**647**	**5.4**
Under age 55	12,886	11,014	85.5	10,407	607	5.5
Aged 55 or older	2,076	971	46.8	931	40	4.1
Aged 55 to 59	666	508	76.3	490	18	3.5
Aged 60 to 64	458	271	59.2	258	13	4.8
Aged 65 or older	953	192	20.1	183	9	4.7
Aged 65 to 69	327	114	34.9	109	5	4.4
Aged 70 to 74	253	45	17.8	42	3	6.7
Aged 75 or older	372	33	8.9	32	1	3.0
WHITE MEN						
Total, aged 16 or older	**90,027**	**66,694**	**74.1**	**63,763**	**2,931**	**4.4**
Under age 55	64,490	55,328	85.8	52,743	2,587	4.7
Aged 55 or older	25,539	11,363	44.5	11,022	344	3.0
Aged 55 to 59	7,113	5,599	78.7	5,431	169	3.0
Aged 60 to 64	5,302	3,134	59.1	3,040	94	3.0
Aged 65 or older	13,123	2,631	20.0	2,550	81	3.1
Aged 65 to 69	4,005	1,383	34.5	1,345	38	2.7
Aged 70 to 74	3,267	685	21.0	663	23	3.4
Aged 75 or older	5,852	562	9.6	543	20	3.6

Note: People who selected more than one race are not included. Hispanics may be of any race. "–" means sample is too small to make a reliable estimate.
Source: Bureau of Labor Statistics, 2005 Current Population Survey, Internet site http://www.bls.gov/cps/home.htm; calculations by New Strategist

Table 5.4 Employment Status of Women by Race, Hispanic Origin, and Age, 2005

(number and percent of women aged 16 or older in the civilian labor force by race, Hispanic origin, and age, 2005; numbers in thousands)

	civilian noninstitutional population	civilian labor force			unemployed	
		total	percent of population	employed	number	percent of labor force
ASIAN WOMEN						
Total, aged 16 or older	**5,163**	**3,002**	**58.1%**	**2,885**	**118**	**3.9%**
Under age 55	3,940	2,572	65.3	2,477	95	3.7
Aged 55 or older	1,222	430	35.2	409	22	5.1
Aged 55 to 59	362	238	65.7	226	12	5.0
Aged 60 to 64	242	116	47.9	109	8	6.9
Aged 65 or older	619	76	12.3	74	2	2.6
Aged 65 to 69	200	45	22.5	43	2	4.4
Aged 70 to 74	140	15	10.7	15	–	–
Aged 75 or older	278	16	5.8	16	–	–
BLACK WOMEN						
Total, aged 16 or older	**14,635**	**9,014**	**61.6**	**8,158**	**856**	**9.5**
Under age 55	11,155	7,916	71.0	7,120	796	10.1
Aged 55 or older	3,479	1,098	31.6	1,037	62	5.6
Aged 55 to 59	948	585	61.7	552	34	5.8
Aged 60 to 64	712	306	43.0	292	14	4.6
Aged 65 or older	1,819	207	11.4	193	14	6.8
Aged 65 to 69	563	122	21.7	114	8	6.6
Aged 70 to 74	452	55	12.2	50	4	7.3
Aged 75 or older	804	–	–	29	1	–
HISPANIC WOMEN						
Total, aged 16 or older	**14,172**	**7,839**	**55.3**	**7,295**	**544**	**6.9**
Under age 55	11,645	7,121	61.2	6,612	509	7.1
Aged 55 or older	2,527	717	28.4	682	36	5.0
Aged 55 to 59	699	404	57.8	385	19	4.7
Aged 60 to 64	539	194	36.0	184	11	5.7
Aged 65 or older	1,289	119	9.2	113	6	5.0
Aged 65 to 69	405	66	16.3	63	3	4.5
Aged 70 to 74	354	35	9.9	33	2	5.7
Aged 75 or older	530	18	3.4	18	1	5.6
WHITE WOMEN						
Total, aged 16 or older	**94,419**	**55,605**	**58.9**	**53,186**	**2,419**	**4.4**
Under age 55	63,867	46,071	72.1	43,939	2,132	4.6
Aged 55 or older	30,552	9,535	31.2	9,247	287	3.0
Aged 55 to 59	7,405	4,906	66.3	4,761	145	3.0
Aged 60 to 64	5,714	2,636	46.1	2,556	79	3.0
Aged 65 or older	17,433	1,993	11.4	1,930	63	3.2
Aged 65 to 69	4,522	1,086	24.0	1,052	34	3.1
Aged 70 to 74	3,948	505	12.8	487	18	3.6
Aged 75 or older	8,964	402	4.5	391	11	2.7

Note: People who selected more than one race are not included. Hispanics may be of any race. "–" means sample is too small to make a reliable estimate.
Source: Bureau of Labor Statistics, 2005 Current Population Survey, Internet site http://www.bls.gov/cps/home.htm; calculations by New Strategist

Few Older Couples Are Dual Earners

Nearly half of couples in the 55-to-64 age group are dual earners, however.

Dual incomes are the norm among married couples. Both husband and wife are in the labor force in 55 percent of the nation's couples. In another 23 percent, the husband is the only worker. Not far behind are the 17 percent of couples in which neither spouse is in the labor force. The wife is the sole worker among 6 percent of couples.

The 68 percent majority of couples under age 55 are dual earners. Among those aged 55 or older, however, both spouses are in the labor force in only 28 percent. The figure is a much higher 47 percent among couples aged 55 to 64. The wife is the only one employed in a substantial 13 percent of couples in the 55-to-64 age group. In these homes, typically, the older husband is retired, while the younger wife is still at work. For 71 percent of couples aged 65 or older, neither husband nor wife is working.

■ As Boomers fill the 55-to-64 age group, the dual-income couple share will rise because fewer Boomers will have the opportunity to retire before age 65.

Dual earners account for nearly half of couples aged 55 to 64

(percent of married couples in which both husband and wife are in the labor force, by age, 2004)

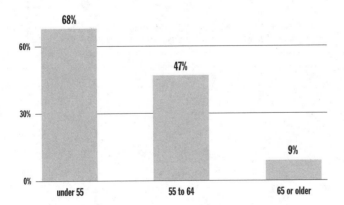

Table 5.5 Labor Force Status of Married-Couple Family Groups by Age of Reference Person, 2004

(number and percent distribution of married-couple family groups by age of reference person and labor force status of husband and wife, 2004; numbers in thousands)

	total	husband and/or wife in labor force husband and wife	husband only	wife only	neither husband nor wife in labor force
Total married-couple family groups	**59,064**	**32,199**	**13,328**	**3,771**	**9,766**
Under age 55	39,081	26,607	9,983	1,564	933
Aged 55 or older	19,983	5,594	3,347	2,210	8,833
Aged 55 to 64	10,013	4,741	2,274	1,257	1,741
Aged 65 or older	9,970	853	1,073	953	7,092
Aged 65 to 74	6,118	748	874	781	3,715
Aged 75 or older	3,852	105	199	172	3,377
PERCENT DISTRIBUTION					
Total married-couple family groups	**100.0%**	**54.5%**	**22.6%**	**6.4%**	**16.5%**
Under age 55	100.0	68.1	25.5	4.0	2.4
Aged 55 or older	100.0	28.0	16.7	11.1	44.2
Aged 55 to 64	100.0	47.3	22.7	12.6	17.4
Aged 65 or older	100.0	8.6	10.8	9.6	71.1
Aged 65 to 74	100.0	12.2	14.3	12.8	60.7
Aged 75 or older	100.0	2.7	5.2	4.5	87.7

Source: Bureau of the Census, 2004 Current Population Survey Annual Demographic Supplement, Internet site http://www .census.gov/population/www/socdemo/hh-fam/cps2004.html; calculations by New Strategist

Few Working Americans Are Aged 55 or Older

Only 17 percent of the nation's 142 million employed are aged 55 or older.

The share of workers aged 55 or older varies by occupation. Only 8 percent of computer software engineers are aged 55 or older, for example, because of the rapid technological change that has occurred since older Americans began their career. Only 6 percent of firefighters and 8 percent of police are aged 55 or older, in part because of the physical requirements of the job and also because of early retirement options in those careers.

Workers aged 55 or older account for a disproportionate share of some occupations, however. They are 53 percent of all legislators, for example. They are 31 percent of writers and authors, 32 percent of farmers and ranchers, 34 percent of real estate agents, and 38 percent of psychologists.

■ As Boomers age into their sixties, expect to see a growing share of older workers in technical jobs.

People aged 55 or older account for few workers in technical occupations

(percent of workers aged 55 or older, by occupation, 2005)

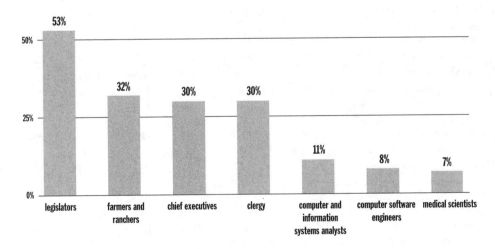

Table 5.6 Occupation of Workers Aged 55 or Older, 2005

(number of employed workers aged 16 or older, median age of workers, and number of workers aged 55 or older, by occupation, 2005; numbers in thousands)

	total	median age	aged 55 or older total	55 to 64	65 or older
TOTAL WORKERS	**141,730**	**40.7**	**23,443**	**18,349**	**5,094**
Management and professional occupations	**49,245**	**43.1**	**9,280**	**7,386**	**1,894**
Management, business and financial operations	20,450	44.3	4,303	3,328	975
Management	14,685	45.1	3,285	2,509	776
Business and financial operations	5,765	42.1	1,018	819	199
Professional and related occupations	28,795	42.2	4,977	4,058	919
Computer and mathematical	3,246	39.4	310	287	23
Architecture and engineering	2,793	42.3	440	350	90
Life, physical, and social sciences	1,406	41.6	245	197	48
Community and social services	2,138	44.0	456	360	96
Legal	1,614	43.9	339	271	68
Education, training, and library	8,114	43.0	1,571	1,322	249
Arts, design, entertainment, sports, and media	2,736	40.5	466	336	130
Health care practitioner and technician	6,748	42.9	1,150	935	215
Service occupations	**23,133**	**36.9**	**3,235**	**2,387**	**848**
Health care support	3,092	38.4	405	321	84
Protective service	2,894	40.6	424	318	106
Food preparation and serving	7,374	28.6	618	450	168
Building and grounds cleaning and maintenance	5,241	41.5	992	729	263
Personal care and service	4,531	38.6	795	568	227
Sales and office occupations	**35,962**	**39.9**	**6,189**	**4,718**	**1,471**
Sales and related occupations	16,433	39.1	2,886	2,084	802
Office and administrative support	19,529	40.5	3,303	2,634	669
Natural resources, construction, and maintenance occupations	**15,348**	**38.9**	**1,819**	**1,515**	**304**
Farming, fishing, and forestry	976	36.8	132	102	30
Construction and extraction	9,145	38.0	922	764	158
Installation, maintenance, and repair	5,226	40.8	766	649	117
Production, transportation, and material-moving occupations	**18,041**	**41.0**	**2,920**	**2,343**	**577**
Production	9,378	41.5	1,467	1,240	227
Transportation and material moving	8,664	40.5	1,453	1,103	350

Source: Bureau of Labor Statistics, unpublished data from the 2005 Current Population Survey; calculations by New Strategist

Table 5.7 Distribution of Workers Aged 55 or Older by Occupation, 2005

(percent distribution of employed people aged 16 or older and aged 55 or older by occupation, 2005)

	total	aged 55 or older		
		total	55 to 64	65 or older
TOTAL WORKERS	**100.0%**	**16.5%**	**12.9%**	**3.6%**
Management and professional occupations	**100.0**	**18.8**	**15.0**	**3.8**
Management, business and financial operations	100.0	21.0	16.3	4.8
Management	100.0	22.4	17.1	5.3
Business and financial operations	100.0	17.7	14.2	3.5
Professional and related occupations	100.0	17.3	14.1	3.2
Computer and mathematical	100.0	9.6	8.8	0.7
Architecture and engineering	100.0	15.8	12.5	3.2
Life, physical, and social sciences	100.0	17.4	14.0	3.4
Community and social services	100.0	21.3	16.8	4.5
Legal	100.0	21.0	16.8	4.2
Education, training, and library	100.0	19.4	16.3	3.1
Arts, design, entertainment, sports, and media	100.0	17.0	12.3	4.8
Health care practitioner and technician	100.0	17.0	13.9	3.2
Service occupations	**100.0**	**14.0**	**10.3**	**3.7**
Health care support	100.0	13.1	10.4	2.7
Protective service	100.0	14.7	11.0	3.7
Food preparation and serving	100.0	8.4	6.1	2.3
Building and grounds cleaning and maintenance	100.0	18.9	13.9	5.0
Personal care and service	100.0	17.5	12.5	5.0
Sales and office occupations	**100.0**	**17.2**	**13.1**	**4.1**
Sales and related occupations	100.0	17.6	12.7	4.9
Office and administrative support	100.0	16.9	13.5	3.4
Natural resources, construction, maintenance occupations	**100.0**	**11.9**	**9.9**	**2.0**
Farming, fishing, and forestry	100.0	13.5	10.5	3.1
Construction and extraction	100.0	10.1	8.4	1.7
Installation, maintenance, and repair	100.0	14.7	12.4	2.2
Production, transportation, material-moving occupations	**100.0**	**16.2**	**13.0**	**3.2**
Production	100.0	15.6	13.2	2.4
Transportation and material moving	100.0	16.8	12.7	4.0

Source: Calculations by New Strategist based on Bureau of Labor Statistics' unpublished 2005 Current Population Survey data

Table 5.8 Share of Workers Aged 55 or Older by Occupation, 2005

(percent distribution of total employed and employed aged 55 or older, by occupation, 2005)

	total	aged 55 or older total	55 to 64	65 or older
TOTAL WORKERS	100.0%	100.0%	100.0%	100.0%
Management and professional occupations	**34.7**	**39.6**	**40.3**	**37.2**
Management, business and financial operations	14.4	18.4	18.1	19.1
Management	10.4	14.0	13.7	15.2
Business and financial operations	4.1	4.3	4.5	3.9
Professional and related occupations	20.3	21.2	22.1	18.0
Computer and mathematical	2.3	1.3	1.6	0.5
Architecture and engineering	2.0	1.9	1.9	1.8
Life, physical, and social sciences	1.0	1.0	1.1	0.9
Community and social services	1.5	1.9	2.0	1.9
Legal	1.1	1.4	1.5	1.3
Education, training, and library	5.7	6.7	7.2	4.9
Arts, design, entertainment, sports, and media	1.9	2.0	1.8	2.6
Health care practitioner and technician	4.8	4.9	5.1	4.2
Service occupations	**16.3**	**13.8**	**13.0**	**16.6**
Health care support	2.2	1.7	1.7	1.6
Protective service	2.0	1.8	1.7	2.1
Food preparation and serving	5.2	2.6	2.5	3.3
Building and grounds cleaning and maintenance	3.7	4.2	4.0	5.2
Personal care and service	3.2	3.4	3.1	4.5
Sales and office occupations	**25.4**	**26.4**	**25.7**	**28.9**
Sales and related occupations	11.6	12.3	11.4	15.7
Office and administrative support	13.8	14.1	14.4	13.1
Natural resources, construction, maintenance occupations	**10.8**	**7.8**	**8.3**	**6.0**
Farming, fishing, and forestry	0.7	0.6	0.6	0.6
Construction and extraction	6.5	3.9	4.2	3.1
Installation, maintenance, and repair	3.7	3.3	3.5	2.3
Production, transportation, material-moving occupations	**12.7**	**12.5**	**12.8**	**11.3**
Production	6.6	6.3	6.8	4.5
Transportation and material moving	6.1	6.2	6.0	6.9

Source: Calculations by New Strategist based on Bureau of Labor Statistics' unpublished 2005 Current Population Survey data

Table 5.9 Workers Aged 55 or Older by Detailed Occupation, 2005

(number of employed workers aged 16 or older, median age, and number and percent aged 55 or older, by selected detailed occupation, 2005; numbers in thousands)

	total workers	median age	total aged 55 or older		aged 55 to 64		aged 65 or older	
			number	percent of total	number	percent of total	number	percent of total
TOTAL WORKERS	**141,730**	**40.7**	**23,443**	**16.5%**	**18,349**	**12.9%**	**5,094**	**3.6%**
Chief executives	1,644	49.3	489	29.7	384	23.4	105	6.4
Legislators	17	54.2	9	52.9	5	29.4	4	23.5
Marketing and sales managers	798	41.2	97	12.2	88	11.0	9	1.1
Computer and information systems managers	351	42.3	36	10.3	32	9.1	4	1.1
Financial managers	1,045	42.2	154	14.7	130	12.4	24	2.3
Human resources managers	272	43.6	47	17.3	42	5.0	5	1.8
Farmers and ranchers	195	48.5	62	31.8	38	19.5	24	12.3
Education administrators	805	47.3	210	26.1	190	23.6	20	2.5
Food service managers	929	39.9	119	12.8	99	10.7	20	2.2
Medical and health services managers	470	47.8	115	24.5	100	21.3	15	3.2
Accountants and auditors	1,683	41.7	269	16.0	214	12.7	55	3.3
Computer scientists and systems analysts	745	40.6	85	11.4	80	10.7	5	0.7
Computer programmers	581	39.6	48	8.3	41	7.1	7	1.2
Computer software engineers	832	39.3	70	8.4	68	8.2	2	0.2
Architects	235	45.3	46	19.6	35	14.9	11	4.7
Civil engineers	319	43.3	66	20.7	49	15.4	17	5.3
Electrical engineers	352	42.1	54	15.3	42	11.9	12	3.4
Mechanical engineers	318	42.2	48	15.1	40	12.6	8	2.5
Medical scientists	125	37.6	9	7.2	7	5.6	2	1.6
Psychologists	188	50.7	71	37.8	52	27.7	19	10.1
Social workers	670	42.9	124	18.5	110	16.4	14	2.1
Clergy	435	48.2	129	29.7	84	19.3	45	10.3
Lawyers	961	45.4	232	24.1	181	18.8	51	5.3
Postsecondary teachers	1,185	45.1	327	27.6	250	21.1	77	6.5
Preschool and kindergarten teachers	719	38.2	79	11.0	69	9.6	10	1.4
Elementary and middle school teachers	2,616	43.1	480	18.3	427	16.3	53	2.0
Secondary school teachers	1,136	44.1	217	19.1	192	16.9	25	2.2
Librarians	214	50.3	65	30.4	59	27.6	6	2.8
Teacher assistants	947	42.6	163	17.2	137	14.5	26	2.7
Artists	234	44.0	57	24.4	38	16.2	19	8.1
Actors	41	34.7	7	17.1	4	9.8	3	7.3
Athletes	273	31.0	26	9.5	18	6.6	8	2.9
Editors	150	41.8	27	18.0	21	14.0	6	4.0
Writers and authors	178	47.5	55	30.9	37	20.8	18	10.1
Dentists	164	48.2	48	29.3	34	20.7	14	8.5
Pharmacists	248	42.6	53	21.4	37	14.9	16	6.5
Physicians and surgeons	830	44.9	189	22.8	133	16.0	56	6.7
Registered nurses	2,416	44.6	437	18.1	375	15.5	62	2.6
Physical therapists	177	39.9	14	7.9	12	6.8	2	1.1
Licensed practical nurses	510	43.8	84	16.5	70	13.7	14	2.7
Nursing, psychiatric, and home health aides	1,900	39.4	284	14.9	222	11.7	62	3.3

(continued)

	total workers	median age	total aged 55 or older		aged 55 to 64		aged 65 or older	
			number	percent of total	number	percent of total	number	percent of total
Firefighters	243	38.2	14	5.8%	13	5.3%	1	0.4%
Police and sheriff's patrol officers	677	39.2	56	8.3	48	7.1	8	1.2
Security guards, gaming surveillance officers	814	42.5	197	24.2	137	16.8	60	7.4
Chefs and head cooks	317	37.5	28	8.8	24	7.6	4	1.3
Cooks	1,838	32.9	187	10.2	145	7.9	42	2.3
Food preparation workers	664	27.6	70	10.5	49	7.4	21	3.2
Waiters and waitresses	1,927	24.4	88	4.6	63	3.3	25	1.3
Janitors and building cleaners	2,074	43.2	468	22.6	333	16.1	135	6.5
Maids and housekeeping cleaners	1,382	42.2	264	19.1	198	14.3	66	4.8
Grounds maintenance workers	1,187	36.1	156	13.1	109	9.2	47	4.0
Hairdressers, hair stylists, cosmetologists	738	39.5	125	16.9	103	14.0	22	3.0
Child care workers	1,329	36.8	217	16.3	151	11.4	66	5.0
Cashiers	3,075	25.8	314	10.2	215	7.0	99	3.2
Retail salespersons	3,248	34.5	566	17.4	390	12.0	176	5.4
Insurance sales agents	531	44.7	137	25.8	112	21.1	25	4.7
Securities, commodities, and financial services sales agents	392	39.7	57	14.5	40	10.2	17	4.3
Sales representatives, wholesale and manufacturing	474	39.9	68	14.3	58	12.2	10	2.1
Real estate brokers and sales agents	995	47.5	336	33.8	230	23.1	106	10.7
Bookkeeping, accounting, auditing clerks	1,456	45.0	368	25.3	275	18.9	93	6.4
Customer service representatives	1,833	35.8	193	10.5	163	8.9	30	1.6
Receptionists and information clerks	1,376	36.9	246	17.9	168	12.2	78	5.7
Stock clerks and order fillers	1,461	32.4	201	13.8	151	10.3	50	3.4
Secretaries and administrative assistants	3,499	44.0	722	20.6	591	16.9	131	3.7
Miscellaneous agricultural workers	698	34.5	76	10.9	56	8.0	20	2.9
Carpenters	1,797	37.4	165	9.2	133	7.4	32	1.8
Construction laborers	1,491	34.6	121	8.1	100	6.7	21	1.4
Automotive service technicians, mechanics	954	38.8	110	11.5	93	9.7	17	1.8
Miscellaneous assemblers and fabricators	1,107	39.8	138	12.5	109	9.8	29	2.6
Machinists	420	44.7	83	19.8	77	18.3	6	1.4
Aircraft pilots and flight engineers	121	44.9	26	21.5	24	19.8	2	1.7
Driver/sales workers and truck drivers	3,409	42.4	616	18.1	470	13.8	146	4.3
Freight, stock, material movers, hand laborers	1,806	33.1	173	9.6	133	7.4	40	2.2

Source: Bureau of Labor Statistics, unpublished tables from the 2005 Current Population Survey; calculations by New Strategist

Part-Time Work Appeals to Many

Workers aged 65 or older are much more likely than average to work part-time.

While only 11 percent of all men in the labor force work part-time, the proportion is 17 percent among men aged 55 or older. Part-time work rises with age among older men, from 10 percent of workers aged 55 to 64 to 40 percent of those aged 65 or older. Among working women aged 55 or older, 30 percent work part-time. The proportion rises to 54 percent among those aged 65 or older.

Because so many older Americans work part-time, they account for a disproportionate share of part-time workers. Men aged 55 or older account for 25 percent of all men with part-time jobs.

■ More older Americans will work part-time as Boomers enter their sixties and look for ways to supplement their retirement income.

Many older workers choose part-time jobs

(percent of workers aged 55 or older who work part-time, by sex and age, 2005)

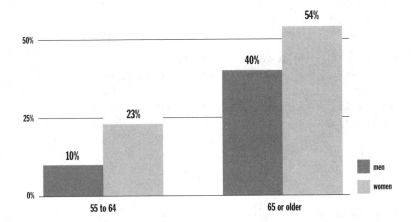

Table 5.10 Full- and Part-Time Workers by Age and Sex, 2005

(number and percent distribution of employed people aged 16 or older in the civilian labor force by age, sex, and employment status, 2005; numbers in thousands)

	men			women		
	total	full-time	part-time	total	full-time	part-time
Total employed	**80,033**	**71,302**	**8,731**	**69,288**	**51,890**	**17,398**
Under age 55	67,029	60,495	6,534	58,034	43,985	14,049
Aged 55 or older	13,004	10,807	2,197	11,253	7,905	3,348
Aged 55 to 64	10,045	9,022	1,023	8,934	6,837	2,097
Aged 65 or older	2,959	1,785	1,174	2,319	1,068	1,251
Aged 65 to 69	1,571	1,064	507	1,275	652	623
Aged 70 to 74	775	424	351	590	239	351
Aged 75 or older	612	296	316	454	177	277
PERCENT DISTRIBUTION BY AGE						
Total employed	**100.0%**	**100.0%**	**100.0%**	**100.0%**	**100.0%**	**100.0%**
Under age 55	83.8	84.8	74.8	83.8	84.8	80.8
Aged 55 or older	16.2	15.2	25.2	16.2	15.2	19.2
Aged 55 to 64	12.6	12.7	11.7	12.9	13.2	12.1
Aged 65 or older	3.7	2.5	13.4	3.3	2.1	7.2
Aged 65 to 69	2.0	1.5	5.8	1.8	1.3	3.6
Aged 70 to 74	1.0	0.6	4.0	0.9	0.5	2.0
Aged 75 or older	0.8	0.4	3.6	0.7	0.3	1.6
PERCENT DISTRIBUTION BY EMPLOYMENT STATUS						
Total employed	**100.0%**	**89.1%**	**10.9%**	**100.0%**	**74.9%**	**25.1%**
Under age 55	100.0	90.3	9.7	100.0	75.8	24.2
Aged 55 or older	100.0	83.1	16.9	100.0	70.2	29.8
Aged 55 to 64	100.0	89.8	10.2	100.0	76.5	23.5
Aged 65 or older	100.0	60.3	39.7	100.0	46.1	53.9
Aged 65 to 69	100.0	67.7	32.3	100.0	51.1	48.9
Aged 70 to 74	100.0	54.7	45.3	100.0	40.5	59.5
Aged 75 or older	100.0	48.4	51.6	100.0	39.0	61.0

Source: Unpublished data from the 2005 Current Population Survey, Bureau of Labor Statistics; calculations by New Strategist

Many Older Americans Are Self-Employed

Men and women aged 65 or older are more likely than average to work for themselves.

While only 7 percent of all employed workers aged 16 or older are self-employed, 20 percent of workers aged 65 or older work for themselves. Self-employment usually requires specialized skills, and those most likely to have such skills are older workers with decades of experience. Men and women aged 55 or older account for 30 percent of the self-employed, a much greater proportion than their share of all workers.

Older men are more likely to be self-employed than older women. While 10 percent of employed women aged 55 or older work for themselves, the proportion is 16 percent among men. Twenty-five percent of working men aged 65 or older are self-employed versus 14 percent of their female counterparts.

■ As Boomers enter the 55-or-older age group, the number of self-employed Americans will rise.

Self-employment is common among older men

(percent of employed men aged 16 or older and aged 55 or older who are self-employed, 2005)

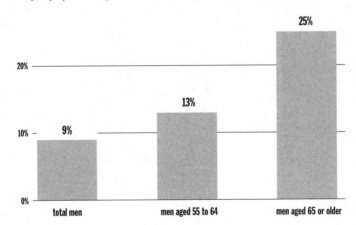

Table 5.11 Self-Employed by Sex and Age, 2005

(number of employed workers aged 16 or older, number and percent who are self-employed, and percent distribution of self-employed, by age, 2005; numbers in thousands)

	total	self-employed number	self-employed percent	percent distribution of self-employed by age
Total workers	**141,729**	**10,464**	**7.4%**	**100.0%**
Under age 55	118,286	7,373	6.2	70.5
Aged 55 or older	23,445	3,091	13.2	29.5
Aged 55 to 64	18,350	2,072	11.3	19.8
Aged 65 or older	5,095	1,019	20.0	9.7
Total men	**75,973**	**6,632**	**8.7**	**100.0**
Under age 55	61,402	4,638	7.6	69.9
Aged 55 or older	12,571	1,995	15.9	30.1
Aged 55 to 64	9,714	1,292	13.3	19.5
Aged 65 or older	2,857	703	24.6	10.6
Total women	**65,757**	**3,832**	**5.8**	**100.0**
Under age 55	54,884	2,739	5.0	71.5
Aged 55 or older	10,874	1,094	10.1	28.5
Aged 55 to 64	8,635	779	9.0	20.3
Aged 65 or older	2,238	315	14.1	8.2

Source: Bureau of Labor Statistics, 2005 Current Population Survey, Internet site http://www.bls.gov/cps/home.htm; calculations by New Strategist

Job Tenure Has Shortened among Older Men

Women's job tenure has been more stable.

Job tenure has decreased for men, and the biggest drop occurred among men aged 55 to 64. In 1991, men aged 55 to 64 had been with their current employer a median of 13.4 years. By 2004, the figure had fallen by nearly four years, to 9.8 years. Job tenure also fell slightly among women aged 55 to 64.

Statistics on long-term employment also reveal erosion in employer-employee relationships. The proportion of men aged 60 to 64 who have worked for their current employer for at least ten years has fallen by 9 percentage points, from 58 to 49 percent between 1991 and 2004. Among women in the age group, long-term employment rose between 1991 and 2000, but fell between 2000 and 2004.

■ Long-term employment may rise if fewer older workers opt for early retirement.

Fewer men aged 55 to 64 have long-term jobs

(percent of men aged 55 to 64 who have worked for their current employer for ten or more years, 1991 and 2004)

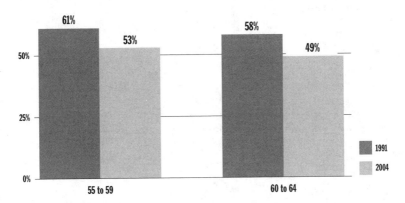

Table 5.12 Job Tenure by Sex and Age, 1991 to 2004

(median number of years employed wage and salary workers aged 25 or older have been with their current employer, by sex and age, 1991 to 2004; change in years, 2000–2004 and 1991–2004)

	2004	2000	1991	change 2000–04	1991–2004
Total workers aged 25 or older	**4.9**	**4.7**	**4.8**	**0.2**	**0.1**
Aged 25 to 34	2.9	2.6	2.9	0.3	0.0
Aged 35 to 44	4.9	4.8	5.4	0.1	−0.5
Aged 45 to 54	7.7	8.2	8.9	−0.5	−1.2
Aged 55 to 64	9.6	10.0	11.1	−0.4	−1.5
Aged 65 or older	9.0	9.4	8.1	−0.4	0.9
Total men aged 25 or older	**5.1**	**4.9**	**5.4**	**0.2**	**−0.3**
Aged 25 to 34	3.0	2.7	3.1	0.3	−0.1
Aged 35 to 44	5.2	5.3	6.5	−0.1	−1.3
Aged 45 to 54	9.6	9.5	11.2	0.1	−1.6
Aged 55 to 64	9.8	10.2	13.4	−0.4	−3.6
Aged 65 or older	8.2	9.0	7.0	−0.8	1.2
Total women aged 25 or older	**4.7**	**4.4**	**4.3**	**0.3**	**0.4**
Aged 25 to 34	2.8	2.5	2.7	0.3	0.1
Aged 35 to 44	4.5	4.3	4.5	0.2	0.0
Aged 45 to 54	6.4	7.3	6.7	−0.9	−0.3
Aged 55 to 64	9.2	9.9	9.9	−0.7	−0.7
Aged 65 or older	9.6	9.7	9.5	−0.1	0.1

Source: Bureau of Labor Statistics, Employee Tenure, Internet site http://www.bls.gov/news.release/tenure.t01.htm; calculations by New Strategist

Table 5.13 Long-Term Employment by Sex and Age, 1991 to 2004

(percent of employed wage and salary workers aged 25 or older who have been with their current employer for ten or more years, by sex and age, 1991 to 2004; percentage point change in share, 2000–2004 and 1991–2004)

	2004	2000	1991	percentage point change 2000–04	percentage point change 1991–2004
Total workers aged 25 or older	**30.6%**	**31.5%**	**32.2%**	**–0.9**	**–1.6**
Aged 25 to 29	2.4	2.5	5.1	–0.1	–2.7
Aged 30 to 34	10.9	13.9	19.3	–3.0	–8.4
Aged 35 to 39	23.2	26.1	31.1	–2.9	–7.9
Aged 40 to 44	32.4	35.9	39.3	–3.5	–6.9
Aged 45 to 49	42.1	45.3	46.5	–3.2	–4.4
Aged 50 to 54	48.5	48.6	51.4	–0.1	–2.9
Aged 55 to 59	50.9	53.1	56.7	–2.2	–5.8
Aged 60 to 64	49.7	53.2	55.4	–3.5	–5.7
Aged 65 or older	48.7	50.0	46.3	–1.3	2.4
Men aged 25 or older	**32.4**	**33.4**	**35.9**	**–1.0**	**–3.5**
Aged 25 to 29	2.7	3.0	5.7	–0.3	–3.0
Aged 30 to 34	11.9	15.1	21.1	–3.2	–9.2
Aged 35 to 39	24.9	29.4	35.6	–4.5	–10.7
Aged 40 to 44	36.2	40.4	46.3	–4.2	–10.1
Aged 45 to 49	48.1	49.0	53.5	–0.9	–5.4
Aged 50 to 54	53.0	51.6	58.5	1.4	–5.5
Aged 55 to 59	53.4	53.7	61.0	–0.3	–7.6
Aged 60 to 64	48.5	52.5	57.5	–4.0	–9.0
Aged 65 or older	46.8	48.9	42.6	–2.1	4.2
Women aged 25 or older	**28.6**	**29.5**	**28.2**	**–0.9**	**0.4**
Aged 25 to 29	1.9	1.9	4.4	0.0	–2.5
Aged 30 to 34	9.8	12.5	17.3	–2.7	–7.5
Aged 35 to 39	21.3	22.3	26.1	–1.0	–4.8
Aged 40 to 44	28.5	31.4	32.0	–2.9	–3.5
Aged 45 to 49	36.2	41.5	39.3	–5.3	–3.1
Aged 50 to 54	44.1	45.6	43.4	–1.5	0.7
Aged 55 to 59	48.4	52.5	51.4	–4.1	–3.0
Aged 60 to 64	51.0	54.0	53.1	–3.0	0.9
Aged 65 or older	50.7	51.2	49.9	–0.5	1.3

Source: Bureau of Labor Statistics, Employee Tenure, Internet site http://www.bls.gov/news.release/tenure.t02.htm; calculations by New Strategist

Independent Contracting Appeals to Older Workers

Nearly one in four workers aged 65 or older has an alternative work arrangement.

Older workers are most likely to have alternative work arrangements. The Bureau of Labor Statistics defines alternative workers as independent contractors, on-call workers (such as substitute teachers), temporary-help agency workers, and people who work for contract firms (such as lawn or janitorial service companies).

The most popular alternative work arrangement is independent contracting—which includes most of the self-employed. Among the 15 million alternative workers, 10 million are independent contractors—or 70 percent. Among alternative workers aged 65 or older, 80 percent are independent contractors, accounting for 18 percent of all workers in the 65-or-older age group. This age group is also more likely than average to do on-call work, such as substitute teaching.

■ Many older workers opt for self-employment because it gives them more control over their work schedule, and their government-provided health insurance coverage allows them the freedom to strike out on their own.

Older workers are most likely to be independent contractors

(percent of employed workers who are independent contractors, by age, 2005)

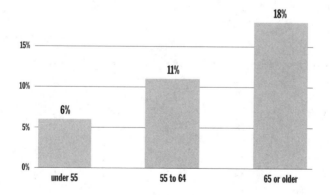

Table 5.14 Alternative Work Arrangements by Age, 2005

(number and percent distribution of employed people aged 16 or older by age and work arrangement, 2005; numbers in thousands)

			alternative workers				
	total employed	total in traditional arrangements	total	independent contractors	on-call workers	temporary-help agency workers	workers provided by contract firms
Total people	**138,952**	**123,843**	**14,826**	**10,342**	**2,454**	**1,217**	**813**
Under age 55	116,155	104,646	11,260	7,518	2,011	1,050	681
Aged 55 to 64	17,980	15,496	2,459	1,943	267	135	114
Aged 65 or older	4,817	3,701	1,107	881	175	33	18
PERCENT DISTRIBUTION BY ALTERNATIVE WORK STATUS							
Total people	**100.0%**	**89.1%**	**10.7%**	**7.4%**	**1.8%**	**0.9%**	**0.6%**
Under age 55	100.0	90.1	9.7	6.5	1.7	0.9	0.6
Aged 55 to 64	100.0	86.2	13.7	10.8	1.5	0.8	0.6
Aged 65 or older	100.0	76.8	23.0	18.3	3.6	0.7	0.4
PERCENT DISTRIBUTION BY AGE							
Total people	**100.0%**	**100.0%**	**100.0%**	**100.0%**	**100.0%**	**100.0%**	**100.0%**
Under age 55	83.6	84.5	75.9	72.7	81.9	86.3	83.8
Aged 55 to 64	12.9	12.5	16.6	18.8	10.9	11.1	14.0
Aged 65 or older	3.5	3.0	7.5	8.5	7.1	2.7	2.2

Note: Numbers may not add to total because the total employed include day laborers, an alternative arrangement not shown separately, and a small number of workers were both "on call" and "provided by contract firms." Independent contractors are workers who obtain customers on their own to provide a product or service, including the self-employed. On-call workers are in a pool of workers who are called to work only as needed, such as substitute teachers and construction workers supplied by a union hiring hall. Temporary-help agency workers are those who said they are paid by a temporary0help agency. Workers provided by contract firms are those employed by a company that provides employees or their services under contract, such as security, landscaping, and computer programming.
Source: Bureau of Labor Statistics, Contingent and Alternative Employment Arrangements, February 2005, Internet site http:// www.bls.gov/news.release/conemp.t05.htm; calculations by New Strategist

Many Workers Have Flexible Schedules

Older men are most likely to have flexible schedules.

Twenty-seven percent of the nation's wage and salary workers have flexible schedules—meaning they can vary the time they begin or end work, according to the Bureau of Labor Statistics. Men are slightly more likely than women to have flexible schedules—28 versus 27 percent in 2004.

The percentage of workers with flexible schedules varies little by age—with one exception. Among men aged 65 or older, fully 41 percent have flexible schedules as compared with 28 percent of all men who work full-time. Among their female counterparts, a much smaller 28 percent have flexibility in their work schedule.

Fifteen percent of wage and salary workers do not work a regular daytime schedule. The youngest workers are most likely to work shifts—22 percent of those aged 20 to 24 work the evening, night, or other shift. The figure bottoms out at 10 percent among workers aged 65 or older.

■ Older men with flexible work schedules may remain in the labor force only because of the flexibility their schedule allows them.

Older workers are least likely to be shift workers

(percent of full-time wage and salary workers who do not work a regular daytime schedule, by age, 2004)

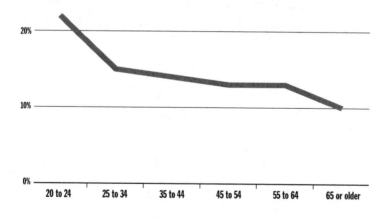

Table 5.15 Workers with Flexible Work Schedules by Sex and Age, 2004

(total number of full-time wage and salary workers aged 16 or older, and number and percent with flexible work schedules, by sex and age, 2004; numbers in thousands)

	total	with flexible schedules number	with flexible schedules percent
Full-time wage and salary workers	**99,778**	**27,411**	**27.5%**
Under age 55	86,692	23,754	27.4
Aged 55 to 64	11,745	3,181	27.1
Aged 65 or older	1,341	475	35.4
Men	**56,412**	**15,853**	**28.1**
Under age 55	49,272	13,675	27.8
Aged 55 to 64	6,383	1,865	29.2
Aged 65 or older	757	314	41.5
Women	**43,366**	**11,558**	**26.7**
Under age 55	37,420	10,079	26.9
Aged 55 to 64	5,361	1,316	24.5
Aged 65 or older	585	161	27.5

Note: Flexible schedules are those that allow workers to vary the time they begin or end work.
Source: Bureau of Labor Statistics, Workers on Flexible and Shift Schedules, Internet site http://www.bls.gov/news.release/flex.t01.htm

Table 5.16 Workers by Age and Shift Usually Worked, 2004

(total number of full-time wage and salary workers aged 20 or older and percent distribution by age and shift usually worked, 2004; numbers in thousands)

	total workers number	total workers percent	regular daytime schedule	shift schedule total	evening shift	night shift	rotating shift	employer-arranged irregular shift	split or other shift
Total aged 20 or older	**98,351**	**100.0%**	**84.9%**	**14.6%**	**4.6%**	**3.2%**	**2.5%**	**3.0%**	**1.2%**
Aged 20 to 24	9,004	100.0	76.8	22.3	8.8	3.7	3.3	4.6	1.8
Aged 25 to 34	24,640	100.0	84.1	15.2	5.0	3.4	2.7	2.8	1.3
Aged 35 to 44	26,766	100.0	85.4	14.1	4.1	3.2	2.5	3.1	1.1
Aged 45 to 54	24,855	100.0	86.8	12.8	3.6	3.2	2.3	2.5	1.2
Aged 55 to 64	11,745	100.0	87.1	12.5	3.8	2.6	2.0	3.0	1.1
Aged 65 or older	1,341	100.0	88.8	10.3	3.5	1.8	1.4	2.9	0.7

Source: Bureau of Labor Statistics, Workers on Flexible and Shift Schedules, Internet site http://www.bls.gov/news.release/flex.t04.htm

Most Minimum-Wage Workers Are Young Adults

The percentage of workers earning minimum wage or less rises in old age, however.

Among the nation's 74 million workers who are paid hourly rates, only 2 million (3 percent) make minimum wage or less, according to the Bureau of Labor Statistics. Fully 91 percent of minimum-wage workers are under age 55. Only 9 percent are aged 55 or older, and just 4 percent are aged 65 or older.

While 3 percent of all workers paid hourly rates make minimum wage or less, the figure falls to about 1 percent among the middle-aged. Among workers aged 65 or older, however, the proportion rises. Four percent of workers aged 65 or older are paid minimum wage or less.

■ Older workers are more likely to earn minimum wage than the middle aged because many are part-timers supplementing their retirement income.

Older workers are more likely than average to earn minimum wage or less

(percent of workers making minimum wage or less, by age, 2004)

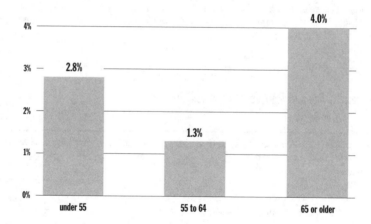

Table 5.17 Workers Earning Minimum Wage by Age, 2004

(number and percent distribution of workers paid hourly rates at or below minimum wage, by age, 2004; numbers in thousands)

	total hourly rates	at or below minimum wage		
		total	at $5.15/hour	below $5.15/hour
Total aged 16 or older	**73,939**	**2,003**	**520**	**1,483**
Under age 55	64,259	1,817	447	1,370
Aged 55 or older	9,678	187	73	114
Aged 55 to 64	7,501	101	40	61
Aged 55 to 59	4,756	60	21	39
Aged 60 to 64	2,745	41	19	22
Aged 65 or older	2,177	86	33	53
Aged 65 to 69	1,196	41	15	26
Aged 70 or older	981	45	18	27
PERCENT DISTRIBUTION BY AGE				
Total aged 16 or older	**100.0%**	**100.0%**	**100.0%**	**100.0%**
Under age 55	86.9	90.7	86.0	92.4
Aged 55 or older	13.1	9.3	14.0	7.7
Aged 55 to 64	10.1	5.0	7.7	4.1
Aged 55 to 59	6.4	3.0	4.0	2.6
Aged 60 to 64	3.7	2.0	3.7	1.5
Aged 65 or older	2.9	4.3	6.3	3.6
Aged 65 to 69	1.6	2.0	2.9	1.8
Aged 70 or older	1.3	2.2	3.5	1.8
PERCENT DISTRIBUTION BY WAGE STATUS				
Total aged 16 or older	**100.0%**	**2.7%**	**0.7%**	**2.0%**
Under age 55	100.0	2.8	0.7	2.1
Aged 55 or older	100.0	1.9	0.8	1.2
Aged 55 to 64	100.0	1.3	0.5	0.8
Aged 55 to 59	100.0	1.3	0.4	0.8
Aged 60 to 64	100.0	1.5	0.7	0.8
Aged 65 or older	100.0	4.0	1.5	2.4
Aged 65 to 69	100.0	3.4	1.3	2.2
Aged 70 or older	100.0	4.6	1.8	2.8

Source: Bureau of Labor Statistics, Characteristics of Minimum Wage Workers, 2004, Internet site http://www.bls.gov/cps/minwage2004.htm; calculations by New Strategist

Union Representation Peaks among Workers Aged 45 to 64

Men are more likely than women to be represented by a union.

Union representation has fallen sharply over the past few decades. In 2005, only 14 percent of workers were represented by a union.

The percentage of workers who are represented by a union peaks among men in the 45-to-54 age group at 20 percent and among women aged 55 to 64 at 17 percent. Men are more likely than women to be represented by a union because men are more likely to work in manufacturing jobs—traditional strongholds of labor unions. In fact, the decline of labor unions is partly the result of the shift in jobs from manufacturing to services.

■ Union representation may rise along with workers' concerns about the cost of health care coverage.

Few workers are represented by a union

(percent of employed wage and salary workers who are represented by unions, by age, 2005)

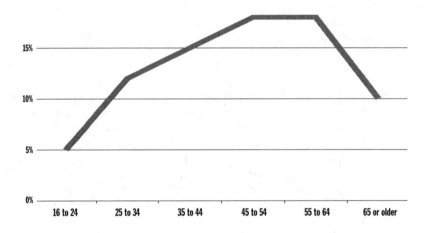

Table 5.18 Union Representation by Sex and Age, 2005

(number and percent of employed wage and salary workers aged 16 or older by union representation status, sex, and age, 2005; numbers in thousands)

	total employed	represented by unions	
		number	percent
Total aged 16 or older	**125,889**	**17,223**	**13.7%**
Aged 16 to 24	19,283	1,019	5.3
Aged 25 to 34	28,450	3,368	11.8
Aged 35 to 44	30,654	4,579	14.9
Aged 45 to 54	28,714	5,158	18.0
Aged 55 to 64	15,158	2,732	18.0
Aged 65 or older	3,631	366	10.1
Men aged 16 or older	**65,466**	**9,597**	**14.7**
Aged 16 to 24	9,860	603	6.1
Aged 25 to 34	15,559	1,915	12.3
Aged 35 to 44	16,196	2,582	15.9
Aged 45 to 54	14,421	2,849	19.8
Aged 55 to 64	7,606	1,458	19.2
Aged 65 or older	1,824	190	10.4
Women aged 16 or older	**60,423**	**7,626**	**12.6**
Aged 16 to 24	9,423	417	4.4
Aged 25 to 34	12,891	1,454	11.3
Aged 35 to 44	14,457	1,997	13.8
Aged 45 to 54	14,293	2,309	16.2
Aged 55 to 64	7,552	1,274	16.9
Aged 65 or older	1,806	176	9.8

Note: Workers represented by unions are either members of a labor union or similar employee association or workers who report no union affiliation but whose jobs are covered by a union or an employee association contract.
Source: Bureau of Labor Statistics, 2005 Current Population Survey, Internet site http://www.bls.gov/cps/home.htm

More Older Americans Will Work

Changes in Social Security, fewer defined-benefit pension plans, and meager savings will keep people at work.

The labor force participation rate of older Americans will rise between 2005 and 2014, according to projections by the Bureau of Labor Statistics. Among men aged 55 or older, labor force participation should rise 2.6 percentage points during those years compared with a decline of 0.3 percentage points among men under age 55. For women, the participation rate of those aged 55 or older should rise 5.4 percentage points versus a much smaller 0.8 percentage point gain for those under age 55.

Behind the rising participation rate of older workers is the end of early retirement as the Baby-Boom generation enters its sixties. The increase in the age at which workers become eligible for full Social Security benefits, the disappearance of defined-benefit pension plans, meager savings, and stock market volatility will keep additional millions of older workers on the job.

According to a survey by Pulte Homes, the Sun City developer, the majority of older Americans are somewhat to extremely excited about the prospect of retirement. The largest share (62 percent) have unfulfilled ambitions to travel in retirement. Health is the biggest retirement concern, followed by not having enough money.

■ Between 2005 and 2014, the number of workers aged 55 or older will increase by more than 10 million, a 42 percent increase.

Expect more older workers in the labor force

(number of people aged 55 or older in the labor force, 2005 and 2014)

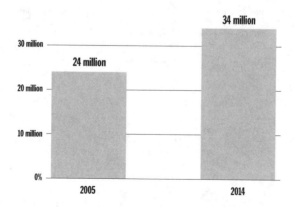

Table 5.19 Projections of the Labor Force by Sex and Age, 2005 to 2014

(number and percent of people aged 16 or older in the civilian labor force by sex and age, 2005 and 2014; percent change in number and percentage point change in participation rate, 2005–14; numbers in thousands)

	number			participation rate		
	2005	2014	percent change	2005	2014	percentage point change
Total labor force	**149,132**	**162,100**	**8.7%**	**66.0%**	**65.6%**	**–0.4**
Total men in labor force	**80,040**	**86,194**	**7.7**	**73.3**	**71.8**	**–1.5**
Under age 55	67,167	68,377	1.8	84.2	83.9	–0.3
Aged 55 or older	12,873	17,817	38.4	43.7	46.3	2.6
Aged 55 to 64	9,975	13,022	30.5	68.8	68.7	–0.1
Aged 55 to 59	6,451	7,849	21.7	77.5	76.6	–0.9
Aged 60 to 64	3,524	5,173	46.8	57.1	59.4	2.3
Aged 60 to 61	1,701	2,412	41.8	65.1	65.7	0.6
Aged 62 to 64	1,823	2,761	51.5	51.2	54.7	3.5
Aged 65 or older	2,898	4,795	65.5	19.4	24.6	5.2
Aged 65 to 74	2,286	2,834	24.0	27.2	31.5	4.3
Aged 65 to 69	1,556	2,815	80.9	33.2	37.9	4.7
Aged 70 to 74	730	1,019	39.6	19.6	21.5	1.9
Aged 75 or older	612	961	57.0	9.4	13.1	3.7
Aged 75 to 79	410	643	56.8	13.0	19.2	6.2
Aged 80 or older	202	317	56.9	6.0	7.9	1.9
Total women in labor force	**69,092**	**75,906**	**9.9**	**59.1**	**59.7**	**0.6**
Under age 55	57,849	59,407	2.7	71.3	72.1	0.8
Aged 55 or older	11,243	16,499	46.7	31.4	36.8	5.4
Aged 55 to 64	8,936	12,606	41.1	57.0	61.9	4.9
Aged 55 to 59	5,806	7,654	31.8	65.6	70.7	5.1
Aged 60 to 64	3,130	4,953	58.2	45.8	51.8	6.0
Aged 60 to 61	1,582	2,490	57.4	54.7	61.4	6.7
Aged 62 to 64	1,547	2,463	59.2	39.3	44.8	5.5
Aged 65 or older	2,307	3,892	68.7	11.5	15.9	4.4
Aged 65 to 74	1,838	3,108	69.1	18.4	22.9	4.5
Aged 65 to 69	1,266	2,243	77.2	23.8	28.7	4.9
Aged 70 to 74	572	865	51.2	12.3	15.0	2.7
Aged 75 or older	469	784	67.2	4.6	7.2	2.6
Aged 75 to 79	296	390	31.8	6.7	8.8	2.1
Aged 80 or older	171	394	130.4	3.0	6.1	3.1

Note: Figures for 2005 are slightly different from those shown elsewhere in this chapter because they are projections rather than estimates.
Source: Bureau of Labor Statistics, Internet site http://www.bls.gov/emp/emplab1.htm; calculations by New Strategist

Table 5.20 Retirement Attitudes by Age, 2005

(percent distribution of people aged 41 to 69 by attitudes toward retirement, 2005)

	total	41 to 49	50 to 59	60 to 69
"How do you feel about the retirement phase of your life?"				
Extremely/somewhat excited	55%	45%	56%	68%
Not sure/haven't thought about it	28	33	25	23
Somewhat/absolutely dreading it	17	21	19	10
"Do you have unfulfilled ambitions that you might consider taking up upon retirement/now that you are retired?"				
Travel	62	65	64	53
Spend more time with friends/family/spouse	42	45	39	43
Exercise more	42	43	41	43
Volunteer	37	37	35	39
Learn/take up a hobby	33	40	29	27
Acquire new skills	29	30	28	29
Take classes/go back to school	25	30	24	20
"Of your retirement concerns, which is the most crucial?"				
Not being healthy enough	30	21	32	40
Not having enough money	17	18	19	14
Ouliving money set aside	12	13	10	13
Having to work	11	12	14	4
Outliving my spouse	10	11	9	9
Depending on family/friends	8	8	6	9
Having to live alone	4	5	4	2
Not having enough to do	3	5	1	2
Losing touch with children/grandchildren	3	3	3	3
Being discriminated against	3	3	2	3

Source: Pulte Homes, 2005 Del Webb Baby Boomer Survey; Internet site http://phx.corporate-ir.net/phoenix.zhtml?c=147717&p=delWebb

6

Living Arrangements

■ Among the 23 million households headed by people aged 65 or older, a 43 percent minority are married couples.

■ Among older Americans, married couples are a much larger share of Asian, Hispanic, and non-Hispanic white households than of black households.

■ Average household size is just over two people in the 60-to-64 age group. It falls below two in the 65-to-74 age group.

■ Among householders aged 55 to 64, a substantial 24 percent have children of any age living with them. The figure falls to 11 percent among householders aged 65 or older.

■ Fifty-seven percent of women aged 85 or older live alone versus only 31 percent of their male counterparts.

■ Among people aged 85 or older, fully 77 percent of women, but only 35 percent of men, are currently widowed.

Married Couples Lose Ground with Age

Only 43 percent of householders aged 65 or older are married couples.

Of the nation's 113 million households in 2005, the 51 percent majority was headed by married couples. But among the 23 million households headed by people aged 65 or older, a 43 percent minority are couples. Older people are less likely than the average American to live with their spouse because an important transition in living arrangements occurs among people in their seventies. While married couples account for the majority of households headed by 65-to-69-year-olds, the proportion falls to 49 percent among householders aged 70 to 74, and drops to 33 percent among those aged 75 or older.

The married-couple share of older households falls as women become widowed and begin to live alone. Women who live alone account for 26 percent of all households headed by people aged 55 or older, ranging from 16 percent of households headed by 55-to-59-year-olds to 42 percent of those headed by people aged 75 or older. In the oldest age group, the most common household type is women who live alone.

■ American women must prepare themselves emotionally and financially for lone living in old age.

Married-couple share of households falls in older age groups

(percent of households headed by married couples, by age, 2005)

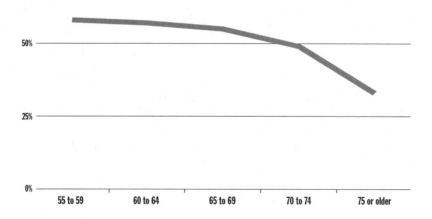

Table 6.1 Households Headed by People Aged 55 or Older by Household Type, 2005: Total Households

(number and percent distribution of total households and households headed by people aged 55 or older, by household type, 2005; numbers in thousands)

	total	aged 55 or older			aged 65 or older			
		total	55 to 59	60 to 64	total	65 to 69	70 to 74	75 or older
TOTAL HOUSEHOLDS	113,146	40,611	9,747	7,729	23,135	6,204	5,315	11,616
Family households	77,010	24,119	6,798	5,179	12,142	4,021	3,088	5,033
Married couples	58,109	19,924	5,632	4,419	9,873	3,407	2,591	3,875
Female hh, no spouse	14,009	3,268	891	576	1,801	461	397	943
Male hh, no spouse	4,893	927	275	184	468	153	99	215
Nonfamily households	36,136	16,492	2,949	2,550	10,993	2,183	2,227	6,583
Female householder	19,792	11,163	1,695	1,577	7,891	1,395	1,561	4,935
Living alone	17,207	10,689	1,524	1,478	7,687	1,326	1,530	4,830
Male householder	16,344	5,329	1,254	973	3,102	788	666	1,648
Living alone	12,652	4,823	1,077	843	2,903	724	632	1,547
PERCENT DISTRIBUTION BY TYPE								
TOTAL HOUSEHOLDS	100.0%	100.0%	100.0%	100.0%	100.0%	100.0%	100.0%	100.0%
Family households	68.1	59.4	69.7	67.0	52.5	64.8	58.1	43.3
Married couples	51.4	49.1	57.8	57.2	42.7	54.9	48.7	33.4
Female hh, no spouse	12.4	8.0	9.1	7.5	7.8	7.4	7.5	8.1
Male hh, no spouse	4.3	2.3	2.8	2.4	2.0	2.5	1.9	1.9
Nonfamily households	31.9	40.6	30.3	33.0	47.5	35.2	41.9	56.7
Female householder	17.5	27.5	17.4	20.4	34.1	22.5	29.4	42.5
Living alone	15.2	26.3	15.6	19.1	33.2	21.4	28.8	41.6
Male householder	14.4	13.1	12.9	12.6	13.4	12.7	12.5	14.2
Living alone	11.2	11.9	11.0	10.9	12.5	11.7	11.9	13.3
PERCENT DISTRIBUTION BY AGE								
TOTAL HOUSEHOLDS	100.0%	35.9%	8.6%	6.8%	20.4%	5.5%	4.7%	10.3%
Family households	100.0	31.3	8.8	6.7	15.8	5.2	4.0	6.5
Married couples	100.0	34.3	9.7	7.6	17.0	5.9	4.5	6.7
Female hh, no spouse	100.0	23.3	6.4	4.1	12.9	3.3	2.8	6.7
Male hh, no spouse	100.0	18.9	5.6	3.8	9.6	3.1	2.0	4.4
Nonfamily households	100.0	45.6	8.2	7.1	30.4	6.0	6.2	18.2
Female householder	100.0	56.4	8.6	8.0	39.9	7.0	7.9	24.9
Living alone	100.0	62.1	8.9	8.6	44.7	7.7	8.9	28.1
Male householder	100.0	32.6	7.7	6.0	19.0	4.8	4.1	10.1
Living alone	100.0	38.1	8.5	6.7	22.9	5.7	5.0	12.2

Source: Bureau of the Census, 2005 Current Population Survey, Annual Social and Economic Supplement, Internet site http://pubdb3.census.gov/macro/032005/hhinc/new02_000.htm; calculations by New Strategist

Households of Older Americans Differ by Race and Hispanic Origin

Among older householders, married couples are a much larger share of Asian, Hispanic, and non-Hispanic white households than of black households.

There are sharp differences in household composition among older people by race and Hispanic origin. Among householders aged 55 or older, 58 percent of Asians, 51 percent of non-Hispanic whites, and 48 percent of Hispanics are married couples. In contrast, married couples head only 32 percent of black households in the age group. Female-headed families are common among older blacks, accounting for nearly one in five households headed by blacks aged 55 or older. The comparable figure for non-Hispanic whites is just 6 percent.

Regardless of race or Hispanic origin, women who live alone account for a large share of the oldest householders. Among householders aged 75 or older, the proportion of households headed by women living alone ranges from a low of 36 percent among Hispanics to a high of 42 percent among non-Hispanic whites.

■ Lone living is likely for many women in old age, regardless of race or Hispanic origin.

The married-couple share of households varies by race and Hispanic origin

(married-couple share of households headed by people aged 55 or older, by race and Hispanic origin, 2005)

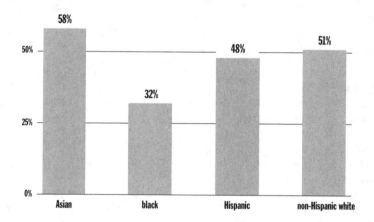

Table 6.2   Households Headed by People Aged 55 or Older by Household Type, 2005: Asian Households

(number and percent distribution of total households headed by Asians and households headed by Asians aged 55 or older, by household type, 2005; numbers in thousands)

| | | aged 55 or older | | | | | | |
| | | | | | aged 65 or older | | | |
	total	total	55 to 59	60 to 64	total	65 to 69	70 to 74	75 or older
TOTAL ASIAN HOUSEHOLDS	**4,360**	**1,106**	**360**	**223**	**523**	**189**	**126**	**208**
Family households	**3,295**	**771**	**280**	**154**	**337**	**147**	**89**	**101**
Married couples	2,649	642	222	130	290	128	75	88
Female hh, no spouse	385	91	48	14	29	10	8	11
Male hh, no spouse	261	38	10	10	18	9	6	2
Nonfamily households	**1,065**	**335**	**79**	**69**	**187**	**42**	**38**	**107**
Female householder	558	228	52	45	131	22	26	83
Living alone	463	220	49	43	128	20	26	83
Male householder	507	107	27	24	56	20	12	24
Living alone	372	94	25	23	46	17	8	21
PERCENT DISTRIBUTION BY TYPE								
TOTAL ASIAN HOUSEHOLDS	**100.0%**	**100.0%**	**100.0%**	**100.0%**	**100.0%**	**100.0%**	**100.0%**	**100.0%**
Family households	**75.6**	**69.7**	**77.8**	**69.1**	**64.4**	**77.8**	**70.6**	**48.6**
Married couples	60.8	58.0	61.7	58.3	55.4	67.7	59.5	42.3
Female hh, no spouse	8.8	8.2	13.3	6.3	5.5	5.3	6.3	5.3
Male hh, no spouse	6.0	3.4	2.8	4.5	3.4	4.8	4.8	1.0
Nonfamily households	**24.4**	**30.3**	**21.9**	**30.9**	**35.8**	**22.2**	**30.2**	**51.4**
Female householder	12.8	20.6	14.4	20.2	25.0	11.6	20.6	39.9
Living alone	10.6	19.9	13.6	19.3	24.5	10.6	20.6	39.9
Male householder	11.6	9.7	7.5	10.8	10.7	10.6	9.5	11.5
Living alone	8.5	8.5	6.9	10.3	8.8	9.0	6.3	10.1
PERCENT DISTRIBUTION BY AGE								
TOTAL ASIAN HOUSEHOLDS	**100.0%**	**25.4%**	**8.3%**	**5.1%**	**12.0%**	**4.3%**	**2.9%**	**4.8%**
Family households	**100.0**	**23.4**	**8.5**	**4.7**	**10.2**	**4.5**	**2.7**	**3.1**
Married couples	100.0	24.2	8.4	4.9	10.9	4.8	2.8	3.3
Female hh, no spouse	100.0	23.6	12.5	3.6	7.5	2.6	2.1	2.9
Male hh, no spouse	100.0	14.6	3.8	3.8	6.9	3.4	2.3	0.8
Nonfamily households	**100.0**	**31.5**	**7.4**	**6.5**	**17.6**	**3.9**	**3.6**	**10.0**
Female householder	100.0	40.9	9.3	8.1	23.5	3.9	4.7	14.9
Living alone	100.0	47.5	10.6	9.3	27.6	4.3	5.6	17.9
Male householder	100.0	21.1	5.3	4.7	11.0	3.9	2.4	4.7
Living alone	100.0	25.3	6.7	6.2	12.4	4.6	2.2	5.6

Note: Asians include those identifying themselves as being of the race alone and those identifying themselves as being of the race in combination with other races.
Source: Bureau of the Census, 2005 Current Population Survey, Annual Social and Economic Supplement, Internet site http:// pubdb3.census.gov/macro/032005/hhinc/new02_000.htm; calculations by New Strategist

Table 6.3 Households Headed by People Aged 55 or Older by Household Type, 2005: Black Households

(number and percent distribution of total black households and black households headed by people aged 55 or older, by household type, 2005; numbers in thousands)

	total	aged 55 or older			aged 65 or older			
		total	55 to 59	60 to 64	total	65 to 69	70 to 74	75 or older
TOTAL BLACK HOUSEHOLDS	14,127	4,053	1,097	821	2,135	683	538	914
Family households	9,109	2,207	719	479	1,009	386	252	372
Married couples	4,272	1,277	479	284	514	219	128	167
Female hh, no spouse	4,084	776	206	160	410	134	104	173
Male hh, no spouse	754	154	34	35	85	33	20	32
Nonfamily households	5,018	1,845	378	342	1,125	298	286	542
Female householder	2,863	1,221	221	235	765	181	197	387
Living alone	2,599	1,162	193	224	745	176	193	377
Male householder	2,155	624	157	107	360	117	89	155
Living alone	1,833	586	146	97	343	109	86	149

PERCENT DISTRIBUTION BY TYPE

	total	total	55 to 59	60 to 64	total	65 to 69	70 to 74	75 or older
TOTAL BLACK HOUSEHOLDS	100.0%	100.0%	100.0%	100.0%	100.0%	100.0%	100.0%	100.0%
Family households	64.5	54.5	65.5	58.3	47.3	56.5	46.8	40.7
Married couples	30.2	31.5	43.7	34.6	24.1	32.1	23.8	18.3
Female hh, no spouse	28.9	19.1	18.8	19.5	19.2	19.6	19.3	18.9
Male hh, no spouse	5.3	3.8	3.1	4.3	4.0	4.8	3.7	3.5
Nonfamily households	35.5	45.5	34.5	41.7	52.7	43.6	53.2	59.3
Female householder	20.3	30.1	20.1	28.6	35.8	26.5	36.6	42.3
Living alone	18.4	28.7	17.6	27.3	34.9	25.8	35.9	41.2
Male householder	15.3	15.4	14.3	13.0	16.9	17.1	16.5	17.0
Living alone	13.0	14.5	13.3	11.8	16.1	16.0	16.0	16.3

PERCENT DISTRIBUTION BY AGE

	total	total	55 to 59	60 to 64	total	65 to 69	70 to 74	75 or older
TOTAL BLACK HOUSEHOLDS	100.0%	28.7%	7.8%	5.8%	15.1%	4.8%	3.8%	6.5%
Family households	100.0	24.2	7.9	5.3	11.1	4.2	2.8	4.1
Married couples	100.0	29.9	11.2	6.6	12.0	5.1	3.0	3.9
Female hh, no spouse	100.0	19.0	5.0	3.9	10.0	3.3	2.5	4.2
Male hh, no spouse	100.0	20.4	4.5	4.6	11.3	4.4	2.7	4.2
Nonfamily households	100.0	36.8	7.5	6.8	22.4	5.9	5.7	10.8
Female householder	100.0	42.6	7.7	8.2	26.7	6.3	6.9	13.5
Living alone	100.0	44.7	7.4	8.6	28.7	6.8	7.4	14.5
Male householder	100.0	29.0	7.3	5.0	16.7	5.4	4.1	7.2
Living alone	100.0	32.0	8.0	5.3	18.7	5.9	4.7	8.1

Note: Blacks include those identifying themselves as being of the race alone and those identifying themselves as being of the race in combination with other races.
Source: Bureau of the Census, 2005 Current Population Survey, Annual Social and Economic Supplement, Internet site http:// pubdb3.census.gov/macro/032005/hhinc/new02_000.htm; calculations by New Strategist

Table 6.4 Households Headed by People Aged 55 or Older by Household Type, 2005: Hispanic Households

(number and percent distribution of total Hispanic households and Hispanic households headed by people aged 55 or older, by household type, 2005; numbers in thousands)

		aged 55 or older						
					aged 65 or older			
	total	total	55 to 59	60 to 64	total	65 to 69	70 to 74	75 or older
TOTAL HISPANIC HOUSEHOLDS	12,181	2,488	724	547	1,217	402	317	497
Family households	9,537	1,645	544	395	706	261	194	252
Married couples	6,367	1,200	389	286	525	205	150	171
Female hh, no spouse	2,240	355	127	84	144	38	40	66
Male hh, no spouse	930	90	28	25	37	18	4	15
Nonfamily households	2,644	843	180	152	511	142	123	246
Female householder	1,177	543	90	96	357	97	77	183
Living alone	981	517	82	88	347	91	76	179
Male householder	1,467	300	90	56	154	45	46	63
Living alone	941	264	72	46	146	41	46	59
PERCENT DISTRIBUTION BY TYPE								
TOTAL HISPANIC HOUSEHOLDS	100.0%	100.0%	100.0%	100.0%	100.0%	100.0%	100.0%	100.0%
Family households	78.3	66.1	75.1	72.2	58.0	64.9	61.2	50.7
Married couples	52.3	48.2	53.7	52.3	43.1	51.0	47.3	34.4
Female hh, no spouse	18.4	14.3	17.5	15.4	11.8	9.5	12.6	13.3
Male hh, no spouse	7.6	3.6	3.9	4.6	3.0	4.5	1.3	3.0
Nonfamily households	21.7	33.9	24.9	27.8	42.0	35.3	38.8	49.5
Female householder	9.7	21.8	12.4	17.6	29.3	24.1	24.3	36.8
Living alone	8.1	20.8	11.3	16.1	28.5	22.6	24.0	36.0
Male householder	12.0	12.1	12.4	10.2	12.7	11.2	14.5	12.7
Living alone	7.7	10.6	9.9	8.4	12.0	10.2	14.5	11.9
PERCENT DISTRIBUTION BY AGE								
TOTAL HISPANIC HOUSEHOLDS	100.0%	20.4%	5.9%	4.5%	10.0%	3.3%	2.6%	4.1%
Family households	100.0	17.2	5.7	4.1	7.4	2.7	2.0	2.6
Married couples	100.0	18.8	6.1	4.5	8.2	3.2	2.4	2.7
Female hh, no spouse	100.0	15.8	5.7	3.8	6.4	1.7	1.8	2.9
Male hh, no spouse	100.0	9.7	3.0	2.7	4.0	1.9	0.4	1.6
Nonfamily households	100.0	31.9	6.8	5.7	19.3	5.4	4.7	9.3
Female householder	100.0	46.1	7.6	8.2	30.3	8.2	6.5	15.5
Living alone	100.0	52.7	8.4	9.0	35.4	9.3	7.7	18.2
Male householder	100.0	20.4	6.1	3.8	10.5	3.1	3.1	4.3
Living alone	100.0	28.1	7.7	4.9	15.5	4.4	4.9	6.3

Source: Bureau of the Census, 2005 Current Population Survey, Annual Social and Economic Supplement, Internet site http:// pubdb3.census.gov/macro/032005/hhinc/new02_000.htm; calculations by New Strategist

Table 6.5 Households Headed by People Aged 55 or Older by Household Type, 2005: Non-Hispanic White Households

(number and percent distribution of total non-Hispanic white households and non-Hispanic white households headed by people aged 55 or older, by household type, 2005; numbers in thousands)

	total	aged 55 or older total	55 to 59	60 to 64	aged 65 or older total	65 to 69	70 to 74	75 or older
TOTAL NON-HISPANIC WHITE HOUSEHOLDS	81,445	32,621	7,482	6,051	19,088	4,882	4,291	9,915
Family households	54,383	19,287	5,201	4,093	9,993	3,194	2,520	4,278
Married couples	44,296	16,649	4,502	3,664	8,483	2,833	2,216	3,433
Female hh, no spouse	7,200	2,001	499	314	1,188	271	237	680
Male hh, no spouse	2,888	637	200	115	322	90	67	165
Nonfamily households	27,062	13,335	2,281	1,958	9,096	1,688	1,771	5,637
Female householder	15,052	9,106	1,312	1,191	6,603	1,092	1,258	4,253
Living alone	13,053	8,728	1,182	1,114	6,432	1,035	1,233	4,164
Male householder	12,009	4,229	969	767	2,493	596	513	1,384
Living alone	9,349	3,813	823	661	2,329	545	487	1,297
PERCENT DISTRIBUTION BY TYPE								
TOTAL NON-HISPANIC WHITE HOUSEHOLDS	100.0%	100.0%	100.0%	100.0%	100.0%	100.0%	100.0%	100.0%
Family households	66.8	59.1	69.5	67.6	52.4	65.4	58.7	43.1
Married couples	54.4	51.0	60.2	60.6	44.4	58.0	51.6	34.6
Female hh, no spouse	8.8	6.1	6.7	5.2	6.2	5.6	5.5	6.9
Male hh, no spouse	3.5	2.0	2.7	1.9	1.7	1.8	1.6	1.7
Nonfamily households	33.2	40.9	30.5	32.4	47.7	34.6	41.3	56.9
Female householder	18.5	27.9	17.5	19.7	34.6	22.4	29.3	42.9
Living alone	16.0	26.8	15.8	18.4	33.7	21.2	28.7	42.0
Male householder	14.7	13.0	13.0	12.7	13.1	12.2	12.0	14.0
Living alone	11.5	11.7	11.0	10.9	12.2	11.2	11.3	13.1
PERCENT DISTRIBUTION BY AGE								
TOTAL NON-HISPANIC WHITE HOUSEHOLDS	100.0%	40.1%	9.2%	7.4%	23.4%	6.0%	5.3%	12.2%
Family households	100.0	35.5	9.6	7.5	18.4	5.9	4.6	7.9
Married couples	100.0	37.6	10.2	8.3	19.2	6.4	5.0	7.8
Female hh, no spouse	100.0	27.8	6.9	4.4	16.5	3.8	3.3	9.4
Male hh, no spouse	100.0	22.1	6.9	4.0	11.1	3.1	2.3	5.7
Nonfamily households	100.0	49.3	8.4	7.2	33.6	6.2	6.5	20.8
Female householder	100.0	60.5	8.7	7.9	43.9	7.3	8.4	28.3
Living alone	100.0	66.9	9.1	8.5	49.3	7.9	9.4	31.9
Male householder	100.0	35.2	8.1	6.4	20.8	5.0	4.3	11.5
Living alone	100.0	40.8	8.8	7.1	24.9	5.8	5.2	13.9

Note: Non-Hispanic whites include only those identifying themselves as being white alone and not Hispanic.
Source: Bureau of the Census, 2005 Current Population Survey, Annual Social and Economic Supplement, Internet site http:// pubdb3.census.gov/macro/032005/hhinc/new02_000.htm; calculations by New Strategist

Household Size Shrinks in the Older Age Groups

Average household size falls below two people in the 65-to-74 age group.

The average American household was home to 2.57 people in 2004. Household size peaks among householders aged 35 to 39, who are most likely to have at least one child at home. As householders age through their forties and fifties, the nest empties. The average number of children per household falls below one in the 45-to-49 age group.

Average household size is just over two people in the 60-to-64 age group. It falls below two, to 1.89, in the 65-to-74 age group as (usually) women become widows. For households headed by people aged 75 or older, average household size is just 1.56 people.

■ Most older householders are either empty-nesters or people living alone. Few have children at home.

Household size shrinks rapidly after age 50

(average household size by age of householder, 2004)

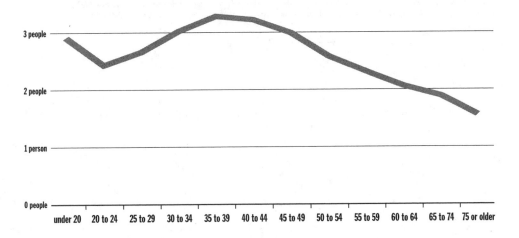

Table 6.6 Average Size of Household by Age of Householder, 2004

(number of households, average number of people per household, and average number of people under age 18 per household, by age of householder, 2004; number of households in thousands)

	number	average number of people	average number of people under age 18
Total households	**112,000**	**2.57**	**0.66**
Under age 20	837	2.91	0.84
Aged 20 to 24	5,772	2.43	0.55
Aged 25 to 29	8,738	2.66	0.85
Aged 30 to 34	10,421	3.02	1.21
Aged 35 to 39	10,997	3.28	1.42
Aged 40 to 44	12,224	3.22	1.22
Aged 45 to 49	12,360	2.99	0.82
Aged 50 to 54	10,778	2.58	0.41
Aged 55 to 59	9,504	2.31	0.23
Aged 60 to 64	7,320	2.06	0.14
Aged 65 to 74	11,499	1.89	0.08
Aged 75 or older	11,550	1.56	0.03

Source: Bureau of the Census, Current Population Survey Annual Social and Economic Supplement, America's Families and Living Arrangements: 2004, detailed tables, Internet site http://www.census.gov/population/www/socdemo/hh-fam/cps2004.html

Few Older Americans Have Children under Age 18 at Home

Many householders aged 55 to 64 have adult children at home, however.

Among householders aged 55 to 64, a substantial 24 percent have children living with them. Seventeen percent have children aged 18 or older, while only 7 percent have children under age 18 at home. Some of these children are in college dormitories, which the Census Bureau classified as living "at home." Among householders aged 65 or older, 11 percent have children at home, almost all of them adults.

The percentage of older householders with children at home varies sharply by race and Hispanic origin. Among Asian householders aged 55 to 64, fully 45 percent have children at home, and 12 percent have children under age 18. Among non-Hispanic whites, only 21 percent have children of any age at home and just 6 percent have children under age 18.

■ The presence of children in the home creates lifestyle differences among older Americans by race and Hispanic origin.

The nest is slow to empty for Asians and Hispanics

(percent of householders aged 55 to 64 with own children in their home, by race and Hispanic origin, 2004)

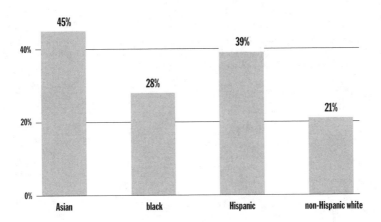

Table 6.7 Households by Presence and Age of Children at Home, 2004: Total Households

(number and percent distribution of households by presence and age of own children at home, by age of children and age of householder, 2004; numbers in thousands)

| | | | aged 55 or older | | | | |
| | | | | | aged 65 or older | | |
	total	under 55	total	55 to 64	total	65 to 74	75 or older
Total households	**112,000**	**72,127**	**39,873**	**16,824**	**23,049**	**11,499**	**11,550**
With children of any age	46,253	39,675	6,578	3,974	2,604	1,428	1,176
Under age 25	41,544	38,918	2,626	2,336	290	223	67
Under age 18	35,944	34,652	1,292	1,128	164	122	42
Under age 12	26,118	25,691	427	340	87	65	22
Under age 6	15,614	15,489	125	98	27	15	12
Aged 12 to 17	16,960	15,952	1,008	896	112	85	27
PERCENT DISTRIBUTION							
Total households	**100.0%**	**100.0%**	**100.0%**	**100.0%**	**100.0%**	**100.0%**	**100.0%**
With children of any age	41.3	55.0	16.5	23.6	11.3	12.4	10.2
Under age 25	37.1	54.0	6.6	13.9	1.3	1.9	0.6
Under age 18	32.1	48.0	3.2	6.7	0.7	1.1	0.4
Under age 12	23.3	35.6	1.1	2.0	0.4	0.6	0.2
Under age 6	13.9	21.5	0.3	0.6	0.1	0.1	0.1
Aged 12 to 17	15.1	22.1	2.5	5.3	0.5	0.7	0.2

Source: Bureau of the Census, Current Population Survey Annual Social and Economic Supplement, America's Families and Living Arrangements: 2004, detailed tables, Internet site http://www.census.gov/population/www/socdemo/hh-fam/cps2004.html; calculations by New Strategist

Table 6.8 Households by Presence and Age of Children at Home, 2004: Asian Households

(number and percent distribution of Asian households by presence and age of own children at home, by age of children and age of householder, 2004; numbers in thousands)

	total	under 55	aged 55 or older				
			total	55 to 64	aged 65 or older		
					total	65 to 74	75 or older
Total Asian households	**4,235**	**3,148**	**1,087**	**547**	**540**	**307**	**233**
With children of any age	2,131	1,788	344	246	98	66	32
Under age 25	1,928	1,762	164	145	19	15	4
Under age 18	1,711	1,635	74	63	11	7	4
Under age 12	1,297	1,268	28	22	6	5	1
Under age 6	829	820	9	5	4	3	1
Aged 12 to 17	714	655	58	51	7	4	3
PERCENT DISTRIBUTION							
Total Asian households	**100.0%**	**100.0%**	**100.0%**	**100.0%**	**100.0%**	**100.0%**	**100.0%**
With children of any age	50.3	56.8	31.6	45.0	18.1	21.5	13.7
Under age 25	45.5	56.0	15.1	26.5	3.5	4.9	1.7
Under age 18	40.4	51.9	6.8	11.5	2.0	2.3	1.7
Under age 12	30.6	40.3	2.6	4.0	1.1	1.6	0.4
Under age 6	19.6	26.0	0.8	0.9	0.7	1.0	0.4
Aged 12 to 17	16.9	20.8	5.3	9.3	1.3	1.3	1.3

Note: Asians include those identifying themselves as being of the race alone and those identifying themselves as being of the race in combination with other races.
Source: Bureau of the Census, Current Population Survey Annual Social and Economic Supplement, America's Families and Living Arrangements: 2004, detailed tables, Internet site http://www.census.gov/population/www/socdemo/hh-fam/cps2004.html; calculations by New Strategist

Table 6.9 Households by Presence and Age of Children at Home, 2004: Black Households

(number and percent distribution of black households by presence and age of own children at home, by age of children and age of householder, 2004; numbers in thousands)

	total	under 55	aged 55 or older				
					aged 65 or older		
			total	55 to 64	total	65 to 74	75 or older
Total black households	**13,969**	**10,058**	**3,912**	**1,827**	**2,085**	**1,143**	**942**
With children of any age	6,629	5,696	933	512	421	256	165
Under age 25	5,865	5,543	322	261	61	47	14
Under age 18	5,104	4,934	170	134	36	24	12
Under age 12	3,716	3,650	65	45	20	15	5
Under age 6	2,185	2,164	20	18	2	–	2
Aged 12 to 17	2,494	2,370	123	100	23	15	8
PERCENT DISTRIBUTION							
Total black households	**100.0%**	**100.0%**	**100.0%**	**100.0%**	**100.0%**	**100.0%**	**100.0%**
With children of any age	47.5	56.6	23.8	28.0	20.2	22.4	17.5
Under age 25	42.0	55.1	8.2	14.3	2.9	4.1	1.5
Under age 18	36.5	49.1	4.3	7.3	1.7	2.1	1.3
Under age 12	26.6	36.3	1.7	2.5	1.0	1.3	0.5
Under age 6	15.6	21.5	0.5	1.0	0.1	–	0.2
Aged 12 to 17	17.9	23.6	3.1	5.5	1.1	1.3	0.8

Note: Blacks include those identifying themselves as being of the race alone and those identifying themselves as being of the race in combination with other races. "–" means number is less than 500 or sample is too small to make a reliable estimate.
Source: Bureau of the Census, Current Population Survey Annual Social and Economic Supplement, America's Families and Living Arrangements: 2004, detailed tables, Internet site http://www.census.gov/population/www/socdemo/hh-fam/cps2004.html; calculations by New Strategist

Table 6.10 Households by Presence and Age of Children at Home, 2004: Hispanic Households

(number and percent distribution of Hispanic households by presence of own children at home, by age of children and age of householder, 2004; numbers in thousands)

| | | | aged 55 or older | | | | |
| | | | | | aged 65 or older | | |
	total	under 55	total	55 to 64	total	65 to 74	75 or older
Total Hispanic households	**11,692**	**9,351**	**2,342**	**1,229**	**1,113**	**683**	**430**
With children of any age	6,971	6,241	729	480	249	150	99
Under age 25	6,485	6,125	360	315	45	33	12
Under age 18	5,837	5,655	183	158	25	17	8
Under age 12	4,701	4,636	66	51	15	10	5
Under age 6	3,015	2,997	18	12	6	4	2
Aged 12 to 17	2,535	2,401	134	120	14	11	3
PERCENT DISTRIBUTION							
Total Hispanic households	**100.0%**	**100.0%**	**100.0%**	**100.0%**	**100.0%**	**100.0%**	**100.0%**
With children of any age	59.6	66.7	31.1	39.1	22.4	22.0	23.0
Under age 25	55.5	65.5	15.4	25.6	4.0	4.8	2.8
Under age 18	49.9	60.5	7.8	12.9	2.2	2.5	1.9
Under age 12	40.2	49.6	2.8	4.1	1.3	1.5	1.2
Under age 6	25.8	32.1	0.8	1.0	0.5	0.6	0.5
Aged 12 to 17	21.7	25.7	5.7	9.8	1.3	1.6	0.7

Source: Bureau of the Census, Current Population Survey Annual Social and Economic Supplement, America's Families and Living Arrangements: 2004, detailed tables, Internet site http://www.census.gov/population/www/socdemo/hh-fam/cps2004.html; calculations by New Strategist

Table 6.11 Households by Presence and Age of Children at Home, 2004: Non-Hispanic White Households

(number and percent distribution of non-Hispanic white households by presence and age of own children at home, by age of children and age of householder, 2004; numbers in thousands)

| | | | aged 55 or older | | | | |
| | | | | | aged 65 or older | | |
	total	under 55	total	55 to 64	total	65 to 74	75 or older
Total non-Hispanic white households	**81,149**	**48,967**	**32,181**	**13,037**	**19,144**	**9,262**	**9,882**
With children of any age	30,133	25,634	4,497	2,701	1,796	925	871
Under age 25	26,950	25,191	1,760	1,597	163	127	36
Under age 18	23,040	22,186	853	761	92	75	17
Under age 12	16,221	15,954	267	221	46	36	10
Under age 6	9,475	9,399	77	61	16	10	6
Aged 12 to 17	11,080	10,399	680	615	65	54	11
PERCENT DISTRIBUTION							
Total non-Hispanic white households	**100.0%**	**100.0%**	**100.0%**	**100.0%**	**100.0%**	**100.0%**	**100.0%**
With children of any age	37.1	52.3	14.0	20.7	9.4	10.0	8.8
Under age 25	33.2	51.4	5.5	12.2	0.9	1.4	0.4
Under age 18	28.4	45.3	2.7	5.8	0.5	0.8	0.2
Under age 12	20.0	32.6	0.8	1.7	0.2	0.4	0.1
Under age 6	11.7	19.2	0.2	0.5	0.1	0.1	0.1
Aged 12 to 17	13.7	21.2	2.1	4.7	0.3	0.6	0.1

Note: Non-Hispanic whites include only those identifying themselves as being white alone and not Hispanic.
Source: Bureau of the Census, Current Population Survey Annual Social and Economic Supplement, America's Families and Living Arrangements: 2004, detailed tables, Internet site http://www.census.gov/population/www/socdemo/hh-fam/cps2004.html; calculations by New Strategist

Lifestyles of Men and Women Diverge in Old Age

Most older men live with their wife, while most older women live alone.

The lifestyles of men and women become increasingly different with age. Because men die at a younger age than women, and because women tend to marry men who are slightly older, most women spend the end of their lives alone, while most men die while still married.

In the 55-to-64 age group, 62 percent of women and 74 percent of men live with their spouse. This 12 percentage point gap in living arrangements grows to a 39 percentage point chasm in the 85-or-older age group—when a substantial 52 percent of men, but only 13 percent of women, still live with their spouse. Fifty-seven percent of women aged 85 or older lived alone in 2004 versus only 31 percent of their male counterparts.

■ The wants and needs of men and women in old age differ because of their contrasting living arrangements.

Many older women live alone

(percent of people aged 85 or older who live alone, by sex, 2004)

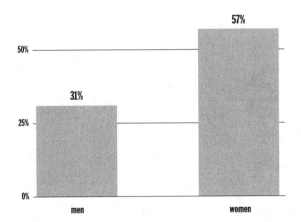

Table 6.12 Living Arrangements of Men by Age, 2004

(number and percent distribution of men aged 15 or older by living arrangement and age, 2004; numbers in thousands)

	total	under 55	aged 55 or older total	55 to 64	aged 65 or older total	65 to 74	75 to 84	85 or older
NUMBER								
Total men	110,048	81,714	28,336	13,543	14,793	8,353	5,238	1,202
Married-couple householder or spouse	57,719	37,128	20,591	10,088	10,503	6,261	3,611	631
Other householder	20,852	14,861	5,990	2,572	3,418	1,626	1,341	451
Male family householder	4,716	3,840	874	430	444	213	165	66
Living alone	12,562	7,953	4,609	1,825	2,784	1,293	1,121	370
Living with nonrelatives	3,574	3,068	507	317	190	120	55	15
Nonhouseholder	31,477	29,723	1,753	883	870	465	286	119
Child of householder	18,936	18,759	177	157	20	20	–	–
Other relative of householder	5,575	4,519	1,057	411	646	315	230	101
Living with nonrelatives	6,965	6,444	520	316	204	130	56	18
PERCENT DISTRIBUTION BY LIVING ARRANGEMENT								
Total men	100.0%	100.0%	100.0%	100.0%	100.0%	100.0%	100.0%	100.0%
Married-couple householder or spouse	52.4	45.4	72.7	74.5	71.0	75.0	68.9	52.5
Other householder	18.9	18.2	21.1	19.0	23.1	19.5	25.6	37.5
Male family householder	4.3	4.7	3.1	3.2	3.0	2.5	3.2	5.5
Living alone	11.4	9.7	16.3	13.5	18.8	15.5	21.4	30.8
Living with nonrelatives	3.2	3.8	1.8	2.3	1.3	1.4	1.1	1.2
Nonhouseholder	28.6	36.4	6.2	6.5	5.9	5.6	5.5	9.9
Child of householder	17.2	23.0	0.6	1.2	0.1	0.2	–	–
Other relative of householder	5.1	5.5	3.7	3.0	4.4	3.8	4.4	8.4
Living with nonrelatives	6.3	7.9	1.8	2.3	1.4	1.6	1.1	1.5
PERCENT DISTRIBUTION BY AGE								
Total men	100.0%	74.3%	25.7%	12.3%	13.4%	7.6%	4.8%	1.1%
Married-couple householder or spouse	100.0	64.3	35.7	17.5	18.2	10.8	6.3	1.1
Other householder	100.0	71.3	28.7	12.3	16.4	7.8	6.4	2.2
Male family householder	100.0	81.4	18.5	9.1	9.4	4.5	3.5	1.4
Living alone	100.0	63.3	36.7	14.5	22.2	10.3	8.9	2.9
Living with nonrelatives	100.0	85.8	14.2	8.9	5.3	3.4	1.5	0.4
Nonhouseholder	100.0	94.4	5.6	2.8	2.8	1.5	0.9	0.4
Child of householder	100.0	99.1	0.9	0.8	0.1	0.1	–	–
Other relative of householder	100.0	81.1	19.0	7.4	11.6	5.7	4.1	1.8
Living with nonrelatives	100.0	92.5	7.5	4.5	2.9	1.9	0.8	0.3

Note: "–" means number is less than 500 or sample is too small to make a reliable estimate.
Source: Bureau of the Census, Current Population Survey Annual Social and Economic Supplement, America's Families and Living Arrangements: 2004, detailed tables, Internet site http://www.census.gov/population/www/socdemo/hh-fam/cps2004.html; calculations by New Strategist

Table 6.13 Living Arrangements of Women by Age, 2004

(number and percent distribution of women aged 15 or older by living arrangement and age, 2004; numbers in thousands)

	total	under 55	aged 55 or older		aged 65 or older			
			total	55 to 64	total	65 to 74	75 to 84	85 or older
NUMBER								
Total women	**117,295**	**82,626**	**34,670**	**14,823**	**19,847**	**9,878**	**7,603**	**2,366**
Married-couple householder or spouse	57,719	40,394	17,326	9,239	8,087	5236	2549	302
Other householder	33,428	19,191	14,237	4,418	9,819	3,853	4,371	1,595
Female family householder	13,781	10,691	3,090	1,357	1,733	823	694	216
Living alone	17,024	6,375	10,649	2,775	7,874	2,904	3,616	1,354
Living with nonrelatives	2,623	2,125	498	286	212	126	61	25
Nonhouseholder	26,147	23,040	3,109	1,166	1,943	790	684	469
Child of householder	14,863	14,688	178	158	20	16	4	–
Other relative of householder	5,926	3,453	2,473	727	1,746	673	635	438
Living with nonrelatives	5,358	4,899	458	281	177	101	45	31
PERCENT DISTRIBUTION BY LIVING ARRANGEMENT								
Total women	**100.0%**	**100.0%**	**100.0%**	**100.0%**	**100.0%**	**100.0%**	**100.0%**	**100.0%**
Married-couple householder or spouse	49.2	48.9	50.0	62.3	40.7	53.0	33.5	12.8
Other householder	28.5	23.2	41.1	29.8	49.5	39.0	57.5	67.4
Female family householder	11.7	12.9	8.9	9.2	8.7	8.3	9.1	9.1
Living alone	14.5	7.7	30.7	18.7	39.7	29.4	47.6	57.2
Living with nonrelatives	2.2	2.6	1.4	1.9	1.1	1.3	0.8	1.1
Nonhouseholder	22.3	27.9	9.0	7.9	9.8	8.0	9.0	19.8
Child of householder	12.7	17.8	0.5	1.1	0.1	0.2	0.1	–
Other relative of householder	5.1	4.2	7.1	4.9	8.8	6.8	8.4	18.5
Living with nonrelatives	4.6	5.9	1.3	1.9	0.9	1.0	0.6	1.3
PERCENT DISTRIBUTION BY AGE								
Total women	**100.0%**	**70.4%**	**29.6%**	**12.6%**	**16.9%**	**8.4%**	**6.5%**	**2.0%**
Married-couple householder or spouse	100.0	70.0	30.0	16.0	14.0	9.1	4.4	0.5
Other householder	100.0	57.4	42.6	13.2	29.4	11.5	13.1	4.8
Female family householder	100.0	77.6	22.4	9.8	12.6	6.0	5.0	1.6
Living alone	100.0	37.4	62.6	16.3	46.3	17.1	21.2	8.0
Living with nonrelatives	100.0	81.0	19.0	10.9	8.1	4.8	2.3	1.0
Nonhouseholder	100.0	88.1	11.9	4.5	7.4	3.0	2.6	1.8
Child of householder	100.0	98.8	1.2	1.1	0.1	0.1	0.0	–
Other relative of householder	100.0	58.3	41.7	12.3	29.5	11.4	10.7	7.4
Living with nonrelatives	100.0	91.4	8.5	5.2	3.3	1.9	0.8	0.6

Note: "–" means number is less than 500 or sample is too small to make a reliable estimate.
Source: Bureau of the Census, Current Population Survey Annual Social and Economic Supplement, America's Families and Living Arrangements: 2004, detailed tables, Internet site http://www.census.gov/population/www/socdemo/hh-fam/cps2004.html; calculations by New Strategist

Table 6.14 People Who Live Alone by Sex and Age, 2005

(number of people aged 15 or older and number and percent who live alone by sex and age, 2005; numbers in thousands)

	total	living alone	
		number	percent
Total people	**230,425**	**29,859**	**13.0%**
Under age 55	165,679	14,347	8.7
Aged 55 or older	64,745	15,512	24.0
Aged 55 to 59	16,763	2,601	15.5
Aged 60 to 64	12,768	2,321	18.2
Aged 65 or older	35,214	10,590	30.1
Aged 65 to 69	10,124	2,050	20.2
Aged 70 to 74	8,264	2,162	26.2
Aged 75 or older	16,825	6,377	37.9
Total men	**111,686**	**12,652**	**11.3**
Under age 55	82,489	7,829	9.5
Aged 55 or older	29,198	4,823	16.5
Aged 55 to 59	8,003	1,077	13.5
Aged 60 to 64	6,044	843	13.9
Aged 65 or older	15,151	2,903	19.2
Aged 65 to 69	4,814	724	15.0
Aged 70 to 74	3,652	632	17.3
Aged 75 or older	6,685	1,547	23.1
Total women	**118,739**	**17,207**	**14.5**
Under age 55	83,190	6,518	7.8
Aged 55 or older	35,547	10,689	30.1
Aged 55 to 59	8,760	1,524	17.4
Aged 60 to 64	6,724	1,478	22.0
Aged 65 or older	20,063	7,687	38.3
Aged 65 to 69	5,310	1,326	25.0
Aged 70 to 74	4,612	1,530	33.2
Aged 75 or older	10,140	4,830	47.6

Source: Bureau of the Census, 2005 Current Population Survey, Annual Social and Economic Supplement, Internet sites http://pubdb3.census.gov/macro/032005/hhinc/new02_000.htm and http://pubdb3.census.gov/macro/032005/perinc/new01_000.htm; calculations by New Strategist

The Widowed Population Rises Sharply in Old Age

Fewer than half of women aged 75 or older are currently married.

Among all women aged 15 or older, only 10 percent are currently widowed. The figure stands at 43 percent among women aged 65 or older. The proportion rises from a 28 percent minority among women aged 65 to 74 to the 77 percent majority of women aged 85 or older. Women are far more likely to be currently widowed than men, since they tend to marry slightly older men and because widowed men are more likely to remarry. Among men aged 85 or older, only 35 percent are currently widowed.

The 55 percent majority of men aged 15 or older are currently married. Among men aged 65 or older, the figure is an even larger 74 percent and remains above 50 percent even among men aged 85 or older. The contrast with older women is stark. Only 43 percent of women aged 65 or older are currently married, and the proportion falls to just 14 percent among women aged 85 or older.

■ The lifestyles of men and women diverge as they age and a growing proportion of women become widows and live alone.

Older women are more likely to be widowed

(percent of people aged 85 or older who are currently married or widowed, by sex, 2004)

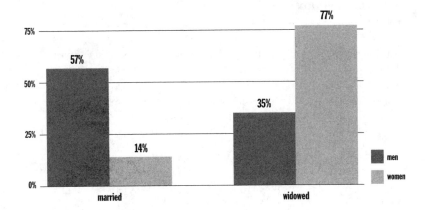

Table 6.15 Marital Status by Sex and Age, 2004: Total People

(number and percent distribution of people aged 15 or older by sex, age, and current marital status, 2004; numbers in thousands)

	total	never married	married	separated or divorced	widowed
NUMBER					
Total men	**110,048**	**35,885**	**60,724**	**10,791**	**2,648**
Under age 55	81,714	34,485	39,269	7,633	322
Aged 55 or older	28,336	1,400	21,453	3,158	2,324
Aged 55 to 64	13,543	797	10,506	1,947	293
Aged 65 or older	14,793	603	10,947	1,211	2,031
Aged 65 to 74	8,353	370	6,507	849	626
Aged 75 to 84	5,238	204	3,758	292	984
Aged 85 or older	1,202	29	682	70	421
Total women	**117,295**	**29,975**	**60,616**	**15,558**	**11,146**
Under age 55	82,626	28,436	42,433	10,700	1,057
Aged 55 or older	34,670	1,539	18,184	4,859	10,091
Aged 55 to 64	14,823	796	9,657	2,912	1,458
Aged 65 or older	19,847	743	8,527	1,947	8,633
Aged 65 to 74	9,878	365	5,453	1,294	2,768
Aged 75 to 84	7,603	270	2,732	559	4,042
Aged 85 or older	2,366	108	342	94	1,823
PERCENT DISTRIBUTION					
Total men	**100.0%**	**32.6%**	**55.2%**	**9.8%**	**2.4%**
Under age 55	100.0	42.2	48.1	9.3	0.4
Aged 55 or older	100.0	4.9	75.7	11.1	8.2
Aged 55 to 64	100.0	5.9	77.6	14.4	2.2
Aged 65 or older	100.0	4.1	74.0	8.2	13.7
Aged 65 to 74	100.0	4.4	77.9	10.2	7.5
Aged 75 to 84	100.0	3.9	71.7	5.6	18.8
Aged 85 or older	100.0	2.4	56.7	5.8	35.0
Total women	**100.0**	**25.6**	**51.7**	**13.3**	**9.5**
Under age 55	100.0	34.4	51.4	12.9	1.3
Aged 55 or older	100.0	4.4	52.4	14.0	29.1
Aged 55 to 64	100.0	5.4	65.1	19.6	9.8
Aged 65 or older	100.0	3.7	43.0	9.8	43.5
Aged 65 to 74	100.0	3.7	55.2	13.1	28.0
Aged 75 to 84	100.0	3.6	35.9	7.4	53.2
Aged 85 or older	100.0	4.6	14.5	4.0	77.0

Source: Bureau of the Census, Current Population Survey Annual Social and Economic Supplement, America's Families and Living Arrangements: 2004, detailed tables, Internet site http://www.census.gov/population/www/socdemo/hh-fam/cps2004.html; calculations by New Strategist

Table 6.16 Marital Status by Sex and Age, 2004: Asians

(number and percent distribution of total Asians aged 15 or older by sex, age, and current marital status, 2004; numbers in thousands)

	total	never married	married	separated or divorced	widowed
NUMBER					
Total Asian men	**4,874**	**1,752**	**2,842**	**213**	**68**
Under age 55	3,895	1,719	2,022	144	10
Aged 55 or older	979	33	819	68	58
Aged 55 to 64	497	24	426	38	9
Aged 65 or older	482	9	393	30	49
Aged 65 to 74	308	9	258	23	17
Aged 75 to 84	144	0	114	5	24
Aged 85 or older	31	–	21	2	8
Total Asian women	**5,247**	**1,327**	**3,197**	**377**	**346**
Under age 55	4,103	1,293	2,479	286	45
Aged 55 or older	1145	35	719	90	301
Aged 55 to 64	562	22	426	57	57
Aged 65 or older	583	13	293	33	244
Aged 65 to 74	342	6	210	21	104
Aged 75 to 84	181	4	71	11	95
Aged 85 or older	60	3	11	1	45
PERCENT DISTRIBUTION					
Total Asian men	**100.0%**	**35.9%**	**58.3%**	**4.4%**	**1.4%**
Under age 55	100.0	44.1	51.9	3.7	0.3
Aged 55 or older	100.0	3.4	83.7	6.9	5.9
Aged 55 to 64	100.0	4.8	85.7	7.6	1.8
Aged 65 or older	100.0	1.9	81.5	6.2	10.2
Aged 65 to 74	100.0	2.9	83.8	7.5	5.5
Aged 75 to 84	100.0	0.0	79.2	3.5	16.7
Aged 85 or older	100.0	–	67.7	6.5	25.8
Total Asian women	**100.0**	**25.3**	**60.9**	**7.2**	**6.6**
Under age 55	100.0	31.5	60.4	7.0	1.1
Aged 55 or older	100.0	3.1	62.8	7.9	26.3
Aged 55 to 64	100.0	3.9	75.8	10.1	10.1
Aged 65 or older	100.0	2.2	50.3	5.7	41.9
Aged 65 to 74	100.0	1.8	61.4	6.1	30.4
Aged 75 to 84	100.0	2.2	39.2	6.1	52.5
Aged 85 or older	100.0	5.0	18.3	1.7	75.0

Note: Asians include those identifying themselves as being the race alone and those identifying themselves as being the race in combination with other races. "–" means number is less than 500 or sample is too small to make a reliable estimate.
Source: Bureau of the Census, Current Population Survey Annual Social and Economic Supplement, America's Families and Living Arrangements: 2004, detailed tables, Internet site http://www.census.gov/population/www/socdemo/hh-fam/cps2004.html; calculations by New Strategist

Table 6.17 Marital Status by Sex and Age, 2004: Blacks

(number and percent distribution of blacks aged 15 or older by sex, age, and current marital status, 2004; numbers in thousands)

	total	never married	married	separated or divorced	widowed
NUMBER					
Total black men	**12,330**	**5,795**	**4,689**	**1,535**	**312**
Under age 55	9,967	5,574	3,262	1,088	44
Aged 55 or older	2,364	222	1,428	445	269
Aged 55 to 64	1,243	141	771	279	51
Aged 65 or older	1,121	81	657	166	218
Aged 65 to 74	662	54	415	109	83
Aged 75 to 84	380	22	215	46	97
Aged 85 or older	78	4	27	11	37
Total black women	**15,110**	**6,417**	**4,587**	**2,715**	**1,390**
Under age 55	11,718	6,074	3,477	1,964	203
Aged 55 or older	3,391	344	1,108	752	1,187
Aged 55 to 64	1,581	217	643	451	270
Aged 65 or older	1,810	127	465	301	917
Aged 65 to 74	966	83	318	201	364
Aged 75 to 84	659	37	135	82	405
Aged 85 or older	185	7	13	16	148
PERCENT DISTRIBUTION					
Total black men	**100.0%**	**47.0%**	**38.0%**	**12.4%**	**2.5%**
Under age 55	100.0	55.9	32.7	10.9	0.4
Aged 55 or older	100.0	9.4	60.4	18.8	11.4
Aged 55 to 64	100.0	11.3	62.0	22.4	4.1
Aged 65 or older	100.0	7.2	58.6	14.8	19.4
Aged 65 to 74	100.0	8.2	62.7	16.5	12.5
Aged 75 to 84	100.0	5.8	56.6	12.1	25.5
Aged 85 or older	100.0	5.1	34.6	14.1	47.4
Total black women	**100.0**	**42.5**	**30.4**	**18.0**	**9.2**
Under age 55	100.0	51.8	29.7	16.8	1.7
Aged 55 or older	100.0	10.1	32.7	22.2	35.0
Aged 55 to 64	100.0	13.7	40.7	28.5	17.1
Aged 65 or older	100.0	7.0	25.7	16.6	50.7
Aged 65 to 74	100.0	8.6	32.9	20.8	37.7
Aged 75 to 84	100.0	5.6	20.5	12.4	61.5
Aged 85 or older	100.0	3.8	7.0	8.6	80.0

Note: Blacks include those identifying themselves as being of the race alone and those identifying themselves as being of the race in combination with other races.
Source: Bureau of the Census, Current Population Survey Annual Social and Economic Supplement, America's Families and Living Arrangements: 2004, detailed tables, Internet site http://www.census.gov/population/www/socdemo/hh-fam/cps2004.html; calculations by New Strategist

Table 6.18 Marital Status by Sex and Age, 2004: Hispanics

(number and percent distribution of Hispanics aged 15 or older by sex, age, and current marital status, 2004; numbers in thousands)

	total	never married	married	separated or divorced	widowed
NUMBER					
Total Hispanic men	**14,640**	**6,003**	**7,248**	**1,199**	**190**
Under age 55	12,736	5,881	5,864	949	43
Aged 55 or older	1,904	123	1,384	249	147
Aged 55 to 64	1,023	72	787	148	15
Aged 65 or older	881	51	597	101	132
Aged 65 to 74	545	24	381	77	63
Aged 75 to 84	282	26	186	23	48
Aged 85 or older	53	–	29	2	22
Total Hispanic women	**13,878**	**4,306**	**6,987**	**1,825**	**761**
Under age 55	11,540	4,166	5,838	1,389	145
Aged 55 or older	2,337	140	1,149	435	615
Aged 55 to 64	1,138	79	681	244	134
Aged 65 or older	1,199	61	468	191	481
Aged 65 to 74	727	37	333	148	210
Aged 75 to 84	366	21	115	38	192
Aged 85 or older	107	3	19	6	79
PERCENT DISTRIBUTION					
Total Hispanic men	**100.0%**	**41.0%**	**49.5%**	**8.2%**	**1.3%**
Under age 55	100.0	46.2	46.0	7.5	0.3
Aged 55 or older	100.0	6.5	72.7	13.1	7.7
Aged 55 to 64	100.0	7.0	76.9	14.5	1.5
Aged 65 or older	100.0	5.8	67.8	11.5	15.0
Aged 65 to 74	100.0	4.4	69.9	14.1	11.6
Aged 75 to 84	100.0	9.2	66.0	8.2	17.0
Aged 85 or older	100.0	–	54.7	3.8	41.5
Total Hispanic women	**100.0**	**31.0**	**50.3**	**13.2**	**5.5**
Under age 55	100.0	36.1	50.6	12.0	1.3
Aged 55 or older	100.0	6.0	49.2	18.6	26.3
Aged 55 to 64	100.0	6.9	59.8	21.4	11.8
Aged 65 or older	100.0	5.1	39.0	15.9	40.1
Aged 65 to 74	100.0	5.1	45.8	20.4	28.9
Aged 75 to 84	100.0	5.7	31.4	10.4	52.5
Aged 85 or older	100.0	2.8	17.8	5.6	73.8

Note: "–" means number is less than 500 or sample is too small to make a reliable estimate.
Source: Bureau of the Census, Current Population Survey Annual Social and Economic Supplement, America's Families and Living Arrangements: 2004, detailed tables, Internet site http://www.census.gov/population/www/socdemo/hh-fam/cps2004.html; calculations by New Strategist

Table 6.19 Marital Status by Sex and Age, 2004: Non-Hispanic Whites

(number and percent distribution of non-Hispanic whites aged 15 or older by sex, age, and current marital status, 2004; numbers in thousands)

	total	never married	married	separated or divorced	widowed
NUMBER					
Total non-Hispanic white men	**77,192**	**22,000**	**45,438**	**7,710**	**2,045**
Under age 55	54,360	20,984	27,796	5,358	220
Aged 55 or older	22,832	1,016	17,640	2,353	1,825
Aged 55 to 64	10,640	551	8,422	1,460	209
Aged 65 or older	12,192	465	9,218	893	1,616
Aged 65 to 74	6,755	282	5,394	623	456
Aged 75 to 84	4,401	158	3,221	215	807
Aged 85 or older	1,035	25	602	55	353
Total non-Hispanic white women	**82,115**	**17,683**	**45,380**	**10,484**	**8,567**
Under age 55	54,589	16,667	30,317	6,945	658
Aged 55 or older	27,526	1,015	15,061	3,541	7,911
Aged 55 to 64	11,400	475	7,816	2,136	974
Aged 65 or older	16,126	540	7,245	1,405	6,937
Aged 65 to 74	7,759	241	4,540	908	2,069
Aged 75 to 84	6,362	206	2,407	425	3,324
Aged 85 or older	2,005	93	298	71	1,544
PERCENT DISTRIBUTION					
Total non-Hispanic white men	**100.0%**	**28.5%**	**58.9%**	**10.0%**	**2.6%**
Under age 55	100.0	38.6	51.1	9.9	0.4
Aged 55 or older	100.0	4.4	77.3	10.3	8.0
Aged 55 to 64	100.0	5.2	79.2	13.7	2.0
Aged 65 or older	100.0	3.8	75.6	7.3	13.3
Aged 65 to 74	100.0	4.2	79.9	9.2	6.8
Aged 75 to 84	100.0	3.6	73.2	4.9	18.3
Aged 85 or older	100.0	2.4	58.2	5.3	34.1
Total non-Hispanic white women	**100.0**	**21.5**	**55.3**	**12.8**	**10.4**
Under age 55	100.0	30.5	55.5	12.7	1.2
Aged 55 or older	100.0	3.7	54.7	12.9	28.7
Aged 55 to 64	100.0	4.2	68.6	18.7	8.5
Aged 65 or older	100.0	3.3	44.9	8.7	43.0
Aged 65 to 74	100.0	3.1	58.5	11.7	26.7
Aged 75 to 84	100.0	3.2	37.8	6.7	52.2
Aged 85 or older	100.0	4.6	14.9	3.5	77.0

Note: Non-Hispanic whites include only those identifying themselves as being white alone and not Hispanic.
Source: Bureau of the Census, Current Population Survey Annual Social and Economic Supplement, America's Families and Living Arrangements: 2004, detailed tables, Internet site http://www.census.gov/population/www/socdemo/hh-fam/cps2004.html; calculations by New Strategist

7

Population

■ According to projections by the Census Bureau, the number of Americans aged 55 or older stood at 67 million in 2005, which accounts for 23 percent of the total population.

■ The number of people aged 55 or older will increase from 67 million in 2005 to 97 million in 2020. The enormous 45 percent gain is much greater than the 14 percent increase projected for the U.S. population as a whole during those years.

■ Eighty percent of people aged 55 or older are non-Hispanic white, according to Census Bureau projections for 2005. This figure is much higher than the 67 percent non-Hispanic white share among all Americans.

■ The 55-or-older age group accounts for only 20 percent of the total foreign-born population, but it represents a much larger 35 percent of the naturalized foreign-born.

■ The diversity of older Americans varies by state of residence, but not dramatically. Only in Hawaii are non-Hispanic whites a minority among the 55-or-older population.

Rapid Growth Is in Store for Older Age Groups

The 55-or-older age group is projected to expand by more than 30 million during the next 15 years.

According to projections by the Census Bureau, the number of Americans aged 55 or older stood at 67 million in 2005, which accounts for 23 percent of the population. The oldest members of the Baby-Boom generation entirely filled the 55-to-59 age group in 2005. Because mortality rates are higher for males than females, most older Americans are women. The sex ratio falls from 94 men per 100 women in the 55-to-59 age group to just 44 men per 100 women among people aged 85 or older.

The number of people aged 55 or older will increase from 67 million in 2005 to 97 million in 2020. The enormous 45 percent gain is much greater than the 14 percent increase projected for the U.S. population as a whole during those years. Behind the expansion is the entry of the Baby-Boom generation into the older age groups.

In the 15 years between 2005 and 2020, the number of people aged 60 to 74 (Boomers will be aged 56 to 74 in 2020) will expand by an enormous 66 percent—a gain of more than 20 million people. By 2020, the generations preceding the Baby Boom will account for only 7 percent of the nation's population—down from 17 percent today. Boomers will account for 21 percent of the population, down from 26 percent.

■ The rapid growth in the number of Americans in their sixties and seventies will focus the nation's attention on the wants and needs of the older population.

The number of older Americans will expand rapidly

(number of people aged 60 to 74, 2005 and 2020)

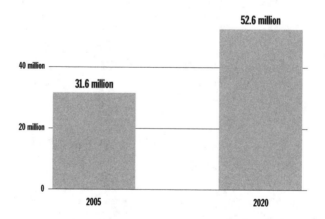

Table 7.1 Population by Age and Generation, 2005

(number and percent distribution of people by age and generation, 2005; numbers in thousands)

	number	percent distribution
Total people	**295,507**	**100.0%**
Under age 5	20,495	6.9
Aged 5 to 9	19,467	6.6
Aged 10 to 14	20,838	7.1
Aged 15 to 19	21,172	7.2
Aged 20 to 24	20,823	7.0
Aged 25 to 29	19,753	6.7
Aged 30 to 34	19,847	6.7
Aged 35 to 39	20,869	7.1
Aged 40 to 44	22,735	7.7
Aged 45 to 49	22,453	7.6
Aged 50 to 54	19,983	6.8
Aged 55 or older	67,072	22.7
Aged 55 to 59	17,359	5.9
Aged 60 to 64	13,017	4.4
Aged 65 or older	36,696	12.4
Aged 65 to 69	10,123	3.4
Aged 70 to 74	8,500	2.9
Aged 75 to 79	7,376	2.5
Aged 80 to 84	5,576	1.9
Aged 85 or older	5,120	1.7
Total people	**295,507**	**100.0**
Post-Millennial (under age 11)	43,978	14.9
Millennial (aged 11 to 28)	74,775	25.3
Generation X (aged 29 to 40)	48,985	16.6
Baby Boom (aged 41 to 59)	78,056	26.4
Older Americans (aged 60 or older)	49,713	16.8

Source: Bureau of the Census, State Interim Population Projections by Age and Sex: 2004–2030, Internet site http://www.census.gov/population/www/projections/projectionsagesex.html; calculations by New Strategist

Table 7.2 Population by Age and Sex, 2005

(number of people by age and sex, and sex ratio by age, 2005; numbers in thousands)

	total	female	male	sex ratio
Total people	**295,507**	**150,394**	**145,113**	**96**
Under age 5	20,495	10,024	10,471	104
Aged 5 to 9	19,467	9,512	9,954	105
Aged 10 to 14	20,838	10,167	10,670	105
Aged 15 to 19	21,172	10,310	10,862	105
Aged 20 to 24	20,823	10,166	10,657	105
Aged 25 to 29	19,753	9,737	10,016	103
Aged 30 to 34	19,847	9,860	9,987	101
Aged 35 to 39	20,869	10,420	10,449	100
Aged 40 to 44	22,735	11,452	11,282	99
Aged 45 to 49	22,453	11,377	11,076	97
Aged 50 to 54	19,983	10,212	9,771	96
Aged 55 or older	67,072	37,156	29,916	81
Aged 55 to 59	17,359	8,944	8,415	94
Aged 60 to 64	13,017	6,814	6,203	91
Aged 65 or older	36,696	21,397	15,299	71
Aged 65 to 69	10,123	5,412	4,712	87
Aged 70 to 74	8,500	4,697	3,804	81
Aged 75 to 79	7,376	4,282	3,094	72
Aged 80 to 84	5,576	3,459	2,117	61
Aged 85 or older	5,120	3,548	1,572	44

Note: The sex ratio is the number of males per 100 females.
Source: Bureau of the Census, State Interim Population Projections by Age and Sex: 2004–2030, Internet site http://www.census
.gov/population/www/projections/projectionsagesex.html; calculations by New Strategist

Table 7.3 Population by Age, 2000 and 2005

(number of people by age, April 1, 2000, and July 1, 2005; percent change 2000–05; numbers in thousands)

	2000	2005	percent change
Total people	**281,422**	**295,507**	**5.0%**
Under age 5	19,176	20,495	6.9
Aged 5 to 9	20,550	19,467	−5.3
Aged 10 to 14	20,528	20,838	1.5
Aged 15 to 19	20,220	21,172	4.7
Aged 20 to 24	18,964	20,823	9.8
Aged 25 to 29	19,381	19,753	1.9
Aged 30 to 34	20,510	19,847	−3.2
Aged 35 to 39	22,707	20,869	−8.1
Aged 40 to 44	22,442	22,735	1.3
Aged 45 to 49	20,092	22,453	11.7
Aged 50 to 54	17,586	19,983	13.6
Aged 55 to 59	13,469	17,359	28.9
Aged 60 to 64	10,805	13,017	20.5
Aged 65 to 69	9,534	10,123	6.2
Aged 70 to 74	8,857	8,500	−4.0
Aged 75 to 79	7,416	7,376	−0.5
Aged 80 to 84	4,945	5,576	12.7
Aged 85 or older	4,240	5,120	20.8

Source: Bureau of the Census, State Interim Population Projections by Age and Sex: 2004–2030, Internet site http://www.census .gov/population/www/projections/projectionsagesex.html; calculations by New Strategist

Table 7.4 Population by Age, 2005 to 2020

(number of people by age, 2005 to 2020; percent change, 2005–20; numbers in thousands)

	2005	2010	2015	2020	percent change 2005–20
Total people	**295,507**	**308,936**	**322,366**	**335,805**	**13.6%**
Under age 5	20,495	21,426	22,358	22,932	11.9
Aged 5 to 9	19,467	20,706	21,623	22,564	15.9
Aged 10 to 14	20,838	19,767	20,984	21,914	5.2
Aged 15 to 19	21,172	21,336	20,243	21,478	1.4
Aged 20 to 24	20,823	21,676	21,810	20,751	–0.3
Aged 25 to 29	19,753	21,375	22,195	22,361	13.2
Aged 30 to 34	19,847	20,271	21,858	22,704	14.4
Aged 35 to 39	20,869	20,137	20,543	22,143	6.1
Aged 40 to 44	22,735	20,984	20,250	20,673	–9.1
Aged 45 to 49	22,453	22,654	20,926	20,219	–9.9
Aged 50 to 54	19,983	22,173	22,376	20,702	3.6
Aged 55 to 59	17,359	19,507	21,649	21,876	26.0
Aged 60 to 64	13,017	16,679	18,761	20,856	60.2
Aged 65 to 69	10,123	12,172	15,621	17,618	74.0
Aged 70 to 74	8,500	9,097	10,987	14,161	66.6
Aged 75 to 79	7,376	7,186	7,761	9,450	28.1
Aged 80 to 84	5,576	5,665	5,600	6,134	10.0
Aged 85 or older	5,120	6,123	6,822	7,269	42.0

Source: Bureau of the Census, State Interim Population Projections by Age and Sex: 2004–2030, Internet site http://www.census .gov/population/www/projections/projectionsagesex.html; calculations by New Strategist

Table 7.5 Population by Generation, 2005 and 2020

(number and percent distribution of people by generation, 2005 and 2020; percent change in number, 2005–20; numbers in thousands)

	2005			2020		
	number	percent distribution		number	percent distribution	percent change 2005–20
Total people	**295,507**	**100.0%**	**Total people**	**335,805**	**100.0%**	**13.6%**
Post-Millennial (under 11)	43,978	14.9	Post-Millennial (under 26)	113,942	33.9	159.1
Millennial (11 to 28)	74,775	25.3	Millennial (26 to 43)	79,639	23.7	6.5
Generation X (29 to 40)	48,985	16.6	Generation X (44 to 55)	49,219	14.7	0.5
Baby Boom (41 to 59)	78,056	26.4	Baby Boom (56 to 74)	70,151	20.9	–10.1
Older Americans (60+)	49,713	16.8	Older Americans (75+)	22,853	6.8	–54.0

Source: Bureau of the Census, State Interim Population Projections by Age and Sex: 2004–2030, Internet site http://www.census .gov/population/www/projections/projectionsagesex.html; calculations by New Strategist

Older Americans Are Less Diverse than Younger Generations

Fewer than one in five older Americans is black, Hispanic, or Asian.

Eighty percent of people aged 55 or older are non-Hispanic white, according to Census Bureau projections for 2005. This figure is much higher than the 67 percent for the population as a whole and dwarfs the share among the youngest Americans—only 56 percent of children under age 5 are non-Hispanic white.

Just 6 percent of people aged 60 or older are Hispanic. The figure is a slightly larger 10 percent among Boomers (aged 41 to 59 in 2005). In comparison, 21 percent of children under age 11 are Hispanic. Only 9 percent of older Americans are black versus 15 percent of Millennials and younger people. Among people aged 55 or older, blacks outnumber Hispanics by more than 1.5 million. Among people under age 55, Hispanics outnumber blacks by more than 5 million.

■ The differences in the racial and ethnic composition of older and younger generations may create political tension in the years ahead.

More than 80 percent of the oldest Americans are non-Hispanic white

(non-Hispanic white share of population by generation, 2005)

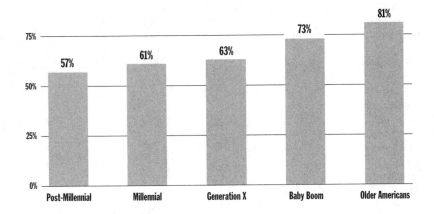

Table 7.6 Population by Age, Race, and Hispanic Origin, 2005

(number and percent distribution of people by age, race, and Hispanic origin, 2005; numbers in thousands)

	number	Asian	black	Hispanic	non-Hispanic white
Total people	**295,507**	**12,419**	**38,056**	**41,801**	**198,451**
Under age 5	20,495	833	3,113	4,397	11,528
Aged 5 to 9	19,467	763	2,941	3,892	11,330
Aged 10 to 14	20,838	787	3,332	3,853	12,370
Aged 15 to 19	21,172	815	3,306	3,576	13,013
Aged 20 to 24	20,823	898	3,078	3,604	12,836
Aged 25 to 29	19,753	985	2,807	3,781	11,881
Aged 30 to 34	19,847	1,190	2,678	3,666	12,060
Aged 35 to 39	20,869	1,117	2,732	3,297	13,480
Aged 40 to 44	22,735	1,033	2,892	2,926	15,606
Aged 45 to 49	22,453	948	2,736	2,375	16,113
Aged 50 to 54	19,983	828	2,276	1,823	14,812
Aged 55 or older	67,072	2,223	6,165	4,611	53,421
Aged 55 to 59	17,359	685	1,788	1,393	13,289
Aged 60 to 64	13,017	480	1,250	978	10,161
Aged 65 or older	36,696	1,058	3,127	2,240	29,971
Aged 65 to 69	10,123	370	972	745	7,931
Aged 70 to 74	8,500	275	767	571	6,811
Aged 75 to 79	7,376	200	591	433	6,097
Aged 80 to 84	5,576	125	407	275	4,733
Aged 85 or older	5,120	87	390	216	4,398

PERCENT DISTRIBUTION BY RACE AND HISPANIC ORIGIN

	number	Asian	black	Hispanic	non-Hispanic white
Total people	**100.0%**	**4.2%**	**12.9%**	**14.1%**	**67.2%**
Under age 5	100.0	4.1	15.2	21.5	56.2
Aged 5 to 9	100.0	3.9	15.1	20.0	58.2
Aged 10 to 14	100.0	3.8	16.0	18.5	59.4
Aged 15 to 19	100.0	3.8	15.6	16.9	61.5
Aged 20 to 24	100.0	4.3	14.8	17.3	61.6
Aged 25 to 29	100.0	5.0	14.2	19.1	60.1
Aged 30 to 34	100.0	6.0	13.5	18.5	60.8
Aged 35 to 39	100.0	5.4	13.1	15.8	64.6
Aged 40 to 44	100.0	4.5	12.7	12.9	68.6
Aged 45 to 49	100.0	4.2	12.2	10.6	71.8
Aged 50 to 54	100.0	4.1	11.4	9.1	74.1
Aged 55 or older	100.0	3.3	9.2	6.9	79.6
Aged 55 to 59	100.0	3.9	10.3	8.0	76.6
Aged 60 to 64	100.0	3.7	9.6	7.5	78.1
Aged 65 or older	100.0	2.9	8.5	6.1	81.7
Aged 65 to 69	100.0	3.7	9.6	7.4	78.3
Aged 70 to 74	100.0	3.2	9.0	6.7	80.1
Aged 75 to 79	100.0	2.7	8.0	5.9	82.7
Aged 80 to 84	100.0	2.2	7.3	4.9	84.9
Aged 85 or older	100.0	1.7	7.6	4.2	85.9

Note: Numbers will not add to total because Asians and blacks include those who identified themselves as being of the respective race alone and those who identified themselves as being the race in combination with one or more other races, and because Hispanics may be of any race. Non-Hispanic whites include only those who identified themselves as being white alone and not Hispanic.
Source: Bureau of the Census, U.S. Interim Projections by Age, Sex, Race, and Hispanic Origin, Internet site http://www.census .gov/ipc/www/usinterimproj/; calculations by New Strategist

Table 7.7 Population by Generation, Race, and Hispanic Origin, 2005

(number and percent distribution of people by generation, race, and Hispanic origin, 2005; numbers in thousands)

	total	Asian	black	Hispanic	non-Hispanic white
Total people	**295,507**	**12,419**	**38,056**	**41,801**	**198,451**
Post-Millennial (under age 11)	43,978	1,751	6,680	9,058	25,223
Millennial (aged 11 to 28)	74,775	3,114	11,375	13,287	45,488
Generation X (aged 29 to 40)	48,985	2,735	6,522	8,353	30,772
Baby Boom (aged 41 to 59)	78,056	3,280	9,101	7,885	56,836
Older Americans (aged 60 or older)	49,713	1,538	4,377	3,218	40,132

PERCENT DISTRIBUTION BY RACE AND HISPANIC ORIGIN

	total	Asian	black	Hispanic	non-Hispanic white
Total people	**100.0%**	**4.2%**	**12.9%**	**14.1%**	**67.2%**
Post-Millennial (under age 11)	100.0	4.0	15.2	20.6	57.4
Millennial (aged 11 to 28)	100.0	4.2	15.2	17.8	60.8
Generation X (aged 29 to 40)	100.0	5.6	13.3	17.1	62.8
Baby Boom (aged 41 to 59)	100.0	4.2	11.7	10.1	72.8
Older Americans (aged 60 or older)	100.0	3.1	8.8	6.5	80.7

PERCENT DISTRIBUTION BY GENERATION

	total	Asian	black	Hispanic	non-Hispanic white
Total people	**100.0%**	**100.0%**	**100.0%**	**100.0%**	**100.0%**
Post-Millennial (under age 11)	14.9	14.1	17.6	21.7	12.7
Millennial (aged 11 to 28)	25.3	25.1	29.9	31.8	22.9
Generation X (aged 29 to 40)	16.6	22.0	17.1	20.0	15.5
Baby Boom (aged 41 to 59)	26.4	26.4	23.9	18.9	28.6
Older Americans (aged 60 or older)	16.8	12.4	11.5	7.7	20.2

Note: Numbers will not add to total because Asians and blacks include those who identified themselves as being of the respective race alone and those who identified themselves as being of the race in combination with one or more other races, and because Hispanics may be of any race. Non-Hispanic whites include only those who identified themselves as being white alone and not Hispanic.
Source: Bureau of the Census, U.S. Interim Projections by Age, Sex, Race, and Hispanic Origin, Internet site http://www.census.gov/ipc/www/usinterimproj/; calculations by New Strategist

One in Nine Older Americans Is Foreign-Born

Many of the older foreign born are from Europe.

A substantial 11.9 percent of all Americans are foreign-born, but the proportion is a slightly smaller 10.9 percent among people aged 55 or older. Of the nearly 7 million people aged 55 or older who were born in a foreign country, the 67 percent majority are naturalized citizens. The 55-or-older age group accounts for only 20 percent of the total foreign-born population, but it represents a much larger 35 percent of the naturalized foreign-born.

Among the foreign-born aged 55 or older, 28 percent are from Europe. This share is much larger than the 19 percent from Central America (a region that includes Mexico in these statistics). Among the foreign-born under age 55, a much larger 42 percent are from Central America. There are fewer differences in the proportion of foreign-born from Asia. The Asian foreign-born account for 28 percent of the foreign-born population aged 55 or older and for 25 percent of the foreign-born under age 55.

■ As younger generations replace older Americans, the European-born population is shrinking.

Among the older foreign-born, more than one-fourth are from Europe

(percent distribution of foreign-born population aged 55 or older, by region of birth, 2004)

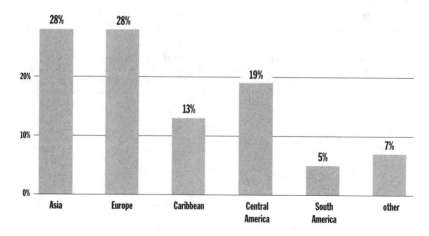

Table 7.8 Population by Age and Citizenship Status, 2004

(number and percent distribution of people by age and citizenship status, 2004; numbers in thousands)

	total	native born	foreign-born total	naturalized citizen	not a citizen
Total people	**288,280**	**254,037**	**34,244**	**13,128**	**21,116**
Under age 55	225,247	197,870	27,377	8,551	18,826
Aged 55 or older	63,036	56,167	6,867	4,576	2,291
Aged 55 to 59	16,158	14,347	1,811	1,077	734
Aged 60 to 64	12,217	10,857	1,359	864	495
Aged 65 or older	34,661	30,963	3,697	2,635	1,062
Aged 65 to 69	9,819	8,624	1,195	790	405
Aged 70 to 74	8,420	7,522	897	606	291
Aged 75 to 79	7,631	6,876	755	563	192
Aged 80 to 84	5,220	4,744	476	383	93
Aged 85 or older	3,571	3,197	374	293	81

PERCENT DISTRIBUTION BY CITIZENSHIP STATUS

	total	native born	foreign-born total	naturalized citizen	not a citizen
Total people	**100.0%**	**88.1%**	**11.9%**	**4.6%**	**7.3%**
Under age 55	100.0	87.8	12.2	3.8	8.4
Aged 55 or older	100.0	89.1	10.9	7.3	3.6
Aged 55 to 59	100.0	88.8	11.2	6.7	4.5
Aged 60 to 64	100.0	88.9	11.1	7.1	4.1
Aged 65 or older	100.0	89.3	10.7	7.6	3.1
Aged 65 to 69	100.0	87.8	12.2	8.0	4.1
Aged 70 to 74	100.0	89.3	10.7	7.2	3.5
Aged 75 to 79	100.0	90.1	9.9	7.4	2.5
Aged 80 to 84	100.0	90.9	9.1	7.3	1.8
Aged 85 or older	100.0	89.5	10.5	8.2	2.3

PERCENT DISTRIBUTION BY AGE

	total	native born	foreign-born total	naturalized citizen	not a citizen
Total people	**100.0%**	**100.0%**	**100.0%**	**100.0%**	**100.0%**
Under age 55	78.1	77.9	79.9	65.1	89.2
Aged 55 or older	21.9	22.1	20.1	34.9	10.8
Aged 55 to 59	5.6	5.6	5.3	8.2	3.5
Aged 60 to 64	4.2	4.3	4.0	6.6	2.3
Aged 65 or older	12.0	12.2	10.8	20.1	5.0
Aged 65 to 69	3.4	3.4	3.5	6.0	1.9
Aged 70 to 74	2.9	3.0	2.6	4.6	1.4
Aged 75 to 79	2.6	2.7	2.2	4.3	0.9
Aged 80 to 84	1.8	1.9	1.4	2.9	0.4
Aged 85 or older	1.2	1.3	1.1	2.2	0.4

Source: Bureau of the Census, Foreign Born Population of the United States, Current Population Survey, March 2004, Internet site http://www.census.gov/population/www/socdemo/foreign/ppl-176.html#cit; calculations by New Strategist

Table 7.9 Foreign-Born Population by Age and World Region of Birth, 2004

(number and percent distribution of people by age, foreign-born status, and region of birth, 2004; numbers in thousands)

		foreign-born							
					Latin America				
	total	total	Asia	Europe	total	Caribbean	Central America	South America	other
Total people	**288,280**	**34,244**	**8,685**	**4,661**	**18,314**	**3,323**	**12,924**	**2,066**	**2,584**
Under age 55	225,247	27,377	6,756	2,754	15,777	2,428	11,633	1,717	2,092
Aged 55 or older	63,036	6,867	1,929	1,908	2,537	896	1,290	349	494
Aged 55 to 59	16,158	1,811	600	346	739	208	422	108	127
Aged 60 to 64	12,217	1,359	389	293	570	186	292	92	108
Aged 65 or older	34,661	3,697	940	1,269	1,228	502	576	149	259
Aged 65 to 69	9,819	1,195	322	353	460	162	239	59	59
Aged 70 to 74	8,420	897	271	258	304	124	127	53	64
Aged 75 to 79	7,631	755	178	298	225	105	98	22	54
Aged 80 to 84	5,220	476	84	209	145	62	78	5	38
Aged 85 or older	3,571	374	85	151	94	49	34	10	44

PERCENT DISTRIBUTION OF FOREIGN-BORN BY REGION OF BIRTH

Total people	–	**100.0%**	**25.4%**	**13.6%**	**53.5%**	**9.7%**	**37.7%**	**6.0%**	**7.5%**
Under age 55	–	100.0	24.7	10.1	57.6	8.9	42.5	6.3	7.6
Aged 55 or older	–	100.0	28.1	27.8	36.9	13.0	18.8	5.1	7.2
Aged 55 to 59	–	100.0	33.1	19.1	40.8	11.5	23.3	6.0	7.0
Aged 60 to 64	–	100.0	28.6	21.6	41.9	13.7	21.5	6.8	7.9
Aged 65 or older	–	100.0	25.4	34.3	33.2	13.6	15.6	4.0	7.0
Aged 65 to 69	–	100.0	26.9	29.5	38.5	13.6	20.0	4.9	4.9
Aged 70 to 74	–	100.0	30.2	28.8	33.9	13.8	14.2	5.9	7.1
Aged 75 to 79	–	100.0	23.6	39.5	29.8	13.9	13.0	2.9	7.2
Aged 80 to 84	–	100.0	17.6	43.9	30.5	13.0	16.4	1.1	8.0
Aged 85 or older	–	100.0	22.7	40.4	25.1	13.1	9.1	2.7	11.8

PERCENT DISTRIBUTION BY AGE

Total people	**100.0%**	**100.0%**	**100.0%**	**100.0%**	**100.0%**	**100.0%**	**100.0%**	**100.0%**	**100.0%**
Under age 55	78.1	79.9	77.8	59.1	86.1	73.1	90.0	83.1	81.0
Aged 55 or older	21.9	20.1	22.2	40.9	13.9	27.0	10.0	16.9	19.1
Aged 55 to 59	5.6	5.3	6.9	7.4	4.0	6.3	3.3	5.2	4.9
Aged 60 to 64	4.2	4.0	4.5	6.3	3.1	5.6	2.3	4.5	4.2
Aged 65 or older	12.0	10.8	10.8	27.2	6.7	15.1	4.5	7.2	10.0
Aged 65 to 69	3.4	3.5	3.7	7.6	2.5	4.9	1.8	2.9	2.3
Aged 70 to 74	2.9	2.6	3.1	5.5	1.7	3.7	1.0	2.6	2.5
Aged 75 to 79	2.6	2.2	2.0	6.4	1.2	3.2	0.8	1.1	2.1
Aged 80 to 84	1.8	1.4	1.0	4.5	0.8	1.9	0.6	0.2	1.5
Aged 85 or older	1.2	1.1	1.0	3.2	0.5	1.5	0.3	0.5	1.7

Note: Central America includes Mexico in these statistics; "–" means not applicable.
Source: Bureau of the Census, Foreign Born Population of the United States, Current Population Survey, March 2004, Internet site http://www.census.gov/population/www/socdemo/foreign/ppl-176.html#cit; calculations by New Strategist

Few Recent Immigrants Are in the Older Age Groups

Only one in ten immigrants in 2004 was aged 55 or older.

The number of legal immigrants admitted to the U.S. numbered over 900,000 in 2004. Only about 97,000 were aged 55 or older, which accounted for 10 percent of the total. Most immigrants are young adults seeking economic opportunity for themselves and their families.

Within the 55-or-older age group, the immigrant share declines with age. Three percent of immigrants admitted to the U.S. in 2004 were aged 55 to 59, the figure falling to just 1 percent in the 75-or-older age group.

■ Because most immigrants are children and young adults, immigration has a much greater impact on the diversity of younger Americans than on the older population.

Immigrants aged 55 or older accounted for just 10 percent of the 2004 total

(percent distribution of immigrants by age, 2004)

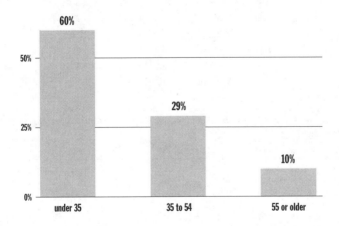

Table 7.10 Immigrants by Age, 2004

(number and percent distribution of immigrants by age, 2004)

	number	percent distribution
Total immigrants	**946,142**	**100.0%**
Under age 1	7,807	0.8
Aged 1 to 4	22,932	2.4
Aged 5 to 9	48,181	5.1
Aged 10 to 14	58,821	6.2
Aged 15 to 19	78,069	8.3
Aged 20 to 24	86,278	9.1
Aged 25 to 29	124,406	13.1
Aged 30 to 34	143,921	15.2
Aged 35 to 39	107,251	11.3
Aged 40 to 44	76,404	8.1
Aged 45 to 49	55,223	5.8
Aged 50 to 54	39,661	4.2
Aged 55 or older	97,148	10.3
Aged 55 to 59	30,037	3.2
Aged 60 to 64	23,829	2.5
Aged 65 or older	43,282	4.6
Aged 65 to 74	32,346	3.4
Aged 75 or older	10,936	1.2

Note: Numbers may not sum to total because "age not stated" is not shown.
Source: Office of Immigration Statistics, 2004 Yearbook of Immigration Statistics, Internet site http://uscis.gov/graphics/shared/statistics/yearbook/YrBk04Im.htm; calculations by New Strategist

Many Americans Do Not Speak English at Home

Most are Spanish speakers, but many also speak English.

Nearly 50 million Americans speak a language other than English at home, according to the Census Bureau's 2004 American Community Survey—19 percent of the population aged 5 or older. Among those who do not speak English at home, 61 percent speak Spanish.

The percentage of Americans who do not speak English at home does not vary much by age—19 percent of school children, 20 percent of working-age adults, and 13 percent of the elderly. But the languages spoken by each age group at home do vary by age. Fully 71 percent of children aged 5 to 17 who do not speak English at home are Spanish speakers. The proportion is a smaller 61 percent among adults aged 18 to 64, and falls to just 43 percent among people aged 65 or older. Thirty-seven percent of the elderly who do not speak English at home speak another Indo-European language, and 17 percent speak an Asian language.

Among school children, most of those who do not speak English at home are able to speak English "very well." Only 29 percent of the Spanish speakers aged 5 to 17, for example, cannot speak English very well. Among working-age adults, a much larger 53 percent of the Spanish speakers cannot speak English very well. Among people aged 65 or older, most of those who speak Spanish or an Asian language at home cannot speak English very well.

■ The language barrier is a bigger problem for adults than for school children.

Few children who speak Spanish at home cannot speak English "very well"

(percent of people aged 5 or older who speak Spanish at home and do not speak English "very well," by age, 2004)

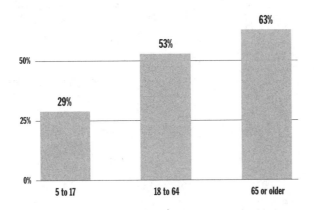

Table 7.11 Language Spoken at Home by Age, 2004

(number and percent distribution of people aged 5 or older who speak a language other than English at home by language spoken at home, and ability to speak English "very well," by age, 2004; numbers in thousands)

	total		aged 5 to 17		aged 18 to 64		aged 65 or older	
	number	percent distribution	number	percent distribution	number	percent distribution	number	percent distribution
Total, aged 5 or older	**265,683**	100.0%	**52,916**	100.0%	178,562	100.0%	34,205	100.0%
Speak only English at home	216,050	81.3	42,939	81.1	143,420	80.3	29,691	86.8
Speak a language other than English at home	49,633	18.7	9,977	18.9	35,142	19.7	4,514	13.2
Speak English less than "very well"	22,305	8.4	2,774	5.2	16,944	9.5	2,587	7.6
Total who speak a language other than English at home	**49,633**	**100.0**	**9,977**	**100.0**	**35,142**	**100.0**	**4,514**	**100.0**
Speak Spanish at home	30,522	61.5	7,103	71.2	21,498	61.2	1,921	42.6
Speak other Indo-European language at home	9,634	19.4	1,440	14.4	6,530	18.6	1,664	36.9
Speak Asian or Pacific Island language at home	7,614	15.3	1,116	11.2	5,730	16.3	769	17.0
Speak other language at home	1,863	3.8	318	3.2	1,384	3.9	161	3.6
Speak Spanish at home	**30,522**	**100.0**	**7,103**	**100.0**	**21,498**	**100.0**	**1,921**	**100.0**
Speak English less than "very well"	14,637	48.0	2,075	29.2	11,358	52.8	1,203	62.6
Speak other Indo-European language at home	**9,634**	**100.0**	**1,440**	**100.0**	**6,530**	**100.0**	**1,664**	**100.0**
Speak English less than "very well"	3,317	34.4	341	23.6	2,237	34.3	740	44.4
Speak Asian or Pacific Island language at home	**7,614**	**100.0**	**1,116**	**100.0**	**5,730**	**100.0**	**769**	**100.0**
Speak English less than "very well"	3,807	50.0	306	27.4	2,932	51.2	569	74.0
Speak other language at home	**1,863**	**100.0**	**318**	**100.0**	**1,384**	**100.0**	**161**	**100.0**
Speak English less than "very well"	545	29.3	53	16.6	417	30.1	75	46.7

Source: Bureau of the Census, 2004 American Community Survey Data Profile, Internet site http://factfinder.census.gov/servlet/ DatasetMainPageServlet?_program=ACS&_submenuId=datasets_2&_lang=en&_ts=; calculations by New Strategist

The Largest Share of Older Americans Lives in the South

People aged 55 or older account for 27 percent of the populations of Florida and West Virginia.

The South is home to the largest share of the population and, consequently, to the largest share of older Americans. The Census Bureau's 2004 American Community Survey found 36 percent of people aged 55 or older living in the South, where they accounted for 22 percent of the population.

Utah and Alaska have the smallest proportions of older residents—just 16 percent of people living in those states are aged 55 or older. Florida's warm climate attracts many retirees, which is why the state ranks first in the proportion of residents aged 55 or older.

The diversity of older Americans varies by state of residence, but not nearly as dramatically as it does among middle-aged and younger Americans. Only in Hawaii are non-Hispanic whites a minority among the 55-or-older population. In the nation's most populous state, California, the 63 percent majority of people aged 55 or older are non-Hispanic white. In contrast, only 31 percent of California's children under age 11 are non-Hispanic white.

■ The diversity of the older population will surge when Generation X enters the 55-or-older age group beginning in 2020.

The smallest share of older Americans lives in the Northeast

(percent distribution of people aged 55 or older, by region of residence, 2004)

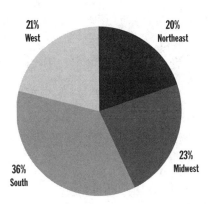

Table 7.12 Population by Age and Region, 2004

(number and percent distribution of people by age and region of residence, 2004; numbers in thousands)

	total	Northeast	Midwest	South	West
Total people	**285,692**	**52,865**	**63,910**	**103,021**	**65,896**
Under age 55	222,640	40,292	49,632	80,182	52,535
Aged 55 or older	63,051	12,572	14,278	22,839	13,361
Aged 55 to 59	16,227	3,191	3,586	5,874	3,575
Aged 60 to 64	12,619	2,443	2,878	4,623	2,675
Aged 65 or older	34,205	6,939	7,814	12,342	7,111
Aged 65 to 69	9,812	1,817	2,162	3,745	2,088
Aged 70 to 74	8,352	1,631	1,876	3,105	1,740
Aged 75 to 79	7,234	1,552	1,688	2,542	1,452
Aged 80 to 84	5,181	1,116	1,215	1,774	1,077
Aged 85 or older	3,626	824	872	1,176	754

PERCENT DISTRIBUTION BY AGE

	total	Northeast	Midwest	South	West
Total people	**100.0%**	**100.0%**	**100.0%**	**100.0%**	**100.0%**
Under age 55	77.9	76.2	77.7	77.8	79.7
Aged 55 or older	22.1	23.8	22.3	22.2	20.3
Aged 55 to 59	5.7	6.0	5.6	5.7	5.4
Aged 60 to 64	4.4	4.6	4.5	4.5	4.1
Aged 65 or older	12.0	13.1	12.2	12.0	10.8
Aged 65 to 69	3.4	3.4	3.4	3.6	3.2
Aged 70 to 74	2.9	3.1	2.9	3.0	2.6
Aged 75 to 79	2.5	2.9	2.6	2.5	2.2
Aged 80 to 84	1.8	2.1	1.9	1.7	1.6
Aged 85 or older	1.3	1.6	1.4	1.1	1.1

PERCENT DISTRIBUTION BY REGION

	total	Northeast	Midwest	South	West
Total people	**100.0%**	**18.5%**	**22.4%**	**36.1%**	**23.1%**
Under age 55	100.0	18.1	22.3	36.0	23.6
Total, aged 55 or older	100.0	19.9	22.6	36.2	21.2
Aged 55 to 59	100.0	19.7	22.1	36.2	22.0
Aged 60 to 64	100.0	19.4	22.8	36.6	21.2
Aged 65 or older	100.0	20.3	22.8	36.1	20.8
Aged 65 to 69	100.0	18.5	22.0	38.2	21.3
Aged 70 to 74	100.0	19.5	22.5	37.2	20.8
Aged 75 to 79	100.0	21.4	23.3	35.1	20.1
Aged 80 to 84	100.0	21.5	23.5	34.2	20.8
Aged 85 or older	100.0	22.7	24.1	32.4	20.8

Source: Bureau of the Census, 2004 American Community Survey, Internet site http://factfinder.census.gov/servlet/ DatasetMainPageServlet?_program=ACS&_lang=en&_ts=143547961449; calculations by New Strategist

Table 7.13 Population by Generation and Region, 2004

(number and percent distribution of people by generation and region of residence, 2004; numbers in thousands)

	total	Northeast	Midwest	South	West
Total people	**285,692**	**52,865**	**63,910**	**103,021**	**65,896**
Post-Millennial (under age 10)	39,667	6,778	8,693	14,542	9,655
Millennial (aged 10 to 27)	70,753	12,274	15,907	25,503	17,069
Generation X (aged 28 to 39)	48,123	8,908	10,445	17,334	11,437
Baby Boom (aged 40 to 58)	77,079	14,885	17,457	27,503	17,235
Older Americans (aged 59 or older)	50,069	10,020	11,409	18,140	10,500

PERCENT DISTRIBUTION BY GENERATION

	total	Northeast	Midwest	South	West
Total people	**100.0%**	**100.0%**	**100.0%**	**100.0%**	**100.0%**
Post-Millennial (under age 10)	13.9	12.8	13.6	14.1	14.7
Millennial (aged 10 to 27)	24.8	23.2	24.9	24.8	25.9
Generation X (aged 28 to 39)	16.8	16.9	16.3	16.8	17.4
Baby Boom (aged 40 to 58)	27.0	28.2	27.3	26.7	26.2
Older Americans (aged 59 or older)	17.5	19.0	17.9	17.6	15.9

PERCENT DISTRIBUTION BY REGION

	total	Northeast	Midwest	South	West
Total people	**100.0%**	**18.5%**	**22.4%**	**36.1%**	**23.1%**
Post-Millennial (under age 10)	100.0	17.1	21.9	36.7	24.3
Millennial (aged 10 to 27)	100.0	17.3	22.5	36.0	24.1
Generation X (aged 28 to 39)	100.0	18.5	21.7	36.0	23.8
Baby Boom (aged 40 to 58)	100.0	19.3	22.6	35.7	22.4
Older Americans (aged 59 or older)	100.0	20.0	22.8	36.2	21.0

Source: Bureau of the Census, 2004 American Community Survey, Internet site http://factfinder.census.gov/servlet/DatasetMainPageServlet?_program=ACS&_lang=en&_ts=143547961449; calculations by New Strategist

Table 7.14 Population Aged 55 or Older by Region, Race, and Hispanic Origin, 2004

(number and percent distribution of people aged 55 or older by region of residence, race, and Hispanic origin, 2004; numbers in thousands)

	total aged 55 or older	Asian	black	Hispanic	non-Hispanic white
United States	**63,051**	**2,091**	**5,612**	**4,263**	**50,375**
Northeast	12,572	387	1,074	696	10,374
Midwest	14,278	179	1,026	287	12,672
South	22,839	340	3,024	1,583	17,635
West	13,361	1,185	487	1,698	9,694

PERCENT DISTRIBUTION BY RACE AND HISPANIC ORIGIN

United States	**100.0%**	**3.3%**	**8.9%**	**6.8%**	**79.9%**
Northeast	100.0	3.1	8.5	5.5	82.5
Midwest	100.0	1.3	7.2	2.0	88.7
South	100.0	1.5	13.2	6.9	77.2
West	100.0	8.9	3.6	12.7	72.6

PERCENT DISTRIBUTION BY REGION

United States	**100.0%**	**100.0%**	**100.0%**	**100.0%**	**100.0%**
Northeast	19.9	18.5	19.1	16.3	20.6
Midwest	22.6	8.5	18.3	6.7	25.2
South	36.2	16.3	53.9	37.1	35.0
West	21.2	56.7	8.7	39.8	19.2

Note: Blacks and Asians are those who identify themselves as being of the respective race alone. Non-Hispanic whites are those who identify themselves as being white alone and not Hispanic. Numbers will not sum to total because Hispanics may be of any race and not all races are shown.
Source: Bureau of the Census, 2004 American Community Survey, Internet site http://factfinder.census.gov/servlet/ DatasetMainPageServlet?_program=ACS&_lang=en&_ts=143547961449; calculations by New Strategist

Table 7.15 Older Generations by Region, Race, and Hispanic Origin, 2004

(number and percent distribution of people aged 59 or older by region of residence, race, and Hispanic origin, 2004; numbers in thousands)

	total aged 59 or older	Asian	black	Hispanic	non-Hispanic white
United States	**50,069**	**1,607**	**4,375**	**3,288**	**40,256**
Northeast	10,020	290	838	531	8,339
Midwest	11,409	130	804	215	10,128
South	18,140	253	2,352	1,235	14,084
West	10,500	934	381	1,308	7,706
PERCENT DISTRIBUTION BY RACE AND HISPANIC ORIGIN					
United States	**100.0%**	**3.2%**	**8.7%**	**6.6%**	**80.4%**
Northeast	100.0	2.9	8.4	5.3	83.2
Midwest	100.0	1.1	7.0	1.9	88.8
South	100.0	1.4	13.0	6.8	77.6
West	100.0	8.9	3.6	12.5	73.4
PERCENT DISTRIBUTION BY REGION					
United States	**100.0%**	**100.0%**	**100.0%**	**100.0%**	**100.0%**
Northeast	20.0	18.0	19.2	16.1	20.7
Midwest	22.8	8.1	18.4	6.5	25.2
South	36.2	15.7	53.8	37.6	35.0
West	21.0	58.2	8.7	39.8	19.1

Note: The older generations included people aged 59 or older in 2004. Blacks and Asians are those who identify themselves as being of the respective race alone. Non-Hispanic whites are those who identify themselves as being white alone and not Hispanic. Numbers will not sum to total because Hispanics may be of any race and not all races are shown.
Source: Bureau of the Census, 2004 American Community Survey, Internet site http://factfinder.census.gov/servlet/ DatasetMainPageServlet?_program=ACS&_lang=en&_ts=143547961449; calculations by New Strategist

Table 7.16 State Populations Aged 55 or Older, 2004

(number of people aged 55 or older by state of residence, 2004; numbers in thousands)

| | | aged 55 or older | | | | | | | |
| | | | | aged 65 or older | | | | | |
	total population	total	55 to 59	60 to 64	total	65 to 69	70 to 74	75 to 79	80 to 84	85 or older
United States	**285,692**	**63,051**	**16,227**	**12,619**	**34,205**	**9,812**	**8,352**	**7,234**	**5,181**	**3,626**
Alabama	4,415	1,044	272	210	562	170	148	119	77	49
Alaska	636	100	38	22	39	14	11	7	4	3
Arizona	5,634	1,250	295	247	709	202	193	152	100	63
Arkansas	2,676	645	159	133	353	104	94	72	49	34
California	35,055	6,850	1,839	1,356	3,655	1,051	888	749	570	398
Colorado	4,499	845	237	176	431	140	106	82	62	42
Connecticut	3,389	814	212	164	438	112	102	100	73	52
Delaware	805	190	48	37	104	30	27	21	16	9
District of Columbia	518	117	29	25	63	18	15	12	11	7
Florida	16,990	4,663	997	855	2,811	775	682	611	443	301
Georgia	8,581	1,592	451	351	791	276	194	149	97	75
Hawaii	1,227	304	77	59	168	41	40	40	27	21
Idaho	1,360	286	78	57	151	46	34	31	21	18
Illinois	12,391	2,627	670	534	1,423	392	352	297	224	158
Indiana	6,059	1,326	330	280	715	205	172	160	105	73
Iowa	2,851	693	165	130	397	102	96	84	62	52
Kansas	2,653	581	139	112	330	89	81	68	58	34
Kentucky	4,031	927	242	196	490	154	125	103	65	42
Louisiana	4,381	928	244	190	494	160	116	101	74	44
Maine	1,279	331	95	58	178	48	46	37	26	21
Maryland	5,422	1,169	315	256	597	167	148	122	94	68
Massachusetts	6,201	1,437	386	260	791	202	182	176	131	99
Michigan	9,859	2,190	568	441	1,180	321	277	268	180	133
Minnesota	4,959	1,050	265	215	570	162	135	111	94	69
Mississippi	2,805	610	157	124	330	105	82	67	44	32
Missouri	5,586	1,303	325	265	713	208	175	148	105	77
Montana	902	225	60	46	119	37	29	24	16	14
Nebraska	1,697	383	97	72	214	59	48	48	31	28
Nevada	2,301	492	135	102	255	92	63	50	31	18
New Hampshire	1,262	287	83	59	145	39	39	34	21	13
New Jersey	8,503	1,941	495	381	1,065	277	254	238	170	126
New Mexico	1,863	418	113	88	217	66	58	43	30	20
New York	18,634	4,290	1,080	866	2,344	643	557	503	367	273
North Carolina	8,270	1,812	468	379	966	305	236	196	137	92
North Dakota	610	148	36	27	86	22	20	18	15	10
Ohio	11,154	2,602	658	520	1,424	396	333	317	223	154
Oklahoma	3,412	800	210	153	437	125	118	93	64	37
Oregon	3,514	814	213	160	441	122	104	90	72	54
Pennsylvania	11,958	3,075	735	577	1,763	441	401	416	292	213
Rhode Island	1,037	247	61	47	139	32	31	33	25	18

(continued)

	total population	aged 55 or older			aged 65 or older					
		toal	55 to 59	60 to 64	total	65 to 69	70 to 74	75 to 79	80 to 84	85 or older
South Carolina	4,060	938	255	194	489	149	132	96	72	42
South Dakota	741	173	40	33	100	26	25	21	15	13
Tennessee	5,748	1,319	341	279	698	220	180	136	103	59
Texas	21,912	4,030	1,123	817	2,090	667	542	416	279	186
Utah	2,349	367	104	66	197	62	46	38	30	22
Vermont	601	150	44	30	76	22	19	16	11	9
Virginia	7,224	1,575	442	331	802	244	201	172	113	72
Washington	6,063	1,296	352	273	671	198	154	137	107	75
West Virginia	1,770	480	120	95	265	77	65	57	37	28
Wisconsin	5,351	1,202	293	249	660	179	160	147	103	71
Wyoming	493	114	33	24	57	18	15	11	8	6

Source: Bureau of the Census, 2004 American Community Survey, Internet site http://factfinder.census.gov/servlet/ DatasetMainPageServlet?_program=ACS&_lang=en&_ts=143547961449; calculations by New Strategist

Table 7.17 Distribution of State Populations by Age, 2004

(percent distribution of people by state of residence and age, 2004; numbers in thousands)

	total population	aged 55 or older								
					aged 65 or older					
		toal	55 to 59	60 to 64	total	65 to 69	70 to 74	75 to 79	80 to 84	85 or older
United States	**100.0%**	**22.1%**	**5.7%**	**4.4%**	**12.0%**	**3.4%**	**2.9%**	**2.5%**	**1.8%**	**1.3%**
Alabama	100.0	23.7	6.2	4.8	12.7	3.8	3.4	2.7	1.7	1.1
Alaska	100.0	15.7	6.0	3.4	6.2	2.2	1.8	1.1	0.6	0.5
Arizona	100.0	22.2	5.2	4.4	12.6	3.6	3.4	2.7	1.8	1.1
Arkansas	100.0	24.1	5.9	5.0	13.2	3.9	3.5	2.7	1.8	1.3
California	100.0	19.5	5.2	3.9	10.4	3.0	2.5	2.1	1.6	1.1
Colorado	100.0	18.8	5.3	3.9	9.6	3.1	2.3	1.8	1.4	0.9
Connecticut	100.0	24.0	6.3	4.8	12.9	3.3	3.0	2.9	2.2	1.5
Delaware	100.0	23.6	6.0	4.7	12.9	3.8	3.4	2.6	2.0	1.2
District of Columbia	100.0	22.6	5.7	4.8	12.1	3.5	2.9	2.3	2.0	1.4
Florida	100.0	27.4	5.9	5.0	16.5	4.6	4.0	3.6	2.6	1.8
Georgia	100.0	18.6	5.3	4.1	9.2	3.2	2.3	1.7	1.1	0.9
Hawaii	100.0	24.8	6.3	4.8	13.7	3.3	3.3	3.2	2.2	1.7
Idaho	100.0	21.0	5.8	4.2	11.1	3.4	2.5	2.3	1.5	1.3
Illinois	100.0	21.2	5.4	4.3	11.5	3.2	2.8	2.4	1.8	1.3
Indiana	100.0	21.9	5.4	4.6	11.8	3.4	2.8	2.6	1.7	1.2
Iowa	100.0	24.3	5.8	4.6	13.9	3.6	3.4	3.0	2.2	1.8
Kansas	100.0	21.9	5.2	4.2	12.4	3.4	3.1	2.6	2.2	1.3
Kentucky	100.0	23.0	6.0	4.9	12.1	3.8	3.1	2.6	1.6	1.0
Louisiana	100.0	21.2	5.6	4.3	11.3	3.7	2.6	2.3	1.7	1.0
Maine	100.0	25.9	7.5	4.6	13.9	3.8	3.6	2.9	2.0	1.7
Maryland	100.0	21.6	5.8	4.7	11.0	3.1	2.7	2.2	1.7	1.2
Massachusetts	100.0	23.2	6.2	4.2	12.8	3.3	2.9	2.8	2.1	1.6
Michigan	100.0	22.2	5.8	4.5	12.0	3.3	2.8	2.7	1.8	1.4
Minnesota	100.0	21.2	5.3	4.3	11.5	3.3	2.7	2.2	1.9	1.4
Mississippi	100.0	21.8	5.6	4.4	11.7	3.7	2.9	2.4	1.6	1.1
Missouri	100.0	23.3	5.8	4.7	12.8	3.7	3.1	2.7	1.9	1.4
Montana	100.0	25.0	6.7	5.1	13.2	4.1	3.2	2.7	1.7	1.5
Nebraska	100.0	22.6	5.7	4.2	12.6	3.5	2.9	2.8	1.8	1.6
Nevada	100.0	21.4	5.9	4.4	11.1	4.0	2.7	2.2	1.3	0.8
New Hampshire	100.0	22.8	6.6	4.7	11.5	3.1	3.1	2.7	1.7	1.0
New Jersey	100.0	22.8	5.8	4.5	12.5	3.3	3.0	2.8	2.0	1.5
New Mexico	100.0	22.4	6.1	4.7	11.6	3.5	3.1	2.3	1.6	1.1
New York	100.0	23.0	5.8	4.6	12.6	3.5	3.0	2.7	2.0	1.5
North Carolina	100.0	21.9	5.7	4.6	11.7	3.7	2.9	2.4	1.7	1.1
North Dakota	100.0	24.3	5.9	4.4	14.1	3.7	3.3	3.0	2.5	1.6
Ohio	100.0	23.3	5.9	4.7	12.8	3.6	3.0	2.8	2.0	1.4
Oklahoma	100.0	23.4	6.1	4.5	12.8	3.7	3.5	2.7	1.9	1.1
Oregon	100.0	23.2	6.1	4.6	12.5	3.5	3.0	2.6	2.0	1.5
Pennsylvania	100.0	25.7	6.1	4.8	14.7	3.7	3.4	3.5	2.4	1.8
Rhode Island	100.0	23.8	5.9	4.5	13.4	3.1	3.0	3.2	2.4	1.7

(continued)

	total population	aged 55 or older			aged 65 or older					
		toal	55 to 59	60 to 64	total	65 to 69	70 to 74	75 to 79	80 to 84	85 or older
South Carolina	100.0%	23.1%	6.3%	4.8%	12.1%	3.7%	3.2%	2.4%	1.8%	1.0%
South Dakota	100.0	23.3	5.3	4.5	13.5	3.5	3.4	2.8	2.0	1.8
Tennessee	100.0	22.9	5.9	4.9	12.1	3.8	3.1	2.4	1.8	1.0
Texas	100.0	18.4	5.1	3.7	9.5	3.0	2.5	1.9	1.3	0.8
Utah	100.0	15.6	4.4	2.8	8.4	2.6	1.9	1.6	1.3	0.9
Vermont	100.0	25.0	7.3	5.0	12.7	3.7	3.1	2.6	1.9	1.4
Virginia	100.0	21.8	6.1	4.6	11.1	3.4	2.8	2.4	1.6	1.0
Washington	100.0	21.4	5.8	4.5	11.1	3.3	2.5	2.3	1.8	1.2
West Virginia	100.0	27.1	6.8	5.4	15.0	4.4	3.7	3.2	2.1	1.6
Wisconsin	100.0	22.5	5.5	4.7	12.3	3.4	3.0	2.8	1.9	1.3
Wyoming	100.0	23.2	6.8	4.8	11.6	3.6	3.0	2.2	1.6	1.2

Source: Bureau of the Census, 2004 American Community Survey, Internet site http://factfinder.census.gov/servlet/ DatasetMainPageServlet?_program=ACS&_lang=en&_ts=143547961449; calculations by New Strategist

Table 7.18 State Populations by Generation, 2004

(number of people by state of residence and generation, 2004; numbers in thousands)

	total population	post-Millennial (under age 10)	Millennial (10 to 27)	Generation X (28 to 39)	Baby Boom (40 to 58)	Older Americans (59 or older)
United States	**285,692**	**39,667**	**70,753**	**48,123**	**77,079**	**50,069**
Alabama	4,415	573	1,110	719	1,186	827
Alaska	636	96	179	100	192	69
Arizona	5,634	877	1,447	938	1,358	1,014
Arkansas	2,676	353	680	423	702	518
California	35,055	5,239	9,111	6,258	9,068	5,379
Colorado	4,499	640	1,162	812	1,229	655
Connecticut	3,389	434	766	559	986	644
Delaware	805	104	193	136	222	151
District of Columbia	518	64	116	112	132	94
Florida	16,990	2,140	3,874	2,633	4,479	3,865
Georgia	8,581	1,315	2,180	1,627	2,228	1,232
Hawaii	1,227	163	288	196	337	243
Idaho	1,360	204	367	209	357	223
Illinois	12,391	1,774	3,112	2,151	3,262	2,091
Indiana	6,059	864	1,535	984	1,614	1,062
Iowa	2,851	364	697	439	791	561
Kansas	2,653	375	672	427	709	470
Kentucky	4,031	535	968	672	1,122	734
Louisiana	4,381	630	1,159	687	1,172	733
Maine	1,279	140	290	195	399	255
Maryland	5,422	764	1,289	906	1,545	917
Massachusetts	6,201	789	1,399	1,108	1,777	1,128
Michigan	9,859	1,353	2,438	1,618	2,714	1,735
Minnesota	4,959	655	1,244	827	1,394	838
Mississippi	2,805	406	739	448	728	485
Missouri	5,586	739	1,386	891	1,528	1,043
Montana	902	106	222	127	269	177
Nebraska	1,697	235	433	267	457	305
Nevada	2,301	338	562	421	597	384
New Hampshire	1,262	154	293	205	389	221
New Jersey	8,503	1,146	1,975	1,440	2,398	1,545
New Mexico	1,863	267	480	288	500	328
New York	18,634	2,451	4,413	3,262	5,083	3,426
North Carolina	8,270	1,170	1,978	1,451	2,233	1,438
North Dakota	610	71	156	87	175	120
Ohio	11,154	1,483	2,705	1,787	3,104	2,075
Oklahoma	3,412	474	854	529	923	632
Oregon	3,514	456	858	600	957	643
Pennsylvania	11,958	1,472	2,754	1,873	3,371	2,487
Rhode Island	1,037	124	249	174	291	198

(continued)

	total population	post-Millennial (under age 10)	Millennial (10 to 27)	Generation X (28 to 39)	Baby Boom (40 to 58)	Older Americans (59 or older)
South Carolina	4,060	549	996	660	1,120	734
South Dakota	741	101	191	110	199	141
Tennessee	5,748	767	1,366	988	1,582	1,046
Texas	21,912	3,529	5,856	3,820	5,576	3,132
Utah	2,349	436	736	387	507	284
Vermont	601	68	135	93	189	115
Virginia	7,224	976	1,737	1,245	2,044	1,221
Washington	6,063	772	1,530	1,031	1,716	1,014
West Virginia	1,770	193	409	277	508	384
Wisconsin	5,351	680	1,336	857	1,510	968
Wyoming	493	60	126	70	149	88

Source: Bureau of the Census, 2004 American Community Survey, Internet site http://factfinder.census.gov/servlet/ DatasetMainPageServlet?_program=ACS&_lang=en&_ts=143547961449; calculations by New Strategist

Table 7.19 Distribution of State Populations by Generation, 2004

(percent distribution of people by state of residence and generation, 2004)

	total population	post-Millennial (under age 10)	Millennial (10 to 27)	Generation X (28 to 39)	Baby Boom (40 to 58)	Older Americans (59 or older)
United States	**100.0%**	**13.9%**	**24.8%**	**16.8%**	**27.0%**	**17.5%**
Alabama	100.0	13.0	25.1	16.3	26.9	18.7
Alaska	100.0	15.2	28.2	15.7	30.2	10.8
Arizona	100.0	15.6	25.7	16.7	24.1	18.0
Arkansas	100.0	13.2	25.4	15.8	26.2	19.4
California	100.0	14.9	26.0	17.9	25.9	15.3
Colorado	100.0	14.2	25.8	18.0	27.3	14.6
Connecticut	100.0	12.8	22.6	16.5	29.1	19.0
Delaware	100.0	12.9	23.9	16.8	27.6	18.8
District of Columbia	100.0	12.3	22.4	21.7	25.6	18.1
Florida	100.0	12.6	22.8	15.5	26.4	22.7
Georgia	100.0	15.3	25.4	19.0	26.0	14.4
Hawaii	100.0	13.3	23.5	16.0	27.5	19.8
Idaho	100.0	15.0	27.0	15.4	26.3	16.4
Illinois	100.0	14.3	25.1	17.4	26.3	16.9
Indiana	100.0	14.3	25.3	16.2	26.6	17.5
Iowa	100.0	12.8	24.4	15.4	27.7	19.7
Kansas	100.0	14.1	25.3	16.1	26.7	17.7
Kentucky	100.0	13.3	24.0	16.7	27.8	18.2
Louisiana	100.0	14.4	26.5	15.7	26.8	16.7
Maine	100.0	11.0	22.6	15.2	31.2	19.9
Maryland	100.0	14.1	23.8	16.7	28.5	16.9
Massachusetts	100.0	12.7	22.6	17.9	28.7	18.2
Michigan	100.0	13.7	24.7	16.4	27.5	17.6
Minnesota	100.0	13.2	25.1	16.7	28.1	16.9
Mississippi	100.0	14.5	26.3	16.0	25.9	17.3
Missouri	100.0	13.2	24.8	15.9	27.3	18.7
Montana	100.0	11.8	24.6	14.1	29.8	19.6
Nebraska	100.0	13.8	25.5	15.7	26.9	18.0
Nevada	100.0	14.7	24.4	18.3	25.9	16.7
New Hampshire	100.0	12.2	23.2	16.3	30.8	17.5
New Jersey	100.0	13.5	23.2	16.9	28.2	18.2
New Mexico	100.0	14.3	25.8	15.5	26.8	17.6
New York	100.0	13.2	23.7	17.5	27.3	18.4
North Carolina	100.0	14.1	23.9	17.5	27.0	17.4
North Dakota	100.0	11.6	25.6	14.3	28.8	19.6
Ohio	100.0	13.3	24.3	16.0	27.8	18.6
Oklahoma	100.0	13.9	25.0	15.5	27.0	18.5
Oregon	100.0	13.0	24.4	17.1	27.2	18.3
Pennsylvania	100.0	12.3	23.0	15.7	28.2	20.8
Rhode Island	100.0	12.0	24.0	16.8	28.0	19.1

(continued)

	total population	post-Millennial (under age 10)	Millennial (10 to 27)	Generation X (28 to 39)	Baby Boom (40 to 58)	Older Americans (59 or older)
South Carolina	100.0%	13.5%	24.5%	16.3%	27.6%	18.1%
South Dakota	100.0	13.6	25.7	14.8	26.8	19.1
Tennessee	100.0	13.3	23.8	17.2	27.5	18.2
Texas	100.0	16.1	26.7	17.4	25.4	14.3
Utah	100.0	18.6	31.3	16.5	21.6	12.1
Vermont	100.0	11.3	22.5	15.4	31.5	19.1
Virginia	100.0	13.5	24.0	17.2	28.3	16.9
Washington	100.0	12.7	25.2	17.0	28.3	16.7
West Virginia	100.0	10.9	23.1	15.7	28.7	21.7
Wisconsin	100.0	12.7	25.0	16.0	28.2	18.1
Wyoming	100.0	12.2	25.6	14.1	30.2	17.8

Source: Bureau of the Census, 2004 American Community Survey, Internet site http://factfinder.census.gov/servlet/ DatasetMainPageServlet?_program=ACS&_lang=en&_ts=143547961449; calculations by New Strategist

Table 7.20 Population Aged 55 or Older by State, Race, and Hispanic Origin, 2004

(number and percent distribution of people aged 55 or older by state of residence, race, and Hispanic origin, 2004; numbers in thousands)

	number					percent distribution				
	total 55 or older	Asian	black	Hispanic	non-Hispanic white	total 55 or older	Asian	black	Hispanic	non-Hispanic white
United States	**63,051**	**2,091**	**5,612**	**4,260**	**50,163**	**100.0%**	**3.3%**	**8.9%**	**6.8%**	**79.6%**
Alabama	1,044	5	199	3	826	100.0	0.4	19.1	0.3	79.1
Alaska	100	4	2	2	77	100.0	3.9	1.6	2.1	76.9
Arizona	1,250	19	24	143	1,028	100.0	1.5	1.9	11.4	82.2
Arkansas	645	2	61	6	568	100.0	0.3	9.5	0.9	88.0
California	6,850	853	370	1,197	4,331	100.0	12.5	5.4	17.5	63.2
Colorado	845	16	23	83	713	100.0	1.9	2.7	9.8	84.4
Connecticut	814	13	55	34	710	100.0	1.6	6.7	4.2	87.2
Delaware	190	3	25	3	158	100.0	1.5	13.0	1.7	83.2
District of Columbia	117	2	74	5	35	100.0	2.0	63.0	4.2	29.7
Florida	4,663	57	376	578	3,626	100.0	1.2	8.1	12.4	77.8
Georgia	1,592	29	328	27	1,193	100.0	1.8	20.6	1.7	74.9
Hawaii	304	171	2	9	80	100.0	56.1	0.5	2.9	26.2
Idaho	286	2	–	8	270	100.0	0.8	–	2.9	94.7
Illinois	2,627	82	305	149	2,078	100.0	3.1	11.6	5.7	79.1
Indiana	1,326	6	79	16	1,212	100.0	0.5	5.9	1.2	91.4
Iowa	693	3	7	5	676	100.0	0.4	1.0	0.7	97.5
Kansas	581	6	18	11	537	100.0	1.1	3.1	1.9	92.5
Kentucky	927	6	46	5	863	100.0	0.6	5.0	0.5	93.0
Louisiana	928	7	225	18	669	100.0	0.7	24.2	1.9	72.1
Maine	331	2	0	0	326	100.0	0.5	0.1	0.1	98.4
Maryland	1,169	45	253	25	838	100.0	3.8	21.6	2.1	71.7
Massachusetts	1,437	34	54	40	1,305	100.0	2.4	3.8	2.8	90.8
Michigan	2,190	24	232	32	1,885	100.0	1.1	10.6	1.5	86.1
Minnesota	1,050	13	14	10	1,001	100.0	1.3	1.4	0.9	95.3
Mississippi	610	3	156	3	445	100.0	0.5	25.5	0.5	72.9
Missouri	1,303	9	102	16	1,162	100.0	0.7	7.8	1.2	89.2
Montana	225	–	–	3	213	100.0	–	–	1.5	94.4
Nebraska	383	3	9	9	358	100.0	0.8	2.4	2.5	93.6
Nevada	492	26	25	42	389	100.0	5.4	5.1	8.5	79.2
New Hampshire	287	3	1	2	279	100.0	0.9	0.5	0.8	97.0
New Jersey	1,941	89	197	154	1,495	100.0	4.6	10.2	8.0	77.0
New Mexico	418	4	6	132	250	100.0	1.0	1.5	31.7	59.8
New York	4,290	204	544	413	3,125	100.0	4.7	12.7	9.6	72.8
North Carolina	1,812	13	294	18	1,462	100.0	0.7	16.2	1.0	80.7
North Dakota	148	1	–	1	143	100.0	0.5	–	0.5	96.4
Ohio	2,602	22	227	25	2,311	100.0	0.9	8.7	1.0	88.8
Oklahoma	800	6	41	19	669	100.0	0.8	5.2	2.3	83.6
Oregon	814	17	7	22	754	100.0	2.1	0.9	2.7	92.6
Pennsylvania	3,075	40	217	42	2,761	100.0	1.3	7.0	1.4	89.8
Rhode Island	247	2	6	9	227	100.0	1.0	2.5	3.5	92.0

	number				percent distribution				
	total 55 or older	Asian	black	Hispanic	non-Hispanic white	total 55 or older	Asian	black	Hispanic	non-Hispanic white
South Carolina	938	6	205	7	715	100.0%	0.7%	21.8%	0.8%	76.2%
South Dakota	173	1	0	1	169	100.0	0.3	0.2	0.4	97.8
Tennessee	1,319	8	140	8	1,150	100.0	0.6	10.6	0.6	87.2
Texas	4,030	97	349	830	2,714	100.0	2.4	8.7	20.6	67.3
Utah	367	4	3	16	341	100.0	1.1	0.9	4.5	92.8
Vermont	150	0	–	1	146	100.0	0.3	–	0.6	97.5
Virginia	1,575	52	242	28	1,242	100.0	3.3	15.4	1.8	78.9
Washington	1,296	67	25	35	1,142	100.0	5.2	1.9	2.7	88.1
West Virginia	480	1	11	2	462	100.0	0.3	2.2	0.4	96.3
Wisconsin	1,202	8	34	12	1,140	100.0	0.7	2.8	1.0	94.8
Wyoming	114	0	1	4	107	100.0	0.4	0.5	3.6	93.4

Note: Blacks and Asians are those who identify themselves as being of the respective race alone. Non-Hispanic whites are those who identify themselves as being white alone and not Hispanic. Numbers will not sum to total because Hispanics may be of any race and not all races are shown. "–" means number is less than 500 or sample is too small to make a reliable estimate.
Source: Bureau of the Census, 2004 American Community Survey, Internet site http://factfinder.census.gov/servlet/ DatasetMainPageServlet?_program=ACS&_lang=en&_ts=143547961449; calculations by New Strategist

Table 7.21 Older Generations by State, Race, and Hispanic Origin, 2004

(number and percent distribution of people aged 59 or older by state of residence, race, and Hispanic origin, 2004; numbers in thousands)

	number				percent distribution				
	total 59 or older	Asian	black	Hispanic	non-Hispanic white	total 59 or older	Asian	black	Hispanic	non-Hispanic white
United States	**50,069**	**1,608**	**4,376**	**3,289**	**40,256**	**100.0%**	**3.2%**	**8.7%**	**6.6%**	**80.4%**
Alabama	827	3	156	2	658	100.0	0.3	18.8	0.3	79.6
Alaska	69	3	1	1	56	100.0	4.3	1.9	2.1	81.5
Arizona	1,014	15	19	110	834	100.0	1.4	1.8	10.9	82.2
Arkansas	518	1	47	5	454	100.0	0.2	9.1	0.9	87.7
California	5,379	670	290	922	3,457	100.0	12.5	5.4	17.1	64.3
Colorado	655	12	18	65	558	100.0	1.9	2.7	10.0	85.2
Connecticut	644	10	41	24	568	100.0	1.6	6.4	3.7	88.2
Delaware	151	2	19	2	126	100.0	1.5	12.7	1.5	83.7
District of Columbia	94	2	59	4	27	100.0	2.0	63.6	4.0	28.5
Florida	3,865	43	292	465	2,993	100.0	1.1	7.6	12.0	77.4
Georgia	1,232	20	252	19	933	100.0	1.7	20.5	1.6	75.7
Hawaii	243	140	1	7	61	100.0	57.9	0.5	2.9	25.2
Idaho	223	2	–	5	214	100.0	0.8	–	2.5	96.0
Illinois	2,091	60	239	111	1,665	100.0	2.9	11.5	5.3	79.6
Indiana	1,062	5	61	12	964	100.0	0.4	5.8	1.1	90.8
Iowa	561	2	5	4	545	100.0	0.4	0.9	0.7	97.2
Kansas	470	5	15	9	432	100.0	1.1	3.1	1.8	91.9
Kentucky	734	4	36	3	681	100.0	0.6	4.9	0.5	92.8
Louisiana	733	4	176	14	532	100.0	0.6	24.0	1.9	72.6
Maine	255	1	–	–	259	100.0	0.5	–	–	101.4
Maryland	917	33	193	18	663	100.0	3.6	21.1	1.9	72.3
Massachusetts	1,128	26	42	28	1,046	100.0	2.3	3.7	2.5	92.7
Michigan	1,735	16	182	25	1,500	100.0	0.9	10.5	1.5	86.4
Minnesota	838	11	11	7	796	100.0	1.3	1.3	0.9	95.0
Mississippi	485	2	122	3	355	100.0	0.4	25.2	0.5	73.2
Missouri	1,043	6	79	12	928	100.0	0.6	7.6	1.1	89.0
Montana	177	–	–	3	168	100.0	–	–	1.6	94.9
Nebraska	305	2	7	7	289	100.0	0.6	2.4	2.3	94.5
Nevada	384	20	20	32	307	100.0	5.3	5.1	8.2	80.0
New Hampshire	221	2	1	2	218	100.0	0.8	0.5	0.7	98.7
New Jersey	1,545	65	154	120	1,204	100.0	4.2	10.0	7.7	78.0
New Mexico	328	3	5	103	199	100.0	0.9	1.6	31.5	60.6
New York	3,426	155	424	318	2,514	100.0	4.5	12.4	9.3	73.4
North Carolina	1,438	10	231	13	1,161	100.0	0.7	16.1	0.9	80.7
North Dakota	120	1	–	1	116	100.0	0.4	–	0.4	96.7
Ohio	2,075	16	178	18	1,846	100.0	0.8	8.6	0.9	88.9
Oklahoma	632	5	33	12	535	100.0	0.8	5.2	2.0	84.7
Oregon	643	13	6	17	599	100.0	2.1	0.9	2.6	93.1
Pennsylvania	2,487	30	171	32	2,233	100.0	1.2	6.9	1.3	89.8
Rhode Island	198	2	5	6	183	100.0	0.8	2.5	3.3	92.3

(continued)

	number					percent distribution				
	total 59 or older	Asian	black	Hispanic	non-Hispanic white	total 59 or older	Asian	black	Hispanic	non-Hispanic white
South Carolina	734	4	159	5	565	100.0%	0.6%	21.6%	0.7%	76.9%
South Dakota	141	–	–	1	137	100.0	–	–	0.4	97.0
Tennessee	1,046	6	111	6	909	100.0	0.6	10.6	0.6	87.0
Texas	3,132	72	269	641	2,149	100.0	2.3	8.6	20.5	68.6
Utah	284	3	2	12	271	100.0	1.2	0.9	4.2	95.5
Vermont	115	–	–	1	114	100.0	–	–	0.6	99.2
Virginia	1,221	39	188	21	973	100.0	3.2	15.4	1.7	79.7
Washington	1,014	52	19	27	898	100.0	5.1	1.8	2.6	88.5
West Virginia	384	1	9	1	369	100.0	0.2	2.3	0.3	96.2
Wisconsin	968	5	26	9	911	100.0	0.6	2.6	0.9	94.1
Wyoming	88	–	–	3	84	100.0	–	–	3.6	95.1

Note: The older generations included people aged 59 or older in 2004. Blacks and Asians are those who identify themselves as being of the respective race alone. Non-Hispanic whites are those who identify themselves as being white alone and not Hispanic. Numbers will not sum to total because Hispanics may be of any race and not all races are shown. "–" means number is less than 500 or sample is too small to make a reliable estimate.
Source: Bureau of the Census, 2004 American Community Survey, Internet site http://factfinder.census.gov/servlet/ DatasetMainPageServlet?_program=ACS&_lang=en&_ts=143547961449; calculations by New Strategist

8

Spending

■ Householders aged 55 to 64 spent 10 percent more in 2004 than in 2000, after adjusting for inflation. The age group's spending is growing because two-earner couples head a growing proportion of households.

■ The spending of householders aged 65 or older is becoming more like the spending of middle-aged householders as better-educated generations fill the older age groups. Spending on entertainment among householders aged 65 or older rose 22 percent between 2000 and 2004, after adjusting for inflation.

■ Older Americans are the most-ardent travelers, and this is reflected in their spending. Householders aged 55 to 64 spend 57 percent more than average on "other" lodging (mostly hotels and motels) and 37 percent more than average on public transportation (mostly airfares).

■ Despite their small household size, householders aged 65 to 74 spend 11 percent more than the average household on "other" lodging and 19 percent more than average on public transportation.

■ Retirees spent more in 2004 than in 2000 on many discretionary items. Their spending on entertainment climbed by a whopping 42 percent during those years, after adjusting for inflation.

Older Householders Open Their Wallets

Householders aged 55 and older boosted their spending between 2000 and 2004.

Householders aged 55 to 64 spent 10 percent more in 2004 than in 2000, after adjusting for inflation—more than double the 4 percent rise in spending by the average household during those years. Householders aged 65 or older boosted their spending by 8 percent, and those aged 75 or older spent 7 percent more. Rising labor force participation rates—and incomes—are behind these increases.

Householders aged 55 to 64 are spending more not only on necessities, but also on discretionary items. Between 2000 and 2004, they spent 10 percent more on food away from home, after adjusting for inflation. They spent 12 percent more on alcoholic beverages, 27 percent more on furniture, and 32 percent more on entertainment. They also spent more on necessities: property tax spending rose 10 percent, vehicle insurance 11 percent, and out-of-pocket health insurance costs 26 percent.

The spending of householders aged 65 or older is becoming more like the spending of middle-aged householders as better-educated generations fill the older age groups. Spending on food away from home grew 12 percent among householders aged 65 or older between 2000 and 2004, after adjusting for inflation. Households in the age group spent 13 percent more on alcoholic beverages, 7 percent more on furniture, and 22 percent more on entertainment.

■ The incomes and spending of older Americans will continue to rise as the labor force participation rate of older workers climbs.

The 55-and-older age groups saw the biggest increases in spending

(percent change in average household spending by age of householder, 2000–04; in 2004 dollars)

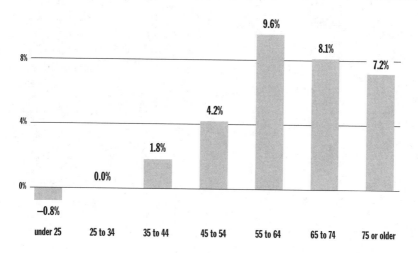

Table 8.1 Average Spending of Householders Aged 55 to 64, 2000 and 2004

(average annual spending of total consumer units and consumer units headed by people aged 55 to 64, 2000 and 2004; percent change, 2000–04; in 2004 dollars)

	total consumer units			aged 55 to 64		
	2004	2000	percent change 2000–04	2004	2000	percent change 2000–04
Number of consumer units (in 000s)	116,282	109,367	6.3%	17,479	14,161	23.4%
Average before-tax income	$54,453	$48,975	11.2	$61,031	$52,769	15.7
Average annual spending	43,395	41,731	4.0	47,299	43,152	9.6
FOOD	5,781	5,658	2.2	5,898	5,669	4.0
Food at home	3,347	3,314	1.0	3,374	3,369	0.2
Cereals and bakery products	461	497	–7.2	437	484	–9.7
Cereals and cereal products	154	171	–10.0	137	154	–10.8
Bakery products	307	326	–5.8	300	330	–9.1
Meats, poultry, fish, and eggs	880	872	0.9	894	913	–2.0
Beef	265	261	1.5	257	267	–3.6
Pork	181	183	–1.2	203	204	–0.5
Other meats	108	111	–2.5	102	109	–6.1
Poultry	156	159	–1.9	156	160	–2.6
Fish and seafood	128	121	6.1	130	126	3.1
Eggs	42	37	12.6	46	47	–2.5
Dairy products	371	356	4.1	371	352	5.4
Fresh milk and cream	144	144	0.2	137	138	–0.9
Other dairy products	226	212	6.8	235	214	9.9
Fruits and vegetables	561	571	–1.8	588	612	–3.9
Fresh fruits	187	179	4.6	199	203	–1.9
Fresh vegetables	183	174	4.9	200	190	5.4
Processed fruits	110	126	–12.8	108	126	–14.4
Processed vegetables	82	92	–11.0	80	95	–16.2
Other food at home	1,075	1,017	5.7	1,083	1,007	7.6
Sugar and other sweets	128	128	–0.3	137	126	8.6
Fats and oils	89	91	–2.2	97	99	–1.7
Miscellaneous foods	527	479	9.9	485	437	11.1
Nonalcoholic beverages	290	274	5.8	295	288	2.3
Food prepared by household on trips	41	44	–6.6	69	57	21.0
Food away from home	2,434	2,344	3.8	2,524	2,300	9.7
ALCOHOLIC BEVERAGES	459	408	12.5	457	407	12.3
HOUSING	13,918	13,513	3.0	14,339	13,560	5.7
Shelter	7,998	7,803	2.5	7,883	7,225	9.1
Owned dwellings	5,324	5,048	5.5	5,970	5,243	13.9
Mortgage interest and charges	2,936	2,895	1.4	2,813	2,499	12.6
Property taxes	1,391	1,249	11.3	1,760	1,604	9.7
Maintenance, repairs, insurance, other expenses	997	905	10.2	1,398	1,141	22.5

	total consumer units			aged 55 to 64		
	2004	2000	percent change 2000–04	2004	2000	percent change 2000–04
Rented dwellings	$2,201	$2,231	−1.3%	$1,169	$1,232	−5.1%
Other lodging	473	524	−9.8	743	751	−1.1
Utilities, fuels, public services	**2,927**	**2,730**	**7.2**	**3,222**	**3,023**	**6.6**
Natural gas	424	337	25.9	477	374	27.5
Electricity	1,064	999	6.5	1,177	1,150	2.4
Fuel oil and other fuels	121	106	13.7	161	124	29.9
Telephone services	990	962	2.9	1,040	997	4.3
Water and other public services	327	325	0.7	367	378	−3.0
Household services	**753**	**750**	**0.4**	**645**	**595**	**8.5**
Personal services	300	358	−16.1	43	102	−57.8
Other household services	453	393	15.4	602	493	22.2
Housekeeping supplies	**594**	**529**	**12.4**	**657**	**642**	**2.4**
Laundry and cleaning supplies	149	144	3.7	158	202	−21.7
Other household products	290	248	17.0	318	287	10.7
Postage and stationery	155	138	12.1	181	152	18.7
Household furnishings and equipment	**1,646**	**1,699**	**−3.1**	**1,932**	**2,074**	**−6.9**
Household textiles	158	116	35.9	203	137	48.1
Furniture	417	429	−2.8	504	396	27.3
Floor coverings	52	48	7.7	87	61	41.6
Major appliances	204	207	−1.6	240	242	−1.0
Small appliances, misc. housewares	105	95	10.0	130	116	11.8
Miscellaneous household equipment	711	802	−11.3	768	1,121	−31.5
APPAREL AND SERVICES	**1,816**	**2,036**	**−10.8**	**1,863**	**1,858**	**0.3**
Men and boys	**406**	**483**	**−15.9**	**338**	**433**	**−22.0**
Men, aged 16 or older	317	377	−16.0	285	386	−26.2
Boys, aged 2 to 15	89	105	−15.5	53	46	15.0
Women and girls	**739**	**795**	**−7.1**	**793**	**754**	**5.2**
Women, aged 16 or older	631	666	−5.2	743	691	7.5
Girls, aged 2 to 15	108	129	−16.6	50	63	−20.0
Children under age 2	**79**	**90**	**−12.2**	**47**	**58**	**−19.2**
Footwear	**329**	**376**	**−12.6**	**351**	**329**	**6.7**
Other apparel products and services	**264**	**292**	**−9.5**	**333**	**284**	**17.2**
TRANSPORTATION	**7,801**	**8,136**	**−4.1**	**8,421**	**8,602**	**−2.1**
Vehicle purchases	**3,397**	**3,749**	**−9.4**	**3,616**	**3,974**	**−9.0**
Cars and trucks, new	1,748	1,761	−0.7	2,311	2,300	0.5
Cars and trucks, used	1,582	1,941	−18.5	1,247	1,654	−24.6
Gasoline and motor oil	**1,598**	**1,416**	**12.8**	**1,666**	**1,480**	**12.6**
Other vehicle expenses	**2,365**	**2,502**	**−5.5**	**2,532**	**2,605**	**−2.8**
Vehicle finance charges	323	360	−10.2	336	383	−12.2
Maintenance and repairs	652	684	−4.7	742	737	0.7
Vehicle insurance	964	853	13.0	973	873	11.4
Vehicle rental, leases, licenses, other charges	426	604	−29.5	481	613	−21.6
Public transportation	**441**	**468**	**−5.8**	**606**	**543**	**11.6**

	total consumer units			aged 55 to 64		
	2004	2000	percent change 2000–04	2004	2000	percent change 2000–04
HEALTH CARE	**$2,574**	**$2,266**	**13.6%**	**$3,262**	**$2,751**	**18.6%**
Health insurance	1,332	1,078	23.5	1,567	1,242	26.2
Medical services	648	623	4.0	892	791	12.8
Drugs	480	456	5.2	642	590	8.8
Medical supplies	114	109	5.0	161	128	25.5
ENTERTAINMENT	**2,218**	**2,044**	**8.5**	**2,823**	**2,144**	**31.6**
Fees and admissions	528	565	–6.5	618	558	10.7
Television, radio, sound equipment	788	682	15.5	810	637	27.1
Pets, toys, and playground equipment	381	366	4.0	428	393	9.0
Other entertainment supplies, services	522	431	21.1	967	556	73.9
PERSONAL CARE PRODUCTS AND SERVICES	**581**	**619**	**–6.1**	**628**	**624**	**0.6**
READING	**130**	**160**	**–18.8**	**177**	**196**	**–9.9**
EDUCATION	**905**	**693**	**30.5**	**730**	**417**	**75.1**
TOBACCO PRODUCTS AND SMOKING SUPPLIES	**288**	**350**	**–17.7**	**301**	**383**	**–21.4**
MISCELLANEOUS	**690**	**851**	**–18.9**	**825**	**904**	**–8.7**
CASH CONTRIBUTIONS	**1,408**	**1,307**	**7.7**	**1,752**	**1,427**	**22.8**
PERSONAL INSURANCE AND PENSIONS	**4,823**	**3,691**	**30.7**	**5,825**	**4,210**	**38.4**
Life and other personal insurance	390	438	–10.9	612	644	–5.0
Pensions and Social Security	4,433	3,253	36.3	5,214	3,567	46.2
PERSONAL TAXES	**2,166**	**3,419**	**–36.6**	**2,987**	**4,386**	**–31.9**
Federal income taxes	1,519	2,642	–42.5	2,168	3,359	–35.5
State and local income taxes	472	616	–23.4	584	770	–24.2
Other taxes	175	160	9.3	236	258	–8.4
GIFTS FOR NONHOUSEHOLD MEMBERS	**1,215**	**1,188**	**2.3**	**1,636**	**1,475**	**10.9**

Note: The Bureau of Labor Statistics uses consumer unit rather than household as the sampling unit in the Consumer Expenditure Survey. For the definition of consumer unit, see the glossary. Spending on gifts is also included in the preceding product and service categories.
Source: Bureau of Labor Statistics, 2000 and 2004 Consumer Expenditure Surveys, Internet site http://www.bls.gov/cex/; calculations by New Strategist

Table 8.2 Average Spending of Householders Aged 65 or Older, 2000 and 2004

(average annual spending of total consumer units and consumer units headed by people aged 65 or older, 2000 and 2004; percent change, 2000–04; in 2004 dollars)

	total consumer units			aged 65 or older		
	2004	2000	percent change 2000–04	2004	2000	percent change 2000–04
Number of consumer units (in 000s)	116,282	109,367	6.3%	22,765	22,155	2.8%
Average before-tax income	$54,453	$48,975	11.2	$34,988	$27,664	26.5
Average annual spending	43,395	41,731	4.0	31,104	29,104	6.9
FOOD	5,781	5,658	2.2	4,206	4,006	5.0
Food at home	3,347	3,314	1.0	2,722	2,685	1.4
Cereals and bakery products	461	497	−7.2	394	412	−4.5
Cereals and cereal products	154	171	−10.0	118	135	−12.5
Bakery products	307	326	−5.8	276	278	−0.5
Meats, poultry, fish, and eggs	880	872	0.9	694	687	1.1
Beef	265	261	1.5	205	200	2.7
Pork	181	183	−1.2	148	157	−5.6
Other meats	108	111	−2.5	91	87	5.0
Poultry	156	159	−1.9	108	118	−8.8
Fish and seafood	128	121	6.1	103	92	11.8
Eggs	42	37	12.6	38	33	15.5
Dairy products	371	356	4.1	313	302	3.8
Fresh milk and cream	144	144	0.2	118	123	−3.9
Other dairy products	226	212	6.8	195	179	9.1
Fruits and vegetables	561	571	−1.8	510	543	−6.1
Fresh fruits	187	179	4.6	174	185	−6.1
Fresh vegetables	183	174	4.9	167	160	4.3
Processed fruits	110	126	−12.8	99	120	−17.2
Processed vegetables	82	92	−11.0	70	78	−10.1
Other food at home	1,075	1,017	5.7	812	741	9.5
Sugar and other sweets	128	128	−0.3	109	102	6.9
Fats and oils	89	91	−2.2	77	81	−5.1
Miscellaneous foods	527	479	9.9	394	333	18.2
Nonalcoholic beverages	290	274	5.8	201	193	4.1
Food prepared by household on trips	41	44	−6.6	31	32	−2.5
Food away from home	2,434	2,344	3.8	1,484	1,322	12.3
ALCOHOLIC BEVERAGES	459	408	12.5	261	231	12.8
HOUSING	13,918	13,513	3.0	10,259	9,608	6.8
Shelter	7,998	7,803	2.5	5,329	5,042	5.7
Owned dwellings	5,324	5,048	5.5	3,523	3,338	5.5
Mortgage interest and charges	2,936	2,895	1.4	863	870	−0.8
Property taxes	1,391	1,249	11.3	1,416	1,289	9.9
Maintenance, repairs, insurance, other expenses	997	905	10.2	1,244	1,179	5.5

	total consumer units			aged 65 or older		
	2004	**2000**	percent change 2000–04	**2004**	**2000**	percent change 2000–04
Rented dwellings	$2,201	$2,231	–1.3%	$1,393	$1,250	11.4%
Other lodging	473	524	–9.8	414	453	–8.6
Utilities, fuels, public services	**2,927**	**2,730**	**7.2**	**2,580**	**2,411**	**7.0**
Natural gas	424	337	25.9	442	340	30.0
Electricity	1,064	999	6.5	957	915	4.6
Fuel oil and other fuels	121	106	13.7	163	150	8.5
Telephone services	990	962	2.9	695	680	2.2
Water and other public services	327	325	0.7	323	327	–1.2
Household services	**753**	**750**	**0.4**	**694**	**725**	**–4.3**
Personal services	300	358	–16.1	201	236	–14.8
Other household services	453	393	15.4	493	489	0.8
Housekeeping supplies	**594**	**529**	**12.4**	**509**	**462**	**10.2**
Laundry and cleaning supplies	149	144	3.7	111	104	6.5
Other household products	290	248	17.0	248	215	15.4
Postage and stationery	155	138	12.1	149	143	4.5
Household furnishings and equipment	**1,646**	**1,699**	**–3.1**	**1,147**	**967**	**18.6**
Household textiles	158	116	35.9	154	80	92.3
Furniture	417	429	–2.8	236	220	7.0
Floor coverings	52	48	7.7	44	42	5.6
Major appliances	204	207	–1.6	175	176	–0.3
Small appliances, misc. housewares	105	95	10.0	90	59	51.9
Miscellaneous household equipment	711	802	–11.3	448	390	14.7
APPAREL AND SERVICES	**1,816**	**2,036**	**–10.8**	**907**	**1,015**	**–10.6**
Men and boys	**406**	**483**	**–15.9**	**204**	**215**	**–5.1**
Men, aged 16 or older	317	377	–16.0	180	194	–7.3
Boys, aged 2 to 15	89	105	–15.5	24	21	15.2
Women and girls	**739**	**795**	**–7.1**	**431**	**439**	**–1.8**
Women, aged 16 or older	631	666	–5.2	404	415	–2.6
Girls, aged 2 to 15	108	129	–16.6	27	24	11.9
Children under age 2	**79**	**90**	**–12.2**	**20**	**22**	**–8.8**
Footwear	**329**	**376**	**–12.6**	**123**	**174**	**–29.5**
Other apparel products and services	**264**	**292**	**–9.5**	**129**	**165**	**–21.6**
TRANSPORTATION	**7,801**	**8,136**	**–4.1**	**4,875**	**4,823**	**1.1**
Vehicle purchases	**3,397**	**3,749**	**–9.4**	**1,966**	**2,088**	**–5.9**
Cars and trucks, new	1,748	1,761	–0.7	1,089	1,180	–7.7
Cars and trucks, used	1,582	1,941	–18.5	872	903	–3.4
Gasoline and motor oil	**1,598**	**1,416**	**12.8**	**963**	**806**	**19.4**
Other vehicle expenses	**2,365**	**2,502**	**–5.5**	**1,546**	**1,507**	**2.6**
Vehicle finance charges	323	360	–10.2	115	126	–8.8
Maintenance and repairs	652	684	–4.7	490	484	1.3
Vehicle insurance	964	853	13.0	711	611	16.4
Vehicle rental, leases, licenses, other charges	426	604	–29.5	230	285	–19.4
Public transportation	**441**	**468**	**–5.8**	**400**	**422**	**–5.3**

	total consumer units			aged 65 or older		
	2004	2000	percent change 2000–04	2004	2000	percent change 2000–04
HEALTH CARE	**$2,574**	**$2,266**	**13.6%**	**$3,899**	**$3,562**	**9.5%**
Health insurance	1,332	1,078	23.5	2,142	1,776	20.6
Medical services	648	623	4.0	678	737	–8.0
Drugs	480	456	5.2	920	902	2.0
Medical supplies	114	109	5.0	158	146	8.3
ENTERTAINMENT	**2,218**	**2,044**	**8.5**	**1,429**	**1,173**	**21.9**
Fees and admissions	528	565	–6.5	361	350	3.2
Television, radio, sound equipment	788	682	15.5	550	438	25.7
Pets, toys, and playground equipment	381	366	4.0	204	205	–0.5
Other entertainment supplies, services	522	431	21.1	314	180	74.6
PERSONAL CARE PRODUCTS AND SERVICES	**581**	**619**	**–6.1**	**468**	**467**	**0.2**
READING	**130**	**160**	**–18.8**	**146**	**162**	**–10.1**
EDUCATION	**905**	**693**	**30.5**	**274**	**118**	**131.3**
TOBACCO PRODUCTS AND SMOKING SUPPLIES	**288**	**350**	**–17.7**	**147**	**179**	**–17.8**
MISCELLANEOUS	**690**	**851**	**–18.9**	**641**	**725**	**–11.6**
CASH CONTRIBUTIONS	**1,408**	**1,307**	**7.7**	**2,000**	**2,005**	**–0.3**
PERSONAL INSURANCE AND PENSIONS	**4,823**	**3,691**	**30.7**	**1,592**	**1,030**	**54.6**
Life and other personal insurance	390	438	–10.9	372	415	–10.3
Pensions and Social Security	4,433	3,253	36.3	1,220	615	98.3
PERSONAL TAXES	**2,166**	**3,419**	**–36.6**	**948**	**1,459**	**–35.0**
Federal income taxes	1,519	2,642	–42.5	648	1,074	–39.7
State and local income taxes	472	616	–23.4	93	159	–41.5
Other taxes	175	160	9.3	207	225	–7.9
GIFTS FOR NONHOUSEHOLD MEMBERS	**1,215**	**1,188**	**2.3**	**1,000**	**950**	**5.3**

Note: The Bureau of Labor Statistics uses consumer unit rather than household as the sampling unit in the Consumer Expenditure Survey. For the definition of consumer unit, see the glossary. Spending on gifts is also included in the preceding product and service categories.
Source: Bureau of Labor Statistics, 2000 and 2004 Consumer Expenditure Surveys, Internet site http://www.bls.gov/cex/; calculations by New Strategist

Table 8.3 Average Spending of Householders Aged 65 to 74, 2000 and 2004

(average annual spending of total consumer units and consumer units headed by people aged 65 to 74, 2000 and 2004; percent change, 2000–04; in 2004 dollars)

	total consumer units			aged 65 to 74		
	2004	2000	percent change 2000–04	2004	2000	percent change 2000–04
Number of consumer units (in 000s)	116,282	109,367	6.3%	11,230	11,538	–2.7%
Average before-tax income	$54,453	$48,975	11.2	$42,137	$32,193	30.9
Average annual spending	43,395	41,731	4.0	36,512	33,764	8.1
FOOD	**5,781**	**5,658**	**2.2**	**4,871**	**4,583**	**6.3**
Food at home	**3,347**	**3,314**	**1.0**	**3,049**	**3,027**	**0.7**
Cereals and bakery products	461	497	–7.2	422	454	–7.1
Cereals and cereal products	154	171	–10.0	126	146	–13.6
Bakery products	307	326	–5.8	296	308	–4.0
Meats, poultry, fish, and eggs	880	872	0.9	799	797	0.2
Beef	265	261	1.5	236	238	–0.9
Pork	181	183	–1.2	173	184	–6.1
Other meats	108	111	–2.5	113	94	19.8
Poultry	156	159	–1.9	123	143	–13.7
Fish and seafood	128	121	6.1	111	104	6.5
Eggs	42	37	12.6	44	35	25.4
Dairy products	371	356	4.1	353	340	3.8
Fresh milk and cream	144	144	0.2	125	129	–3.4
Other dairy products	226	212	6.8	227	211	7.8
Fruits and vegetables	561	571	–1.8	548	580	–5.6
Fresh fruits	187	179	4.6	183	180	1.7
Fresh vegetables	183	174	4.9	191	178	7.5
Processed fruits	110	126	–12.8	97	131	–25.7
Processed vegetables	82	92	–11.0	77	92	–16.4
Other food at home	1,075	1,017	5.7	927	854	8.5
Sugar and other sweets	128	128	–0.3	127	115	10.3
Fats and oils	89	91	–2.2	84	95	–12.0
Miscellaneous foods	527	479	9.9	446	382	16.8
Nonalcoholic beverages	290	274	5.8	226	218	3.5
Food prepared by household on trips	41	44	–6.6	45	44	2.6
Food away from home	**2,434**	**2,344**	**3.8**	**1,822**	**1,555**	**17.1**
ALCOHOLIC BEVERAGES	**459**	**408**	**12.5**	**329**	**286**	**14.9**
HOUSING	**13,918**	**13,513**	**3.0**	**11,152**	**10,608**	**5.1**
Shelter	**7,998**	**7,803**	**2.5**	**5,784**	**5,609**	**3.1**
Owned dwellings	5,324	5,048	5.5	4,134	3,970	4.1
Mortgage interest and charges	2,936	2,895	1.4	1,317	1,293	1.8
Property taxes	1,391	1,249	11.3	1,534	1,395	9.9
Maintenance, repairs, insurance, other expenses	997	905	10.2	1,283	1,281	0.1

	total consumer units			aged 65 to 74		
	2004	2000	percent change 2000–04	2004	2000	percent change 2000–04
Rented dwellings	$2,201	$2,231	−1.3%	$1,123	$1,044	7.5%
Other lodging	473	524	−9.8	527	596	−11.5
Utilities, fuels, public services	**2,927**	**2,730**	**7.2**	**2,881**	**2,674**	**7.7**
Natural gas	424	337	25.9	478	349	37.0
Electricity	1,064	999	6.5	1,072	1,010	6.1
Fuel oil and other fuels	121	106	13.7	163	166	−1.6
Telephone services	990	962	2.9	815	790	3.2
Water and other public services	327	325	0.7	353	360	−1.9
Household services	**753**	**750**	**0.4**	**522**	**546**	**−4.4**
Personal services	300	358	−16.1	27	109	−75.1
Other household services	453	393	15.4	495	438	13.1
Housekeeping supplies	**594**	**529**	**12.4**	**569**	**561**	**1.5**
Laundry and cleaning supplies	149	144	3.7	122	121	1.1
Other household products	290	248	17.0	285	264	7.8
Postage and stationery	155	138	12.1	162	176	−7.7
Household furnishings and equipment	**1,646**	**1,699**	**−3.1**	**1,395**	**1,218**	**14.6**
Household textiles	158	116	35.9	122	111	10.1
Furniture	417	429	−2.8	322	281	14.7
Floor coverings	52	48	7.7	61	44	39.0
Major appliances	204	207	−1.6	208	215	−3.3
Small appliances, misc. housewares	105	95	10.0	109	75	46.1
Miscellaneous household equipment	711	802	−11.3	573	494	16.1
APPAREL AND SERVICES	**1,816**	**2,036**	**−10.8**	**1,200**	**1,239**	**−3.2**
Men and boys	**406**	**483**	**−15.9**	**312**	**295**	**5.7**
Men, aged 16 or older	317	377	−16.0	273	263	3.7
Boys, aged 2 to 15	89	105	−15.5	39	32	22.6
Women and girls	**739**	**795**	**−7.1**	**543**	**495**	**9.8**
Women, aged 16 or older	631	666	−5.2	504	462	9.1
Girls, aged 2 to 15	108	129	−16.6	39	34	14.7
Children under age 2	**79**	**90**	**−12.2**	**28**	**34**	**−17.7**
Footwear	**329**	**376**	**−12.6**	**153**	**204**	**−25.0**
Other apparel products and services	**264**	**292**	**−9.5**	**165**	**211**	**−21.7**
TRANSPORTATION	**7,801**	**8,136**	**−4.1**	**6,506**	**6,359**	**2.3**
Vehicle purchases	**3,397**	**3,749**	**−9.4**	**2,822**	**2,886**	**−2.2**
Cars and trucks, new	1,748	1,761	−0.7	1,561	1,587	−1.7
Cars and trucks, used	1,582	1,941	−18.5	1,251	1,287	−2.8
Gasoline and motor oil	**1,598**	**1,416**	**12.8**	**1,259**	**1,051**	**19.8**
Other vehicle expenses	**2,365**	**2,502**	**−5.5**	**1,902**	**1,937**	**−1.8**
Vehicle finance charges	323	360	−10.2	182	200	−8.8
Maintenance and repairs	652	684	−4.7	585	612	−4.4
Vehicle insurance	964	853	13.0	825	738	11.8
Vehicle rental, leases, licenses, other charges	426	604	−29.5	309	387	−20.2
Public transportation	**441**	**468**	**−5.8**	**524**	**485**	**8.1**

	total consumer units			aged 65 to 74		
	2004	2000	percent change 2000–04	2004	2000	percent change 2000–04
HEALTH CARE	**$2,574**	**$2,266**	**13.6%**	**$3,799**	**$3,469**	**9.5%**
Health insurance	1,332	1,078	23.5	2,171	1,764	23.1
Medical services	648	623	4.0	631	752	−16.1
Drugs	480	456	5.2	854	816	4.6
Medical supplies	114	109	5.0	144	138	4.2
ENTERTAINMENT	**2,218**	**2,044**	**8.5**	**1,879**	**1,539**	**22.1**
Fees and admissions	528	565	−6.5	463	456	1.5
Television, radio, sound equipment	788	682	15.5	628	513	22.3
Pets, toys, and playground equipment	381	366	4.0	261	287	−9.2
Other entertainment supplies, services	522	431	21.1	527	282	86.9
PERSONAL CARE PRODUCTS AND SERVICES	**581**	**619**	**−6.1**	**514**	**525**	**−2.2**
READING	**130**	**160**	**−18.8**	**158**	**182**	**−13.2**
EDUCATION	**905**	**693**	**30.5**	**352**	**163**	**115.4**
TOBACCO PRODUCTS AND SMOKING SUPPLIES	**288**	**350**	**−17.7**	**197**	**245**	**−19.5**
MISCELLANEOUS	**690**	**851**	**−18.9**	**735**	**835**	**−11.9**
CASH CONTRIBUTIONS	**1,408**	**1,307**	**7.7**	**2,471**	**2,218**	**11.4**
PERSONAL INSURANCE AND PENSIONS	**4,823**	**3,691**	**30.7**	**2,348**	**1,513**	**55.2**
Life and other personal insurance	390	438	−10.9	472	564	−16.3
Pensions and Social Security	4,433	3,253	36.3	1,875	949	97.6
PERSONAL TAXES	**2,166**	**3,419**	**−36.6**	**1,010**	**1,970**	**−48.7**
Federal income taxes	1,519	2,642	−42.5	679	1,468	−53.7
State and local income taxes	472	616	−23.4	119	219	−45.8
Other taxes	175	160	9.3	213	282	−24.4
GIFTS FOR NONHOUSEHOLD MEMBERS	**1,215**	**1,188**	**2.3**	**1,068**	**1,062**	**0.6**

Note: The Bureau of Labor Statistics uses consumer unit rather than household as the sampling unit in the Consumer Expenditure Survey. For the definition of consumer unit, see the glossary. Spending on gifts is also included in the preceding product and service categories.
Source: Bureau of Labor Statistics, 2000 and 2004 Consumer Expenditure Surveys, Internet site http://www.bls.gov/cex/; calculations by New Strategist

Table 8.4 Average Spending of Householders Aged 75 or Older, 2000 and 2004

(average annual spending of total consumer units and consumer units headed by people aged 75 or older, 2000 and 2004; percent change, 2000–04; in 2004 dollars)

	total consumer units			aged 75 or older		
	2004	2000	percent change 2000–04	2004	2000	percent change 2000–04
Number of consumer units (in 000s)	116,282	109,367	6.3%	11,536	10,617	8.7%
Average before-tax income	$54,453	$48,975	11.2	$28,028	$22,555	24.3
Average annual spending	43,395	41,731	4.0	25,763	24,031	7.2
FOOD	5,781	5,658	2.2	3,518	3,375	4.2
Food at home	3,347	3,314	1.0	2,380	2,310	3.0
Cereals and bakery products	461	497	−7.2	364	366	−0.6
Cereals and cereal products	154	171	−10.0	110	123	−10.5
Bakery products	307	326	−5.8	255	244	4.7
Meats, poultry, fish, and eggs	880	872	0.9	584	565	3.4
Beef	265	261	1.5	172	158	8.9
Pork	181	183	−1.2	122	127	−4.1
Other meats	108	111	−2.5	68	77	−11.4
Poultry	156	159	−1.9	93	92	0.9
Fish and seafood	128	121	6.1	95	80	18.6
Eggs	42	37	12.6	33	31	7.4
Dairy products	371	356	4.1	271	259	4.7
Fresh milk and cream	144	144	0.2	110	114	−3.6
Other dairy products	226	212	6.8	161	145	11.2
Fruits and vegetables	561	571	−1.8	470	501	−6.2
Fresh fruits	187	179	4.6	166	192	−13.5
Fresh vegetables	183	174	4.9	142	140	1.1
Processed fruits	110	126	−12.8	100	106	−6.0
Processed vegetables	82	92	−11.0	62	63	−0.8
Other food at home	1,075	1,017	5.7	692	618	12.1
Sugar and other sweets	128	128	−0.3	91	88	3.7
Fats and oils	89	91	−2.2	69	66	4.8
Miscellaneous foods	527	479	9.9	340	281	21.1
Nonalcoholic beverages	290	274	5.8	175	166	5.7
Food prepared by household on trips	41	44	−6.6	18	19	−3.5
Food away from home	2,434	2,344	3.8	1,138	1,065	6.8
ALCOHOLIC BEVERAGES	459	408	12.5	190	170	11.8
HOUSING	13,918	13,513	3.0	9,381	8,518	10.1
Shelter	7,998	7,803	2.5	4,886	4,425	10.4
Owned dwellings	5,324	5,048	5.5	2,928	2,652	10.4
Mortgage interest and charges	2,936	2,895	1.4	421	411	2.3
Property taxes	1,391	1,249	11.3	1,302	1,174	10.9
Maintenance, repairs, insurance, other expenses	997	905	10.2	1,205	1,067	12.9

	total consumer units			aged 75 or older		
	2004	**2000**	**percent change 2000–04**	**2004**	**2000**	**percent change 2000–04**
Rented dwellings	$2,201	$2,231	−1.3%	$1,655	$1,474	12.3%
Other lodging	473	524	−9.8	303	298	1.6
Utilities, fuels, public services	**2,927**	**2,730**	**7.2**	**2,287**	**2,125**	**7.6**
Natural gas	424	337	25.9	406	330	23.0
Electricity	1,064	999	6.5	845	812	4.1
Fuel oil and other fuels	121	106	13.7	164	133	23.6
Telephone services	990	962	2.9	579	561	3.3
Water and other public services	327	325	0.7	294	290	1.5
Household services	**753**	**750**	**0.4**	**861**	**920**	**−6.4**
Personal services	300	358	−16.1	370	373	−0.8
Other household services	453	393	15.4	491	546	−10.1
Housekeeping supplies	**594**	**529**	**12.4**	**445**	**353**	**26.0**
Laundry and cleaning supplies	149	144	3.7	100	87	15.4
Other household products	290	248	17.0	210	160	31.1
Postage and stationery	155	138	12.1	136	106	27.8
Household furnishings and equipment	**1,646**	**1,699**	**−3.1**	**901**	**695**	**29.6**
Household textiles	158	116	35.9	188	47	298.6
Furniture	417	429	−2.8	153	155	−1.1
Floor coverings	52	48	7.7	26	39	−34.2
Major appliances	204	207	−1.6	143	134	6.9
Small appliances, misc. housewares	105	95	10.0	71	43	66.0
Miscellaneous household equipment	711	802	−11.3	321	279	15.2
APPAREL AND SERVICES	**1,816**	**2,036**	**−10.8**	**604**	**769**	**−21.4**
Men and boys	**406**	**483**	**−15.9**	**93**	**128**	**−27.5**
Men, aged 16 or older	317	377	−16.0	84	118	−29.1
Boys, aged 2 to 15	89	105	−15.5	9	10	−8.8
Women and girls	**739**	**795**	**−7.1**	**315**	**376**	**−16.3**
Women, aged 16 or older	631	666	−5.2	300	363	−17.4
Girls, aged 2 to 15	108	129	−16.6	15	13	14.0
Children under age 2	**79**	**90**	**−12.2**	**13**	**9**	**48.1**
Footwear	**329**	**376**	**−12.6**	**91**	**143**	**−36.2**
Other apparel products and services	**264**	**292**	**−9.5**	**93**	**113**	**−17.7**
TRANSPORTATION	**7,801**	**8,136**	**−4.1**	**3,286**	**3,154**	**4.2**
Vehicle purchases	**3,397**	**3,749**	**−9.4**	**1,132**	**1,222**	**−7.4**
Cars and trucks, new	1,748	1,761	−0.7	630	738	−14.7
Cars and trucks, used	1,582	1,941	−18.5	502	484	3.8
Gasoline and motor oil	**1,598**	**1,416**	**12.8**	**675**	**539**	**25.3**
Other vehicle expenses	**2,365**	**2,502**	**−5.5**	**1,200**	**1,039**	**15.5**
Vehicle finance charges	323	360	−10.2	48	47	1.8
Maintenance and repairs	652	684	−4.7	398	344	15.6
Vehicle insurance	964	853	13.0	600	473	26.9
Vehicle rental, leases, licenses, other charges	426	604	−29.5	153	174	−12.3
Public transportation	**441**	**468**	**−5.8**	**280**	**353**	**−20.7**

	total consumer units			aged 75 or older		
	2004	2000	percent change 2000–04	2004	2000	percent change 2000–04
HEALTH CARE	**$2,574**	**$2,266**	**13.6%**	**$3,995**	**$3,661**	**9.1%**
Health insurance	1,332	1,078	23.5	2,115	1,789	18.2
Medical services	648	623	4.0	723	722	0.2
Drugs	480	456	5.2	985	996	−1.1
Medical supplies	114	109	5.0	172	155	11.2
ENTERTAINMENT	**2,218**	**2,044**	**8.5**	**990**	**776**	**27.7**
Fees and admissions	528	565	−6.5	262	235	11.6
Television, radio, sound equipment	788	682	15.5	474	356	33.0
Pets, toys, and playground equipment	381	366	4.0	147	114	28.9
Other entertainment supplies, services	522	431	21.1	107	69	54.8
PERSONAL CARE PRODUCTS AND SERVICES	**581**	**619**	**−6.1**	**421**	**404**	**4.3**
READING	**130**	**160**	**−18.8**	**135**	**140**	**−3.8**
EDUCATION	**905**	**693**	**30.5**	**198**	**69**	**186.5**
TOBACCO PRODUCTS AND SMOKING SUPPLIES	**288**	**350**	**−17.7**	**98**	**109**	**−9.8**
MISCELLANEOUS	**690**	**851**	**−18.9**	**547**	**607**	**−9.8**
CASH CONTRIBUTIONS	**1,408**	**1,307**	**7.7**	**1,542**	**1,775**	**−13.1**
PERSONAL INSURANCE AND PENSIONS	**4,823**	**3,691**	**30.7**	**856**	**505**	**69.6**
Life and other personal insurance	390	438	−10.9	275	252	9.0
Pensions and Social Security	4,433	3,253	36.3	582	253	129.7
PERSONAL TAXES	**2,166**	**3,419**	**−36.6**	**887**	**882**	**0.6**
Federal income taxes	1,519	2,642	−42.5	618	630	−1.8
State and local income taxes	472	616	−23.4	67	91	−26.4
Other taxes	175	160	9.3	201	161	24.7
GIFTS FOR NONHOUSEHOLD MEMBERS	**1,215**	**1,188**	**2.3**	**926**	**828**	**11.8**

Note: The Bureau of Labor Statistics uses consumer unit rather than household as the sampling unit in the Consumer Expenditure Survey. For the definition of consumer unit, see the glossary. Spending on gifts is also included in the preceding product and service categories.
Source: Bureau of Labor Statistics, 2000 and 2004 Consumer Expenditure Surveys, Internet site http://www.bls.gov/cex/; calculations by New Strategist

The Spending of Householders Aged 55 to 64 Is above Average

As Boomers fill the age group, spending patterns are changing.

The spending of householders aged 55 to 64 is growing faster than that of any other age group, rising 10 percent between 2000 and 2004 after adjusting for inflation. Households headed by 55-to-64-year-olds spent $47,299 in 2004, 9 percent more than the average household. The age group's spending is growing because lifestyles are changing. Two-earner couples are heading a growing proportion of households, and most of those couples are postponing retirement as early retirement options diminish. Rather than coping with reduced incomes in retirement, many 55-to-64-year-olds are continuing to enjoy peak earnings well into their sixties.

On many discretionary items, householders aged 55 to 64 spend well above average. People in this age group are the most ardent travelers, and this is reflected in their spending. Householders aged 55 to 64 spend 57 percent more than average on "other" lodging (mostly hotels and motels) and 37 percent more than average on public transportation (mostly airfares). They spend 67 percent more than average on floor coverings, 32 percent more on new cars and trucks, and 27 percent more on entertainment.

■ The spending patterns of householders aged 55 to 64 will continue to change as Boomers fill the age group.

Householders aged 55 to 64 spend 32 percent more than average on new cars and trucks

(indexed spending of householders aged 55 to 64 on selected items, 2004)

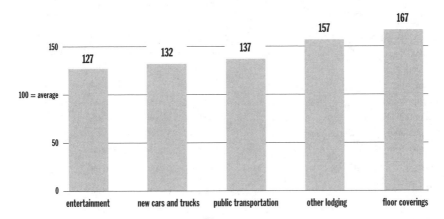

Table 8.5 Average, Indexed, and Market Share of Spending by Householders Aged 55 to 64, 2004

(average annual spending of total consumer units and average annual, indexed, and market share of spending by consumer units headed by 55-to-64-year-olds, 2004)

	total consumer units	consumer units headed by 55-to-64-year-olds		
		average spending	indexed spending	market share
Number of consumer units (in 000s)	116,282	17,479	–	15.0%
Average before-tax income	$54,453	$61,031	112	16.8
Average annual spending	43,395	47,299	109	16.4
FOOD	5,781	5,898	102	15.3
Food at home	3,347	3,374	101	15.2
Cereals and bakery products	461	437	95	14.2
Cereals and cereal products	154	137	89	13.4
Bakery products	307	300	98	14.7
Meats, poultry, fish, and eggs	880	894	102	15.3
Beef	265	257	97	14.6
Pork	181	203	112	16.9
Other meats	108	102	94	14.2
Poultry	156	156	100	15.0
Fish and seafood	128	130	102	15.3
Eggs	42	46	110	16.5
Dairy products	371	371	100	15.0
Fresh milk and cream	144	137	95	14.3
Other dairy products	226	235	104	15.6
Fruits and vegetables	561	588	105	15.8
Fresh fruits	187	199	106	16.0
Fresh vegetables	183	200	109	16.4
Processed fruits	110	108	98	14.8
Processed vegetables	82	80	98	14.7
Other food at home	1,075	1,083	101	15.1
Sugar and other sweets	128	137	107	16.1
Fats and oils	89	97	109	16.4
Miscellaneous foods	527	485	92	13.8
Nonalcoholic beverages	290	295	102	15.3
Food prepared by household on trips	41	69	168	25.3
Food away from home	2,434	2,524	104	15.6
ALCOHOLIC BEVERAGES	459	457	100	15.0
HOUSING	13,918	14,339	103	15.5
Shelter	7,998	7,883	99	14.8
Owned dwellings	5,324	5,970	112	16.9
Mortgage interest and charges	2,936	2,813	96	14.4
Property taxes	1,391	1,760	127	19.0
Maintenance, repairs, insurance, other expenses	997	1,398	140	21.1

	total consumer units	consumer units headed by 55-to-64-year-olds		
		average spending	indexed spending	market share
Rented dwellings	$2,201	$1,169	53	8.0%
Other lodging	473	743	157	23.6
Utilities, fuels, public services	**2,927**	**3,222**	**110**	**16.5**
Natural gas	424	477	113	16.9
Electricity	1,064	1,177	111	16.6
Fuel oil and other fuels	121	161	133	20.0
Telephone services	990	1,040	105	15.8
Water and other public services	327	367	112	16.9
Household services	**753**	**645**	**86**	**12.9**
Personal services	300	43	14	2.2
Other household services	453	602	133	20.0
Housekeeping supplies	**594**	**657**	**111**	**16.6**
Laundry and cleaning supplies	149	158	106	15.9
Other household products	290	318	110	16.5
Postage and stationery	155	181	117	17.6
Household furnishings and equipment	**1,646**	**1,932**	**117**	**17.6**
Household textiles	158	203	128	19.3
Furniture	417	504	121	18.2
Floor coverings	52	87	167	25.1
Major appliances	204	240	118	17.7
Small appliances, misc. housewares	105	130	124	18.6
Miscellaneous household equipment	711	768	108	16.2
APPAREL AND SERVICES	**1,816**	**1,863**	**103**	**15.4**
Men and boys	**406**	**338**	**83**	**12.5**
Men, aged 16 or older	317	285	90	13.5
Boys, aged 2 to 15	89	53	60	9.0
Women and girls	**739**	**793**	**107**	**16.1**
Women, aged 16 or older	631	743	118	17.7
Girls, aged 2 to 15	108	50	46	7.0
Children under age 2	**79**	**47**	**59**	**8.9**
Footwear	**329**	**351**	**107**	**16.0**
Other apparel products and services	**264**	**333**	**126**	**19.0**
TRANSPORTATION	**7,801**	**8,421**	**108**	**16.2**
Vehicle purchases	**3,397**	**3,616**	**106**	**16.0**
Cars and trucks, new	1,748	2,311	132	19.9
Cars and trucks, used	1,582	1,247	79	11.8
Gasoline and motor oil	**1,598**	**1,666**	**104**	**15.7**
Other vehicle expenses	**2,365**	**2,532**	**107**	**16.1**
Vehicle finance charges	323	336	104	15.6
Maintenance and repairs	652	742	114	17.1
Vehicle insurance	964	973	101	15.2
Vehicle rental, leases, licenses, other charges	426	481	113	17.0
Public transportation	**441**	**606**	**137**	**20.7**

	total consumer units	consumer units headed by 55-to-64-year-olds		
		average spending	indexed spending	market share
HEALTH CARE	**$2,574**	**$3,262**	**127**	**19.0%**
Health insurance	1,332	1,567	118	17.7
Medical services	648	892	138	20.7
Drugs	480	642	134	20.1
Medical supplies	114	161	141	21.2
ENTERTAINMENT	**2,218**	**2,823**	**127**	**19.1**
Fees and admissions	528	618	117	17.6
Television, radio, sound equipment	788	810	103	15.5
Pets, toys, and playground equipment	381	428	112	16.9
Other entertainment supplies, services	522	967	185	27.8
PERSONAL CARE PRODUCTS, SERVICES	**581**	**628**	**108**	**16.2**
READING	**130**	**177**	**136**	**20.5**
EDUCATION	**905**	**730**	**81**	**12.1**
TOBACCO PRODUCTS, SMOKING SUPPLIES	**288**	**301**	**105**	**15.7**
MISCELLANEOUS	**690**	**825**	**120**	**18.0**
CASH CONTRIBUTIONS	**1,408**	**1,752**	**124**	**18.7**
PERSONAL INSURANCE AND PENSIONS	**4,823**	**5,825**	**121**	**18.2**
Life and other personal insurance	390	612	157	23.6
Pensions and Social Security	4,433	5,214	118	17.7
PERSONAL TAXES	**2,166**	**2,987**	**138**	**20.7**
Federal income taxes	1,519	2,168	143	21.5
State and local income taxes	472	584	124	18.6
Other taxes	175	236	135	20.3
GIFTS FOR NONHOUSEHOLD MEMBERS	**1,215**	**1,636**	**135**	**20.2**

Note: The Bureau of Labor Statistics uses consumer unit rather than household as the sampling unit in the Consumer Expenditure Survey. For the definition of consumer unit, see the glossary. Spending on gifts is also included in the preceding product and service categories; "–" means not applicable.
Source: Bureau of Labor Statistics, 2004 Consumer Expenditure Survey, Internet site http://www.bls.gov/cex/; calculations by New Strategist

Householders Aged 65 or Older Can Be Big Spenders

Those aged 65 to 74 spend 77 percent as much as the average household.

In 2004, householders aged 65 or older spent $31,104, much less than the $43,395 spent by the average household. The spending of older householders is below average because their households are small and most are retired.

Householders aged 65 to 74 spend more than those aged 75 or older. In 2004, householders aged 65 to 74 spent $36,512, while householders aged 75 or older spent $25,763. Together, the two age groups control 14 percent of household spending. They account for 31 percent of out-of-pocket health insurance spending, however, and 38 percent of spending on drugs.

Despite their small household size, householders aged 65 to 74 spend 11 percent more than the average household on "other" lodging, a category that includes hotel and motel expenses. They spend 19 percent more than average on public transportation, a category that includes airfares. They spend 22 percent more than the average household on reading material and 75 percent more than average on cash contributions to churches, charities, and family members.

Householders aged 75 or older spend only 51 percent as much as the average household. Their spending is above average for items required by the frail elderly. Some of these are household personal services (a category that includes adult care centers) and health care. This age group also spends slightly more than average on reading material.

■ As better-educated generations age into their sixties and seventies, older Americans are not acting so old anymore. The revolution in the older market will continue as Boomers enter the age group.

Many older Americans spend more than average on a variety of items

(indexed spending of householders aged 65 to 74, 2004)

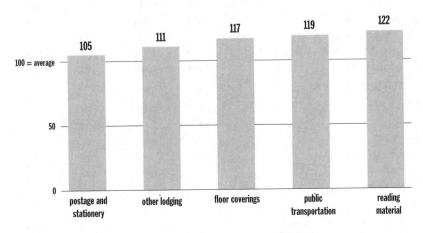

Table 8.6 Average, Indexed, and Market Share of Spending by Householders Aged 65 or Older, 2004

(average annual spending of total consumer units and average annual, indexed, and market share of spending by consumer units headed by people aged 65 or older, 2004)

	total consumer units	consumer units headed by people aged 65 or older		
		average spending	indexed spending	market share
Number of consumer units (in 000s)	116,282	22,765	–	19.6%
Average before-tax income	$54,453	$34,988	64	12.6
Average annual spending	43,395	31,104	72	14.0
FOOD	5,781	4,206	73	14.2
Food at home	3,347	2,722	81	15.9
Cereals and bakery products	461	394	85	16.7
Cereals and cereal products	154	118	77	15.0
Bakery products	307	276	90	17.6
Meats, poultry, fish, and eggs	880	694	79	15.4
Beef	265	205	77	15.1
Pork	181	148	82	16.0
Other meats	108	91	84	16.5
Poultry	156	108	69	13.6
Fish and seafood	128	103	80	15.8
Eggs	42	38	90	17.7
Dairy products	371	313	84	16.5
Fresh milk and cream	144	118	82	16.0
Other dairy products	226	195	86	16.9
Fruits and vegetables	561	510	91	17.8
Fresh fruits	187	174	93	18.2
Fresh vegetables	183	167	91	17.9
Processed fruits	110	99	90	17.6
Processed vegetables	82	70	85	16.7
Other food at home	1,075	812	76	14.8
Sugar and other sweets	128	109	85	16.7
Fats and oils	89	77	87	16.9
Miscellaneous foods	527	394	75	14.6
Nonalcoholic beverages	290	201	69	13.6
Food prepared by household on trips	41	31	76	14.8
Food away from home	2,434	1,484	61	11.9
ALCOHOLIC BEVERAGES	459	261	57	11.1
HOUSING	13,918	10,259	74	14.4
Shelter	7,998	5,329	67	13.0
Owned dwellings	5,324	3,523	66	13.0
Mortgage interest and charges	2,936	863	29	5.8
Property taxes	1,391	1,416	102	19.9
Maintenance, repairs, insurance, other expenses	997	1,244	125	24.4

	total consumer units	consumer units headed by people aged 65 or older		
		average spending	indexed spending	market share
Rented dwellings	$2,201	$1,393	63	12.4%
Other lodging	473	414	88	17.1
Utilities, fuels, public services	**2,927**	**2,580**	**88**	**17.3**
Natural gas	424	442	104	20.4
Electricity	1,064	957	90	17.6
Fuel oil and other fuels	121	163	135	26.4
Telephone services	990	695	70	13.7
Water and other public services	327	323	99	19.3
Household services	**753**	**694**	**92**	**18.0**
Personal services	300	201	67	13.1
Other household services	453	493	109	21.3
Housekeeping supplies	**594**	**509**	**86**	**16.8**
Laundry and cleaning supplies	149	111	74	14.6
Other household products	290	248	86	16.7
Postage and stationery	155	149	96	18.8
Household furnishings and equipment	**1,646**	**1,147**	**70**	**13.6**
Household textiles	158	154	97	19.1
Furniture	417	236	57	11.1
Floor coverings	52	44	85	16.6
Major appliances	204	175	86	16.8
Small appliances, misc. housewares	105	90	86	16.8
Miscellaneous household equipment	711	448	63	12.3
APPAREL AND SERVICES	**1,816**	**907**	**50**	**9.8**
Men and boys	**406**	**204**	**50**	**9.8**
Men, aged 16 or older	317	180	57	11.1
Boys, aged 2 to 15	89	24	27	5.3
Women and girls	**739**	**431**	**58**	**11.4**
Women, aged 16 or older	631	404	64	12.5
Girls, aged 2 to 15	108	27	25	4.9
Children under age 2	**79**	**20**	**25**	**5.0**
Footwear	**329**	**123**	**37**	**7.3**
Other apparel products and services	**264**	**129**	**49**	**9.6**
TRANSPORTATION	**7,801**	**4,875**	**62**	**12.2**
Vehicle purchases	**3,397**	**1,966**	**58**	**11.3**
Cars and trucks, new	1,748	1,089	62	12.2
Cars and trucks, used	1,582	872	55	10.8
Gasoline and motor oil	**1,598**	**963**	**60**	**11.8**
Other vehicle expenses	**2,365**	**1,546**	**65**	**12.8**
Vehicle finance charges	323	115	36	7.0
Maintenance and repairs	652	490	75	14.7
Vehicle insurance	964	711	74	14.4
Vehicle rental, leases, licenses, other charges	426	230	54	10.6
Public transportation	**441**	**400**	**91**	**17.8**

	total consumer units	consumer units headed by people aged 65 or older		
		average spending	indexed spending	market share
HEALTH CARE	**$2,574**	**$3,899**	**151**	**29.7%**
Health insurance	1,332	2,142	161	31.5
Medical services	648	678	105	20.5
Drugs	480	920	192	37.5
Medical supplies	114	158	139	27.1
ENTERTAINMENT	**2,218**	**1,429**	**64**	**12.6**
Fees and admissions	528	361	68	13.4
Television, radio, sound equipment	788	550	70	13.7
Pets, toys, and playground equipment	381	204	54	10.5
Other entertainment supplies, services	522	314	60	11.8
PERSONAL CARE PRODUCTS, SERVICES	**581**	**468**	**81**	**15.8**
READING	**130**	**146**	**112**	**22.0**
EDUCATION	**905**	**274**	**30**	**5.9**
TOBACCO PRODUCTS, SMOKING SUPPLIES	**288**	**147**	**51**	**10.0**
MISCELLANEOUS	**690**	**641**	**93**	**18.2**
CASH CONTRIBUTIONS	**1,408**	**2,000**	**142**	**27.8**
PERSONAL INSURANCE AND PENSIONS	**4,823**	**1,592**	**33**	**6.5**
Life and other personal insurance	390	372	95	18.7
Pensions and Social Security	4,433	1,220	28	5.4
PERSONAL TAXES	**2,166**	**948**	**44**	**8.6**
Federal income taxes	1,519	648	43	8.4
State and local income taxes	472	93	20	3.9
Other taxes	175	207	118	23.2
GIFTS FOR NONHOUSEHOLD MEMBERS	**1,215**	**1,000**	**82**	**16.1**

Note: The Bureau of Labor Statistics uses consumer unit rather than household as the sampling unit in the Consumer Expenditure Survey. For the definition of consumer unit, see the glossary. Spending on gifts is included in the preceding product and service categories; "–" means not applicable.
Source: Bureau of Labor Statistics, 2004 Consumer Expenditure Survey, Internet site http://www.bls.gov/cex/; calculations by New Strategist

Table 8.7 Average, Indexed, and Market Share of Spending by Householders Aged 65 to 74, 2004

(average annual spending of total consumer units and average annual, indexed, and market share of spending by consumer units headed by 65-to-74-year-olds, 2004)

	total consumer units	consumer units headed by 65-to-74-year-olds		
		average spending	indexed spending	market share
Number of consumer units (in 000s)	116,282	11,230	–	9.7%
Average before-tax income	$54,453	$42,137	77	7.5
Average annual spending	43,395	36,512	84	8.1
FOOD	5,781	4,871	84	8.1
Food at home	3,347	3,049	91	8.8
Cereals and bakery products	461	422	92	8.8
Cereals and cereal products	154	126	82	7.9
Bakery products	307	296	96	9.3
Meats, poultry, fish, and eggs	880	799	91	8.8
Beef	265	236	89	8.6
Pork	181	173	96	9.2
Other meats	108	113	105	10.1
Poultry	156	123	79	7.6
Fish and seafood	128	111	87	8.4
Eggs	42	44	105	10.1
Dairy products	371	353	95	9.2
Fresh milk and cream	144	125	87	8.4
Other dairy products	226	227	100	9.7
Fruits and vegetables	561	548	98	9.4
Fresh fruits	187	183	98	9.5
Fresh vegetables	183	191	104	10.1
Processed fruits	110	97	88	8.5
Processed vegetables	82	77	94	9.1
Other food at home	1,075	927	86	8.3
Sugar and other sweets	128	127	99	9.6
Fats and oils	89	84	94	9.1
Miscellaneous foods	527	446	85	8.2
Nonalcoholic beverages	290	226	78	7.5
Food prepared by household on trips	41	45	110	10.6
Food away from home	2,434	1,822	75	7.2
ALCOHOLIC BEVERAGES	459	329	72	6.9
HOUSING	13,918	11,152	80	7.7
Shelter	7,998	5,784	72	7.0
Owned dwellings	5,324	4,134	78	7.5
Mortgage interest and charges	2,936	1,317	45	4.3
Property taxes	1,391	1,534	110	10.7
Maintenance, repairs, insurance, other expenses	997	1,283	129	12.4

	total consumer units	consumer units headed by 65-to-74-year-olds		
		average spending	indexed spending	market share
Rented dwellings	$2,201	$1,123	51	4.9%
Other lodging	473	527	111	10.8
Utilities, fuels, public services	**2,927**	**2,881**	**98**	**9.5**
Natural gas	424	478	113	10.9
Electricity	1,064	1,072	101	9.7
Fuel oil and other fuels	121	163	135	13.0
Telephone services	990	815	82	8.0
Water and other public services	327	353	108	10.4
Household services	**753**	**522**	**69**	**6.7**
Personal services	300	27	9	0.9
Other household services	453	495	109	10.6
Housekeeping supplies	**594**	**569**	**96**	**9.3**
Laundry and cleaning supplies	149	122	82	7.9
Other household products	290	285	98	9.5
Postage and stationery	155	162	105	10.1
Household furnishings and equipment	**1,646**	**1,395**	**85**	**8.2**
Household textiles	158	122	77	7.5
Furniture	417	322	77	7.5
Floor coverings	52	61	117	11.3
Major appliances	204	208	102	9.8
Small appliances, misc. housewares	105	109	104	10.0
Miscellaneous household equipment	711	573	81	7.8
APPAREL AND SERVICES	**1,816**	**1,200**	**66**	**6.4**
Men and boys	**406**	**312**	**77**	**7.4**
Men, aged 16 or older	317	273	86	8.3
Boys, aged 2 to 15	89	39	44	4.2
Women and girls	**739**	**543**	**73**	**7.1**
Women, aged 16 or older	631	504	80	7.7
Girls, aged 2 to 15	108	39	36	3.5
Children under age 2	**79**	**28**	**35**	**3.4**
Footwear	**329**	**153**	**47**	**4.5**
Other apparel products and services	**264**	**165**	**63**	**6.0**
TRANSPORTATION	**7,801**	**6,506**	**83**	**8.1**
Vehicle purchases	**3,397**	**2,822**	**83**	**8.0**
Cars and trucks, new	1,748	1,561	89	8.6
Cars and trucks, used	1,582	1,251	79	7.6
Gasoline and motor oil	**1,598**	**1,259**	**79**	**7.6**
Other vehicle expenses	**2,365**	**1,902**	**80**	**7.8**
Vehicle finance charges	323	182	56	5.4
Maintenance and repairs	652	585	90	8.7
Vehicle insurance	964	825	86	8.3
Vehicle rental, leases, licenses, other charges	426	309	73	7.0
Public transportation	**441**	**524**	**119**	**11.5**

	total consumer units	consumer units headed by 65-to-74-year-olds		
		average spending	indexed spending	market share
HEALTH CARE	**$2,574**	**$3,799**	**148**	**14.3%**
Health insurance	1,332	2,171	163	15.7
Medical services	648	631	97	9.4
Drugs	480	854	178	17.2
Medical supplies	114	144	126	12.2
ENTERTAINMENT	**2,218**	**1,879**	**85**	**8.2**
Fees and admissions	528	463	88	8.5
Television, radio, sound equipment	788	628	80	7.7
Pets, toys, and playground equipment	381	261	69	6.6
Other entertainment supplies, services	522	527	101	9.8
PERSONAL CARE PRODUCTS, SERVICES	**581**	**514**	**88**	**8.5**
READING	**130**	**158**	**122**	**11.7**
EDUCATION	**905**	**352**	**39**	**3.8**
TOBACCO PRODUCTS, SMOKING SUPPLIES	**288**	**197**	**68**	**6.6**
MISCELLANEOUS	**690**	**735**	**107**	**10.3**
CASH CONTRIBUTIONS	**1,408**	**2,471**	**175**	**16.9**
PERSONAL INSURANCE AND PENSIONS	**4,823**	**2,348**	**49**	**4.7**
Life and other personal insurance	390	472	121	11.7
Pensions and Social Security	4,433	1,875	42	4.1
PERSONAL TAXES	**2,166**	**1,010**	**47**	**4.5**
Federal income taxes	1,519	679	45	4.3
State and local income taxes	472	119	25	2.4
Other taxes	175	213	122	11.8
GIFTS FOR NONHOUSEHOLD MEMBERS	**1,215**	**1,068**	**88**	**8.5**

Note: The Bureau of Labor Statistics uses consumer unit rather than household as the sampling unit in the Consumer Expenditure Survey. For the definition of consumer unit, see the glossary. Spending on gifts is included in the preceding product and service categories; "–" means not applicable.
Source: Bureau of Labor Statistics, 2004 Consumer Expenditure Survey, Internet site http://www.bls.gov/cex/; calculations by New Strategist

Table 8.8 **Average, Indexed, and Market Share of Spending by Householders Aged 75 or Older, 2004**

(average annual spending of total consumer units and average annual, indexed, and market share of spending by consumer units headed by people aged 75 or older, 2004)

	total consumer units	consumer units headed by people aged 75 or older		
		average spending	indexed spending	market share
Number of consumer units (in 000s)	116,282	11,536	–	9.9%
Average before-tax income	$54,453	$28,028	51	5.1
Average annual spending	43,395	25,763	59	5.9
FOOD	5,781	3,518	61	6.0
Food at home	3,347	2,380	71	7.1
Cereals and bakery products	461	364	79	7.8
Cereals and cereal products	154	110	71	7.1
Bakery products	307	255	83	8.2
Meats, poultry, fish, and eggs	880	584	66	6.6
Beef	265	172	65	6.4
Pork	181	122	67	6.7
Other meats	108	68	63	6.2
Poultry	156	93	60	5.9
Fish and seafood	128	95	74	7.4
Eggs	42	33	79	7.8
Dairy products	371	271	73	7.2
Fresh milk and cream	144	110	76	7.6
Other dairy products	226	161	71	7.1
Fruits and vegetables	561	470	84	8.3
Fresh fruits	187	166	89	8.8
Fresh vegetables	183	142	78	7.7
Processed fruits	110	100	91	9.0
Processed vegetables	82	62	76	7.5
Other food at home	1,075	692	64	6.4
Sugar and other sweets	128	91	71	7.1
Fats and oils	89	69	78	7.7
Miscellaneous foods	527	340	65	6.4
Nonalcoholic beverages	290	175	60	6.0
Food prepared by household on trips	41	18	44	4.4
Food away from home	2,434	1,138	47	4.6
ALCOHOLIC BEVERAGES	459	190	41	4.1
HOUSING	13,918	9,381	67	6.7
Shelter	7,998	4,886	61	6.1
Owned dwellings	5,324	2,928	55	5.5
Mortgage interest and charges	2,936	421	14	1.4
Property taxes	1,391	1,302	94	9.3
Maintenance, repairs, insurance, other expenses	997	1,205	121	12.0

	total consumer units	consumer units headed by people aged 75 or older		
		average spending	indexed spending	market share
Rented dwellings	$2,201	$1,655	75	7.5%
Other lodging	473	303	64	6.4
Utilities, fuels, public services	**2,927**	**2,287**	**78**	**7.8**
Natural gas	424	406	96	9.5
Electricity	1,064	845	79	7.9
Fuel oil and other fuels	121	164	136	13.4
Telephone services	990	579	58	5.8
Water and other public services	327	294	90	8.9
Household services	**753**	**861**	**114**	**11.3**
Personal services	300	370	123	12.2
Other household services	453	491	108	10.8
Housekeeping supplies	**594**	**445**	**75**	**7.4**
Laundry and cleaning supplies	149	100	67	6.7
Other household products	290	210	72	7.2
Postage and stationery	155	136	88	8.7
Household furnishings and equipment	**1,646**	**901**	**55**	**5.4**
Household textiles	158	188	119	11.8
Furniture	417	153	37	3.6
Floor coverings	52	26	50	5.0
Major appliances	204	143	70	7.0
Small appliances, misc. housewares	105	71	68	6.7
Miscellaneous household equipment	711	321	45	4.5
APPAREL AND SERVICES	**1,816**	**604**	**33**	**3.3**
Men and boys	**406**	**93**	**23**	**2.3**
Men, aged 16 or older	317	84	26	2.6
Boys, aged 2 to 15	89	9	10	1.0
Women and girls	**739**	**315**	**43**	**4.2**
Women, aged 16 or older	631	300	48	4.7
Girls, aged 2 to 15	108	15	14	1.4
Children under age 2	**79**	**13**	**16**	**1.6**
Footwear	**329**	**91**	**28**	**2.7**
Other apparel products and services	**264**	**93**	**35**	**3.5**
TRANSPORTATION	**7,801**	**3,286**	**42**	**4.2**
Vehicle purchases	**3,397**	**1,132**	**33**	**3.3**
Cars and trucks, new	1,748	630	36	3.6
Cars and trucks, used	1,582	502	32	3.1
Gasoline and motor oil	**1,598**	**675**	**42**	**4.2**
Other vehicle expenses	**2,365**	**1,200**	**51**	**5.0**
Vehicle finance charges	323	48	15	1.5
Maintenance and repairs	652	398	61	6.1
Vehicle insurance	964	600	62	6.2
Vehicle rental, leases, licenses, other charges	426	153	36	3.6
Public transportation	**441**	**280**	**63**	**6.3**

	total consumer units	consumer units headed by people aged 75 or older		
		average spending	indexed spending	market share
HEALTH CARE	$2,574	$3,995	155	15.4%
Health insurance	1,332	2,115	159	15.8
Medical services	648	723	112	11.1
Drugs	480	985	205	20.4
Medical supplies	114	172	151	15.0
ENTERTAINMENT	2,218	990	45	4.4
Fees and admissions	528	262	50	4.9
Television, radio, sound equipment	788	474	60	6.0
Pets, toys, and playground equipment	381	147	39	3.8
Other entertainment supplies, services	522	107	20	2.0
PERSONAL CARE PRODUCTS, SERVICES	581	421	72	7.2
READING	130	135	104	10.3
EDUCATION	905	198	22	2.2
TOBACCO PRODUCTS, SMOKING SUPPLIES	288	98	34	3.4
MISCELLANEOUS	690	547	79	7.9
CASH CONTRIBUTIONS	1,408	1,542	110	10.9
PERSONAL INSURANCE AND PENSIONS	4,823	856	18	1.8
Life and other personal insurance	390	275	71	7.0
Pensions and Social Security	4,433	582	13	1.3
PERSONAL TAXES	2,166	887	41	4.1
Federal income taxes	1,519	618	41	4.0
State and local income taxes	472	67	14	1.4
Other taxes	175	201	115	11.4
GIFTS FOR NONHOUSEHOLD MEMBERS	1,215	926	76	7.6

Note: The Bureau of Labor Statistics uses consumer unit rather than household as the sampling unit in the Consumer Expenditure Survey. For the definition of consumer unit, see the glossary. Spending on gifts is included in the preceding product and service categories; "–" means not applicable.
Source: Bureau of Labor Statistics, 2004 Consumer Expenditure Survey, Internet site http://www.bls.gov/cex/; calculations by New Strategist

Retirees Are Spending More

The spending of retirees grew substantially between 2000 and 2004.

Households headed by retirees spent $30,450 in 2004—7 percent more than they spent in 2000, after adjusting for inflation. This spending gain was greater than the 4 percent increase in spending by the average household.

Retirees spent more in 2004 than in 2000 on many discretionary items. Their spending on food away from home rose 10 percent during those years, after adjusting for inflation. Spending on alcoholic beverages grew 21 percent, and spending on entertainment climbed by a whopping 42 percent.

Retirees spent only 70 percent as much as the average household in 2004 because their households are small. Retirees spend more than the average household on some items, such as fuel oil, reading material, and health care. They control 32 percent of out-of-pocket spending on drugs.

■ As Baby Boomers begin to retire, the spending patterns of retirees are likely to change, reflecting Boomer preferences.

Retirees boosted their spending on many items between 2000 and 2004

(percent change in spending by retirees on selected items, 2000 to 2004; in 2004 dollars)

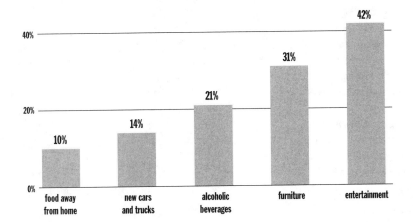

Table 8.9 Average Spending of Retirees, 2000 and 2004

(average annual spending of consumer units headed by retirees, 2000 and 2004; percent change, 2000–04; in 2004 dollars)

	2004	2000	percent change 2000–04
Number of consumer units (in 000s)	20,060	19,499	2.9%
Average before-tax income	$30,399	$24,467	24.2
Average annual spending	30,450	28,451	7.0
FOOD	4,200	4,043	3.9
Food at home	2,711	2,691	0.8
Cereals and bakery products	386	410	–5.9
Cereals and cereal products	124	132	–5.8
Bakery products	262	279	–6.0
Meats, poultry, fish, and eggs	688	698	–1.4
Beef	199	203	–1.9
Pork	153	159	–3.8
Other meats	84	87	–3.1
Poultry	104	118	–12.2
Fish and seafood	108	95	13.2
Eggs	39	34	14.7
Dairy products	310	304	2.0
Fresh milk and cream	117	124	–5.6
Other dairy products	193	180	7.3
Fruits and vegetables	502	534	–6.0
Fresh fruits	171	179	–4.4
Fresh vegetables	164	160	2.4
Processed fruits	98	117	–16.5
Processed vegetables	69	76	–8.8
Other food at home	825	746	10.6
Sugar and other sweets	112	105	6.4
Fats and oils	75	80	–6.3
Miscellaneous foods	391	332	17.6
Nonalcoholic beverages	207	194	6.6
Food prepared by household on trips	39	33	18.5
Food away from home	1,489	1,352	10.1
ALCOHOLIC BEVERAGES	299	248	20.6
HOUSING	10,363	9,502	9.1
Shelter	5,329	4,841	10.1
Owned dwellings	3,526	3,222	9.4
Mortgage interest and charges	917	827	10.9
Property taxes	1,367	1,246	9.7
Maintenance, repairs, insurance, other expenses	1,242	1,148	8.1

	2004	2000	percent change 2000–04
Rented dwellings	$1,398	$1,204	16.1%
Other lodging	406	416	–2.3
Utilities, fuels, public services	**2,559**	**2,390**	**7.1**
Natural gas	430	339	26.9
Electricity	945	916	3.2
Fuel oil and other fuels	163	136	19.8
Telephone services	702	672	4.4
Water and other public services	319	326	–2.1
Household services	**668**	**630**	**6.1**
Personal services	205	213	–3.7
Other household services	463	417	11.1
Housekeeping supplies	**536**	**478**	**12.1**
Laundry and cleaning supplies	117	107	8.8
Other household products	261	218	19.6
Postage and stationery	158	152	3.6
Household furnishings and equipment	**1,270**	**1,163**	**9.2**
Household textiles	173	89	94.7
Furniture	293	224	30.9
Floor coverings	47	36	29.8
Major appliances	204	194	5.1
Small appliances, misc. housewares	90	63	43.9
Miscellaneous household equipment	465	557	–16.6
APPAREL AND SERVICES	**970**	**1,016**	**–4.5**
Men and boys	**224**	**197**	**13.5**
Men, aged 16 or older	197	177	11.6
Boys, aged 2 to 15	28	21	34.4
Women and girls	**426**	**475**	**–10.3**
Women, aged 16 or older	393	441	–10.9
Girls, aged 2 to 15	33	33	0.3
Children under age 2	**19**	**25**	**–24.7**
Footwear	**156**	**173**	**–10.0**
Other apparel products and services	**145**	**145**	**0.1**
TRANSPORTATION	**4,976**	**4,825**	**3.1**
Vehicle purchases	**2,050**	**2,047**	**0.2**
Cars and trucks, new	1,231	1,077	14.3
Cars and trucks, used	801	970	–17.4
Gasoline and motor oil	**998**	**835**	**19.6**
Other vehicle expenses	**1,571**	**1,540**	**2.0**
Vehicle finance charges	127	143	–10.9
Maintenance and repairs	471	496	–5.0
Vehicle insurance	729	629	16.0
Vehicle rental, leases, licenses, other charges	245	273	–10.3
Public transportation	**357**	**404**	**–11.6**

	2004	2000	percent change 2000–04
HEALTH CARE	**$3,868**	**$3,479**	**11.2%**
Health insurance	2,096	1,733	20.9
Medical services	738	733	0.7
Drugs	879	870	1.1
Medical supplies	155	143	8.7
ENTERTAINMENT	**1,722**	**1,212**	**42.1**
Fees and admissions	359	373	–3.7
Television, radio, sound equipment	577	437	32.2
Pets, toys, and playground equipment	208	210	–0.7
Other entertainment supplies, services	578	193	199.4
PERSONAL CARE PRODUCTS AND SERVICES	**483**	**468**	**3.1**
READING	**143**	**156**	**–8.2**
EDUCATION	**167**	**135**	**23.8**
TOBACCO PRODUCTS, SMOKING SUPPLIES	**168**	**196**	**–14.4**
MISCELLANEOUS	**583**	**668**	**–12.7**
CASH CONTRIBUTIONS	**1,476**	**1,844**	**–20.0**
PERSONAL INSURANCE AND PENSIONS	**1,031**	**658**	**56.7**
Life and other personal insurance	339	371	–8.6
Pensions and Social Security	692	287	140.8
PERSONAL TAXES	**693**	**971**	**–28.6**
Federal income taxes	451	633	–28.7
State and local income taxes	51	107	–52.6
Other taxes	192	229	–16.2
GIFTS FOR NONHOUSEHOLD MEMBERS	**927**	**879**	**5.5**

Note: The Bureau of Labor Statistics uses consumer unit rather than household as the sampling unit in the Consumer Expenditure Survey. For the definition of consumer unit, see the glossary. Spending on gifts is also included in the preceding product and service categories.
Source: Bureau of Labor Statistics, 2000 and 2004 Consumer Expenditure Surveys, Internet site http://www.bls.gov/cex/; calculations by New Strategist

Table 8.10 Average, Indexed, and Market Share of Spending by Retirees, 2004

(average annual spending of total consumer units, and average annual, indexed, and market share of spending by consumer units headed by retirees, 2004)

	total consumer units	consumer units headed by retirees		
		average spending	indexed spending	market share
Number of consumer units (in 000s)	116,282	20,060	–	17.3%
Average before-tax income	$54,453	$30,399	56	9.6
Average annual spending	43,395	30,450	70	12.1
FOOD	**5,781**	**4,200**	**73**	**12.5**
Food at home	**3,347**	**2,711**	**81**	**14.0**
Cereals and bakery products	461	386	84	14.4
Cereals and cereal products	154	124	81	13.9
Bakery products	307	262	85	14.7
Meats, poultry, fish, and eggs	880	688	78	13.5
Beef	265	199	75	13.0
Pork	181	153	85	14.6
Other meats	108	84	78	13.4
Poultry	156	104	67	11.5
Fish and seafood	128	108	84	14.6
Eggs	42	39	93	16.0
Dairy products	371	310	84	14.4
Fresh milk and cream	144	117	81	14.0
Other dairy products	226	193	85	14.7
Fruits and vegetables	561	502	89	15.4
Fresh fruits	187	171	91	15.8
Fresh vegetables	183	164	90	15.5
Processed fruits	110	98	89	15.4
Processed vegetables	82	69	84	14.5
Other food at home	1,075	825	77	13.2
Sugar and other sweets	128	112	88	15.1
Fats and oils	89	75	84	14.5
Miscellaneous foods	527	391	74	12.8
Nonalcoholic beverages	290	207	71	12.3
Food prepared by household on trips	41	39	95	16.4
Food away from home	**2,434**	**1,489**	**61**	**10.6**
ALCOHOLIC BEVERAGES	**459**	**299**	**65**	**11.2**
HOUSING	**13,918**	**10,363**	**74**	**12.8**
Shelter	**7,998**	**5,329**	**67**	**11.5**
Owned dwellings	5,324	3,526	66	11.4
Mortgage interest and charges	2,936	917	31	5.4
Property taxes	1,391	1,367	98	17.0
Maintenance, repairs, insurance, other expenses	997	1,242	125	21.5

	total consumer units	consumer units headed by retirees		
		average spending	indexed spending	market share
Rented dwellings	$2,201	$1,398	64	11.0%
Other lodging	473	406	86	14.8
Utilities, fuels, public services	**2,927**	**2,559**	**87**	**15.1**
Natural gas	424	430	101	17.5
Electricity	1,064	945	89	15.3
Fuel oil and other fuels	121	163	135	23.2
Telephone services	990	702	71	12.2
Water and other public services	327	319	98	16.8
Household services	**753**	**668**	**89**	**15.3**
Personal services	300	205	68	11.8
Other household services	453	463	102	17.6
Housekeeping supplies	**594**	**536**	**90**	**15.6**
Laundry and cleaning supplies	149	117	79	13.5
Other household products	290	261	90	15.5
Postage and stationery	155	158	102	17.6
Household furnishings and equipment	**1,646**	**1,270**	**77**	**13.3**
Household textiles	158	173	109	18.9
Furniture	417	293	70	12.1
Floor coverings	52	47	90	15.6
Major appliances	204	204	100	17.3
Small appliances, misc. housewares	105	90	86	14.8
Miscellaneous household equipment	711	465	65	11.3
APPAREL AND SERVICES	**1,816**	**970**	**53**	**9.2**
Men and boys	**406**	**224**	**55**	**9.5**
Men, aged 16 or older	317	197	62	10.7
Boys, aged 2 to 15	89	28	31	5.4
Women and girls	**739**	**426**	**58**	**9.9**
Women, aged 16 or older	631	393	62	10.7
Girls, aged 2 to 15	108	33	31	5.3
Children under age 2	**79**	**19**	**24**	**4.1**
Footwear	**329**	**156**	**47**	**8.2**
Other apparel products and services	**264**	**145**	**55**	**9.5**
TRANSPORTATION	**7,801**	**4,976**	**64**	**11.0**
Vehicle purchases	**3,397**	**2,050**	**60**	**10.4**
Cars and trucks, new	1,748	1,231	70	12.1
Cars and trucks, used	1,582	801	51	8.7
Gasoline and motor oil	**1,598**	**998**	**62**	**10.8**
Other vehicle expenses	**2,365**	**1,571**	**66**	**11.5**
Vehicle finance charges	323	127	39	6.8
Maintenance and repairs	652	471	72	12.5
Vehicle insurance	964	729	76	13.0
Vehicle rental, leases, licenses, other charges	426	245	58	9.9
Public transportation	**441**	**357**	**81**	**14.0**

	total consumer units	consumer units headed by retirees		
		average spending	indexed spending	market share
HEALTH CARE	**$2,574**	**$3,868**	**150**	**25.9%**
Health insurance	1,332	2,096	157	27.1
Medical services	648	738	114	19.6
Drugs	480	879	183	31.6
Medical supplies	114	155	136	23.5
ENTERTAINMENT	**2,218**	**1,722**	**78**	**13.4**
Fees and admissions	528	359	68	11.7
Television, radio, sound equipment	788	577	73	12.6
Pets, toys, and playground equipment	381	208	55	9.4
Other entertainment supplies, services	522	578	111	19.1
PERSONAL CARE PRODUCTS AND SERVICES	**581**	**483**	**83**	**14.3**
READING	**130**	**143**	**110**	**19.0**
EDUCATION	**905**	**167**	**18**	**3.2**
TOBACCO PRODUCTS, SMOKING SUPPLIES	**288**	**168**	**58**	**10.1**
MISCELLANEOUS	**690**	**583**	**84**	**14.6**
CASH CONTRIBUTIONS	**1,408**	**1,476**	**105**	**18.1**
PERSONAL INSURANCE AND PENSIONS	**4,823**	**1,031**	**21**	**3.7**
Life and other personal insurance	390	339	87	15.0
Pensions and Social Security	4,433	692	16	2.7
PERSONAL TAXES	**2,166**	**693**	**32**	**5.5**
Federal income taxes	1,519	451	30	5.1
State and local income taxes	472	51	11	1.9
Other taxes	175	192	110	18.9
GIFTS FOR NONHOUSEHOLD MEMBERS	**1,215**	**927**	**76**	**13.2**

Note: The Bureau of Labor Statistics uses consumer unit rather than household as the sampling unit in the Consumer Expenditure Survey. For the definition of consumer unit, see the glossary. Spending on gifts is also included in the preceding product and service categories; "–" means not applicable.
Source: Bureau of Labor Statistics, 2004 Consumer Expenditure Survey, Internet site http://www.bls.gov/cex/; calculations by New Strategist

9

Time Use

■ Time use varies sharply by age. Older Americans have the most leisure time (49 percent more than average), but also spend the most time in household activities (44 percent more than average).

■ Teenagers get the most sleep, while men aged 45 to 54 get the least amount of sleep. Sleeping time increases after middle age, although it never again matches the levels achieved by teenagers.

■ People aged 65 or older spend the most time watching television—3.86 hours per day. Women aged 35 to 44 spend the least amount of time watching TV (1.91 hours per day).

■ Thirty-two percent of Americans aged 18 or older have a grandchild, the proportion surpassing 50 percent in the 50-to-64 age group. Among people aged 65 or older, 82 percent have grandchildren.

■ Emailing is the most popular online activity, engaged in by 91 percent of Internet users. The oldest Internet users are just as likely to email as young adults.

■ Older Americans accounted for 28 percent of voters in the 2004 presidential election, less than the 40 percent share accounted for by Baby Boomers.

■ Sewing and needlework is especially popular among older Americans, with more than one in five 65-to-74-year-olds participating.

Americans Spend More Time in Leisure than at Work

Driving around ranks fifth in time use, ahead of eating and drinking.

The average person spends 9.33 hours a day in personal care activities, primarily sleeping. Socializing, relaxing, and leisure activities take up 4.62 hours a day, and work accounts for another 3.37 hours, according to the Bureau of Labor Statistics' American Time Use Survey. Household activities (i.e., housework) rank fourth in importance in the time use statistics, followed by traveling—a category that includes driving to work, to stores, to leisure activities, and to children's events.

Time use varies sharply by age. Not surprisingly, people aged 25 to 54 spend the most time working (29 to 36 percent more than the average person) and consequently they have the least amount of leisure time (12 to 20 percent less than average). People aged 25 to 44 spend the most time caring for and helping household members (mostly children). Older Americans have the most leisure time (49 percent more than average), but also spend the most time in household activities (44 percent more than average).

Time use also varies greatly by sex. Among people aged 65 or older, for example, men spend more time than women working, eating and drinking, socializing, and playing sports. Women spend more time than men doing most other activities including household activities (housework), shopping, volunteering, and making phone calls.

■ As leisure time expands, older Americans devote more time to housework and home maintenance.

All but the oldest Americans spend more than one hour a day driving around

(average number of hours per day spent traveling, by age, 2004)

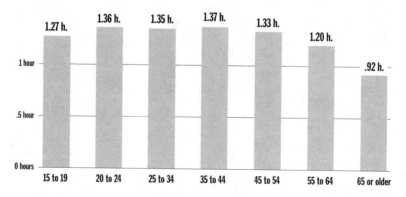

1.27 h.	1.36 h.	1.35 h.	1.37 h.	1.33 h.	1.20 h.	.92 h.
15 to 19	20 to 24	25 to 34	35 to 44	45 to 54	55 to 64	65 or older

Table 9.1 Time Use by Primary Activity and Age, 2004

(average and indexed hours per day spent in primary activities, by age, 2004)

	total	15–19	20–24	25–34	35–44	45–54	55–64	65+
Total hours	24.00	24.00	24.00	24.00	24.00	24.00	24.00	24.00
Personal care activities	9.33	10.25	9.66	9.23	9.02	9.00	9.08	9.65
Household activities	1.82	0.69	1.02	1.53	1.89	2.07	2.18	2.62
Caring for and helping household members	0.48	0.10	0.44	1.01	0.88	0.32	0.14	0.09
Caring for and helping nonhousehold members	0.19	0.11	0.18	0.17	0.14	0.23	0.31	0.19
Work and related activities	3.37	1.14	3.49	4.35	4.60	4.50	3.49	0.65
Education	0.46	2.98	0.94	0.26	0.14	0.09	0.05	0.03
Consumer purchases	0.41	0.31	0.35	0.46	0.41	0.41	0.46	0.40
Professional and personal care services	0.09	0.05	0.03	0.07	0.08	0.11	0.09	0.16
Household services	0.02	–	–	0.01	0.01	0.02	0.02	0.03
Government services and civic obligations	0.01	–	0.01	0.01	0.01	–	0.01	–
Eating and drinking	1.11	0.86	0.97	1.05	1.06	1.12	1.23	1.38
Socializing, relaxing, and leisure	4.62	4.82	4.71	3.87	3.68	4.05	4.97	6.87
Sports, exercise, and recreation	0.33	0.71	0.44	0.30	0.28	0.25	0.26	0.25
Religious and spiritual activities	0.12	0.15	0.10	0.10	0.10	0.11	0.13	0.20
Volunteer activities	0.15	0.17	0.06	0.07	0.15	0.18	0.15	0.20
Telephone calls	0.12	0.26	0.14	0.08	0.08	0.11	0.10	0.14
Traveling	1.26	1.27	1.36	1.35	1.37	1.33	1.20	0.92
Unencodeable	0.12	0.14	0.09	0.07	0.09	0.10	0.13	0.22
Index of time use by age to total								
Personal care activities	100	110	104	99	97	96	97	103
Household activities	100	38	56	84	104	114	120	144
Caring for and helping household members	100	21	92	210	183	67	29	19
Caring for and helping nonhousehold members	100	58	95	89	74	121	163	100
Work and related activities	100	34	104	129	136	134	104	19
Education	100	648	204	57	30	20	11	7
Consumer purchases	100	76	85	112	100	100	112	98
Professional and personal care services	100	56	33	78	89	122	100	178
Household services	100	–	–	50	50	100	100	150
Government services and civic obligations	100	–	100	100	100	–	100	–
Eating and drinking	100	77	87	95	95	101	111	124
Socializing, relaxing, and leisure	100	104	102	84	80	88	108	149
Sports, exercise, and recreation	100	215	133	91	85	76	79	76
Religious and spiritual activities	100	125	83	83	83	92	108	167
Volunteer activities	100	113	40	47	100	120	100	133
Telephone calls	100	217	117	67	67	92	83	117
Traveling	100	101	108	107	109	106	95	73
Unencodeable	100	117	75	58	75	83	108	183

Note: "–" means number is less than .005 or sample is too small to make a reliable estimate.
Source: Bureau of Labor Statistics, unpublished tables from the American Time Use Survey, Internet site http://www.bls.gov/tus/home.htm; calculations by New Strategist

Table 9.2 Time Use by Age and Sex, 2004: Aged 55 to 64

(hours per day spent in primary activities by people aged 15 or older and aged 55 to 64 by sex; index of age group time use to total time use by sex, and index of time use by people aged 55 to 64 by sex, 2004)

	total men	men aged 55 to 64		total women	women aged 55 to 64		aged 55 to 64 index of women's time
		hours	index to total men		hours	index to total women	to men's
Total hours	**24.00**	**24.00**	**100**	**24.00**	**24.00**	**100**	**100**
Personal care activities	9.14	8.93	98	9.50	9.22	97	103
Household activities	1.33	1.69	127	2.28	2.64	116	156
Caring for/helping household members	0.29	0.10	34	0.65	0.18	28	180
Caring for/helping nonhousehold members	0.16	0.20	125	0.22	0.41	186	205
Work and related activities	4.03	4.11	102	2.76	2.91	105	71
Education	0.46	0.03	7	0.46	0.06	13	200
Consumer purchases	0.30	0.30	100	0.50	0.60	120	200
Professional and personal care services	0.07	0.08	114	0.11	0.10	91	125
Household services	0.01	0.02	200	0.02	0.02	100	100
Government services, civic obligations	–	–	–	0.01	0.01	100	–
Eating and drinking	1.17	1.30	111	1.06	1.17	110	90
Socializing, relaxing, and leisure	4.89	5.29	108	4.38	4.69	107	89
Sports, exercise, and recreation	0.43	0.37	86	0.23	0.15	65	41
Religious and spiritual activities	0.12	0.09	75	0.13	0.16	123	178
Volunteer activities	0.12	0.14	117	0.17	0.16	94	114
Telephone calls	0.07	0.04	57	0.17	0.16	94	400
Traveling	1.29	1.19	92	1.22	1.21	99	102
Unencodeable	0.11	0.11	100	0.13	0.14	108	127

Note: "–" means number is less than .005 or sample is too small to make a reliable estimate.
Source: Bureau of Labor Statistics, unpublished tables from the American Time Use Survey, Internet site http://www.bls.gov/tus/home.htm; calculations by New Strategist

Table 9.3 Time Use by Age and Sex, 2004: Aged 65 or Older

(hours per day spent in primary activities by people aged 15 or older and aged 65 or older by sex; index of age group time use to total time use by sex, and index of time use by people aged 65 or older by sex, 2004)

		men aged 65 or older		total women	women aged 65 or older		aged 65 or older index of women's time to men's
	total men	hours	index to total men		hours	index to total women	
Total hours	**24.00**	**24.00**	**100**	**24.00**	**24.00**	**100**	**100**
Personal care activities	9.14	9.42	103	9.50	9.82	103	104
Household activities	1.33	2.12	159	2.28	3.00	132	142
Caring for/helping household members	0.29	0.10	34	0.65	0.08	12	80
Caring for/helping nonhousehold members	0.16	0.17	106	0.22	0.20	91	118
Work and related activities	4.03	0.89	22	2.76	0.48	17	54
Education	0.46	0.02	4	0.46	0.03	7	150
Consumer purchases	0.30	0.36	120	0.50	0.43	86	119
Professional and personal care services	0.07	0.17	243	0.11	0.15	136	88
Household services	0.01	0.04	400	0.02	0.03	150	75
Government services, civic obligations	–	0.01	–	0.01	–	–	–
Eating and drinking	1.17	1.49	127	1.06	1.30	123	87
Socializing, relaxing, and leisure	4.89	7.23	148	4.38	6.60	151	91
Sports, exercise, and recreation	0.43	0.33	77	0.23	0.19	83	58
Religious and spiritual activities	0.12	0.18	150	0.13	0.21	162	117
Volunteer activities	0.12	0.16	133	0.17	0.24	141	150
Telephone calls	0.07	0.06	86	0.17	0.19	112	317
Traveling	1.29	1.02	79	1.22	0.84	69	82
Unencodeable	0.11	0.22	200	0.13	0.21	162	95

Note: "–" means number is less than .005 or sample is too small to make a reliable estimate.
Source: Bureau of Labor Statistics, unpublished tables from the American Time Use Survey, Internet site http://www.bls.gov/tus/home.htm; calculations by New Strategist

Most Americans Get More than Eight Hours of Sleep

The middle aged sleep the least.

On an average day, people aged 15 or older get 8.56 hours of sleep, according to the American Time Use Survey. Not surprisingly, teenagers get the most sleep. People aged 15 to 19 sleep 9.46 hours a night (or day), or 11 percent more than the average person. Men aged 45 to 54 get the least amount of sleep—just 8.08 hours a day, or 6 percent less than average. After middle-age, sleeping time increases, although it never again matches the levels achieved by teenagers.

The average person spends 0.67 hours (or 40 minutes) per day grooming—a category that includes bathing, hair care, dressing, and putting on make-up. Again, teens aged 15 to 19 spend the most time grooming, with teen girls devoting 39 percent more time than average to this task. In every age group, men spend less time than average grooming, with the oldest men spending 25 percent less time than average on grooming activities.

■ Women of all ages spend more than the average amount of time grooming.

Older Americans sleep more than the middle aged

(average number of hours per day spent sleeping, by age, 2004)

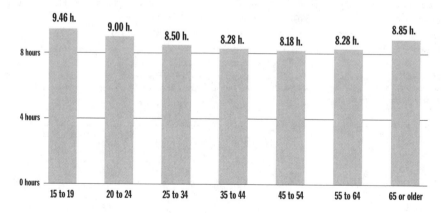

Table 9.4 Time Spent Sleeping by Age and Sex, 2004

(average hours per day spent sleeping as a primary activity and index of time to average, by age and sex, 2004)

	total	men	women
Aged 15 or older	**8.56**	**8.51**	**8.61**
Aged 15 to 19	9.46	9.44	9.49
Aged 20 to 24	9.00	8.83	9.16
Aged 25 to 34	8.50	8.47	8.54
Aged 35 to 44	8.28	8.26	8.29
Aged 45 to 54	8.18	8.08	8.27
Aged 55 to 64	8.28	8.29	8.27
Aged 65 or older	8.85	8.76	8.92
INDEX OF TIME TO AVERAGE			
Aged 15 or older	**100**	**99**	**101**
Aged 15 to 19	111	110	111
Aged 20 to 24	105	103	107
Aged 25 to 34	99	99	100
Aged 35 to 44	97	96	97
Aged 45 to 54	96	94	97
Aged 55 to 64	97	97	97
Aged 65 or older	103	102	104

Source: Bureau of Labor Statistics, unpublished tables from the American Time Use Survey, Internet site http://www.bls.gov/tus/ home.htm; calculations by New Strategist

Table 9.5 Time Spent Grooming by Age and Sex, 2004

(average hours per day spent grooming as a primary activity and index of time to average, by age and sex, 2004)

	total	men	women
Aged 15 or older	**0.67**	**0.55**	**0.77**
Aged 15 to 19	0.74	0.56	0.93
Aged 20 to 24	0.66	0.58	0.73
Aged 25 to 34	0.65	0.57	0.73
Aged 35 to 44	0.66	0.55	0.76
Aged 45 to 54	0.69	0.57	0.80
Aged 55 to 64	0.68	0.54	0.80
Aged 65 or older	0.62	0.50	0.70
INDEX OF TIME TO AVERAGE			
Aged 15 or older	**100**	**82**	**115**
Aged 15 to 19	110	84	139
Aged 20 to 24	99	87	109
Aged 25 to 34	97	85	109
Aged 35 to 44	99	82	113
Aged 45 to 54	103	85	119
Aged 55 to 64	101	81	119
Aged 65 or older	93	75	104

Note: Time spent on this activity does not include travel time or professional grooming services.
Source: Bureau of Labor Statistics, unpublished tables from the American Time Use Survey, Internet site http://www.bls.gov/tus/home.htm; calculations by New Strategist

People Aged 55 to 64 Spend the Most Time Caring for Children from Other Households

People aged 25 to 34 spend the most time caring for household children.

The time spent caring for household children peaks in the 25-to-44 age group, when most families have children under age 18 at home. Women spend far more time on this activity than men. Women aged 25 to 34 spend 1.38 hours a day caring for household children as a primary activity. Their male counterparts spend only 0.40 hours (24 minutes) doing so.

Time spent caring for children from other households as a primary activity peaks in the 55-to-64 age group. Most of those engaged in this activity are grandparents helping out with grandchildren. Women aged 55 to 64 spend three times the average on this activity, while men in the age group spend just 13 percent more time than average caring for children from other households.

The time spent caring for adults in other households varies by age, with peaks in the 25-to-34 and 45-to-64 age groups. The older age group is probably caring for aging parents. The younger age group may be helping ex-spouses or friends with household tasks.

■ Women aged 20 to 24 spend more than the average amount of time caring for children in other households, helping with the children of relatives or friends.

Women aged 45 or older spend less than the average amount of time caring for household children

(index of time women spend caring for household children to the average, by age, 2004; 100 equals the average for all people aged 15 or older)

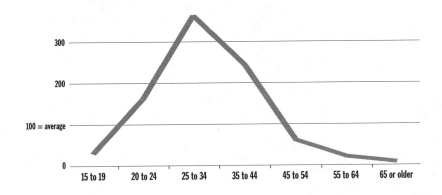

Table 9.6 Time Spent Caring for Household Children, Children in Other Households, and Adults in Other Households by Age and Sex, 2004

(average hours per day spent caring for and helping household children, children in other households, and adults in other households as primary activities, and index of time to average, by age and sex, 2004)

	caring for and helping household children			caring for and helping children in other households			caring for and helping adults in other households		
	total	men	women	total	men	women	total	men	women
Aged 15 or older	**0.38**	**0.23**	**0.52**	**0.08**	**0.05**	**0.11**	**0.11**	**0.11**	**0.09**
Aged 15 to 19	0.08	0.04	0.11	0.05	0.03	0.08	0.05	0.05	0.07
Aged 20 to 24	0.36	0.08	0.62	0.09	0.05	0.13	0.09	0.10	0.08
Aged 25 to 34	0.89	0.40	1.38	0.03	0.03	0.03	0.14	0.15	0.14
Aged 35 to 44	0.73	0.53	0.93	0.06	0.06	0.05	0.09	0.10	0.07
Aged 45 to 54	0.21	0.19	0.23	0.09	0.03	0.14	0.13	0.12	0.13
Aged 55 to 64	0.06	0.04	0.08	0.17	0.09	0.24	0.13	0.11	0.14
Aged 65 or older	0.02	–	0.03	0.10	0.06	0.14	0.08	0.11	0.05
INDEX OF TIME TO AVERAGE									
Aged 15 or older	**100**	**61**	**137**	**100**	**63**	**138**	**100**	**100**	**82**
Aged 15 to 19	21	11	29	63	38	100	45	45	64
Aged 20 to 24	95	21	163	113	63	163	82	91	73
Aged 25 to 34	234	105	363	38	38	38	127	136	127
Aged 35 to 44	192	139	245	75	75	63	82	91	64
Aged 45 to 54	55	50	61	113	38	175	118	109	118
Aged 55 to 64	16	11	21	213	113	300	118	100	127
Aged 65 or older	5	–	8	125	75	175	73	100	45

Note: Time spent on these activities does not include travel time. "–" means number is less than .005 or sample is too small to make a reliable estimate.
Source: Bureau of Labor Statistics, unpublished tables from the American Time Use Survey, Internet site http://www.bls.gov/tus/home.htm; calculations by New Strategist

Women Still Do the Housework

The oldest women spend the most time cooking and cleaning.

Women spend 0.75 hours (45 minutes) a day preparing meals and 0.20 hours (12 minutes) cleaning up in the kitchen afterwards. Men spend much less time on these tasks—only 15 minutes cooking, on average, and 3 minutes cleaning up. These figures are low because they include those who participated in cooking and cleaning and those who did not. The many men who do not cook or clean on an average day drive the numbers to these low levels. Women aged 45 or older spend the most time cooking as a primary activity, at least 20 percent more than average. Two age groups spend the most time cleaning up the kitchen—those aged 35 to 44 (many of whom have teens at home) and those aged 65 or older.

The average woman spends 0.54 hours a day cleaning her house, or 32 minutes. Men spend only 9 minutes a day housecleaning. Women aged 65 or older devote the most time to housecleaning—97 percent more than average. Perhaps the biggest gap in men's and women's housework time can be found in the laundry room. Women spend 18 minutes a day doing the laundry, while men spend less than 4 minutes a day on this task. Women aged 65 or older spend 89 percent more time than average doing the laundry although they are most likely to live alone.

■ As leisure time expands in retirement, people fill some of it with household tasks such as cleaning and laundry.

Older women spend the most time housecleaning

*(index of time women spend housecleaning to the average, by age, 2004;
100 equals the average for all people aged 15 or older)*

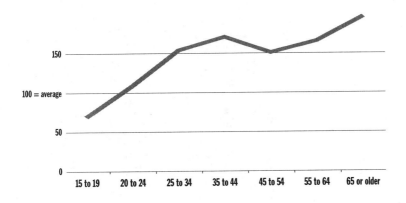

Table 9.7 Time Spent Preparing and Cleaning Up Meals by Age and Sex, 2004

(average hours per day spent on food and drink preparation and kitchen and food cleanup as primary activities, and index of time to average, by age and sex, 2004)

	food and drink preparation			kitchen and food cleanup		
	total	men	women	total	men	women
Aged 15 or older	**0.51**	**0.25**	**0.75**	**0.13**	**0.05**	**0.20**
Aged 15 to 19	0.10	0.05	0.15	0.03	0.01	0.05
Aged 20 to 24	0.23	0.11	0.34	0.05	0.02	0.08
Aged 25 to 34	0.37	0.16	0.58	0.11	0.04	0.18
Aged 35 to 44	0.42	0.24	0.59	0.15	0.05	0.24
Aged 45 to 54	0.43	0.23	0.61	0.15	0.06	0.22
Aged 55 to 64	0.43	0.22	0.63	0.15	0.06	0.23
Aged 65 or older	0.51	0.32	0.66	0.17	0.08	0.24
INDEX OF TIME TO AVERAGE						
Aged 15 or older	**100**	**49**	**147**	**100**	**38**	**154**
Aged 15 to 19	20	10	29	23	8	38
Aged 20 to 24	45	22	67	38	15	62
Aged 25 to 34	73	31	114	85	31	138
Aged 35 to 44	82	47	116	115	38	185
Aged 45 to 54	84	45	120	115	46	169
Aged 55 to 64	84	43	124	115	46	177
Aged 65 or older	100	63	129	131	62	185

Note: Time spent on these activities does not include travel time.
Source: Bureau of Labor Statistics, unpublished tables from the American Time Use Survey, Internet site http://www.bls.gov/tus/home.htm; calculations by New Strategist

Table 9.8 Time Spent Housecleaning and Doing Laundry by Age and Sex, 2004

(average hours per day spent on housecleaning and doing laundry as primary activities, and index of time to average, by age and sex, 2004)

	housecleaning			laundry		
	total	men	women	total	men	women
Aged 15 or older	**0.35**	**0.15**	**0.54**	**0.19**	**0.06**	**0.30**
Aged 15 to 19	0.15	0.08	0.24	0.05	0.03	0.07
Aged 20 to 24	0.23	0.08	0.38	0.09	0.05	0.11
Aged 25 to 34	0.34	0.15	0.54	0.18	0.06	0.29
Aged 35 to 44	0.38	0.15	0.60	0.23	0.07	0.38
Aged 45 to 54	0.35	0.16	0.53	0.23	0.08	0.37
Aged 55 to 64	0.38	0.16	0.58	0.20	0.05	0.33
Aged 65 or older	0.48	0.20	0.69	0.23	0.05	0.36
INDEX OF TIME TO AVERAGE						
Aged 15 or older	**100**	**43**	**154**	**100**	**32**	**158**
Aged 15 to 19	43	23	69	26	16	37
Aged 20 to 24	66	23	109	47	26	58
Aged 25 to 34	97	43	154	95	32	153
Aged 35 to 44	109	43	171	121	37	200
Aged 45 to 54	100	46	151	121	42	195
Aged 55 to 64	109	46	166	105	26	174
Aged 65 or older	137	57	197	121	26	189

Note: Time spent on these activities does not include travel time.
Source: Bureau of Labor Statistics, unpublished tables from the American Time Use Survey, Internet site http://www.bls.gov/tus/home.htm; calculations by New Strategist

Television Takes Up Time

Older Americans devote one-fourth of their waking hours to television.

Watching television is by far the most popular leisure time activity—so popular, in fact, that the average person spends more time watching TV as a primary activity than eating and drinking or doing household chores. People aged 65 or older spend the most time watching TV—3.86 hours per day, or one-fourth of the waking hours of people in the age group. Women aged 35 to 44 spend the least amount of time watching TV (1.91 hours per day).

Even among teenagers, television is more popular than playing on a computer. Teen boys aged 15 to 19 spend 1.24 hours per day on their computer versus 2.45 hours per day watching TV. Teen boys spend the most time playing on a computer, more than three times the average.

People aged 65 or older spend the most time reading, an average of about one hour a day—more than twice the average. Teens and young adults spend much more time on a computer than reading. For men, reading is more popular than leisure computer use only among those aged 45 or older. Among women, reading becomes more popular than computer use in the 25-to-34 age group.

■ As younger generations age, they may spend more time reading and less time on the computer.

Television is especially popular among people aged 65 or older

(average hours per day spent watching television as a primary activity, by age, 2004)

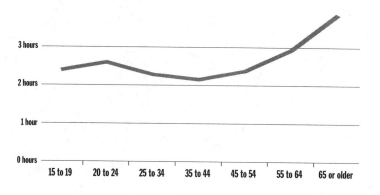

Table 9.9   Time Spent Watching TV, Reading, and Leisure Computer Use and Playing Games by Age and Sex, 2004

(average hours per day spent watching television, reading for personal interest, and leisure computer use and playing games as primary activities, and index of time to average, by age and sex, 2004)

	television			reading			computer use for leisure, games		
	total	men	women	total	men	women	total	men	women
Aged 15 or older	**2.64**	**2.85**	**2.43**	**0.38**	**0.32**	**0.44**	**0.34**	**0.44**	**0.26**
Aged 15 to 19	2.39	2.45	2.33	0.15	0.11	0.19	0.84	1.24	0.40
Aged 20 to 24	2.60	2.87	2.35	0.10	0.07	0.13	0.55	0.79	0.31
Aged 25 to 34	2.28	2.42	2.14	0.16	0.14	0.18	0.28	0.42	0.15
Aged 35 to 44	2.15	2.40	1.91	0.24	0.21	0.27	0.24	0.25	0.23
Aged 45 to 54	2.38	2.68	2.11	0.35	0.30	0.40	0.24	0.26	0.21
Aged 55 to 64	2.93	3.35	2.55	0.57	0.48	0.65	0.25	0.25	0.26
Aged 65 or older	3.86	4.16	3.64	0.99	0.94	1.03	0.35	0.35	0.36
INDEX OF TIME TO AVERAGE									
Aged 15 or older	**100**	**108**	**92**	**100**	**84**	**116**	**100**	**129**	**76**
Aged 15 to 19	91	93	88	39	29	50	247	365	118
Aged 20 to 24	98	109	89	26	18	34	162	232	91
Aged 25 to 34	86	92	81	42	37	47	82	124	44
Aged 35 to 44	81	91	72	63	55	71	71	74	68
Aged 45 to 54	90	102	80	92	79	105	71	76	62
Aged 55 to 64	111	127	97	150	126	171	74	74	76
Aged 65 or older	146	158	138	261	247	271	103	103	106

Note: Time spent on these activities does not include travel time.
Source: Bureau of Labor Statistics, unpublished tables from the American Time Use Survey, Internet site http://www.bls.gov/tus/home.htm; calculations by New Strategist

Many Parents and Adult Children Live Near One Another

Most adult children see their parents at least once a week.

Americans are known for their mobility, but despite the lure of distant places most parents and adult children live less than one hour's drive from each other, according to a survey by the Pew Research Center. Sixty-five percent of people aged 18 or older live less than an hour's drive from their parents. Conversely, 72 percent of parents live less than an hour away from an adult child.

The 54 percent majority of adults see a parent at least once a week. Adding telephone contact to the mix drives the proportion of Americans who see or talk on the telephone with a parent on a weekly basis up to a near-universal 86 percent. Women talk on the phone with their parents much more frequently than men, with 42 percent doing so daily compared with 23 percent of men. Women are also more likely than men to stay in touch with an adult child, 47 percent talking on the phone with a child every day compared with 24 percent of men.

Seventy-three percent of Americans aged 18 or older have children, and 68 percent have a living parent. Only 29 percent of adults have a grandparent still living. Thirty-two percent have a grandchild, with the proportion surpassing 50 percent in the 50-to-64 age group. Among people aged 65 or older, 82 percent have grandchildren.

■ Ninety percent of American adults have a brother or sister, making it the most common family relationship.

Few adult children live far from their parents

(percent distribution of people aged 18 or older by distance from parents' home, 2005)

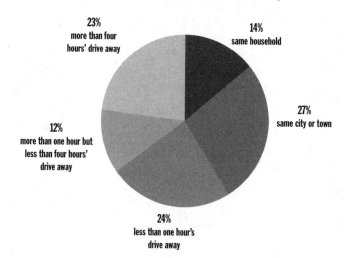

23%
more than four
hours' drive away

14%
same household

27%
same city or town

12%
more than one hour but
less than four hours'
drive away

24%
less than one hour's
drive away

Table 9.10 The Generations: Relationships and Contacts, 2005

(percent of people aged 18 or older with selected living relatives, by age; proximity of parents and adult children; frequency of contact with parents by type of contact; and telephone contact between parents and adult children by sex, 2005)

GENERATIONAL RELATIONSHIPS

	total	18 to 29	30 to 49	50 to 64	65 or older
Have grandchildren	32%	–	11%	56%	82%
Have children	73	39%	78	84	89
Have a brother or sister	90	92	94	91	78
Have at least one living parent	68	98	88	51	9
Have any living grandparents	29	79	31	2	–

PARENT/CHILD PROXIMITY

(among respondents with at least one living parent and among respondents with at least one financially independent adult child)

	parent(s)	adult child
Live in same household	14%	14%
Live in same city or town	27	30
Live less than an hour away	24	28
Live less than four hour's drive away	12	11
Live more than 4 hour's drive away	23	17

FREQUENCY OF CONTACT WITH PARENT(S)

(among respondents with at least one living parent)

	email	see	phone	see or phone
Every day	3%	24%	32%	42%
Once a week or more	10	30	47	44
Once a month or more	8	15	11	10
Several times a year	3	17	2	2
Once a year	–	7	1	1
Less often than once a year	–	7	5	1
Never	76	–	–	–
Don't know	–	–	2	–

TELEPHONE CONTACT WITH PARENT(S)

(among respondents with at least one living parent)

	total	men	women
Daily	32%	23%	42%
Weekly	47	52	41
Less often	19	23	15
Don't know	2	2	2

TELEPHONE CONTACT WITH ADULT CHILD

(among respondents with a financially independent adult child aged 18 or older)

	total	men	women
Daily	37%	24%	47%
Weekly	48	55	43
Less often	13	19	9
Don't know	2	2	1

Note: "–" means zero or sample too small to make a reliable estimate.
Source: Pew Research Center, Families Drawn Together by Communications Revolution, February 21, 2006; Internet site http://pewresearch.org/reports/?ReportID=9

More than Two-Thirds of Americans Are Online

Young adults are most likely to go online.

Sixty-eight percent of Americans aged 18 or older were Internet users in 2005, up substantially from the 46 percent of 2000, according to surveys by the Pew Internet & American Life Project. Fully 84 percent of young adults—those aged 18 to 29—use the Internet, but those aged 30 to 49 are not far behind at 80 percent. The 30-to-49 age group is most likely to have been online yesterday (64 percent).

Emailing is the most popular online activity, engaged in by 91 percent of Internet users. The oldest Internet users are just as likely to email as young adults. But young adults are far more likely to do instant messaging. The 62 percent majority of 18-to-29-year-olds uses instant messaging versus only 26 to 36 percent of older adults. Downloading music shows the biggest gap in Internet use by age, with 46 percent of young adults doing downloads compared with only 6 percent of people aged 65 or older.

■ The Internet is changing the way young and middle-aged adults interact with the world, affecting both government and business.

The oldest Americans are least likely to use the Internet

(percent of people using the Internet, by age, 2005)

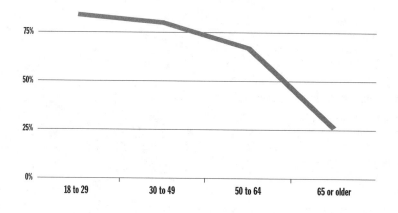

Table 9.11 Computer and Internet Use by Age, 2005

(percent of people aged 18 or older who use a computer, go online, and went online yesterday, by age, 2005)

	use a computer	go online	went online yesterday
Total people	**72%**	**68%**	**60%**
Aged 18 to 29	87	84	58
Aged 30 to 49	84	80	64
Aged 50 to 64	71	67	58
Aged 65 or older	29	26	49

Source: Pew Internet & American Life Project, Internet site http://www.pewinternet.org/trends.asp#demographics; calculations by New Strategist

Table 9.12 Online Activities Ever Done by Age, 2005

(percent of Internet users who have ever used the Internet for selected activities, by age, 2005)

	total	18 to 29	30 to 49	50 to 64	65 or older
Send or read email	91%	91%	91%	92%	91%
Research a product or service	78	79	82	78	65
Get news	72	75	75	71	56
Buy a product	67	68	69	66	48
Do research for job	51	44	59	51	17
Bank	41	40	48	35	27
Instant messaging	40	62	36	31	26
Download computer programs	39	46	40	32	26
Play a game	36	54	33	26	30
Use online classified ads to sell/buy/ find job, meet people	36	44	40	26	15
Read someone else's blog	27	32	27	24	17
Share files with others	27	39	24	22	14
Search for information about someone you know or might meet	27	32	27	23	29
Download music	25	46	22	12	6
Participate in an auction	24	27	27	19	12
Download screensavers	23	28	22	24	20
Download computer games	21	29	19	15	14
Download video files	18	28	18	8	3
Take part in chat rooms or discussions	17	34	15	7	5
View live remote images via a webcam	16	18	17	16	6
Visit an adult web site	13	18	13	9	2
Make a donation to charity	11	10	13	11	4
Create a blog	7	13	6	4	3

Source: Pew Internet & American Life Project, Internet site http://www.pewinternet.org/trends.asp#demographics

Voting Has Decreased among All but the Oldest Americans

Older Americans have considerable influence because so many vote.

The older people are, the more likely they are to vote. This has long been true, but the gap between young and old has widened over the years. In the 1972 presidential election (the first in which 18-to-20-year-olds could vote), 64 percent of people aged 65 or older voted compared with 50 percent of those aged 18 to 24—a gap of 14 percentage points. In the 2004 election, 69 percent of people aged 65 or older voted versus only 42 percent of people aged 18 to 24—a 27 percentage point difference.

A look at voting patterns in 2004 by generation reveals that voting rates rose from a low of 42 percent among Millennials to just over 50 percent among Gen Xers. Sixty-four percent of Boomers voted in 2004, as did 69 percent of Americans aged 59 or older. Because of their numbers, Boomers accounted for the largest share (40 percent) of voters in 2004. Older Americans were 28 percent of voters, while Gen Xers and Millennials were far behind at 19 and 13 percent, respectively.

■ The political power of older Americans will increase as Boomers enter the older age groups and their voting rate rises.

Older Americans rank second in power as a voting block

(percent distribution of people voting in the 2004 presidential election, by generation)

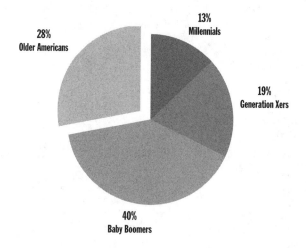

28%
Older Americans

13%
Millennials

19%
Generation Xers

40%
Baby Boomers

Table 9.13 Voting Rate by Age, 1964 to 2004

(percent of people who reported voting in presidential elections by age, and percentage point change, 1964 to 2004)

		presidential election years			
	total	18–24	25–44	45–64	65+
2004	58.3%	41.9%	52.2%	66.6%	68.9%
2000	54.7	32.3	49.8	64.1	67.6
1996	54.2	32.4	49.2	64.4	67.0
1992	61.3	42.8	58.3	70.0	70.1
1988	57.4	36.2	54.0	67.9	68.8
1984	59.9	40.8	58.4	69.8	67.7
1980	59.3	39.9	58.7	69.3	65.1
1976	59.2	42.2	58.7	68.7	62.2
1972	63.0	49.6	62.7	70.8	63.5
1968	67.8	50.4	66.6	74.9	65.8
1964	69.3	50.9	69.0	75.9	66.3
Percentage point change					
1964 to 2004	−11.0	−9.0	−16.8	−9.3	2.6

Note: Before 1972, data for 18-to-24-year-olds include only 21-to-24-year-olds.
Source: Bureau of the Census, Voting and Registration in the Election of November 2004, detailed tables, Internet site http://www.census.gov/population/www/socdemo/voting/cps2004.html; calculations by New Strategist

Table 9.14 Voting by Generation, 2004

(total number of people aged 18 or older, number and percent who reported voting in the presidential election, and percent distribution of voters, by generation, 2004; numbers in thousands)

		voted		
	total	number	percent	percent distribution
Total people aged 18 or older	**215,694**	**125,736**	**58.3%**	**100.0%**
Millennials (aged 18 to 27)	39,335	16,636	42.3	13.2
Generation X (aged 28 to 39)	47,972	24,352	50.8	19.4
Baby Boom (aged 40 to 58)	78,253	50,060	64.0	39.8
Older Americans (aged 59 or older)	50,132	34,689	69.2	27.6

Source: Bureau of the Census, Voting and Registration in the Election of November 2004, detailed tables, Internet site http://www.census.gov/population/www/socdemo/voting/cps2004.html; calculations by New Strategist

Young Adults Dominate Some Religious Groups

Presbyterians and Methodists are much older than Catholics or Baptists.

The religious affiliations of Americans are changing, in large part because younger adults adhere to different religious groups than older adults. The American Religious Identification Survey, taken in 2001 through the efforts of Egon Mayer, Barry A. Kosmin, and Ariela Keysar and sponsored by the Graduate Center of the City University of New York, reveals the differing age distributions of religious groups. In the nationally representative survey, respondents were asked to identify the religious group to which they belonged.

Catholics are by far the most numerous, with an estimated 51 million American adults identifying themselves as belonging to the Catholic Church.

Twenty-four percent of Catholics are aged 18 to 29, 62 percent are aged 30 to 64, and only 14 percent are aged 65 or older. Many religious groups are much older. Fully 35 percent of people who identify themselves as Congregational/UCC are aged 65 or older, as are 30 percent of self-identified Protestants, 29 percent of Presbyterians, and 27 percent of Methodists. At the other extreme, more than half of Muslims and Buddhists are aged 18 to 29. Typically, younger denominations have a greater potential for growth.

■ Twenty-nine million Americans do not identify with any religious group. Among those with no religion, only 8 percent are aged 65 or older.

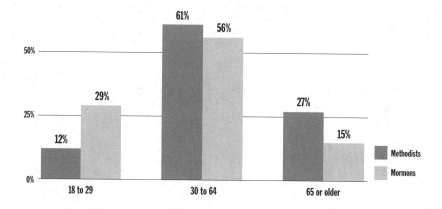

Mormons are much younger than Methodists

(percent distribution of self-identified Methodists and Mormons, by age, 2001)

Table 9.15 Age Distribution of Religious Groups, 2001

(total number of adult members of selected religious groups and percent distribution by age, 2001; numbers in thousands)

	number	percent distribution			
		total	18–29	30–64	65 or older
Total U.S. adults	**208,000**	**100%**	**23%**	**61%**	**16%**
Catholic	50,873	100	24	62	14
Baptist	33,830	100	21	63	16
No religion	29,481	100	35	57	8
Christian	14,190	100	35	58	7
Methodist	14,140	100	12	61	27
Lutheran	9,580	100	15	63	22
Presbyterian	5,596	100	10	61	29
Protestant	4,647	100	13	57	30
Pentecostal	4,407	100	24	67	9
Episcopalian/Anglican	3,451	100	10	62	28
Jewish	2,831	100	14	58	28
Mormon	2,787	100	29	56	15
Churches of Christ	2,503	100	17	58	25
Nondenominational	2,489	100	23	65	12
Congregational/UCC	1,378	100	11	54	35
Jehovah's Witnesses	1,331	100	24	66	10
Assemblies of God	1,105	100	21	69	10
Muslim/Islamic	1,104	100	58	42	–
Buddhist	1,082	100	56	41	3
Evangelical/born again	1,032	100	19	72	9
Church of God	944	100	16	65	19
Seventh Day Adventist	724	100	10	64	26

Note: Religious group is self-identified; numbers will not add to total because not all groups are shown. "–" means sample is too small to make a reliable estimate.
Source: American Religious Indentification Survey 2001, Barry A. Kosmin, Egon Mayer, and Ariela Keysar. For further details see: Barry A. Kosmin and Ariela Keysar, Religion in a Free Market, Paramount Market Publishing, Inc. Ithaca, NY, 2006.

More Than One in Four Volunteer

The middle aged are most likely to volunteer.

Among people aged 16 or older, 29 percent volunteered their time between September 2004 and September 2005, according to the Bureau of Labor Statistics, which defines volunteers as those who performed unpaid activities for an organization at least once during the time period. Volunteering peaks in middle age at 29 percent among men aged 35 to 54 and 40 percent among women aged 35 to 44. Many are volunteering at their children's school or for their children's extracurricular organizations.

Volunteers donate a median of 50 hours a year to the task, or an average of one hour a week. Among volunteers under age 45, the largest share donates time to educational and youth service organizations. Among volunteers aged 45 or older, the largest share works for a religious organization.

■ The most important reason people say they volunteer is because someone asked them to, cited by 43 percent. A slightly smaller share (40 percent) say they volunteered to volunteer.

Volunteering is lowest among young adults

(percent of people volunteering, by age, 2005)

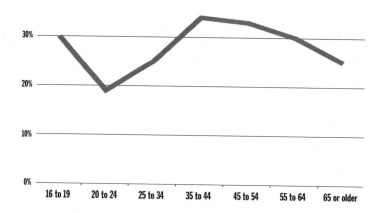

Table 9.16 Volunteering by Sex and Age, 2005

(number of people aged 16 or older, and number and percent who performed unpaid volunteer activities for an organization at any point during the past year, by sex and age, September 2005; numbers in thousands)

		volunteers	
	total	number	percent of total
Total people	**226,693**	**65,357**	**28.8%**
Aged 16 to 19	16,443	5,000	30.4
Aged 20 to 24	20,291	3,956	19.5
Aged 25 to 34	39,118	9,881	25.3
Aged 35 to 44	42,968	14,809	34.5
Aged 45 to 54	42,316	13,826	32.7
Aged 55 to 64	30,410	9,173	30.2
Aged 65 or older	35,146	8,712	24.8
Total men	**109,475**	**27,370**	**25.0**
Aged 16 to 19	8,339	2,282	27.4
Aged 20 to 24	10,193	1,576	15.5
Aged 25 to 34	19,479	3,949	20.3
Aged 35 to 44	21,165	6,105	28.8
Aged 45 to 54	20,701	5,999	29.0
Aged 55 to 64	14,622	3,999	27.3
Aged 65 or older	14,975	3,460	23.1
Total women	**117,218**	**37,987**	**32.4**
Aged 16 to 19	8,104	2,718	33.5
Aged 20 to 24	10,098	2,380	23.6
Aged 25 to 34	19,639	5,931	30.2
Aged 35 to 44	21,803	8,704	39.9
Aged 45 to 54	21,615	7,828	36.2
Aged 55 to 64	15,788	5,174	32.8
Aged 65 or older	20,170	5,252	26.0

Source: Bureau of Labor Statistics, Volunteering in the United States, 2005, Internet site http://www.bls.gov/news.release/volun .toc.htm

Table 9.17 Volunteering by Age and Type of Organization, 2005

(number of people aged 16 or older who performed unpaid volunteer activities for an organization at any point in the past year, median annual hours of volunteer work performed, and percent distribution by type of organization for which the volunteer worked the most hours, by age, September 2005)

	total	16 to 19	20 to 24	25 to 34	35 to 44	45 to 54	55 to 64	65 or older
Total volunteers (in 000s)	**65,357**	**5,000**	**3,956**	**9,881**	**14,809**	**13,826**	**9,173**	**8,712**
Median annual hours	50	36	40	36	48	50	56	96
TYPE OF ORGANIZATION								
Total volunteers	**100.0%**	**100.0%**	**100.0%**	**100.0%**	**100.0%**	**100.0%**	**100.0%**	**100.0%**
Civic, political, professional, or international	6.4	3.4	5.3	6.8	4.8	6.8	8.0	8.2
Educational or youth service	26.2	36.5	27.3	33.6	37.9	25.6	13.5	6.2
Environmental or animal care	1.8	2.1	2.9	2.1	1.3	2.1	2.1	0.9
Hospital or other health	7.7	7.6	9.0	6.6	5.8	7.7	8.9	10.1
Public safety	1.3	1.0	2.3	1.7	1.1	1.3	1.4	0.8
Religious	34.8	27.7	27.3	29.1	31.2	36.8	41.2	45.0
Social or community service	13.4	13.6	16.6	13.1	10.5	11.4	15.5	18.0
Sport, hobby, cultural, or arts	3.3	2.8	2.7	3.0	3.0	3.6	3.8	3.7
Other	3.5	2.9	4.5	3.1	3.1	3.1	4.0	4.7
Not determined	1.7	2.5	2.1	1.0	1.3	1.7	1.7	2.3

Source: Bureau of Labor Statistics, Volunteering in the United States, 2005, Internet site http://www.bls.gov/news.release/volun .toc.htm

Table 9.18 Volunteering by Age and Type of Work Performed, 2005

(number of people aged 16 or older who performed unpaid volunteer activities for an organization at any point in the past year, and percent distribution by type of work performed for the organization for which the volunteer worked the most hours, by age, September 2005)

	total	16 to 19	20 to 24	25 to 34	35 to 44	45 to 54	55 to 64	65 or older
Total volunteers (in 000s)	**65,357**	**5,000**	**3,956**	**9,881**	**14,809**	**13,826**	**9,173**	**8,712**

TYPE OF WORK PERFORMED FOR MAIN ORGANIZATION

	total	16 to 19	20 to 24	25 to 34	35 to 44	45 to 54	55 to 64	65 or older
Total volunteers	**100.0%**	**100.0%**	**100.0%**	**100.0%**	**100.0%**	**100.0%**	**100.0%**	**100.0%**
Coach, referee, or surpervise sports teams	8.9	12.0	11.1	11.6	13.0	9.1	3.4	1.5
Tutor or teach	21.3	21.4	22.8	24.0	24.6	21.4	19.4	13.6
Mentor youth	17.6	20.2	24.6	20.5	20.9	18.0	13.9	7.3
Be an usher, greeter, or minister	13.1	10.0	8.7	9.5	11.0	15.0	17.1	17.7
Collect, prepare, distribute, or serve food	26.3	25.2	21.4	23.4	25.5	27.3	28.5	29.9
Collect, make, distribute goods other than food	16.2	14.5	14.5	15.7	16.4	15.7	16.7	18.6
Fundraise or sell items to raise money	29.7	29.3	23.3	29.7	32.9	32.6	30.1	22.9
Provide counseling, medical care, fire/ EMS or protective services	7.4	3.9	9.1	7.9	6.6	8.3	8.7	6.8
Provide general office services	12.8	9.5	8.8	10.8	13.2	13.0	14.4	15.9
Provide professional or management assistance, including serving on a board or committee	17.7	4.4	8.1	12.8	18.9	21.6	23.8	20.6
Engage in music performance or other artistic activity	11.5	16.3	14.9	12.5	11.3	10.3	10.7	8.7
Engage in general labor, supply transportation	22.5	23.2	19.7	22.2	23.1	24.4	22.9	19.6
Other or not reported	15.3	14.9	15.8	15.4	14.0	14.5	14.3	19.9

Note: Percentages will sum to more than 100 because more than one type of activity may have been performed.
Source: Bureau of Labor Statistics, Volunteering in the United States, 2005, Internet site http://www.bls.gov/news.release/volun
.toc.htm

Table 9.19 Volunteering by Method of Involvement and Age, 2005

(number of people aged 16 or older who performed unpaid volunteer activities for an organization at any point in the past year, and percent distribution by how they became involved with main organization for which they volunteered, by age, September, 2005)

	total	16 to 19	20 to 24	25 to 34	35 to 44	45 to 54	55 to 64	65 or older
Total volunteers (in 000s)	**65,357**	**5,000**	**3,956**	**9,881**	**14,809**	**13,826**	**9,173**	**8,712**

HOW VOLUNTEERS BECAME INVOLVED WITH MAIN ORGANIZATION

	total	16 to 19	20 to 24	25 to 34	35 to 44	45 to 54	55 to 64	65 or older
Total volunteers	**100.0%**	**100.0%**	**100.0%**	**100.0%**	**100.0%**	**100.0%**	**100.0%**	**100.0%**
Approached the organization	40.3	40.0	39.0	39.4	40.2	40.2	40.6	42.1
Were asked to volunteer	42.8	40.0	41.5	44.9	43.3	43.7	42.4	41.0
Asked by boss or employer	1.5	0.5	2.3	2.6	1.5	1.6	1.2	0.4
Asked by relative, friend, or co-worker	14.1	14.8	18.7	15.3	13.3	12.8	14.1	13.7
Asked by someone in organization/school	25.9	23.1	18.4	25.5	27.5	28.0	25.8	25.2
Asked by someone else	1.2	1.4	1.8	1.4	0.9	1.0	1.1	1.6
Other or not reported	16.9	20.0	19.6	15.7	16.5	16.0	17.1	16.9

Source: Bureau of Labor Statistics, Volunteering in the United States, 2005, Internet site http://www.bls.gov/news.release/volun
.toc.htm

Vietnam Veterans Outnumber Others

One-third of veterans served in Vietnam.

Twenty-five million Americans are veterans, and 38 percent of them are aged 65 or older. Despite the older age of the nation's veterans, the largest share of vets served not in World War II, but in Vietnam. Seventeen percent served in the Gulf war, which includes anyone serving in the military from August 2, 1990, to the present.

World War II veterans, once most numerous, now number only 3.9 million and account for just 16 percent of the veteran population. The 8.1 million Vietnam vets account for a much larger 33 percent of the veteran population. Only 3.4 million veterans served during the Korean conflict, accounting for 14 percent of the total.

■ Women account for 7 percent of all veterans, but for 16 percent of Gulf war veterans.

Few living veterans served during World War II

(percent distribution of veterans by time of service, 2004)

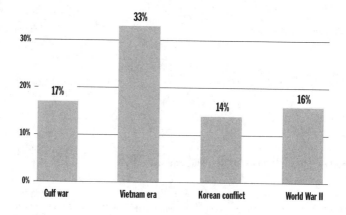

Table 9.20 Veterans by Age and Service, 2004

(number and percent distribution of living veterans by age and service, 2004; numbers in thousands)

	total veterans	wartime veterans total	Gulf war	Vietnam era	Korean conflict	World War II	peacetime veterans
Total veterans	**24,793**	**18,477**	**4,105**	**8,147**	**3,423**	**3,916**	**6,316**
Under age 35	2,007	1,946	1,946	0	0	0	61
Aged 35 to 39	1,332	768	768	0	0	0	564
Aged 40 to 44	1,732	520	520	0	0	0	1,212
Aged 45 to 49	1,906	738	383	393	0	0	1,168
Aged 50 to 54	2,172	1,858	267	1,731	0	0	314
Aged 55 to 59	3,572	3,448	151	3,409	0	0	124
Aged 60 to 64	2,553	1,762	48	1,755	0	0	791
Aged 65 or older	9,520	7,437	22	859	3,423	3,916	2,083
Female	1,692	1,130	647	262	80	178	562

PERCENT DISTRIBUTION BY AGE

	total veterans	wartime veterans total	Gulf war	Vietnam era	Korean conflict	World War II	peacetime veterans
Total veterans	**100.0%**	**100.0%**	**100.0%**	**100.0%**	**100.0%**	**100.0%**	**100.0%**
Under age 35	8.1	10.5	47.4	0.0	0.0	0.0	1.0
Aged 35 to 39	5.4	4.2	18.7	0.0	0.0	0.0	8.9
Aged 40 to 44	7.0	2.8	12.7	0.0	0.0	0.0	19.2
Aged 45 to 49	7.7	4.0	9.3	4.8	0.0	0.0	18.5
Aged 50 to 54	8.8	10.1	6.5	21.2	0.0	0.0	5.0
Aged 55 to 59	14.4	18.7	3.7	41.8	0.0	0.0	2.0
Aged 60 to 64	10.3	9.5	1.2	21.5	0.0	0.0	12.5
Aged 65 or older	38.4	40.3	0.5	10.5	100.0	100.0	33.0
Percent female	6.8	6.1	15.8	3.2	2.3	4.5	8.9

PERCENT DISTRIBUTION BY SERVICE

	total veterans	wartime veterans total	Gulf war	Vietnam era	Korean conflict	World War II	peacetime veterans
Total veterans	**100.0%**	**74.5%**	**16.6%**	**32.9%**	**13.8%**	**15.8%**	**25.5%**
Under age 35	100.0	97.0	97.0	0.0	0.0	0.0	3.0
Aged 35 to 39	100.0	57.7	57.7	0.0	0.0	0.0	42.3
Aged 40 to 44	100.0	30.0	30.0	0.0	0.0	0.0	70.0
Aged 45 to 49	100.0	38.7	20.1	20.6	0.0	0.0	61.3
Aged 50 to 54	100.0	85.5	12.3	79.7	0.0	0.0	14.5
Aged 55 to 59	100.0	96.5	4.2	95.4	0.0	0.0	3.5
Aged 60 to 64	100.0	69.0	1.9	68.7	0.0	0.0	31.0
Aged 65 or older	100.0	78.1	0.2	9.0	36.0	41.1	21.9
Female	100.0	66.8	38.2	15.5	4.7	10.5	33.2

Note: Veterans who served in more than one wartime period are counted only once in the wartime veterans total. Gulf war veterans are those serving from August 2, 1990, to present.
Source: Bureau of the Census, Statistical Abstract of the United States: 2006, Internet site http://www.census.gov/statab/www/; calculations by New Strategist

The Young Are Most Likely to Be Crime Victims

Victimization rate drops sharply with age.

Although older Americans are most fearful of crime, young people are more likely to become victims of crime. Among people aged 12 to 24, the violent-crime victimization rate stands at 43 to 50 crimes per 1,000 people in the age group. This is more than twice the rate for all Americans aged 12 or older. Among people aged 65 or older, the violent-crime victimization rate is just 2 per 1,000.

A variety of factors contribute to the higher victimization rate of young people, who are also more likely than their elders to commit crimes. Because older Americans are more fearful of crime, they take steps to protect themselves—such as avoiding going out at night or venturing into certain areas. Young people, on the other hand, are notorious for living on the edge, believing they are invulnerable to danger. As people enter middle age, they become increasingly aware of their vulnerability, which in turn reduces their chances of becoming a crime victim. People aged 35 or older are less likely than average to be victims of violent crime.

■ The crime rate has dropped over the past few years, but young adults are still most likely to be victims of crime.

The oldest Americans are least likely to be victims of crime

(number of crimes per 1,000 people in age group, by age of victim, 2004)

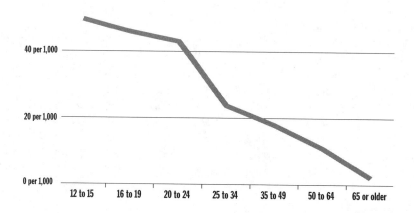

Table 9.21 Violent Crime and Personal Theft Victimization by Age, 2004

(population aged 12 or older, and number of victimizations per 1,000 people aged 12 or older, by age and type of crime, 2004)

		victimizations per 1,000 persons aged 12 or older						
		violent crime						
					assault			
	number (in 000s)	total	rape, sexual assault	robbery	total	aggravated	simple	personal theft
Total people	**241,704**	**21.4**	**0.9**	**2.1**	**18.5**	**4.3**	**14.2**	**0.9**
Aged 12 to 15	17,083	49.7	2.2	3.8	43.6	6.2	37.5	2.1
Aged 16 to 19	16,256	45.9	2.5	4.8	38.6	11.3	27.2	3.3
Aged 20 to 24	20,273	43.0	2.5	3.1	37.4	9.4	28.0	0.7
Aged 25 to 34	39,510	23.7	0.7	2.4	20.6	4.8	15.8	0.6
Aged 35 to 49	65,580	17.9	0.5	2.1	15.2	3.9	11.4	0.7
Aged 50 to 64	48,412	11.0	0.3	1.1	9.6	1.9	7.8	0.5
Aged 65 or older	34,590	2.1	0.1	0.3	1.8	0.5	1.3	0.8

Note: Violent crime as defined in the National Crime Victimization Survey includes rape/sexual assault, robbery, and assault. It does not include murder or manslaughter because it is based on interviews with victims. Personal theft includes pocket picking, purse snatching, and attempted purse snatching.
Source: Bureau of Justice Statistics, Criminal Victimization 2004, Internet site http://www.ojp.usdoj.gov/bjs/abstract/cv04.htm

Movies Lure Most People out of Their Home

Young adults are most likely to go to the movies.

Among the arts, movies attract the largest audience, according to a study by the National Endowment for the Arts. Eighty-three percent of 18-to-24-year-olds attended at least one movie in the past year. Movie attendance falls slowly with age, dropping below 50 percent in the 55-to-64 age group. But even among people aged 75 or older, about one in five went to a movie in the past year.

Literature also has a large audience. Forty-seven percent of people aged 18 or older read literature during the past year, with the figure peaking at 52 percent among people aged 45 to 54. Arts and crafts fairs or festivals attract about one-third of Americans each year, with attendance ranging from a low of 16 percent among people aged 75 or older to a high of 39 percent among those aged 45 to 54.

The most popular personal arts activity is purchasing original pieces of art—24 percent of people aged 65 to 74 have done so in the past year. Sewing and needlework are also popular among older Americans, with more than one in five 65-to-74-year-olds participating.

■ The arts audience is huge and diverse, spanning the age groups.

Movie attendance falls slowly with age

(percent of people aged 18 or older who went to the movies in the past year, by age, 2002)

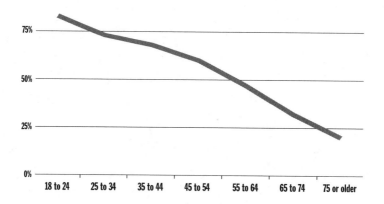

Table 9.22 Attendance at Arts Events by Age, 2002

(percent of people aged 18 or older who attended/visited/read selected arts during the past year, by age, 2002)

	total	18–24	25–34	35–44	45–54	55–64	65–74	75+
Read literature (novels, poetry, or plays)	46.7%	42.8%	47.7%	46.6%	51.6%	48.9%	45.3%	36.7%
Attended art fair/festival or craft fair/festival	33.4	29.2	33.5	37.2	38.8	35.1	31.1	15.7
Visited historic site	31.6	28.3	33.3	35.8	38.0	31.6	24.2	12.8
Visited art museum or gallery	26.5	23.7	26.7	27.4	32.9	27.8	23.4	13.4
Attended musical	17.1	14.8	15.4	19.1	19.3	19.7	16.6	10.1
Attended nonmusical play	12.3	11.4	10.7	13.0	15.2	13.8	13.0	5.4
Attended classical music performance	11.6	7.8	9.0	10.7	15.2	15.6	12.5	9.5
Attended jazz performance	10.8	10.5	10.8	13.0	13.9	8.8	7.6	3.9
Attended dance performance (except ballet)	6.3	6.2	5.9	7.0	8.0	6.0	5.4	3.0
Attended ballet	3.9	2.6	3.5	4.9	5.1	3.3	3.3	2.2
Attended opera	3.2	2.0	3.0	2.8	4.0	4.2	4.0	1.8

Source: National Endowment for the Arts, 2002 Survey of Public Participation in the Arts: Summary Report, Research Division

Table 9.23 Participation in the Arts through Media, 2002

(percent of people aged 18 or older who participated in the arts through media during the past year, by age, 2002)

	total	18–24	25–34	35–44	45–54	55–64	65–74	75+
Jazz								
TV	16.4%	10.7%	13.8%	17.7%	20.7%	17.0%	18.5%	15.1%
Radio	23.5	16.1	23.8	28.1	29.6	24.1	18.4	11.9
Recordings	17.2	13.1	17.5	21.1	21.8	16.8	11.8	7.7
Classical music								
TV	18.1	8.9	12.4	15.9	20.9	23.8	28.3	25.8
Radio	23.9	13.8	21.1	23.9	29.9	29.5	26.5	20.8
Recordings	19.3	14.1	18.1	19.3	23.1	22.9	20.8	14.2
Opera								
TV	5.8	3.0	3.7	4.5	5.7	8.1	10.5	9.7
Radio	5.7	2.0	4.5	4.3	6.4	8.7	9.4	7.7
Recordings	5.5	2.7	4.4	4.7	6.8	8.1	7.9	5.4
Musical play								
TV	11.7	7.2	9.8	11.8	13.3	12.3	16.2	14.1
Radio	2.4	1.9	1.7	2.5	2.6	2.8	3.2	2.6
Recordings	4.3	3.1	3.2	4.4	5.9	5.1	4.4	2.9
Non-musical play								
TV	9.4	7.0	7.3	8.5	9.7	12.3	13.6	11.1
Radio	2.1	1.3	2.1	2.3	2.8	1.6	2.4	1.4
Dance (on TV)	**12.6**	**8.7**	**10.0**	**13.0**	**13.8**	**15.0**	**15.1**	**14.4**
Artists, art work, or art museums (on TV)	**25.0**	**21.1**	**25.3**	**24.8**	**28.5**	**27.2**	**24.5**	**19.1**

Source: National Endowment for the Arts, 2002 Survey of Public Participation in the Arts: Summary Report, Research Division Report No. 45, Internet site http://www.nea.gov/pub/ResearchReports_chrono.html

Table 9.24 Personal Participation in the Arts, 2002

(percent of people aged 18 or older who personally participated in the arts during the past year, by age, 2002)

	total	18–24	25–34	35–44	45–54	55–64	65–74	75+
Purchased art in past year	29.5%	41.0%	39.1%	31.2%	27.9%	26.1%	23.7%	11.4%
Own original pieces of art	19.3	9.4	15.3	20.9	25.8	24.5	20.1	14.8
Sewing, weaving, crocheting, quilting, or needlepoint	16.0	10.4	13.0	15.3	18.6	19.1	20.5	18.0
Photography	11.5	12.9	12.3	14.1	12.1	10.5	8.1	3.8
Painting, drawing, sculpture, or printmaking	8.6	15.4	10.2	8.1	8.2	6.7	4.8	3.1
Writing	7.0	12.7	7.9	6.7	6.8	5.0	4.1	3.7
Pottery, jewelry, leatherwork, or metalwork	6.9	9.3	7.8	7.4	7.5	5.6	4.6	2.4
Choir/chorale	4.8	4.9	3.9	4.8	5.1	5.6	5.3	3.7
Dance (except ballet)	4.2	6.0	4.5	3.9	4.2	3.4	3.7	2.5
Musical play	2.4	2.5	2.1	2.1	2.7	2.6	2.1	2.2
Music composition	2.3	5.7	3.3	2.3	1.8	0.9	0.4	0.1
Classical music performance	1.8	2.5	1.4	1.8	2.5	1.5	1.4	0.7
Act in play	1.4	3.0	1.4	1.7	1.1	0.9	0.6	0.2
Jazz performance	1.3	1.9	1.2	1.5	2.0	0.8	0.5	0.4
Opera	0.7	0.7	0.6	0.6	0.9	0.9	0.8	0.7
Ballet	0.3	1.1	0.2	0.4	0.2	0.2	0.0	0.2

Source: National Endowment for the Arts, 2002 Survey of Public Participation in the Arts: Summary Report, Research Division Report No. 45, Internet site http://www.nea.gov/pub/ResearchReports_chrono.html

Table 9.25 Participation in Selected Leisure Activities, 2002

(percent of people aged 18 or older who participated in selected leisure activities during the past year, by age, 2002)

	total	18–24	25–34	35–44	45–54	55–64	65–74	75+
Go to the movies	60.0%	82.8%	73.3%	68.0%	60.4%	46.6%	32.2%	19.5%
Jog, lift weights, walk, or participate in any other exercise routine	55.1	61.3	60.2	59.5	58.6	48.4	47.0	31.3
Garden indoor or outdoor	47.3	20.7	41.4	51.0	55.4	56.6	57.2	47.9
Participate in home improvement or repair to own home	42.4	21.1	41.1	53.0	54.9	44.8	38.4	22.1
Go to an amusement park or carnival	41.7	57.6	56.2	53.3	37.1	27.1	18.4	9.6
Attend sports events (except youth sports)	35.0	46.0	41.8	42.2	35.8	25.5	19.7	11.1
Participate in outdoor activities such as camping, hiking, or canoeing	30.9	37.7	38.8	39.0	33.0	21.7	14.9	5.8
Participate in sports, such as golf, bowling, skiing, or basketball	30.4	49.4	39.6	36.6	28.6	16.0	13.7	6.0
Perform volunteer or charity work	29.0	25.3	26.0	33.2	33.4	28.1	28.8	21.3

Source: National Endowment for the Arts, 2002 Survey of Public Participation in the Arts: Summary Report, Research Division Report No. 45, Internet site http://www.nea.gov/pub/ResearchReports_chrono.html

10

Wealth

■ The median net worth of householders aged 55 to 64 rose by a substantial 29 percent between 2001 and 2004, after adjusting for inflation—the biggest gain among age groups. Their $248,700 median net worth was higher than the median of any other age group.

■ Householders aged 55 to 64 were the only ones to see their financial assets grow between 2001 and 2004, a 30 percent rise to a median of $78,000, after adjusting for inflation. Householders aged 65 to 74 saw their financial assets fall by 34 percent during those years, while those aged 75 or older experienced a smaller 9 percent decline.

■ The nonfinancial assets owned by householders aged 55 to 64 rose twice as fast as average, up 44 percent to a median of $226,300, after adjusting for inflation. Householders aged 65 or older saw their nonfinancial assets grow only 1 to 5 percent between 2001 and 2004.

■ The median debt of householders aged 65 to 74 rose by 79 percent between 2001 and 2004, to $25,000 after adjusting for inflation. The median debt of householders aged 75 or older nearly tripled during those years, rising from $5,300 to $15,400. The percentage of the oldest householders with debt climbed from 29 to 40 percent during those years.

■ Only 20 percent of workers aged 55 or older are "very confident" they will have enough money to live comfortably throughout retirement, according to the Employee Benefit Research Institute's Retirement Confidence Survey.

The Net Worth of Many Older Americans Only Inched Up

Net worth rose sharply among 55-to-64-year-olds, however.

Net worth is one of the most important measures of wealth. It is the amount remaining after a household's debts are subtracted from its assets. The median net worth of householders aged 55 to 64 rose by a substantial 29 percent between 2001 and 2004, the biggest gain among age groups. The $248,700 median net worth of householders aged 55 to 64 in 2004 was higher than that of any other age group. Householders aged 65 or older saw their net worth rise only 1 percent between 2001 and 2004.

Several factors account for the substantial rise in the net worth of 55-to-64-year-olds, such as the increase in housing values. Homeowners aged 55 to 64 saw more of an increase in the median value of their home than any other age group—up 44 percent to $200,000 between 2001 and 2004, after adjusting for inflation. Among homeowners aged 65 or older, median home values grew by only 6 to 9 percent during those years. The 55-to-64 age group also saw its financial assets grow substantially. The median value of the financial assets owned by householders aged 55 to 64 climbed 30 percent between 2001 and 2004, after adjusting for inflation. Every other age group saw its financial assets decline. Behind the growing financial assets of 55-to-64-year-olds is the postponement of retirement. As older workers remained on the job, they contributed to retirement accounts rather than draining them as retirees.

■ As more older workers postpone retirement, the median net worth of householders aged 55 or older should continue to rise.

Householders aged 55 to 64 made the biggest gains between 2001 and 2004

(percent change in net worth of households by age of householder, 2001 to 2004; in 2004 dollars)

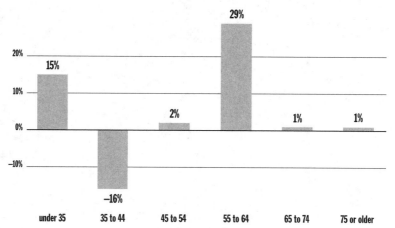

Table 10.1 Net Worth of Households by Age of Householder, 1995 to 2004

(median net worth of households by age of householder, 1995 to 2004; percent change, 1995–2004 and 2001–04; in 2004 dollars)

					percent change	
	2004	2001	1998	1995	2001–04	1995–2004
Total households	**$93,100**	**$91,700**	**$83,100**	**$70,800**	**1.5%**	**31.5%**
Under age 35	14,200	12,300	10,600	14,800	15.4	–4.1
Aged 35 to 44	69,400	82,600	73,500	64,200	–16.0	8.1
Aged 45 to 54	144,700	141,600	122,300	116,800	2.2	23.9
Aged 55 to 64	248,700	193,300	148,200	141,900	28.7	75.3
Aged 65 to 74	190,100	187,800	169,800	136,600	1.2	39.2
Aged 75 or older	163,100	161,200	145,600	114,500	1.2	42.4

Source: Federal Reserve Board, "Recent Changes in U.S. Family Finances: Evidence from the 2001 and 2004 Survey of Consumer Finances," Federal Reserve Bulletin, February 23, 2006, Internet site http://www.federalreserve.gov/pubs/bulletin/default.htm; calculations by New Strategist

Older Householders Are More Likely to Own Stock

But stock values fell in every age group between 2001 and 2004.

Between 2001 and 2004, the financial assets of the average American household fell 23 percent after adjusting for inflation—to a median of $23,000, according to the Federal Reserve Board's Survey of Consumer Finances. Householders aged 55 to 64 were the only ones to see their financial assets grow between 2001 and 2004, a 30 percent rise to $78,000. Householders aged 65 to 74 saw their financial assets fall by 34 percent during those years, while those aged 75 or older experienced a smaller 9 percent decline. Behind the rise in the financial assets of householders aged 55 to 64 is the postponement of retirement, allowing more to accumulate assets rather than spend them.

The percentage of households owning stock fell from 52 to 49 percent between 2001 and 2004, but stock ownership among householders aged 55 or older climbed during those years—up by 4.5 percentage points for those aged 55 to 64, up by 6.6 percentage points for those aged 65 to 74, and up by less than 1 percentage point for those aged 75 or older. Despite the increase, fewer than half of householders aged 65 or older own stock.

Slightly less than half of households owned a retirement account in 2004, but among householders aged 55 to 64 the figure stood at 63 percent. Householders aged 55 to 64 who own a retirement account had saved a median of $83,000. Householders aged 65 or older are less likely to have retirement accounts and have less in their accounts—in part because most are retired and spending their savings.

■ Nonfinancial assets are more important than financial assets to household wealth, even among householders aged 55 to 64.

Financial assets are modest for most households regardless of age

(median value of financial assets of households by age of householder, 2004)

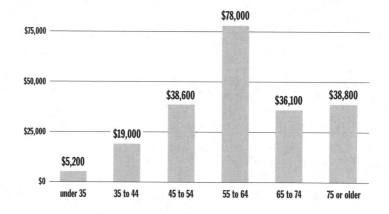

Table 10.2 Financial Assets of Households by Age of Householder, 2001 and 2004

(percentage of households owning financial assets and median value of assets for owners, by age of householder, 2001 and 2004; percentage point change in ownership and percent change in value of asset, 2001–04; in 2004 dollars)

	2004	2001	percentage point change
PERCENT OWNING ANY FINANCIAL ASSET			
Total households	**93.8%**	**93.4%**	**0.4**
Under age 35	90.1	89.7	0.4
Aged 35 to 44	93.6	93.5	0.1
Aged 45 to 54	93.6	94.7	–1.1
Aged 55 to 64	95.2	95.0	0.2
Aged 65 to 74	96.5	94.6	1.9
Aged 75 or older	97.6	95.1	2.5
	2004	**2001**	**percent change**
MEDIAN VALUE OF FINANCIAL ASSETS			
Total households	**$23,000**	**$29,800**	**–22.8%**
Under age 35	5,200	6,600	–21.2
Aged 35 to 44	19,000	28,600	–33.6
Aged 45 to 54	38,600	48,000	–19.6
Aged 55 to 64	78,000	59,800	30.4
Aged 65 to 74	36,100	54,700	–34.0
Aged 75 or older	38,800	42,600	–8.9

Source: Federal Reserve Board, "Recent Changes in U.S. Family Finances: Evidence from the 2001 and 2004 Survey of Consumer Finances," Federal Reserve Bulletin, February 23, 2006, Internet site http://www.federalreserve.gov/pubs/bulletin/default.htm; calculations by New Strategist

Table 10.3 Financial Assets of Households by Type of Asset and Age of Householder, 2004

(percentage of households owning financial assets, and median value of asset for owners, by type of asset and age of householder, 2004)

	total	under 35	35 to 44	45 to 54	55 to 64	65 to 74	75 or older
PERCENT OWNING ASSET							
Any financial asset	**93.8%**	**90.1%**	**93.6%**	**93.6%**	**95.2%**	**96.5%**	**97.6%**
Transaction accounts	91.3	86.4	90.8	91.8	93.2	93.9	96.4
Certificates of deposit	12.7	5.6	6.7	11.9	18.1	19.9	25.7
Savings bonds	17.6	15.3	23.3	21.0	15.2	14.9	11.0
Bonds	1.8	–	0.6	1.8	3.3	4.3	3.0
Stocks	20.7	13.3	18.5	23.2	29.1	25.4	18.4
Pooled investment funds	15.0	8.3	12.3	18.2	20.6	18.6	16.6
Retirement accounts	49.7	40.2	55.9	57.7	62.9	43.2	29.2
Cash value life insurance	24.2	11.0	20.1	26.0	32.1	34.8	34.0
Other managed assets	7.3	2.9	3.7	6.2	9.4	12.8	16.7
Other financial assets	10.0	11.6	10.0	12.1	7.2	8.1	8.1
MEDIAN VALUE OF ASSET							
Any financial asset	**$23,000**	**$5,200**	**$19,000**	**$38,600**	**$78,000**	**$36,100**	**$38,800**
Transaction accounts	3,800	1,800	3,000	4,800	6,700	5,500	6,500
Certificates of deposit	15,000	4,000	10,000	11,000	29,000	20,000	22,000
Savings bonds	1,000	500	500	1,000	2,500	3,000	5,000
Bonds	65,000	–	10,000	30,000	80,000	40,000	295,000
Stocks	15,000	4,400	10,000	14,500	25,000	42,000	50,000
Pooled investment funds	40,400	8,000	15,900	50,000	75,000	60,000	60,000
Retirement accounts	35,200	11,000	27,900	55,500	83,000	80,000	30,000
Cash value life insurance	6,000	3,000	5,000	8,000	10,000	8,000	5,000
Other managed assets	45,000	5,000	18,300	43,000	65,000	60,000	50,000
Other financial assets	4,000	1,000	3,500	5,000	7,000	10,000	22,000

Note: "–" means sample is too small to make a reliable estimate.
Source: Federal Reserve Board, "Recent Changes in U.S. Family Finances: Evidence from the 2001 and 2004 Survey of Consumer Finances," Federal Reserve Bulletin, February 23, 2006, Internet site http://www.federalreserve.gov/pubs/bulletin/default.htm; calculations by New Strategist

Table 10.4 Stock Ownership of Households by Age of Householder, 2001 and 2004

(percentage of householders owning stocks directly or indirectly, median value of stock for owners, and share of total household financial assets accounted for by stock holdings, by age of householder, 2001 and 2004; percent and percentage point change, 2001–04; in 2004 dollars)

	2004	2001	percentage point change
PERCENT OWNING STOCK			
Total households	**48.6%**	**51.9%**	**–3.3**
Under age 35	38.8	48.9	–10.1
Aged 35 to 44	52.3	59.5	–7.2
Aged 45 to 54	54.4	59.2	–4.8
Aged 55 to 64	61.6	57.1	4.5
Aged 65 to 74	45.8	39.2	6.6
Aged 75 or older	34.8	34.2	0.6

	2004	2001	percent change
MEDIAN VALUE OF STOCK			
Total households	**$24,300**	**$36,700**	**–33.8%**
Under age 35	5,200	7,500	–30.7
Aged 35 to 44	12,700	29,300	–56.7
Aged 45 to 54	30,600	53,300	–42.6
Aged 55 to 64	59,500	86,500	–31.2
Aged 65 to 74	75,000	159,800	–53.1
Aged 75 or older	85,900	127,800	–32.8

	2004	2001	percentage point change
STOCK AS SHARE OF FINANCIAL ASSETS			
Total households	**47.4%**	**56.0%**	**–8.6**
Under age 35	30.0	52.5	–22.5
Aged 35 to 44	47.7	57.3	–9.6
Aged 45 to 54	46.8	59.1	–12.3
Aged 55 to 64	51.1	56.2	–5.1
Aged 65 to 74	51.1	55.2	–4.1
Aged 75 or older	39.1	51.4	–12.3

Source: Federal Reserve Board, "Recent Changes in U.S. Family Finances: Evidence from the 2001 and 2004 Survey of Consumer Finances," Federal Reserve Bulletin, February 23, 2006, Internet site http://www.federalreserve.gov/pubs/bulletin/default.htm; calculations by New Strategist

The Nonfinancial Assets of Older Americans Have Grown

Householders aged 55 to 64 have made the biggest gains.

The median value of the nonfinancial assets owned by the average American household stood at $147,800 in 2004, a gain of 22 percent since 2001, after adjusting for inflation. The nonfinancial assets owned by householders aged 55 to 64 rose twice as fast as average, up 44 percent to a median of $226,300, after adjusting for inflation. The value of the nonfinancial assets owned by householders aged 55 to 64 is greater than for any other age group. Householders aged 65 or older saw their nonfinancial assets grow only 1 to 5 percent between 2001 and 2004.

Because housing equity accounts for the largest share of nonfinancial assets, the rise in home values is the biggest contributor to gains in this category. Among homeowners aged 55 to 64, median home value rose by 44 percent, to $200,000, between 2001 and 2004, after adjusting for inflation. Householders aged 65 or older are more likely to own a home than any other age group. The median value of their homes climbed only 6 to 9 percent between 2001 and 2004, after adjusting for inflation.

■ Nonfinancial assets grew as a share of the average household's total assets between 2001 and 2004, rising from 58 to 64 percent.

The value of nonfinancial assets peaks in the 55-to-64 age group

(median value of nonfinancial assets of households by age of householder, 2004)

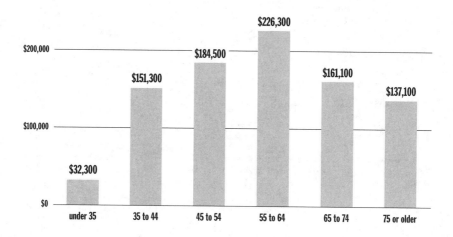

Table 10.5 Nonfinancial Assets of Households by Age of Householder, 2001 and 2004

(percentage of households owning nonfinancial assets and median value of assets for owners, by age of house-holder, 2001 and 2004; percentage point change in ownership and percent change in value of asset, 2001–04; in 2004 dollars)

	2004	2001	percentage point change
PERCENT OWNING ANY NONFINANCIAL ASSET			
Total households	**92.5%**	**90.7%**	**1.8**
Under age 35	88.6	83.0	5.6
Aged 35 to 44	93.0	93.2	–0.2
Aged 45 to 54	94.7	95.2	–0.5
Aged 55 to 64	92.6	95.4	–2.8
Aged 65 to 74	95.6	91.6	4.0
Aged 75 or older	92.5	86.4	6.1
	2004	**2001**	**percent change**
MEDIAN VALUE OF NONFINANCIAL ASSETS			
Total households	**$147,800**	**$120,900**	**22.2%**
Under age 35	32,300	31,700	1.9
Aged 35 to 44	151,300	125,500	20.6
Aged 45 to 54	184,500	150,800	22.3
Aged 55 to 64	226,300	157,500	43.7
Aged 65 to 74	161,100	158,900	1.4
Aged 75 or older	137,100	130,600	5.0

Source: Federal Reserve Board, "Recent Changes in U.S. Family Finances: Evidence from the 2001 and 2004 Survey of Consumer Finances," Federal Reserve Bulletin, February 23, 2006, Internet site http://www.federalreserve.gov/pubs/bulletin/default.htm; calculations by New Strategist

Table 10.6 Nonfinancial Assets of Households by Type of Asset and Age of Householder, 2004

(percentage of households owning nonfinancial assets, and median value of asset for owners, by type of asset and age of householder, 2004)

	total	under 35	35 to 44	45 to 54	55 to 64	65 to 74	75 or older
PERCENT OWNING ASSET							
Any nonfinancial asset	**92.5%**	**88.6%**	**93.0%**	**94.7%**	**92.6%**	**95.6%**	**92.5%**
Vehicles	86.3	82.9	89.4	88.8	88.6	89.1	76.9
Primary residence	69.1	41.6	68.3	77.3	79.1	81.3	85.2
Other residential property	12.5	5.1	9.4	16.3	19.5	19.9	9.7
Equity in nonresidential property	8.3	3.3	6.4	11.4	12.8	10.6	7.7
Business equity	11.5	6.9	13.9	15.7	15.8	8.0	5.3
Other nonfinancial assets	7.8	5.5	6.0	9.7	9.2	9.0	8.5
MEDIAN VALUE OF ASSET							
Total nonfinancial assets	**$147,800**	**$32,300**	**$151,300**	**$184,500**	**$226,300**	**$161,100**	**$137,100**
Vehicles	14,200	11,300	15,600	18,800	18,600	12,400	8,400
Primary residence	160,000	135,000	160,000	170,000	200,000	150,000	125,000
Other residential property	100,000	82,500	80,000	90,000	135,000	80,000	150,000
Equity in nonresidential property	60,000	55,000	42,200	43,000	75,000	78,000	85,800
Business equity	100,000	50,000	100,000	144,000	190,900	100,000	80,300
Other nonfinancial assets	15,000	5,000	10,000	20,000	25,000	30,000	11,000

Source: Federal Reserve Board, "Recent Changes in U.S. Family Finances: Evidence from the 2001 and 2004 Survey of Consumer Finances," Federal Reserve Bulletin, February 23, 2006, Internet site http://www.federalreserve.gov/pubs/bulletin/default.htm; calculations by New Strategist

Table 10.7 Household Ownership of Primary Residence by Age of Householder, 2001 and 2004

(percentage of households owning their primary residence, median value of asset for owners, and median value of home-secured debt for owners, by age of householder, 2001 and 2004; percentage point change in ownership and percent change in value of asset, 2001–04; in 2004 dollars)

	2004	2001	percentage point change
PERCENT OWNING PRIMARY RESIDENCE			
Total households	**69.1%**	**67.7%**	**1.4**
Under age 35	41.6	39.9	1.7
Aged 35 to 44	68.3	67.8	0.5
Aged 45 to 54	77.3	76.2	1.1
Aged 55 to 64	79.1	83.2	−4.1
Aged 65 to 74	81.3	82.5	−1.2
Aged 75 or older	85.2	76.2	9.0

	2004	2001	percent change
MEDIAN VALUE OF PRIMARY RESIDENCE			
Total households	**$160,000**	**$131,000**	**22.1%**
Under age 35	135,000	101,200	33.4
Aged 35 to 44	160,000	133,100	20.2
Aged 45 to 54	170,000	143,800	18.2
Aged 55 to 64	200,000	138,500	44.4
Aged 65 to 74	150,000	137,400	9.2
Aged 75 or older	125,000	118,200	5.8

	2004	2001	percent change
MEDIAN VALUE OF HOME-SECURED DEBT			
Total households	**$95,000**	**$74,600**	**27.3%**
Under age 35	107,000	82,000	30.5
Aged 35 to 44	110,000	85,200	29.1
Aged 45 to 54	97,000	79,900	21.4
Aged 55 to 64	83,000	58,600	41.6
Aged 65 to 74	51,000	41,500	22.9
Aged 75 or older	31,000	47,700	−35.0

Source: Federal Reserve Board, "Recent Changes in U.S. Family Finances: Evidence from the 2001 and 2004 Survey of Consumer Finances," Federal Reserve Bulletin, February 23, 2006, Internet site http://www.federalreserve.gov/pubs/bulletin/default.htm; calculations by New Strategist

The Oldest Americans Saw the Biggest Increase in Debt

The middle-aged are most likely to be in debt, however.

The debt of the average American household grew by a substantial 34 percent between 2001 and 2004—to $55,300 after adjusting for inflation. Among householders aged 55 to 64, debt rose by a smaller 30 percent during those years. But among householders aged 65 or older, debt levels soared. The median debt of householders aged 65 to 74 rose by 79 percent to $25,000. The median debt of householders aged 75 or older nearly tripled, rising from $5,300 to $15,400 during those years. The percentage of the oldest householders with debt climbed from 29 to 40 percent during those years.

Home-secured debt accounts for the largest share of debt by far. Forty-eight percent of households have home-secured debt, owing a median of $95,000. The size of home-secured debt peaks in the 35-to-44 age group, then falls with age. Just over half of householders aged 55 to 64 have home-secured debt, owing a median of $83,000. This figure falls to $51,000 in the 65-to-74 age group, and bottoms out at $31,000 among householders aged 75 or older. Only 19 percent of the oldest householders have home-secured debt. A larger share (24 percent) have credit card debt, owing a median of $1,000 in 2004.

■ By paying down their mortgage debt, older Americans build net worth.

Debt declines in the older age groups

(median amount of debt owed by households by age of householder, 2004)

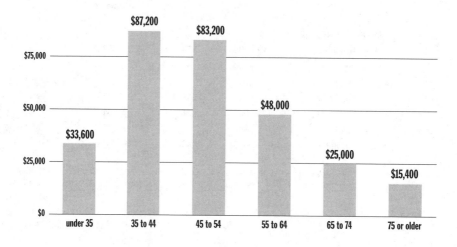

Table 10.8 Debt of Households by Age of Householder, 2001 and 2004

(percentage of households with debt and median amount of debt for debtors, by age of householder, 2001 and 2004; percentage point change in households with debt and percent change in amount of debt, 2001–04; in 2004 dollars)

	2004	2001	percentage point change
PERCENT WITH DEBT			
Total households	**76.4%**	**75.1%**	**1.3**
Under age 35	79.8	82.7	–2.9
Aged 35 to 44	88.6	88.6	0.0
Aged 45 to 54	88.4	84.6	3.8
Aged 55 to 64	76.3	75.4	0.9
Aged 65 to 74	58.8	56.8	2.0
Aged 75 or older	40.3	29.2	11.1

	2004	2001	percent change
MEDIAN AMOUNT OF DEBT			
Total households	**$55,300**	**$41,300**	**33.9%**
Under age 35	33,600	26,500	26.8
Aged 35 to 44	87,200	65,500	33.1
Aged 45 to 54	83,200	57,800	43.9
Aged 55 to 64	48,000	36,900	30.1
Aged 65 to 74	25,000	14,000	78.6
Aged 75 or older	15,400	5,300	190.6

Source: Federal Reserve Board, "Recent Changes in U.S. Family Finances: Evidence from the 2001 and 2004 Survey of Consumer Finances," Federal Reserve Bulletin, February 23, 2006, Internet site http://www.federalreserve.gov/pubs/bulletin/default.htm; calculations by New Strategist

Table 10.9 Debt of Households by Type of Debt and Age of Householder, 2004

(percentage of householders with debt, and median value of debt for those with debt, by type of debt and age of householder, 2004)

	total	under 35	35 to 44	45 to 54	55 to 64	65 to 74	75 or older
PERCENT WITH DEBT							
Any debt	**76.4%**	**79.8%**	**88.6%**	**88.4%**	**76.3%**	**58.8%**	**40.3%**
Secured by residential property							
Primary residence	47.9	37.7	62.8	64.6	51.0	32.1	18.7
Other	4.0	2.1	4.0	6.3	5.9	3.2	1.5
Lines of credit not secured by residential property	1.6	2.2	1.5	2.9	0.7	0.4	–
Installment loans	46.0	59.4	55.7	50.2	42.8	27.5	13.9
Credit card balances	46.2	47.5	58.8	54.0	42.1	31.9	23.6
Other debt	7.6	6.2	11.3	9.4	8.4	4.0	2.5
MEDIAN AMOUNT OF DEBT							
Any debt	**$55,300**	**$33,600**	**$87,200**	**$83,200**	**$48,000**	**$25,000**	**$15,400**
Secured by residential property							
Primary residence	95,000	107,000	110,000	97,000	83,000	51,000	31,000
Other	87,000	62,500	75,000	87,000	108,800	100,000	39,000
Lines of credit not secured by residential property	3,000	1,000	1,900	7,000	14,000	4,000	–
Installment loans	11,500	11,900	12,000	12,000	12,900	8,300	6,700
Credit card balances	2,200	1,500	2,500	2,900	2,200	2,200	1,000
Other debt	4,000	3,000	4,000	4,000	5,500	5,000	2,000

Note: "–" means sample is too small to make a reliable estimate.
Source: Federal Reserve Board, "Recent Changes in U.S. Family Finances: Evidence from the 2001 and 2004 Survey of Consumer Finances," Federal Reserve Bulletin, February 23, 2006, Internet site http://www.federalreserve.gov/pubs/bulletin/default.htm; calculations by New Strategist

Most Workers Aged 55 to 64 Participate in a Workplace Retirement Plan

Only 20 percent of older workers are confident in having enough money for retirement.

Only 42 percent of American workers were included in an employer's retirement plan in 2004, according to an analysis of government statistics by the Employee Benefit Research Institute (EBRI). Retirement coverage peaks among workers aged 45 to 64, at 53 to 54 percent. It falls to 26 percent among workers aged 65 or older.

Another EBRI study shows only 51 percent of workers aged 55 to 64 own an IRA or participate in a 401(k)-type (defined-contribution) retirement plan. Among participants in 401(k)-type plans, the median balance was just $25,000.

Having minimal savings, it is no surprise that many older workers are worried about retirement. Only 20 percent of workers aged 55 or older are "very confident" they will have enough money to live comfortably throughout retirement. Just 42 percent have savings of $100,000 or more. The largest share (33 percent) expects Social Security to be their most important source of income in retirement.

■ The substitution of defined-contribution for defined-benefit pension plans puts the burden of retirement savings on workers rather than employers.

Among workers aged 55 to 64, just over half participate in an employer-sponsored retirement plan

(percent of workers participating in an employer-sponsored retirement plan, by age, 2004)

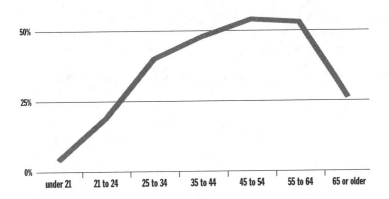

Table 10.10 Retirement-Plan Coverage by Age, 2004

(total number of workers, percent whose employer offers a retirement plan, and percent participating in plan, by type of employment and age of worker, 2004; numbers in thousands)

	number of workers	percent with an employer who sponsors a retirement plan	percent participating in employer's retirement plan
Total workers	**152,708**	**53.2%**	**41.9%**
Under age 21	10,824	24.9	4.1
Aged 21 to 24	12,602	41.0	19.4
Aged 25 to 34	32,468	52.8	39.7
Aged 35 to 44	36,214	57.3	48.3
Aged 45 to 54	34,585	61.2	53.9
Aged 55 to 64	19,654	60.3	53.0
Aged 65 or older	6,361	38.4	25.8
Private wage and salary workers aged 21 to 64			
Total workers	**105,703**	**54.5**	**43.0**
Aged 21 to 24	11,163	39.4	18.2
Aged 25 to 34	26,949	51.0	37.1
Aged 35 to 44	28,344	56.7	46.8
Aged 45 to 54	25,497	59.8	51.5
Aged 55 to 64	13,750	59.3	51.1
Public wage and salary workers aged 21 to 64			
Total workers	**20,529**	**85.1**	**75.8**
Aged 21 to 24	1,156	64.4	35.6
Aged 25 to 34	3,985	82.5	69.8
Aged 35 to 44	5,216	85.1	77.0
Aged 45 to 54	6,319	88.4	82.5
Aged 55 to 64	3,853	88.8	81.7

Source: Employee Benefit Research Institute, "Employment-Based Retirement Plan Participation: Geographic Differences and Trends, 2004," Issue Brief, No. 286, October 2005, Internet site http://www.ebri.org/publications/ib/index.cfm?fa=ibDisp&content_id=3590

Table 10.11 Ownership of IRAs and Participation in 401(k)s by Age, 2002

(percentage of workers aged 21 to 64 owning IRAs and/or participating in a 401(k)-type plan, by age, 2002)

	IRA and/or 401(k)-type plan	IRA only	401(k)-type plan only	both IRA and 401(k)-type plan	neither IRA nor 401(k)-type plan
Total workers	**40.4%**	**9.6%**	**21.7%**	**9.2%**	**59.6%**
Aged 21 to 24	10.6	1.5	8.4	0.7	89.4
Aged 25 to 34	34.3	5.7	22.9	5.7	65.7
Aged 35 to 44	43.0	9.1	24.4	9.6	57.0
Aged 45 to 54	48.3	12.0	23.9	12.4	51.7
Aged 55 to 64	50.6	18.3	18.5	13.8	49.4

Source: Employee Benefit Research Institute, "401(k)-Type Plan and IRA Ownership," by Craig Copeland, Notes, Vol. 26, No. 1, January 2005; Internet site http://www.ebri.org/

Table 10.12 Amount Saved in IRAs and 401(k)s by Age, 2002

(percentage of workers aged 21 to 64 owning an IRA or participating in a 401(k)-type plan, and average and median balance of IRA and 401(k), by age, 2002)

	percent owning IRA	IRA balance		percent participating in 401(k)	401(k) balance	
		average	median		average	median
Total workers	**18.7%**	**$26,951**	**$10,000**	**30.9%**	**$33,647**	**$14,000**
Aged 21 to 24	2.3	3,841	2,000	9.1	4,641	2,500
Aged 25 to 34	11.4	10,146	5,000	28.6	12,067	6,000
Aged 35 to 44	18.7	21,235	9,000	33.9	32,026	15,000
Aged 45 to 54	24.5	29,600	13,000	36.3	44,829	20,000
Aged 55 to 64	32.1	42,003	19,000	32.3	53,184	25,000

Source: Employee Benefit Research Institute, "401(k)-Type Plan and IRA Ownership," by Craig Copeland, Notes, Vol. 26, No. 1, January 2005, Internet site http://www.ebri.org/

Table 10.13 Retirement Planning by Age, 2005

(percentage of workers aged 25 or older responding by age, 2005)

	total	25 to 34	35 to 44	45 to 54	55 or older
Very confident in having enough money to live comfortably throughout retirement	25%	26%	25%	26%	20%
Very confident in having enough money to take care of medical expenses in retirement	20	21	19	20	19
Worker and/or spouse have saved for retirement	69	60	71	73	71
Worker and/or spouse are currently saving for retirement	62	53	67	65	66
Contribute to a workplace retirement savings plan	42	40	44	45	36
Have an IRA opened with money saved outside of an employer's retirement plan	31	25	27	38	38
Expected retirement age					
Less than 60	16	24	15	14	6
Aged 60 to 64	19	15	14	20	31
Aged 65	26	28	30	25	19
Aged 66 or older	24	19	28	26	24
Never retire	6	6	4	8	8
Don't know/refused	9	9	8	7	11
Expected sources of income in retirement					
Money from a workplace retirement savings plan	69	79	73	66	51
Money from a defined-benefit plan	33	34	37	29	33
Largest expected source of income in retirement					
A workplace retirement savings plan, such as a 401(k)	21	26	27	15	12
Other personal savings such as an IRA	18	22	17	19	15
Social Security	18	7	16	22	33
Employer-provided pension that pays a set amount each month for life	16	12	15	18	20
Employment	14	26	14	10	5
Sale or refinancing of your home	3	1	3	3	6
An inheritance	3	2	5	2	2
Other/don't know	6	4	4	11	7
Total savings and investments (not including value of primary residence)					
Less than $25,000	52	70	50	41	39
$25,000 to $49,999	13	12	15	14	12
$50,000 to $99,999	11	9	14	13	7
$100,000 to $249,999	12	5	10	17	23
$250,000 or more	11	4	10	16	19

Source: 2005 Retirement Confidence Survey, Employee Benefit Research Institute, American Savings Education Council, and Mathew Greenwald & Associates; Internet site http://www.ebri.org/surveys/rcs/

Glossary

adjusted for inflation Income or a change in income that has been adjusted for the rise in the cost of living, or the consumer price index (CPI-U-RS).

age Classification by age is based on the age of the person at his/her last birthday.

American Freshman Survey This is an annual survey taken each fall of students entering American colleges and universities as first-time, full-time freshmen. Initiated in Fall 1966, the survey is a project of the Cooperative Institutional Research Program sponsored by the American Council on Education and the Graduate School of Education & Information Studies at the University of California, Los Angeles. Survey results are based on the answers to the Student Information Form filled out by nearly 300,000 freshmen at more than 400 baccalaureate institutions during registration, freshman orientation, or the first few weeks of classes. Results are weighted to provide a normative picture of the American college freshman population.

American Housing Survey The AHS collects national and metropolitan-level data on the nation's housing, including apartments, single-family homes, and mobile homes. The nationally representative survey, with a sample of 55,000 homes, is conducted by the Census Bureau for the Department of Housing and Urban Development every other year.

American Indians In this book, American Indians include Alaska Natives (Eskimos and Aleuts) unless those groups are shown separately.

American Religious Identification Survey The 2001 ARIS, sponsored by the Graduate Center of the City University of New York, was based on a random telephone survey of 50,281 households in the continental U.S. Interviewers asked respondents aged 18 or older for their demographic characteristics and their religion. The 2001 ARIS updates the 1990 National Survey of Religious Identification.

American Time Use Survey Under contract with the Bureau of Labor Statistics, the Census Bureau collects ATUS information, revealing how people spend their time. The ATUS sample is drawn from U.S. households that have completed their final month of interviews for the Current Population Survey. One individual from each selected household is chosen to participate in the ATUS. Respondents are interviewed by telephone only once about their time use on the previous day. In 2003, the sample consisted of approximately 3,000 cases each month, which yielded about 1,700 completed interviews.

Asian The term "Asian" includes Native Hawaiians and other Pacific Islanders unless those groups are shown separately.

Baby Boom Americans born between 1946 and 1964.

Baby Bust Americans born between 1965 and 1976, also known as Generation X.

Behavioral Risk Factor Surveillance System The BRFSS is a collaborative project of the Centers for Disease Control and Prevention and U.S. states and territories. It is an ongoing data collection program designed to measure behavioral risk factors in the adult population aged 18 or older. All 50 states, three territories, and the District of Columbia take part in the survey, making the BRFSS the primary source of information on the health-related behaviors of Americans.

black The black racial category includes those who identified themselves as "black" or "African American."

central cities The largest city in a metropolitan area is called the central city. The balance of the metropolitan area outside the central city is regarded as the "suburbs."

Consumer Expenditure Survey The Consumer Expenditure Survey (CEX) is an ongoing study of the day-to-day spending of American households administered by the Bureau of Labor Statistics. The CEX includes an interview survey and a diary survey. The average spending figures shown in this book are the integrated data from both the diary and interview components of the survey. Two separate, nationally representative samples are used for the interview and diary surveys. For the interview survey, about 7,500 consumer units are interviewed on a rotating panel basis each quarter for five consecutive quarters. For the diary survey, 7,500 consumer units keep weekly diaries of spending for two consecutive weeks.

consumer unit *(on spending tables only)* For convenience, the term consumer unit and households are used interchangeably in the spending section of this book, although consumer units are somewhat different from the Census Bureau's households. Consumer units are all related members of a household, or financially independent members of a household. A household may include more than one consumer unit.

Current Population Survey The CPS is a nationally representative survey of the civilian noninstitutional population aged 15 or older. It is taken monthly by the Census Bureau for the Bureau of Labor Statistics, collecting information from more than 50,000 households on employment and unemployment. In March of each year, the survey includes the Annual Social and Economic Supplement (formerly called the Annual Demographic Survey), which is the source of most national data on the characteristics of Americans, such as educational attainment, living arrangements, and incomes.

disability As defined by the American Community Survey, respondents are asked whether they have a sensory, physical, mental, or self-care disability. Those who answer "yes" are classified as disabled.

disability As defined by the National Health Interview Survey, respondents aged 18 or older are asked whether they have difficulty in physical functioning, probing whether they can perform nine activities by themselves without using special equipment. The categories are walking a quarter mile; standing for two hours; sitting for two hours; walking up 10 steps without resting; stooping, bending, kneeling; reaching over one's head; grasping or handling small objects; carrying a 10-pound object; and pushing/pulling a large object. Adults who report that any of these activities is very difficult or they cannot do it at all are defined as having physical difficulties.

disability, work The Current Population Survey defines a work disability as a specific physical or mental condition that prevents an individual from working. The disability must be so severe that it completely incapacitates the individual and prevents him/her from doing any kind of work for at least the next six months.

dual-earner couple A married couple in which both the householder and the householder's spouse are in the labor force.

earnings A type of income, earnings is the amount of money a person receives from his or her job. *See also* Income.

employed All civilians who did any work as a paid employee or farmer/self-employed worker, or who worked 15 hours or more as an unpaid farm worker or in a family-owned business, during the reference period. All those who have jobs but who are temporarily absent from their jobs due to illness, bad weather, vacation, labor management dispute, or personal reasons are considered employed.

expenditure The transaction cost including excise and sales taxes of goods and services acquired during the survey period. The full cost of each purchase is recorded even though full payment may not have been made at the date of purchase. Average expenditure figures may be artificially low for infrequently purchased items such as cars because figures are calculated using all consumer units within a demographic segment rather than just purchasers. Expenditure estimates include money spent on gifts for others.

family A group of two or more people (one of whom is the householder) related by birth, marriage, or adoption and living in the same household.

family household A household maintained by a householder who lives with one or more people related to him or her by blood, marriage, or adoption.

female/male householder A woman or man who maintains a household without a spouse present. May head family or nonfamily households.

foreign-born population People who are not United States citizens at birth.

full-time employment Full-time is 35 or more hours of work per week during a majority of the weeks worked.

full-time, year-round Indicates 50 or more weeks of full-time employment during the previous calendar year.

Generation X Americans born between 1965 and 1976, also known as the baby-bust generation.

Hispanic Because Hispanic is an ethnic origin rather than a race, Hispanics may be of any race. While most Hispanics are white, there are black, Asian, and American Indian Hispanics.

household All the persons who occupy a housing unit. A household includes the related family members and all the unrelated persons, if any, such as lodgers, foster children, wards, or employees who share the housing unit. A person living alone is counted as a household. A group of unrelated people who share a housing unit as roommates or unmarried partners is also counted as a household. Households do not include group quarters such as college dormitories, prisons, or nursing homes.

household, race/ethnicity of Households are categorized according to the race or ethnicity of the householder only.

householder The householder is the person (or one of the persons) in whose name the housing unit is owned or rented or, if there is no such person, any adult member. With married couples, the householder may be either the husband or wife. The householder is the reference person for the household.

householder, age of The age of the householder is used to categorize households into age groups such as those used in this book. Married couples, for example, are classified according to the age of either the husband or wife, depending on which one identified him or herself as the householder.

housing unit A housing unit is a house, an apartment, a group of rooms, or a single room occupied or intended for occupancy as separate living quarters. Separate living quarters are those in which the occupants do not live and eat with any other persons in the structure and that have direct access from the outside of the building or through a common hall that is used or intended for use by the occupants of another unit or by the general public. The occupants may be a single family, one person living alone, two or more families living together, or any other group of related or unrelated persons who share living arrangements.

Housing Vacancy Survey The HVS is a supplement to the Current Population Survey, providing quarterly and annual data on rental and homeowner vacancy rates, characteristics of units available for occupancy, and homeownership rates by age, household type,

region, state, and metropolitan area. The Current Population Survey sample includes 51,000 occupied housing units and 9,000 vacant units.

housing value The respondent's estimate of how much his or her house and lot would sell for if it were for sale.

immigration The relatively permanent movement (change of residence) of people into the country of reference.

income Money received in the preceding calendar year by each person aged 15 or older from each of the following sources: (1) earnings from longest job (or self-employment); (2) earnings from jobs other than longest job; (3) unemployment compensation; (4) workers' compensation; (5) Social Security; (6) Supplemental Security income; (7) public assistance; (8) veterans' payments; (9) survivor benefits; (10) disability benefits; (11) retirement pensions; (12) interest; (13) dividends; (14) rents and royalties or estates and trusts; (15) educational assistance; (16) alimony; (17) child support; (18) financial assistance from outside the household, and other periodic income. Income is reported in several ways in this book. Household income is the combined income of all household members. Income of persons is all income accruing to a person from all sources. Earnings are the money a person receives from his or her job.

industry Refers to the industry in which a person worked longest in the preceding calendar year.

job tenure The length of time a person has been employed continuously by the same employer.

labor force The labor force tables in this book show the civilian labor force only. The labor force includes both the employed and the unemployed (people who are looking for work). People are counted as in the labor force if they were working or looking for work during the reference week in which the Census Bureau fields the Current Population Survey.

labor force participation rate The percent of the civilian noninstitutional population that is in the civilian labor force, which includes both the employed and the unemployed.

married couples with or without children under age 18 Refers to married couples with or without own children under age 18 living in the same household. Couples without children under age 18 may be parents of grown children who live elsewhere, or they could be childless couples.

median The median is the amount that divides the population or households into two equal portions: one below and one above the median. Medians can be calculated for income, age, and many other characteristics.

median income The amount that divides the income distribution into two equal groups, half having incomes above the median, half having incomes below the median. The medians for households or families are based on all households or families. The median for persons are based on all persons aged 15 or older with income.

Medical Expenditure Panel Survey MEPS is a nationally representative survey that collects detailed information on the health status, access to care, health care use and expenses and health insurance coverage of the civilian noninstitutionalized population of the U.S. and nursing home residents. MEPS comprises four component surveys: the Household Component, the Medical Provider Component, the Insurance Component, and the Nursing Home Component. The Household Component, which is the core survey, is conducted each year and includes 15,000 households and 37,000 people.

metropolitan statistical area To be defined as a metropolitan statistical area (or MSA), an area must include a city with 50,000 or more inhabitants, or a Census Bureau-defined urbanized area of at least 50,000 inhabitants and a total metropolitan population of at least 100,000 (75,000 in New England). The county (or counties) that contains the largest city becomes the "central county" (counties), along with any adjacent counties that have at least 50 percent of their population in the urbanized area surrounding the largest city. Additional "outlying counties" are included in the MSA if they meet specified requirements of commuting to the central counties and other selected requirements of metropolitan character (such as population density and percent urban). In New England, MSAs are defined in terms of cities and towns rather than counties. For this reason, the concept of NECMA is used to define metropolitan areas in the New England division.

Millennial generation Americans born between 1977 and 1994.

mobility status People are classified according to their mobility status on the basis of a comparison between their place of residence at the time of the March Current Population Survey and their place of residence in March of the previous year. Nonmovers are people living in the same house at the end of the period as at the beginning of the period. Movers are people living in a different house at the end of the period than at the beginning of the period. Movers from abroad are either citizens or aliens whose place of residence is outside the United States at the beginning of the period, that is, in an outlying area under the jurisdiction of the United States or in a foreign country. The mobility status for children is fully allocated from the mother if she is in the household; otherwise it is allocated from the householder.

Monitoring the Future Project The MTF survey is conducted by the University of Michigan Survey Research Center. The survey is administered to approximately 50,000 students in 420 public and private secondary schools every year. High school seniors have been surveyed annually since 1975. Students in 8th and 10th grade have been surveyed annually since 1991.

National Ambulatory Medical Care Survey The NAMCS is an annual survey of visits to nonfederally employed office-based physicians who are primarily engaged in direct patient care. Data are collected from physicians rather than patients, with each physician assigned a one-week reporting period. During that week, a systematic random sample of visit characteristics are recorded by the physician or office staff.

National Crime Victimization Survey The NCVS collects data each year on nonfatal crimes against people age 12 or older, reported and not reported to the police, from a nationally representative sample of 42,000 households and 76,000 persons in the United States. The NCVS provides information about victims, offenders, and criminal offenses.

National Health and Nutrition Examination Survey The NHANES is a continuous survey of a representative sample of the U.S. civilian noninstitutionalized population. Respondents are interviewed at home about their health and nutrition, and the interview is followed up by a physical examination that measures such things as height and weight in mobile examination centers.

National Health Interview Survey The NHIS is a continuing nationwide sample survey of the civilian noninstitutional population of the U.S. conducted by the Census Bureau for the National Center for Health Statistics. Each year, data are collected from more than 100,000 people about their illnesses, injuries, impairments, chronic and acute conditions, activity limitations, and the use of health services.

National Home and Hospice Care Survey These are a series of surveys of a nationally representative sample of home and hospice care agencies in the U.S., sponsored by the National Center for Health Statistics. Data on the characteristics of patients and services provided are collected through personal interviews with administrators and staff.

National Hospital Ambulatory Medical Care Survey The NHAMCS, sponsored by the National Center for Health Statistics, is an annual national probability sample survey of visits to emergency departments and outpatient departments at non-Federal, short stay and general hospitals. Data are collected by hospital staff from patient records.

National Hospital Discharge Survey This survey has been conducted annually since 1965, sponsored by the National Center for Health Statistics, to collect nationally representative information on the characteristics of inpatients discharged from nonfederal, short-stay hospitals in the U.S. The survey collects data from a sample of approximately 270,000 inpatient records acquired from a national sample of about 500 hospitals.

National Household Education Survey The NHES, sponsored by the National Center for Education Statistics, provides descriptive data on the educational activities of the U.S. population, including after-school care and adult education. The NHES is a system of telephone surveys of a representative sample of 45,000 to 60,000 households in the U.S. It has been conducted in 1991, 1993, 1995, 1996, 1999, 2001, and 2003.

National Nursing Home Survey This is a series of national sample surveys of nursing homes, their residents, and staff conducted at various intervals since 1973-74 and sponsored by the National Center for Health Statistics. The latest survey was taken in 1999. data for the survey are obtained through personal interviews with administrators and staff, and occasionally with self-administered questionnaires, in a sample of about 1,500 facilities.

National Survey of Family Growth The 2002 NSFG, sponsored by the National Center for Health Statistics, is a nationally representative survey of the civilian noninstitutional population aged 15 to 44. In-**National Survey of Family Growth** The 2002 NSFG, sponsored by the National Center for Health Statistics, is a nationally representative survey of the civilian noninstitutional population aged 15 to 44. In-person interviews were completed with 12,571 men and women, collecting data on marriage, divorce, contraception, and infertility. The 2002 survey updates previous NSFG surveys taken in 1973, 1976, 1988, and 1995.

National Survey on Drug Use and Health *(formerly called the National Household Survey on Drug Abuse)* This survey, sponsored by the Substance Abuse and Mental Health Services Administration, has been conducted since 1971. It is the primary source of information on the use of illegal drugs by the U.S. population. Each year, a nationally representative sample of about 70,000 individuals aged 12 or older are surveyed in the 50 states and the District of Columbia.

net worth The amount of money left over after a household's debts are subtracted from its assets.

nonfamily household A household maintained by a householder who lives alone or who lives with people to whom he or she is not related.

nonfamily householder A householder who lives alone or with nonrelatives.

non-Hispanic People who do not identify themselves as Hispanic are classified as non-Hispanic. Non-Hispanics may be of any race.

non-Hispanic white People who identify their race as white and who do not indicate a Hispanic origin.

nonmetropolitan area Counties that are not classified as metropolitan areas.

occupation Occupational classification is based on the kind of work a person did at his or her job during the previous calendar year. If a person changed jobs during the year, the data refer to the occupation of the job held the longest during that year.

occupied housing units A housing unit is classified as occupied if a person or group of people is living in it or if the occupants are only temporarily absent—on vacation, example. By definition, the count of occupied housing units is the same as the count of households.

outside central city The portion of a metropolitan county or counties that falls outside of the central city or cities; generally regarded as the suburbs.

count of occupied housing units is the same as the count of households.

outside central city The portion of a metropolitan county or counties that falls outside of the central city or cities; generally regarded as the suburbs.

own children Own children are sons and daughters, including stepchildren and adopted children, of the householder. The totals include never-married children living away from home in college dormitories.

owner occupied A housing unit is "owner occupied" if the owner lives in the unit, even if it is mortgaged or not fully paid for. A cooperative or condominium unit is "owner occupied" only if the owner lives in it. All other occupied units are classified as "renter occupied."

part-time employment Part-time is less than 35 hours of work per week in a majority of the weeks worked during the year.

percent change The change (either positive or negative) in a measure that is expressed as a proportion of the starting measure. When median income changes from $20,000 to $25,000, for example, this is a 25 percent increase.

percentage point change The change (either positive or negative) in a value which is already expressed as a percentage. When a labor force participation rate changes from 70 percent of 75 percent, for example, this is a 5 percentage point increase.

poverty level The official income threshold below which families and people are classified as living in poverty. The threshold rises each year with inflation and varies depending on family size and age of householder.

primary activity In the time use tables, primary activities are those that respondents identify as their main activity. Other activities done simultaneously are not included.

proportion or share The value of a part expressed as a percentage of the whole. If there are 4 million people aged 25 and 3 million of them are white, then the white proportion is 75 percent.

race Race is self-reported and can be defined in three ways. The "race alone" population comprises people who identify themselves as only one race. The "race in combination" population comprises people who identify themselves as more than one race, such as white and black. The "race, alone or in combination" population includes both those who identify themselves as one race and those who identify themselves as more than one race.

regions The four major regions and nine census divisions of the United States are the state groupings as shown below:

Northeast:
—New England: Connecticut, Maine, Massachusetts, New Hampshire, Rhode Island, and Vermont
—Middle Atlantic: New Jersey, New York, and Pennsylvania

Midwest:
—East North Central: Illinois, Indiana, Michigan, Ohio, and Wisconsin
—West North Central: Iowa, Kansas, Minnesota, Missouri, Nebraska, North Dakota, and South Dakota

South:
—South Atlantic: Delaware, District of Columbia, Florida, Georgia, Maryland, North Carolina, South Carolina, Virginia, and West Virginia
—East South Central: Alabama, Kentucky, Mississippi, and Tennessee
—West South Central: Arkansas, Louisiana, Oklahoma, and Texas

West:
—Mountain: Arizona, Colorado, Idaho, Montana, Nevada, New Mexico, Utah, and Wyoming
—Pacific: Alaska, California, Hawaii, Oregon, and Washington

renter occupied *See* Owner occupied.

Retirement Confidence Survey The RCS, sponsored by the Employee Benefit Research Institute (EBRI), the American Savings Education Council (ASEC), and Mathew Greenwald & Associates (Greenwald), is an annual survey of a nationally representative sample of 1,000 people aged 25 or older. Respondents are asked a core set of questions that have been asked since 1996, measuring attitudes and behavior towards retirement. Additional questions are also asked about current retirement issues such as 401(k) participation.

rounding Percentages are rounded to the nearest tenth of a percent; therefore, the percentages in a distribution do not always add exactly to 100.0 percent. The totals, however, are always shown as 100.0. Moreover, individual figures are rounded to the nearest thousand without being adjusted to group totals, which are independently rounded; percentages are based on the unrounded numbers.

self-employment A person is categorized as self-employed if he or she was self-employed in the job held longest during the reference period. Persons who report self-employment from a second job are excluded, but those who report wage-and-salary income from a second job are included. Unpaid workers in family businesses are excluded. Self-employment statistics include only nonagricultural workers and exclude people who work for themselves in incorporated business.

sex ratio The number of men per 100 women.

suburbs See Outside central city.

Survey of Consumer Finances The Survey of Consumer Finances is a triennial survey taken by the Federal Reserve Board. It collects data on the assets, debts, and net worth of American households. For the 2004 survey, the Federal Reserve Board interviewed more than 4,000 households.

Survey of Public Participation in the Arts Initiated in 1982 by the National Endowment for the Arts, this survey examines the public's participation in the performing arts, visual arts, historic site visits, music, and literature. The 2002 survey is the fifth (earlier surveys were in 1982, 1985, 1992, and 1997) and was conducted as a supplement to the Current Population Survey. More than 17,000 respondents to the August 2002 Current Population Survey were asked about their arts participation and involvement.

unemployed Unemployed people are those who, during the survey period, had no employment but were available and looking for work. Those who were laid off from their jobs and were waiting to be recalled are also classified as unemployed.

white The "white" racial category includes many Hispanics (who may be of any race) unless the term "non-Hispanic white" is used.

Youth Risk Behavior Surveillance System The YRBSS was created by the Centers for Disease Control to monitor health risks being taken by young people at the national, state, and local level. The national survey is taken every two years based on a nationally representative sample of 16,000 students in 9th through 12th grade in public and private schools.

Bibliography

Agency for Healthcare Research and Quality
Internet site http://www.ahrq.gov/
—Medical Expenditure Panel Survey, Internet site http://www.meps.ahrq.gov/
CompendiumTables/TC_TOC.htm

Bureau of Justice Statistics
Internet site http://www.ojp.usdoj.gov/bjs/welcome.html
—*Criminal Victimization 2004*, Internet site http://www.ojp.usdoj.gov/bjs/abstract/cv04.htm
—Sourcebook of Criminal Justice Statistics Online, Internet site http://www.albany.edu/
sourcebook

Bureau of Labor Statistics
Internet site http://www.bls.gov
—American Time Use Survey, Internet site http://www.bls.gov/tus/home.htm and unpub-
lished data
—Characteristics of Minimum Wage Workers, Internet site http://www.bls.gov/cps/
minwage2004.htm
—Consumer Expenditure Survey, Internet site http://www.bls.gov/cex/
—Contingent and Alternative Employment Arrangements, Internet site http://www.bls
.gov/news.release/conemp.toc.htm
—Current Population Survey, Internet site http://www.bls.gov/cps/home.htm and unpub-
lished data
—Employee Tenure, Internet site http://www.bls.gov/news.release/tenure.toc.htm
—Employment Characteristics of Families, Internet site http://www.bls.gov/news.release/
famee.toc.htm
—Labor force participation rates, historical, Public Query Data Tool, Internet site http://
www.bls.gov/data
—Labor force projections, 2004–2014, Internet site http://www.bls.gov/emp/emplab1.htm
—Statistical Abstract of the United States: 2006, Internet site, http://www.census.gov/
statab/www/
—Volunteering in the United States, Internet site http://www.bls.gov/news.release/volun
.toc.htm
—Workers on Flexible and Shift Schedules, Internet site http://www.bls.gov/news.release/
flex.toc.htm

Bureau of the Census
Internet site http://www.census.gov
—*Adopted Children and Stepchildren: 2000*, Census 2000 Special Reports, CENSR-GRV, 2003,
Internet site http://www.census.gov/population/www/cen2000/phc-t21.html
—American Community Survey, 2004 custom tables, Internet site http://factfinder.census
.gov/servlet/DatasetMainPageServlet?_program=ACS&_lang=en
—American Housing Survey National Tables: 2003, Internet site http://www.census.gov/
hhes/www/housing/ahs/ahs03/ahs03.html
—America's Families and Living Arrangements: 2004, Internet site http://www.census.gov/
population/www/socdemo/hh-fam/cps2004.html

—Current Population Survey, Detailed Income Tabulations, 2005 Annual Social and Economic Supplement, Internet site http://www.census.gov/hhes/www/income/dinctabs.html

—Current Population Survey, Historical Income Tables, Internet site http://www.census.gov/hhes/income/histinc/histinctb.html

—Disability, 2003, Internet site http://www.census.gov/hhes/www/disability/data_title.html#2003

—Educational Attainment, Historical Tables, Internet site http://www.census.gov/population/www/socdemo/educ-attn.html

—Educational Attainment in the United States: 2004, Detailed Tables, Internet site http://www.census.gov/population/www/socdemo/education/cps2004.html

—Fertility of American Women, Current Population Survey—June 2004, Detailed Tables, Internet site http://www.census.gov/population/www/socdemo/fertility/cps2004.html

—Foreign Born Population of the United States, Current Population Survey—March 2004, Detailed Tables, (PPL-176), Internet site http://www.census.gov/population/www/socdemo/foreign/ppl-176.html

—Geographic Mobility: 2004, Detailed Tables, Internet site http://www.census.gov/population/www/socdemo/migrate/cps2004.html

—Health Insurance Coverage: 2004, Internet site http://pubdb3.census.gov/macro/032005/health/toc.htm

—Housing Vacancy Survey, Annual Statistics: 2005, Internet site http://www.census.gov/hhes/www/housing/hvs/annual05/ann05ind.html

—National and State Population Estimates, Internet site http://www.census.gov/popest/states/NST-ann-est.html

—Population Estimates by State, Internet site http://www.census.gov/popest/states/asrh/SC-est2004-02.html

—Poverty, Detailed Tables, Internet site http://pubdb3.census.gov/macro/032005/pov/toc.htm

—School Enrollment, Historical Tables, Internet site http://www.census.gov/population/www/socdemo/school.html

—School Enrollment—Social and Economic Characteristics of Students: October 2004, Internet site http://www.census.gov/population/www/socdemo/school/cps2004.html

—State Interim Population Projections by Age and Sex, Internet site http://www.census.gov/population/www/projections/projectionsagesex.html

—U.S. Interim Projections by Age, Sex, Race, and Hispanic Origin; Internet site http://www.census.gov/ipc/www/usinterimproj/

—Voting and Registration, Historical Time Series Tables, Internet site http://www.census.gov/population/www/socdemo/voting.html

—Voting and Registration in the Election of November 2004, Detailed Tables, Internet site http://www.census.gov/population/www/socdemo/voting/cps2004.html

Centers for Disease Control and Prevention
Internet site http://www.cdc.gov

—Behavioral Risk Factor Surveillance System Prevalence Data, Internet site http://apps.nccd.cdc.gov/brfss/index.asp

—"Youth Risk Behavior Surveillance–United States, 2003," *Mortality and Morbidity Weekly Report*, Vol. 53/SS-2, May 21, 2004; Internet site http://www.cdc.gov/mmwr/indss_2004.html

Employee Benefit Research Institute
Internet site http://www.ebri.org/
—"401(k)-Type Plan and IRA Ownership," Craig Copeland, *Notes*, Vol. 26, No. 1, January 2005
—"Employment-Based Retirement Plan Participation: Geographic Differences and Trends, 2004," *Issue Brief*, No. 286, October 2005
—"Income and the Elderly Population, Age 65 and Over, 2004," by Ken McDonnell, *Notes*, Vol. 27, No. 1, January 2006

Employee Benefit Research Institute, American Savings Education Council, and Mathew Greenwald & Associates
Internet site http://www.ebri.org/
—2005 Retirement Confidence Survey, Internet site http://www.ebri.org/surveys/rcs/2005/

Federal Interagency Forum on Child and Family Statistics
Internet site http://www.childstats.gov/index.asp
—America's Children: Key National Indicators of Well-Being, Internet site http://www.childstats.gov/americaschildren/index.asp

Federal Reserve Board
Internet site http://www.federalreserve.gov/
—"Recent Changes in U.S. Family Finances: Evidence from the 2001 and 2004 Survey of Consumer Finances," Federal Reserve Board, Internet site http://www.federalreserve.gov/pubs/oss/oss2/2004/scf2004home.html

Graduate Center of the City University of New York
Internet site http://www.gc.cuny.edu/index.htm
—American Religious Identification Survey 2001, Egon Mayer, Barry A. Kosmin, and Ariela Keysar, Internet site http://www.gc.cuny.edu/faculty/research_briefs/aris/aris_index.htm

Higher Education Research Institute
Internet site http://www.gseis.ucla.edu/heri/whatis.html
—*The American Freshman: National Norms for Fall 2005*, John H. Pryor, Sylvia Hurtado, Victor B. Saenz, Jennifer A. Lindholm, William S. Korn, and Kathryn M. Mahoney, Higher Education Research Institute, UCLA, 2005, Internet site http://www.gseis.ucla.edu/heri/american_freshman.html

Institute for Social Research, University of Michigan
Internet site http://www.isr.umich.edu/
—Monitoring the Future Survey, Internet site http://monitoringthefuture.org/index.html

National Center for Education Statistics
Internet site http://nces.ed.gov
—Digest of Education Statistics, 2004, Internet site http://nces.ed.gov/programs/digest/d04_tf.asp

National Center for Health Statistics
Internet site http://www.cdc.gov/nchs
—*2003 National Hospital Discharge Survey*, Advance Data, No. 359, 2005, Internet site http://www.cdc.gov/nchs/about/major/hdasd/listpubs.htm

—1999 National Nursing Home Survey, Internet site http://www.cdc.gov/nchs/nnhs.htm

—*Births: Final Data for 2003*, National Vital Statistics Reports, Vol. 54, No. 2, 2005, Internet site http://www.cdc.gov/nchs/products/pubs/pubd/nvsr/54/54-pre.htm

—*Births: Preliminary Data for 2004*, National Vital Statistics Reports, Vol. 54, No. 8, 2005, Internet site http://www.cdc.gov/nchs/products/pubs/pubd/nvsr/54/54-pre.htm

—*Characteristics of Hospice Care Discharges and Their Length of Service: United States, 2000*, Vital and Health Statistics, Series 13, No. 154, 2003; Internet site http://www.cdc.gov/nchs/pressroom/03facts/hospicecare.htm

—*Deaths: Final Data for 2002*, National Vital Statistics Reports, Vol. 53, No. 5, 2004, Internet site http://www.cdc.gov/nchs/about/major/dvs/mortdata.htm

—*Deaths: Preliminary Data for 2003*, National Vital Statistics Reports, Vol. 53, No. 15, 2005, Internet site http://www.cdc.gov/nchs/products/pubs/pubd/nvsr/53/53-21.htm

—*Fertility, Family Planning, and Reproductive Health of U.S. Women: Data from the 2002 National Survey of Family Growth*, Vital and Health Statistics, Series 23, No. 25, 2005; Internet site http://www.cdc.gov/nchs/nsfg.htm

—*Health, United States, 2005*, Internet site http://www.cdc.gov/nchs/hus.htm

—*Mean Body Weight, Height, and Body Mass Index, United States 1960–2002*, Advance Data, No. 347, 2004, Internet site http://www.cdc.gov/nchs/pressroom/04news/americans.htm

—*National Ambulatory Medical Care Survey: 2003 Summary*, Advance Data No. 365, 2005, Internet site http://www.cdc.gov/nchs/about/major/ahcd/adata.htm

—*National Hospital Ambulatory Medical Care Survey: 2003 Emergency Department Summary*, Advance Data No. 358, 2005, Internet site http://www.cdc.gov/nchs/about/major/ahcd/adata.htm

—*National Hospital Ambulatory Medical Care Survey: 2003 Outpatient Department Summary*, Advance Data, No. 366, 2005, Internet site http://www.cdc.gov/nchs/about/major/ahcd/adata.htm

—*Revised Birth and Fertility Rates for the 1990s and New Rates for the Hispanic Populations 2000 and 2001: United States*, National Vital Statistics Reports, Vol. 51, No. 12, 2003

—*Sexual Behavior and Selected Health Measures: Men and Women 15-44 Years of Age, United States, 2002*, Advance Data, No. 362, 2005; Internet site http://www.cdc.gov/nchs/nsfg.htm

—*Summary Health Statistics for U.S. Adults: National Health Interview Survey, 2003*, Vital and Health Statistics, Series 10, No. 225, 2005; Internet site http://www.cdc.gov/nchs/nhis.htm

—*Summary Health Statistics for U.S. Children: National Health Interview Survey, 2004*, Vital and Health Statistics, Series 10, No. 227, 2003; Internet site http://www.cdc.gov/nchs/nhis.htm

—*Teenagers in the United States: Sexual Activity, Contraceptive Use, and Childbearing, 2002*; Vital and Health Statistics, Series 23, No. 24, 2004; Internet site http://www.cdc.gov/nchs/nsfg.htm

National Endowment for the Arts

Internet site http://www.arts.endow.gov/

—*2002 Survey of Public Participation in the Arts: Summary Report*, Research Division Report No. 45, Internet site http://www.nea.gov/pub/ResearchReports_chrono.html

National Sporting Goods Association

Internet site http://www.nsga.org

—Sports Participation, Internet site http://www.nsga.org/public/pages/index.cfm?pageid=158

Office of Immigration Statistics
—2004 Yearbook of Immigration Statistics, Internet site http://uscis.gov/graphics/shared/statistics/index.htm

Pew Internet & American Life Project
Internet site http://www.pewinternet.org
—Latest Trends, Internet site http://www.pewinternet.org/trends.asp#usage

Pew Research Center
Internet site http://people-press.org/
—"Families Drawn Together by Communications Revolution," February 21, 2006

Pulte Homes
Internet site http://www.pulte.com
—2005 Del Webb Baby Boomer Survey, Internet site http://phx.corporate-ir.net/phoenix.zhtml?c=147717&p=delWebb

Substance Abuse and Mental Health Services Administration
Internet site http://www.samhsa.gov/
—National Survey on Drug Use and Health, Internet site http://oas.samhsa.gov/nsduh.htm

Index

cholesterol, high, 44–45, 47, 49, 51
chronic liver disease and cirrhosis, as cause of death, 68–72
chronic lower respiratory disease, as cause of death, 69–73
cigarette smoking, 33–34. *See also* Tobacco products.
citizens, 240–241
clothes dryer, homes with, 97–98
college enrollment, 20–21
computer:
    time spent playing on, 314–315
    use, 318–319
congenital anomalies, 63
contractors. *See* Independent contractors.
coronary, 45, 47, 49
credit card debt, 346, 348
crime:
    as neighborhood problem, 102, 104
    rate, 330–331

death, causes of, 68–73
debt, household, 336, 345–348
deck, houses with, 97–98
dental services: *See also* Teeth, absence of.
    spending on, 40, 42–43
    use of, 42–43
diabetes:
    as cause of death, 69–73
    as reason for home health care, 66
    health condition, 45, 47, 49
    hospital diagnosis, 63
dieting, 28–30
digestive diseases, 63
dining room, houses with, 98
disability:
    benefits, as source of income, 160–167
    by education, 56, 58
    by type, 56–57
    of nursing home residents, 65, 67
    work, 56, 68
dishwashers, houses with, 97–98
dividends, as source of income, 160–167
divorce, 225–230
doctor visits. *See* Physician visits.
drinking, alcoholic beverages, 33–34
drugs:
    illicit, use of, 33, 35
    prescription, 40, 42–43, 53–55
    spending on, 53, 55, 266–299

dryers, houses with, 97–98
dual-income couples, 179–180

earnings: *See also* Income.
    as source of income, 159–168
    by educational attainment, 150–158
    minimum wage, 198–199
eating, time spent, 302–305
education:
    adult, 22–23
    spending on, 266–299
    time spent, 303–305
educational assistance, as source of income, 160–167
educational attainment:
    by race and Hispanic origin, 15–17
    by sex, 6–17
    earnings by, 150–158
    work disability status by, 56, 58
electricity: *See also* Utilities, fuels, and public services.
    as heating fuel, 95–96
    cost of, monthly, 107
email, 318–319
emergency department services. *See* Hospital emergency services.
emphysema, 45, 47, 49
employment: *See also* Labor force.
    as source of income in retirement, 352
    based health insurance, 36, 38
    long-term, 191, 193
endocrine diseases, 63
English speakers, 245–246
entertainment, spending on, 266–299
exercise:
    as way to lose weight, 28, 30
    percent participating in, 31–32, 334
    plans for in retirement, 204
    time spent, 302–305

face pain, 45, 47, 49
families. *See* Households.
family, as a reason for moving, 111, 113–114
female-headed household. *See* Households, female-headed.
fireplace, houses with, 97–98
food:
    preparation and cleanup, time spent, 311–312
    spending on, 266–299

labor force: *See also* Workers.
    by occupation, 181–186
    by race and Hispanic origin, 176–178
    by sex, 172–178, 202–203
    full-time, 138–158, 187–188
    participation, 172–178, 202–203
    part-time, 187–188
    projections, 202–203
    self-employed, 189–190, 194–195
    trends, 172–173, 202–203
    unemployed, 174–178
language spoken at home, 245–246
laundry, time spent, 311, 314
leisure:
    activities, 334
    time, 302–305, 314–315
life expectancy, 74–76
life insurance:
    as financial asset, 340
    spending on, 266–299
liver disease:
    as cause of death, 69–72
    health condition, 45, 47, 49
living alone, fear of in retirement, 204. *See also*
        Households, single-person.
living arrangements, 221–224

male-headed households. *See* Households,
        male-headed.
marital status:
    by race and Hispanic origin, 225, 227–230
    by sex, 225–230
married couples. *See* Households, married-
        couple.
media, percent participating in arts through,
    333
Medicaid, 36, 39, 41–43, 55
Medicare, 36, 39–43, 53, 55
men:
    earnings by educational attainment,
        150–154
    educational attainment, 6–7, 11–12, 15–16
    employment, long-term, 191, 193
    exercise, participation in, 31–32
    full-time workers, 138–143, 150–154,
        187–188
    high blood pressure, 44, 52
    high cholesterol, 51
    home health care patients, 66
    income, 135–136, 138–143

    job tenure of, 191–192
    labor force participation, 172–177, 202–203
    labor force projections, 202–203
    life expectancy, 74, 76
    living alone, 221–222, 224
    living arrangements, 221–222, 224
    marital status, 225–230
    nursing home residents, 65, 67
    part-time workers, 187–188
    physician visits, 59–60
    population, 232, 234
    prescription drug use, 53–54
    school enrollment, 18–19
    self-employed, 189–190
    source of income, 159–163, 168
    telephone contact with parents/children,
        316–317
    time use, 302–315
    unemployed, 174–178
    union representation, 200–201
    volunteers, 324–325
    weight, 28–29
    with flexible schedules, 196–197
mental health problems, 26–27, 46, 48, 50, 63
metropolitan status, homeownership by, 86, 88
migraines. *See* Headaches.
military:
    health insurance, 39
    retirement, 160–167
minimum wage workers, 198–199
mobile homes:
    living in, 89–91
    nearby, 103
mobility, geographic:
    plans after retirement, 111, 114
    rate, 111–112
    reason for, 111, 113–114
mortgage:
    cost of, monthly, 107
    debt, 345–346, 348
    interest, spending on, 266–299
    percent with, 105, 107
movers. *See* Mobility, geographic.
movies, percent attending, 332, 334
musculoskeletal system, 63
mutual funds, 340–341

naturalized citizens, 240–241
neck pain, 45, 47, 49

neighborhood:
    characteristics of, 102–103
    opinion of, 99, 101
    problems with, 102, 104
nephritis, as cause of death, 69–73
nervous system, 63, 66
net worth, household, 336–337
never-married, 225–230
noise, as neighborhood problem, 102, 104
non-Hispanic whites. *See* White, Non-
        Hispanic Americans.
nonmetropolitan areas, homeownership in,
        86, 88
nursing home residents, 65, 67

obesity. *See* Weight.
occupation, 181–186
on-call workers, 194–195
online, 318–319
outpatient department. *See* Hospital
        outpatient services.
overweight. *See* Weight.

parents, contact with, 316–317
part-time workers, 187–188
pensions:
    as source of income, 159–168
    percent covered by, 349–350
    spending on, 266–299
personal care products and services, spending
        on, 266–299
physical activity: *See also* Exercise.
    as a way to lose weight, 28, 30
    percent participating, 31–32, 334
physician visits:
    number of, 59–60
    rating of health care received, 59, 64
    spending on, 40, 42–43
pneumonia, as cause of death, 68–73
population:
    by citizenship status, 240–241
    by generation, 232–233, 236–237, 239, 247,
        249, 251, 256–259, 262–263
    by race and Hispanic origin, 237–239, 247,
        250–251, 260–263
    by region, 247–251
    by sex, 232, 234
    by state, 247, 252–263
    foreign-born, 240–242

projections, 232, 236
    trends, 232, 235–236
porches, houses with, 97–98
poverty rate, 169–170
prescription drugs:
    spending on, 40, 42–43, 53, 55
    use of, 42–43, 53–54
private health insurance, 36–38, 40–43, 55
projections:
    labor force, 202–203
    population, 232, 236
property:
    insurance, cost of, 107
    taxes, spending on, 107, 266–299
public assistance, as source of income, 160–167
public transportation, spending on, 266–299

race. *See* Asian Americans, Black Americans,
        Hispanic Americans, and
        White non-Hispanic Americans.
reading:
    percent participating in, 333
    spending on, 266–299
    time spent, 314–315
recreation room, houses with, 98
regions:
    homeownership by, 86–87
    population of, 247–251
religious:
    activities, time spent on, 302–305
    group membership, 322–323
renters: *See also* Shelter.
    amenities in housing unit, 97–98
    by heating fuel used, 95–96
    by metropolitan status, 86, 88
    by opinion of home, 99–100
    by opinion of neighborhood, 99, 101
    by region, 86–87
    by size of housing unit, 89, 92
    by type of structure, 89, 91
    housing cost of, 105–107
    in new housing, 93–94
    neighborhood characteristics, 102–103
    neighborhood problems, 102, 104
    number of, 80–81
respiratory disease:
    as cause of death, 68–73
    as reason for home health care, 66
    hospital diagnosis, 63